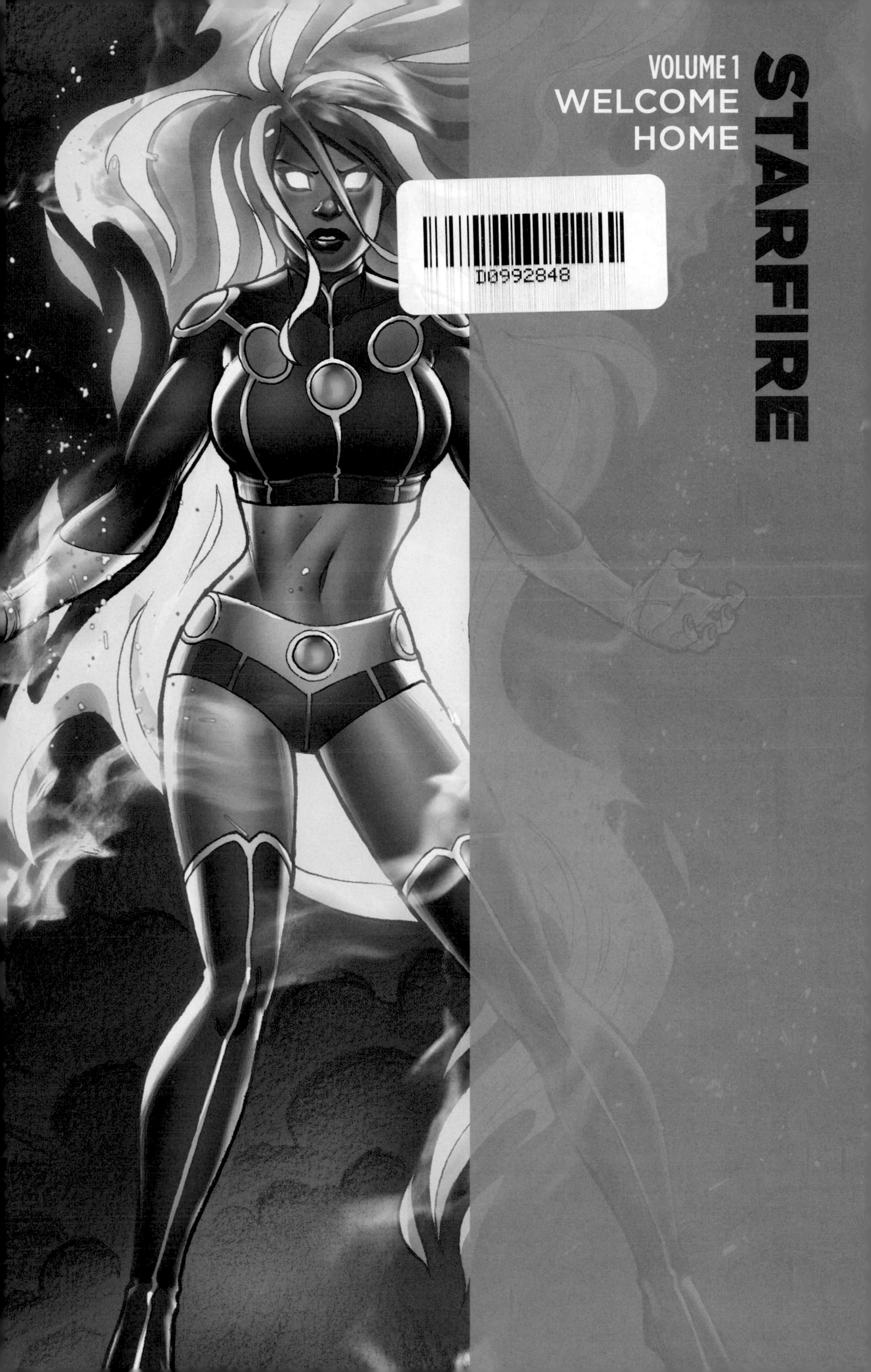
STARFIRE
VOLUME 1
WELCOME
HOME
D0992848

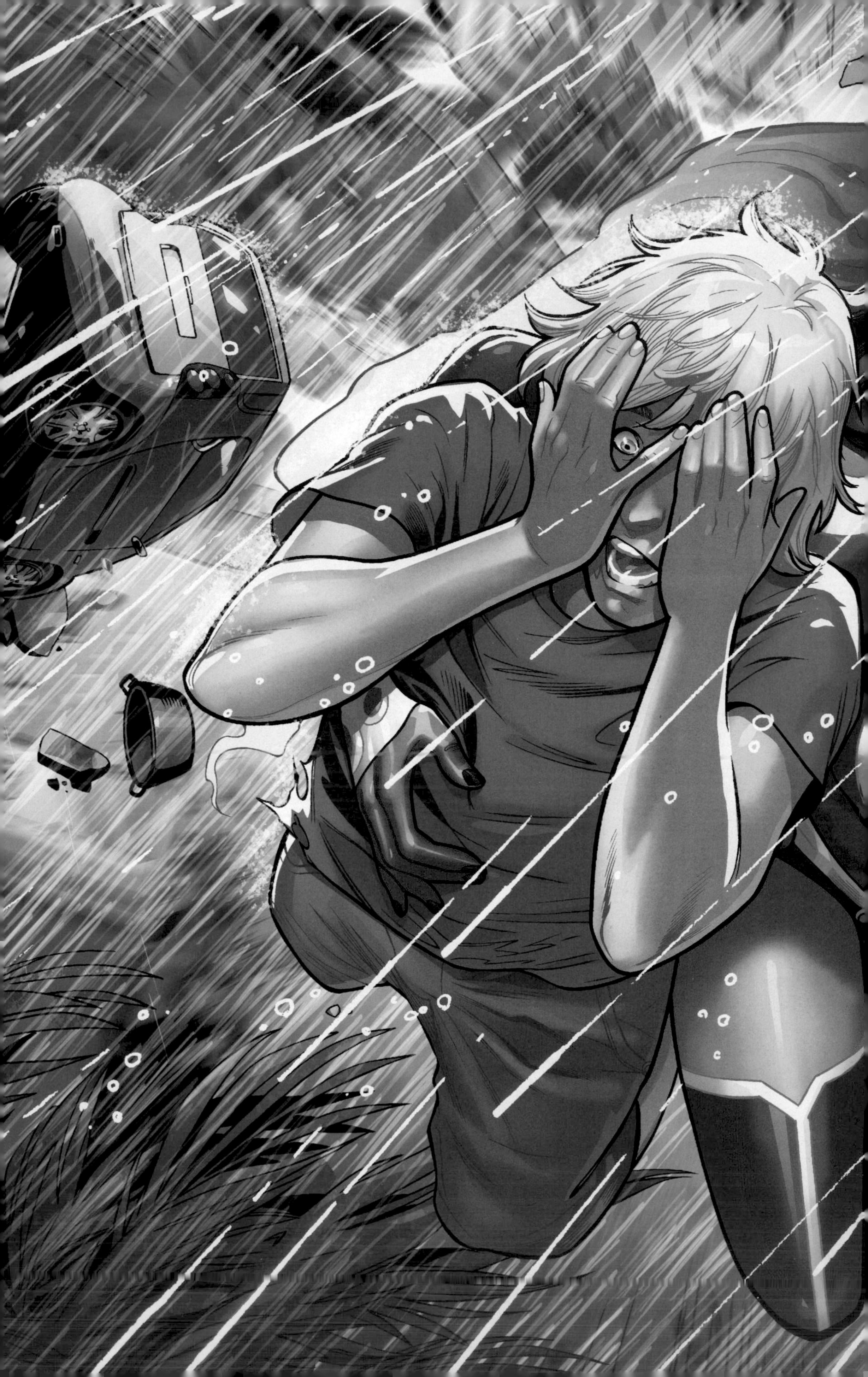

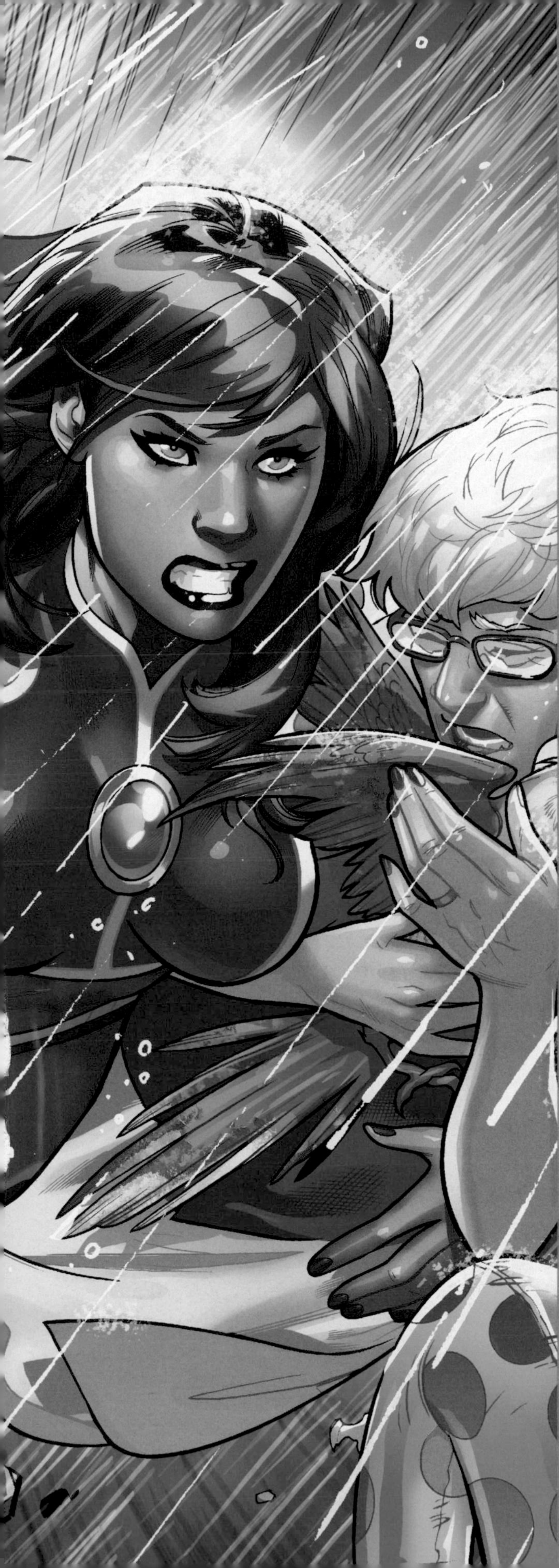

STARFIRE

VOLUME 1
WELCOME HOME

WRITTEN BY
AMANDA CONNER
JIMMY PALMIOTTI

PENCILS BY
EMANUELA LUPACCHINO
PENCIL ASSISTS BY
MIRCO PIERFEDERICI

INKS BY
RAY McCARTHY
TREVOR SCOTT

COLOR BY
HI-FI

LETTERS BY
TOM NAPOLITANO

ORIGINAL SERIES AND
COLLECTION COVER ART BY
AMANDA CONNER &
PAUL MOUNTS

STARFIRE CREATED BY
MARV WOLFMAN AND
GEORGE PÉREZ

PAUL KAMINSKI Editor – Original Series
JEB WOODARD Group Editor – Collected Editions
ROBIN WILDMAN Editor – Collected Edition
STEVE COOK Design Director – Books
DAMIAN RYLAND Publication Design

BOB HARRAS Senior VP – Editor-in-Chief, DC Comics

DIANE NELSON President
DAN DIDIO and JIM LEE Co-Publishers
GEOFF JOHNS Chief Creative Officer
AMIT DESAI Senior VP – Marketing & Global Franchise Management
NAIRI GARDINER Senior VP – Finance
SAM ADES VP – Digital Marketing
BOBBIE CHASE VP – Talent Development
MARK CHIARELLO Senior VP – Art, Design & Collected Editions
JOHN CUNNINGHAM VP – Content Strategy
ANNE DEPIES VP – Strategy Planning & Reporting
DON FALLETTI VP – Manufacturing Operations
LAWRENCE GANEM VP – Editorial Administration & Talent Relations
ALISON GILL Senior VP – Manufacturing & Operations
HANK KANALZ Senior VP – Editorial Strategy & Administration
JAY KOGAN VP – Legal Affairs
DEREK MADDALENA Senior VP – Sales & Business Development
JACK MAHAN VP – Business Affairs
DAN MIRON VP – Sales Planning & Trade Development
NICK NAPOLITANO VP – Manufacturing Administration
CAROL ROEDER VP – Marketing
EDDIE SCANNELL VP – Mass Account & Digital Sales
COURTNEY SIMMONS Senior VP – Publicity & Communications
JIM (SKI) SOKOLOWSKI VP – Comic Book Specialty & Newsstand Sales
SANDY YI Senior VP – Global Franchise Management

STARFIRE VOL. 1: WELCOME HOME

DC Comics, 2900 West Alameda Avenue, Burbank, CA 91505
Printed by RR Donnelley, Salem, VA, USA. 2/19/16. First Printing.
ISBN: 978-1-4012-6160-3

Library of Congress Cataloging-in-Publication Data is Available.

THAT'S AN *INTERESTING QUESTION* AND NOT ONE THAT'S *EASY* TO ANSWER. KNOWING YOU, I WOULD SAY SOMEPLACE WHERE YOU CAN GET AWAY WITH WEARING *NEXT* TO *NOTHING*...MAYBE AN UNPOPULATED ISLAND.

WAIT. SCRATCH THAT. YOU TRIED THAT ALREADY. YOU WOULD GO *NUTS*.

MAYBE A CITY WHERE YOU CAN GET LOST IN THE MASSES. SOMEPLACE LIKE *METROPOLIS?* GET A JOB BARTENDING? YEAH, I DON'T REALLY KNOW.

OH! *PARIS!*

ARE YOU *SERIOUS?* START A *NEW LIFE?* WHAT'S WRONG WITH THE ONE YOU GOT *NOW?* DOES THIS HAVE ANYTHING TO DO WITH ME? GIVE IT TO ME STRAIGHT.

I CAN *HANDLE* IT.

SERIOUSLY, THOUGH.

WHAT WOULD YOU DO ABOUT *MONEY?*

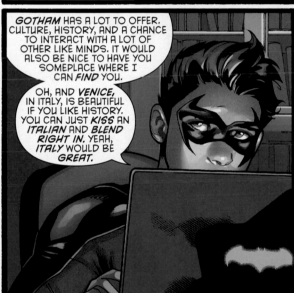

GOTHAM HAS A LOT TO OFFER. CULTURE, HISTORY, AND A CHANCE TO INTERACT WITH A LOT OF OTHER LIKE MINDS. IT WOULD ALSO BE NICE TO HAVE YOU SOMEPLACE WHERE I CAN *FIND* YOU.

OH, AND *VENICE*, IN *ITALY*, IS BEAUTIFUL IF YOU LIKE HISTORY. YOU CAN JUST *KISS* AN *ITALIAN* AND *BLEND RIGHT IN*. YEAH, *ITALY* WOULD BE *GREAT*.

A MONASTERY IS A GOOD PLACE TO LOOK *INSIDE* YOURSELF, AND LEARN WHO YOU REALLY *ARE*, AND WHAT YOUR PURPOSE ON THE PLANET IS.

IT WOULD NOT BE THE BEST OF PLACES TO SOCIALIZE, BUT I THINK IT WOULD HELP REIN IN YOUR *HEDONISTIC ATTITUDES* A BIT.

THE *SHORT DAYS* AND *LACK OF SUNLIGHT* MAY BE A PROBLEM. I *PREFER* THE DARKNESS, BUT FOR *YOU*... IT MAY BE A BAD CHOICE.

I THINK IT'S *IMPORTANT* WHEN STARTING OVER TO FIND A PLACE WHERE PEOPLE CAN *APPRECIATE* YOU FOR THE PERSON YOU *ARE*. YOU HAVE A *BEAUTIFUL SOUL* AND I *TOTALLY UNDERSTAND* YOUR WANTING TO GET AWAY FROM ALL THIS. YOU EVER THINK OF *NEW ZEALAND?*

WAIT. IS THIS ABOUT *SETTLING DOWN* AND HAVING *BABIES?*

ANYWHERE BUT WHERE I AM. *HONEST*. IT'S A *BIG PLANET*.

DO ME A FAVOR AND *GET LOST* IN IT.

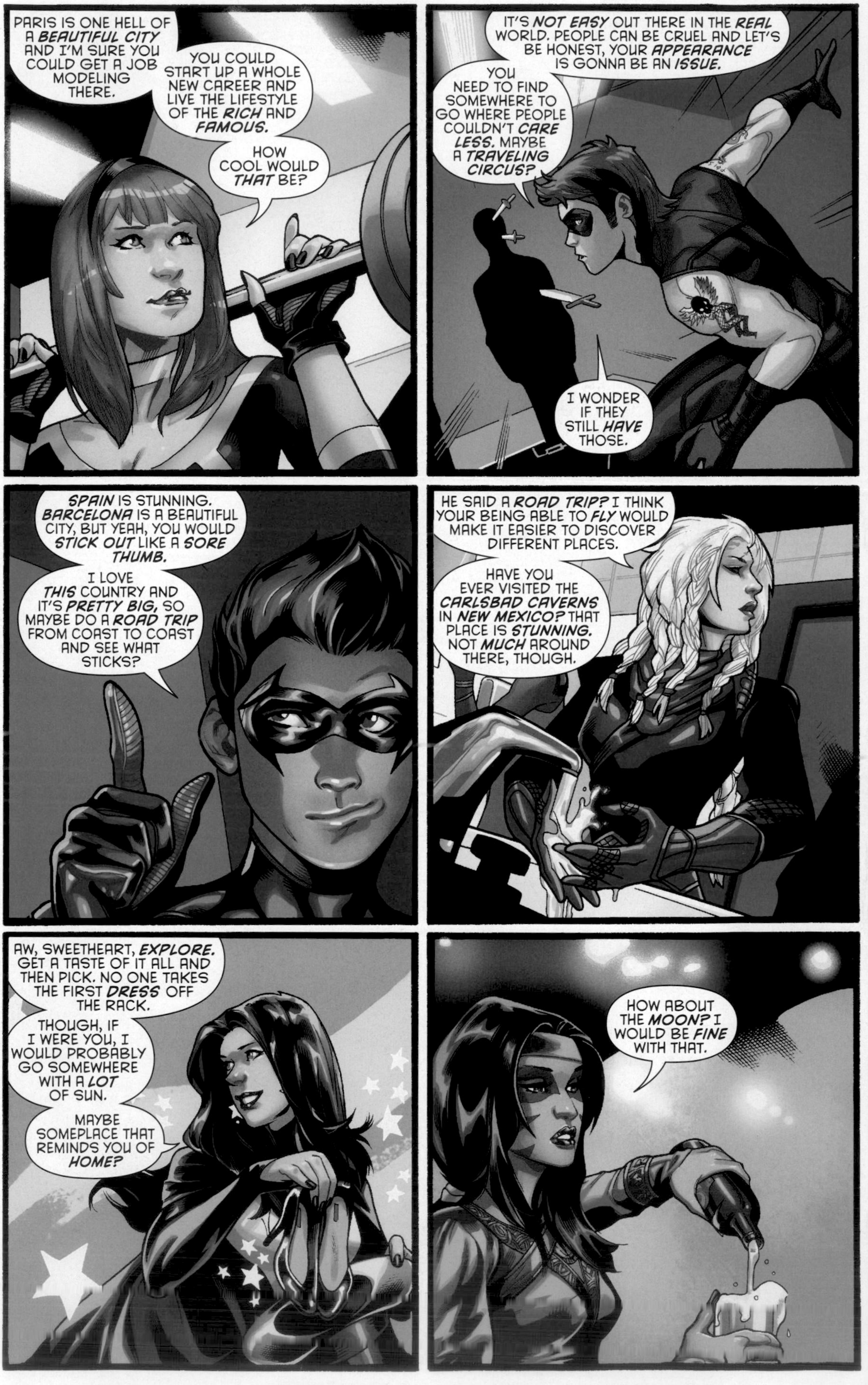
PARIS IS ONE HELL OF A BEAUTIFUL CITY AND I'M SURE YOU COULD GET A JOB MODELING THERE.
YOU COULD START UP A WHOLE NEW CAREER AND LIVE THE LIFESTYLE OF THE RICH AND FAMOUS.
HOW COOL WOULD THAT BE?
IT'S NOT EASY OUT THERE IN THE REAL WORLD. PEOPLE CAN BE CRUEL AND LET'S BE HONEST, YOUR APPEARANCE IS GONNA BE AN ISSUE.
YOU NEED TO FIND SOMEWHERE TO GO WHERE PEOPLE COULDN'T CARE LESS. MAYBE A TRAVELING CIRCUS?
I WONDER IF THEY STILL HAVE THOSE.
SPAIN IS STUNNING. BARCELONA IS A BEAUTIFUL CITY, BUT YEAH, YOU WOULD STICK OUT LIKE A SORE THUMB.
I LOVE THIS COUNTRY AND IT'S PRETTY BIG, SO MAYBE DO A ROAD TRIP FROM COAST TO COAST AND SEE WHAT STICKS?
HE SAID A ROAD TRIP? I THINK YOUR BEING ABLE TO FLY WOULD MAKE IT EASIER TO DISCOVER DIFFERENT PLACES.
HAVE YOU EVER VISITED THE CARLSBAD CAVERNS IN NEW MEXICO? THAT PLACE IS STUNNING. NOT MUCH AROUND THERE, THOUGH.
AW, SWEETHEART, EXPLORE. GET A TASTE OF IT ALL AND THEN PICK. NO ONE TAKES THE FIRST DRESS OFF THE RACK.
THOUGH, IF I WERE YOU, I WOULD PROBABLY GO SOMEWHERE WITH A LOT OF SUN.
MAYBE SOMEPLACE THAT REMINDS YOU OF HOME?
HOW ABOUT THE MOON? I WOULD BE FINE WITH THAT.

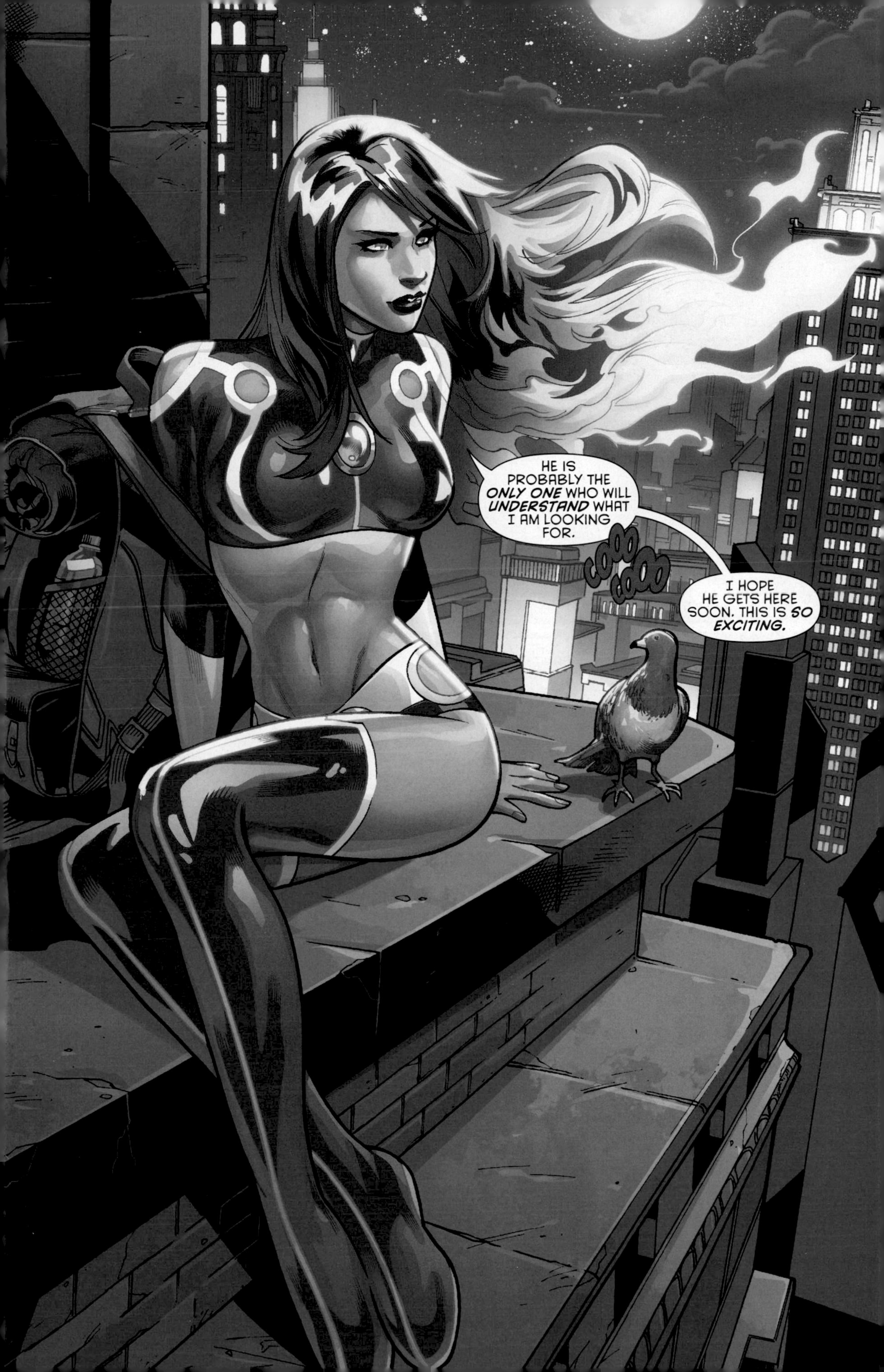
HE IS PROBABLY THE *ONLY ONE* WHO WILL *UNDERSTAND* WHAT I AM LOOKING FOR.
COOO COOO
I HOPE HE GETS HERE SOON. THIS IS *SO EXCITING.*

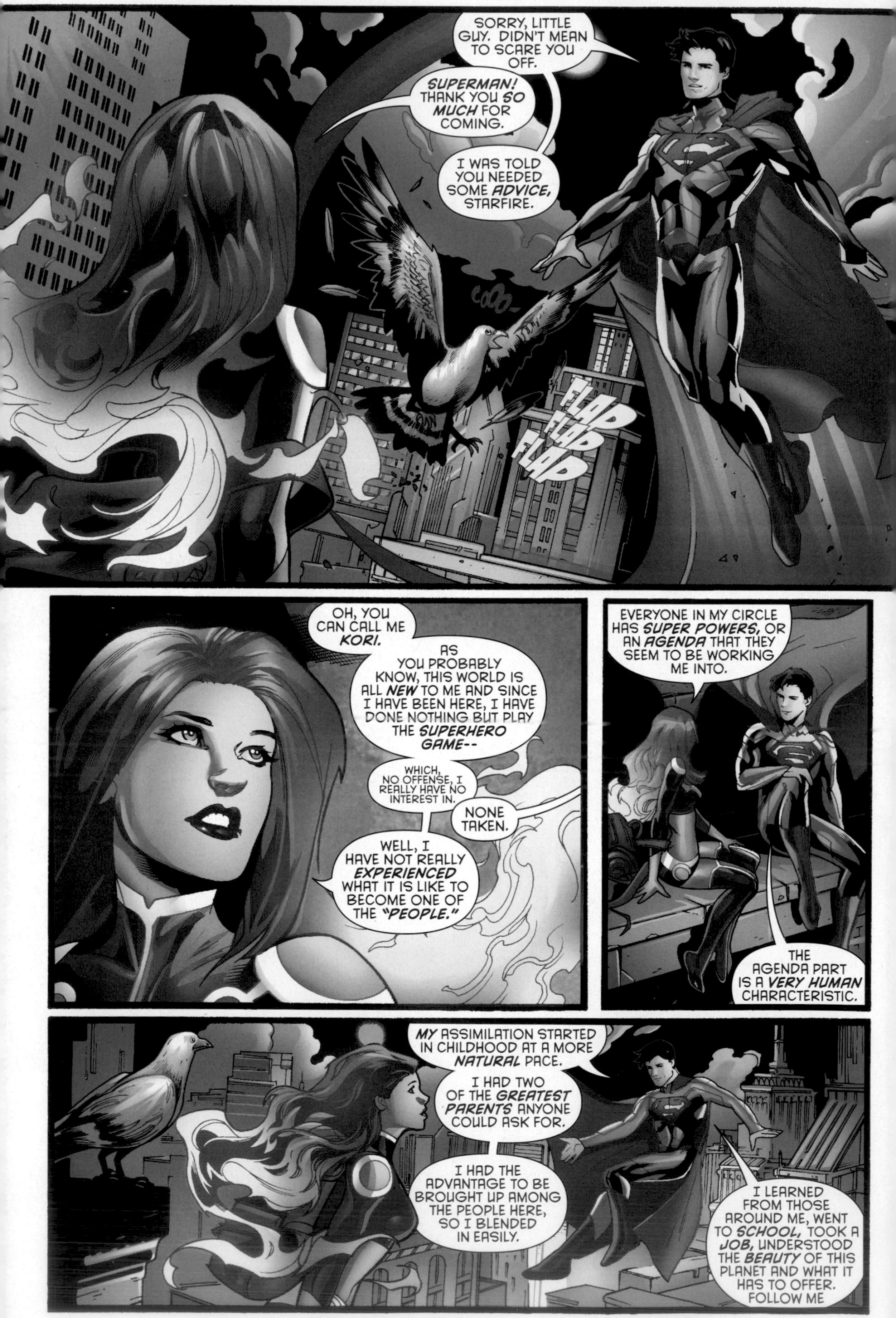
SORRY, LITTLE GUY. DIDN'T MEAN TO SCARE YOU OFF.
SUPERMAN! THANK YOU SO MUCH FOR COMING.
I WAS TOLD YOU NEEDED SOME ADVICE, STARFIRE.
COOO--
FLAP FLAP FLAP
OH, YOU CAN CALL ME KORI.
AS YOU PROBABLY KNOW, THIS WORLD IS ALL NEW TO ME AND SINCE I HAVE BEEN HERE, I HAVE DONE NOTHING BUT PLAY THE SUPERHERO GAME--
WHICH, NO OFFENSE, I REALLY HAVE NO INTEREST IN.
NONE TAKEN.
WELL, I HAVE NOT REALLY EXPERIENCED WHAT IT IS LIKE TO BECOME ONE OF THE "PEOPLE."
EVERYONE IN MY CIRCLE HAS SUPER POWERS, OR AN AGENDA THAT THEY SEEM TO BE WORKING ME INTO.
THE AGENDA PART IS A VERY HUMAN CHARACTERISTIC.
MY ASSIMILATION STARTED IN CHILDHOOD AT A MORE NATURAL PACE.
I HAD TWO OF THE GREATEST PARENTS ANYONE COULD ASK FOR.
I HAD THE ADVANTAGE TO BE BROUGHT UP AMONG THE PEOPLE HERE, SO I BLENDED IN EASILY.
I LEARNED FROM THOSE AROUND ME, WENT TO SCHOOL, TOOK A JOB, UNDERSTOOD THE BEAUTY OF THIS PLANET AND WHAT IT HAS TO OFFER. FOLLOW ME

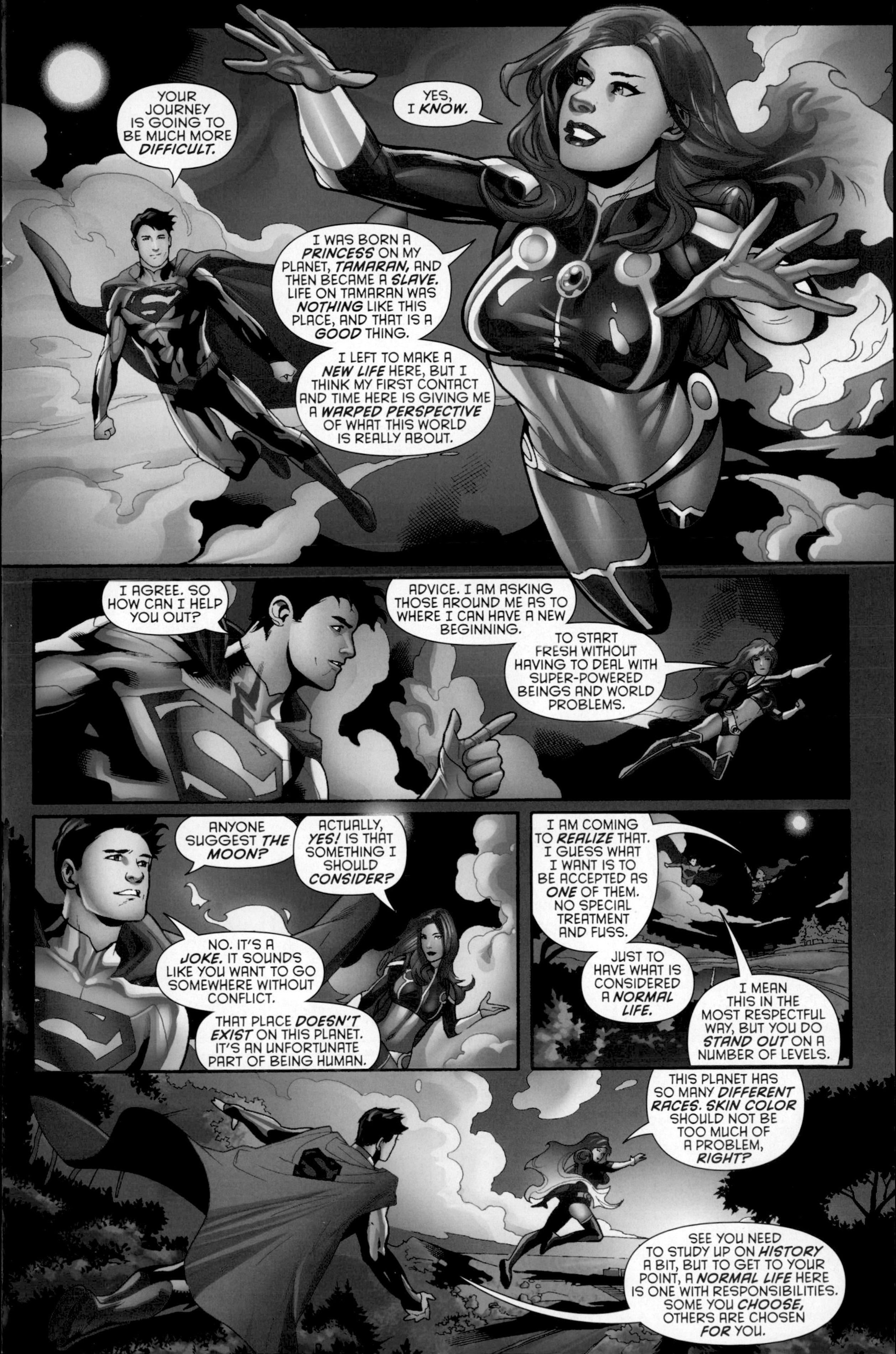
YOUR JOURNEY IS GOING TO BE MUCH MORE DIFFICULT.
YES, I KNOW.
I WAS BORN A PRINCESS ON MY PLANET, TAMARAN, AND THEN BECAME A SLAVE. LIFE ON TAMARAN WAS NOTHING LIKE THIS PLACE, AND THAT IS A GOOD THING.
I LEFT TO MAKE A NEW LIFE HERE, BUT I THINK MY FIRST CONTACT AND TIME HERE IS GIVING ME A WARPED PERSPECTIVE OF WHAT THIS WORLD IS REALLY ABOUT.
I AGREE. SO HOW CAN I HELP YOU OUT?
ADVICE. I AM ASKING THOSE AROUND ME AS TO WHERE I CAN HAVE A NEW BEGINNING.
TO START FRESH WITHOUT HAVING TO DEAL WITH SUPER-POWERED BEINGS AND WORLD PROBLEMS.
ANYONE SUGGEST THE MOON?
ACTUALLY, YES! IS THAT SOMETHING I SHOULD CONSIDER?
NO. IT'S A JOKE. IT SOUNDS LIKE YOU WANT TO GO SOMEWHERE WITHOUT CONFLICT.
THAT PLACE DOESN'T EXIST ON THIS PLANET. IT'S AN UNFORTUNATE PART OF BEING HUMAN.
I AM COMING TO REALIZE THAT. I GUESS WHAT I WANT IS TO BE ACCEPTED AS ONE OF THEM. NO SPECIAL TREATMENT AND FUSS.
JUST TO HAVE WHAT IS CONSIDERED A NORMAL LIFE.
I MEAN THIS IN THE MOST RESPECTFUL WAY, BUT YOU DO STAND OUT ON A NUMBER OF LEVELS.
THIS PLANET HAS SO MANY DIFFERENT RACES. SKIN COLOR SHOULD NOT BE TOO MUCH OF A PROBLEM, RIGHT?
SEE YOU NEED TO STUDY UP ON HISTORY A BIT, BUT TO GET TO YOUR POINT, A NORMAL LIFE HERE IS ONE WITH RESPONSIBILITIES. SOME YOU CHOOSE, OTHERS ARE CHOSEN FOR YOU.

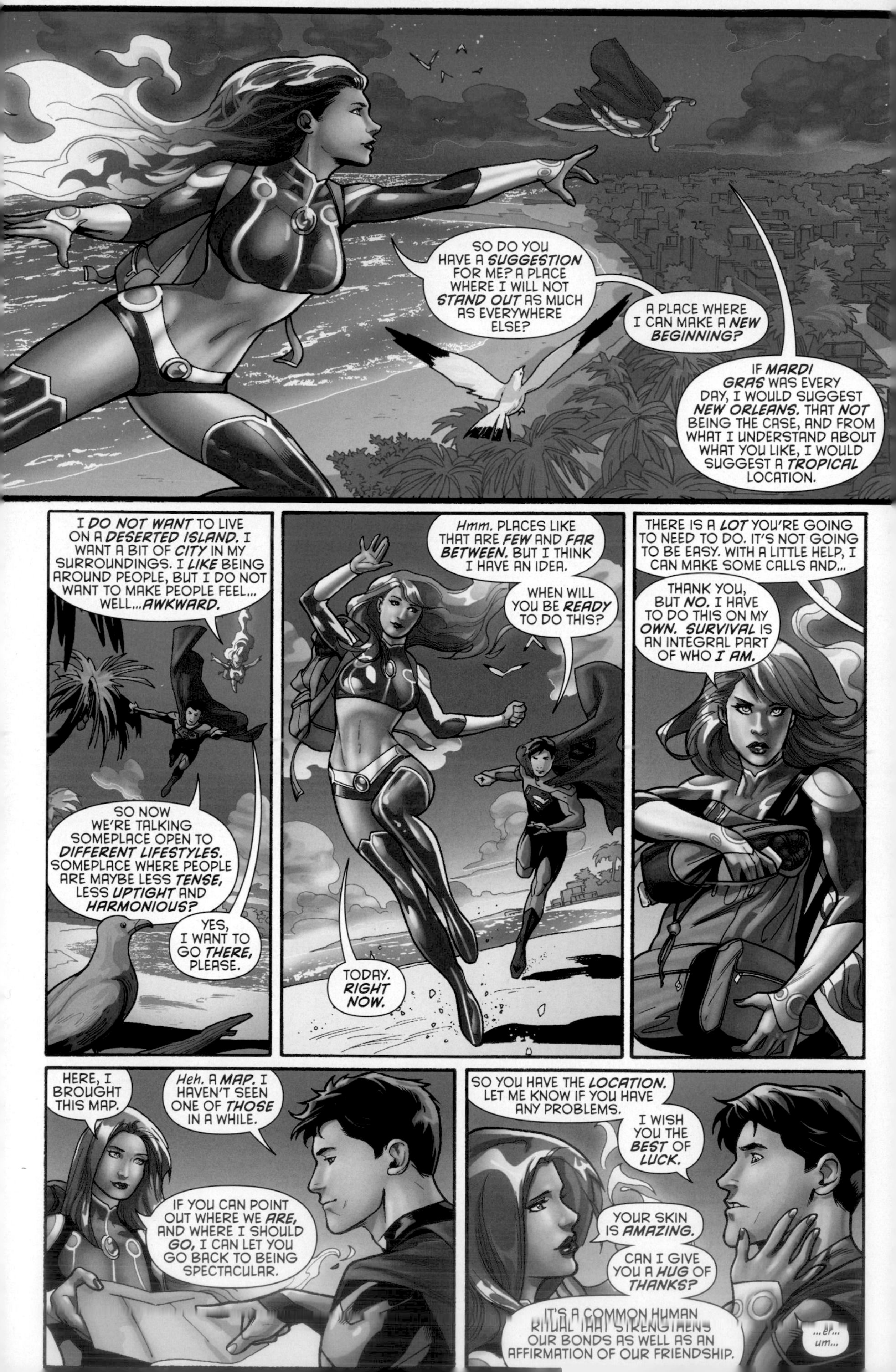
SO DO YOU HAVE A SUGGESTION FOR ME? A PLACE WHERE I WILL NOT STAND OUT AS MUCH AS EVERYWHERE ELSE?
A PLACE WHERE I CAN MAKE A NEW BEGINNING?
IF MARDI GRAS WAS EVERY DAY, I WOULD SUGGEST NEW ORLEANS. THAT NOT BEING THE CASE, AND FROM WHAT I UNDERSTAND ABOUT WHAT YOU LIKE, I WOULD SUGGEST A TROPICAL LOCATION.
I DO NOT WANT TO LIVE ON A DESERTED ISLAND. I WANT A BIT OF CITY IN MY SURROUNDINGS. I LIKE BEING AROUND PEOPLE, BUT I DO NOT WANT TO MAKE PEOPLE FEEL... WELL...AWKWARD.
SO NOW WE'RE TALKING SOMEPLACE OPEN TO DIFFERENT LIFESTYLES. SOMEPLACE WHERE PEOPLE ARE MAYBE LESS TENSE, LESS UPTIGHT AND HARMONIOUS?
YES, I WANT TO GO THERE, PLEASE.
Hmm. PLACES LIKE THAT ARE FEW AND FAR BETWEEN. BUT I THINK I HAVE AN IDEA.
WHEN WILL YOU BE READY TO DO THIS?
TODAY. RIGHT NOW.
THERE IS A LOT YOU'RE GOING TO NEED TO DO. IT'S NOT GOING TO BE EASY. WITH A LITTLE HELP, I CAN MAKE SOME CALLS AND...
THANK YOU, BUT NO. I HAVE TO DO THIS ON MY OWN. SURVIVAL IS AN INTEGRAL PART OF WHO I AM.
HERE, I BROUGHT THIS MAP.
Heh. A MAP. I HAVEN'T SEEN ONE OF THOSE IN A WHILE.
IF YOU CAN POINT OUT WHERE WE ARE, AND WHERE I SHOULD GO, I CAN LET YOU GO BACK TO BEING SPECTACULAR.
SO YOU HAVE THE LOCATION. LET ME KNOW IF YOU HAVE ANY PROBLEMS.
I WISH YOU THE BEST OF LUCK.
YOUR SKIN IS AMAZING.
CAN I GIVE YOU A HUG OF THANKS?
IT'S A COMMON HUMAN RITUAL THAT STRENGTHENS OUR BONDS AS WELL AS AN AFFIRMATION OF OUR FRIENDSHIP.
...er... um...

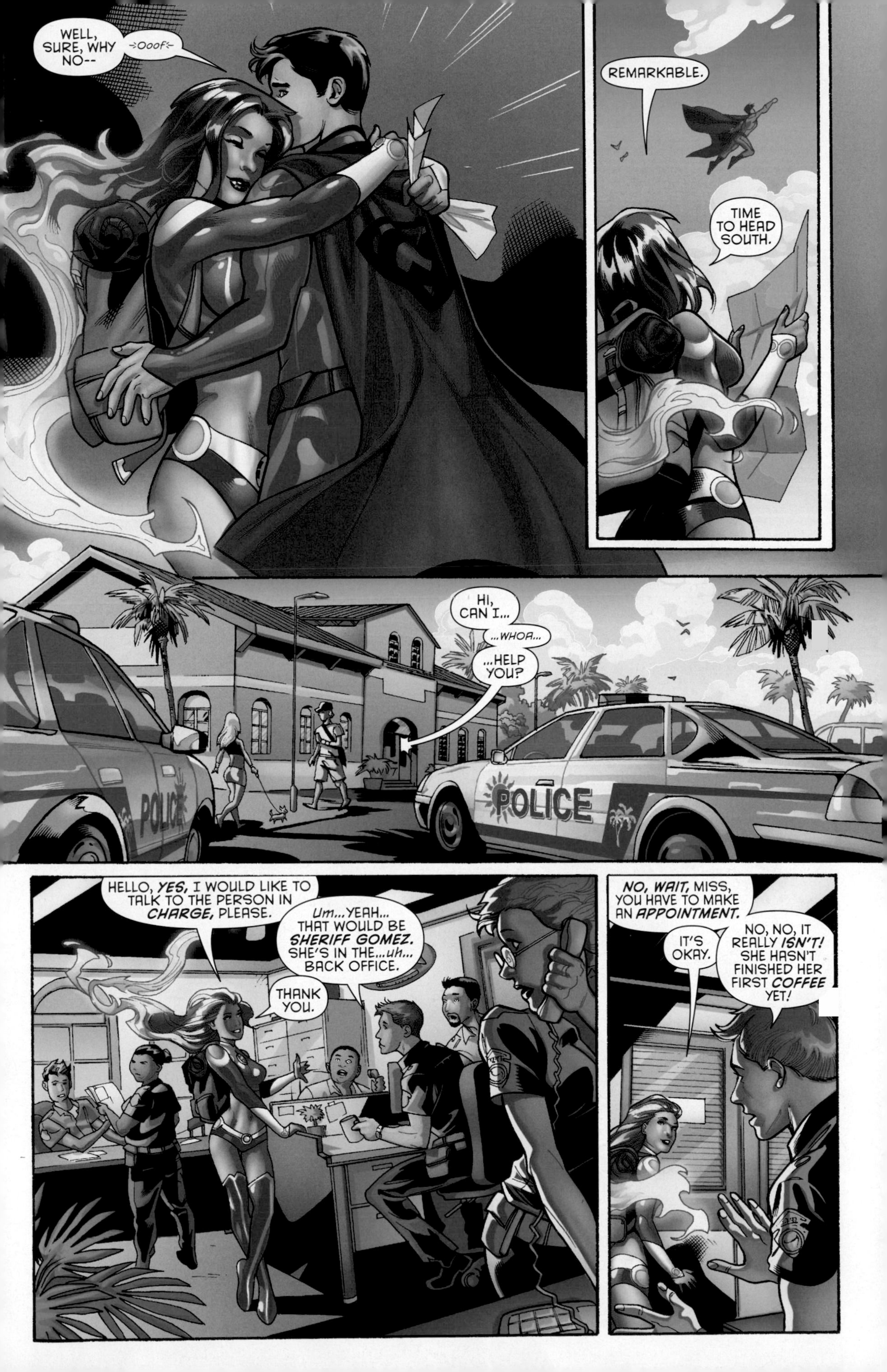
WELL, SURE, WHY NO--
>OOOF<
REMARKABLE.
TIME TO HEAD SOUTH.
HI, CAN I...
...WHOA...
...HELP YOU?
POLICE
POLICE
HELLO, *YES,* I WOULD LIKE TO TALK TO THE PERSON IN *CHARGE,* PLEASE.
Um...YEAH... THAT WOULD BE *SHERIFF GOMEZ.* SHE'S IN THE...*uh*... BACK OFFICE.
THANK YOU.
NO, WAIT, MISS, YOU HAVE TO MAKE AN *APPOINTMENT.*
IT'S OKAY.
NO, NO, IT REALLY *ISN'T!* SHE HASN'T FINISHED HER FIRST *COFFEE* YET!

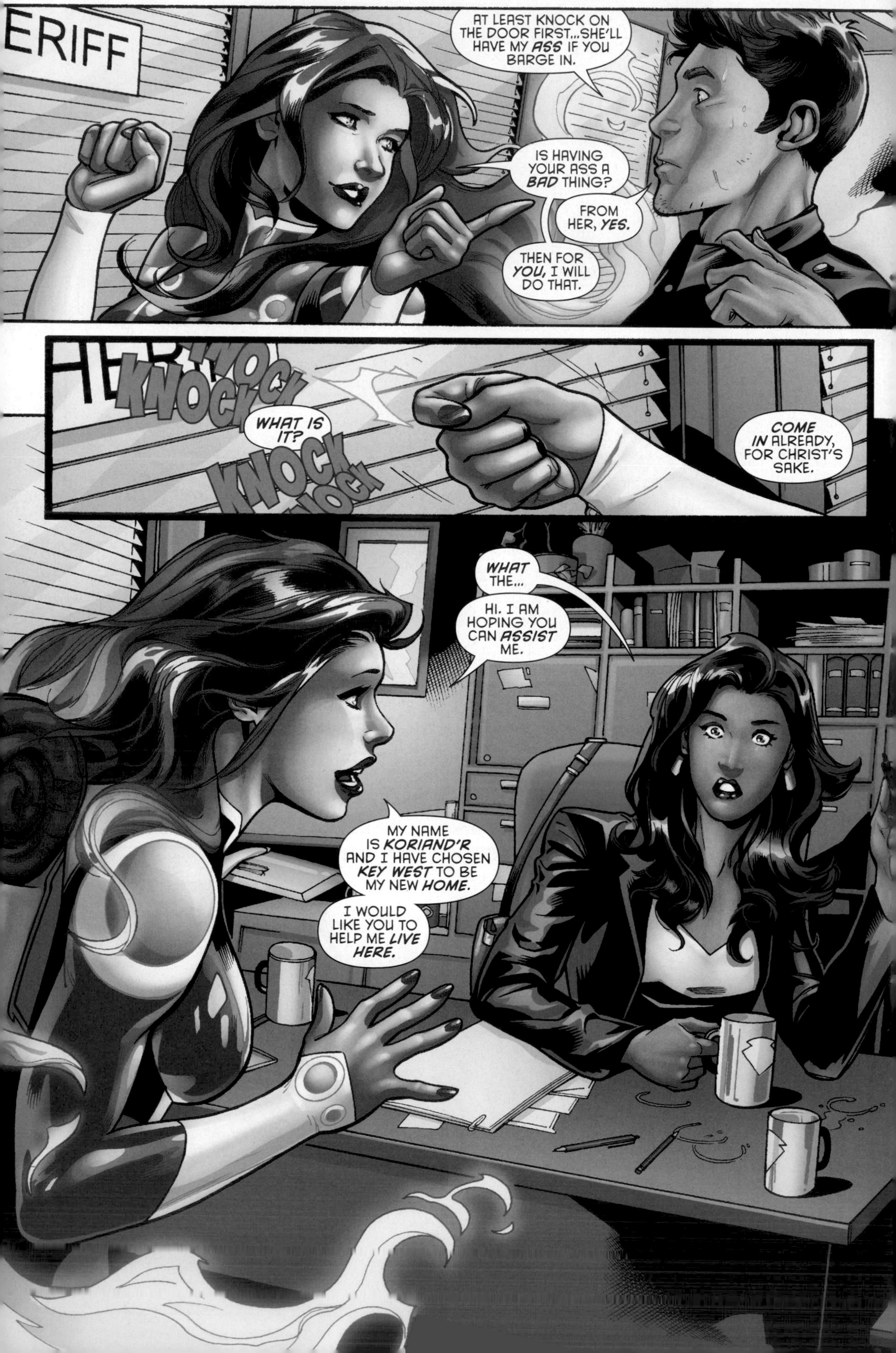
ERIFF
AT LEAST KNOCK ON THE DOOR FIRST...SHE'LL HAVE MY ASS IF YOU BARGE IN.
IS HAVING YOUR ASS A BAD THING?
FROM HER, YES.
THEN FOR YOU, I WILL DO THAT.
KNOCK KNOCK
WHAT IS IT?
KNOCK
COME IN ALREADY, FOR CHRIST'S SAKE.
WHAT THE...
HI. I AM HOPING YOU CAN ASSIST ME.
MY NAME IS KORIAND'R AND I HAVE CHOSEN KEY WEST TO BE MY NEW HOME.
I WOULD LIKE YOU TO HELP ME LIVE HERE.

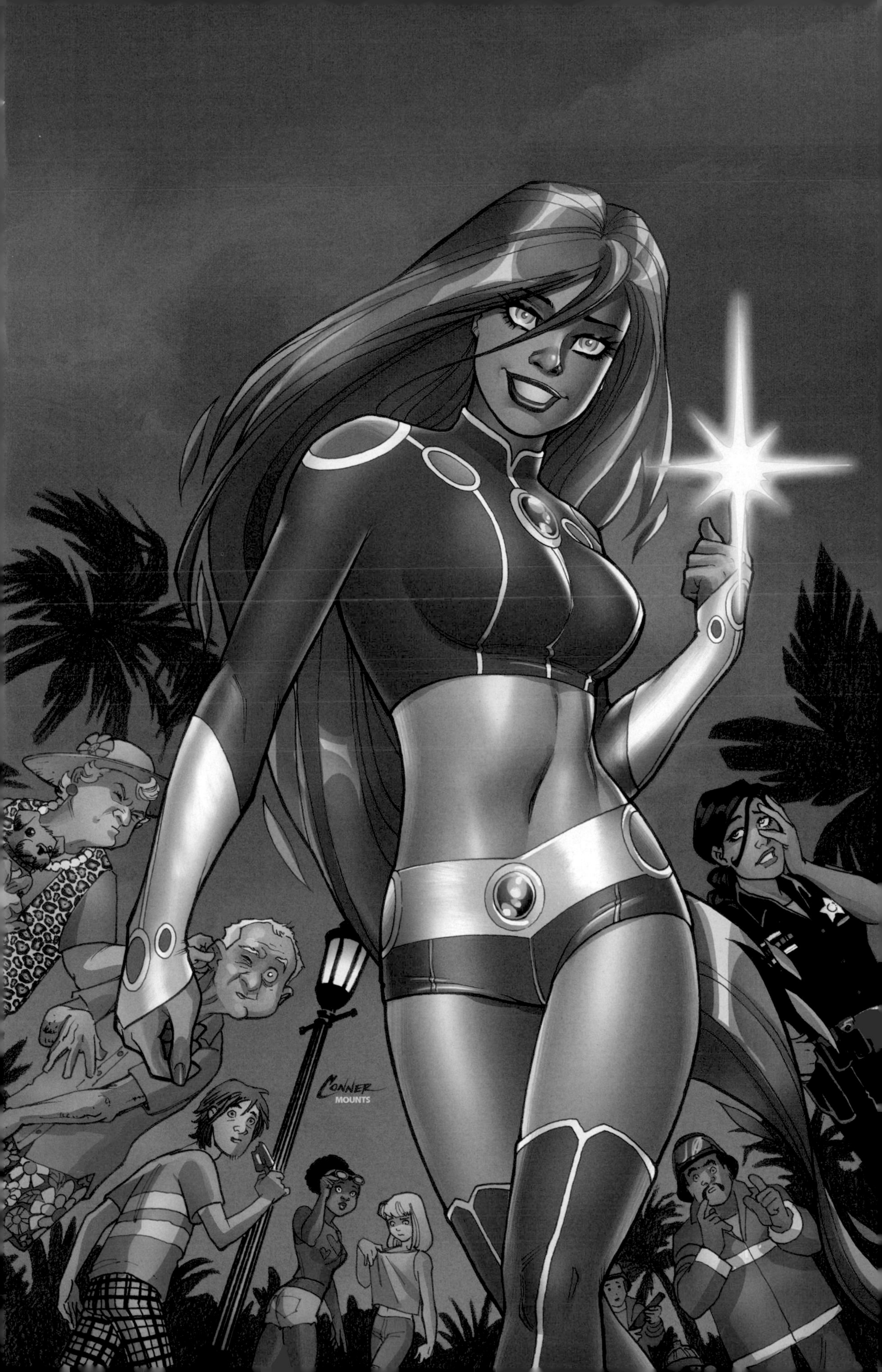
CONNER
MOUNTS

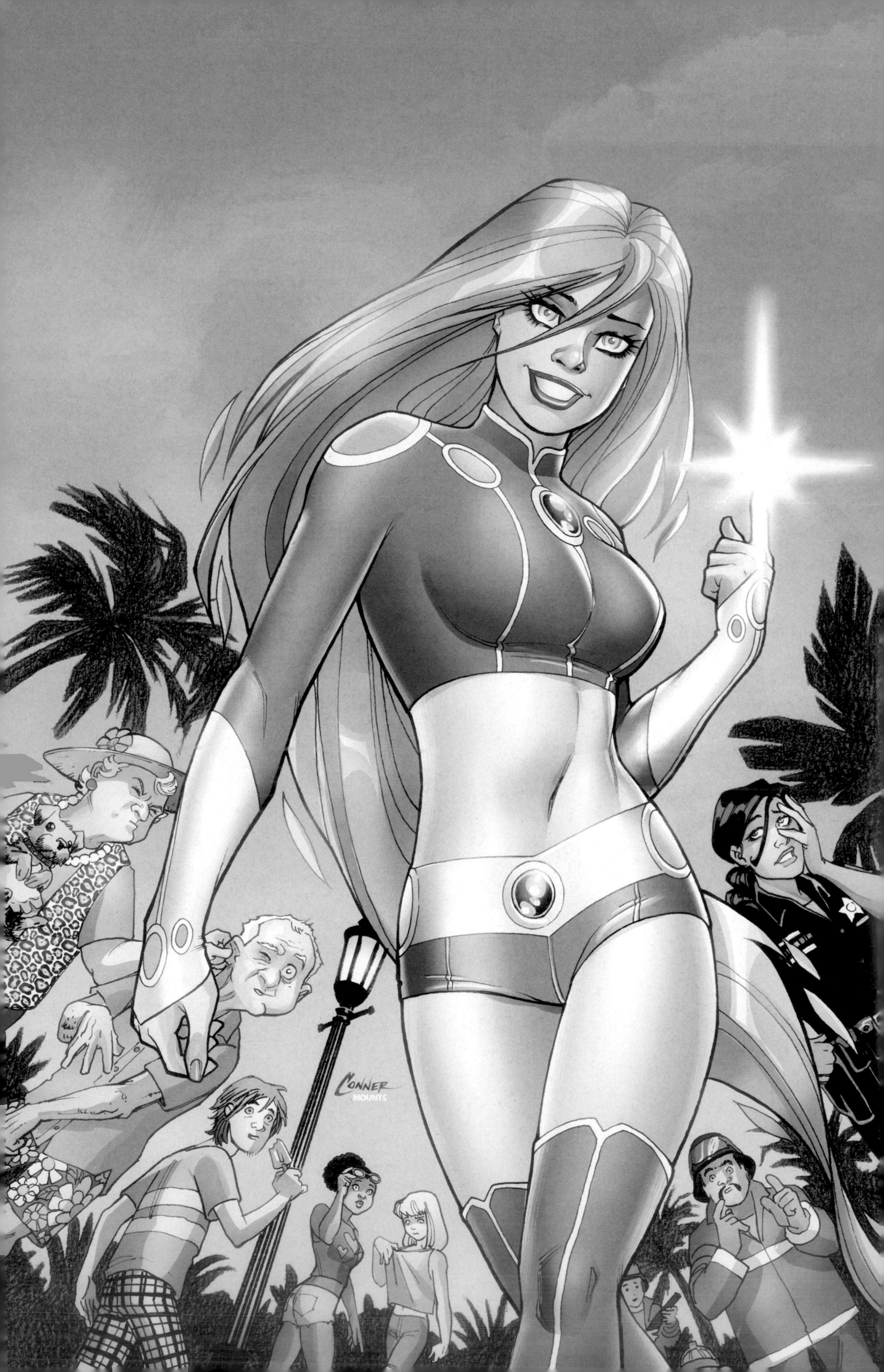
CONNER
MOUNTS

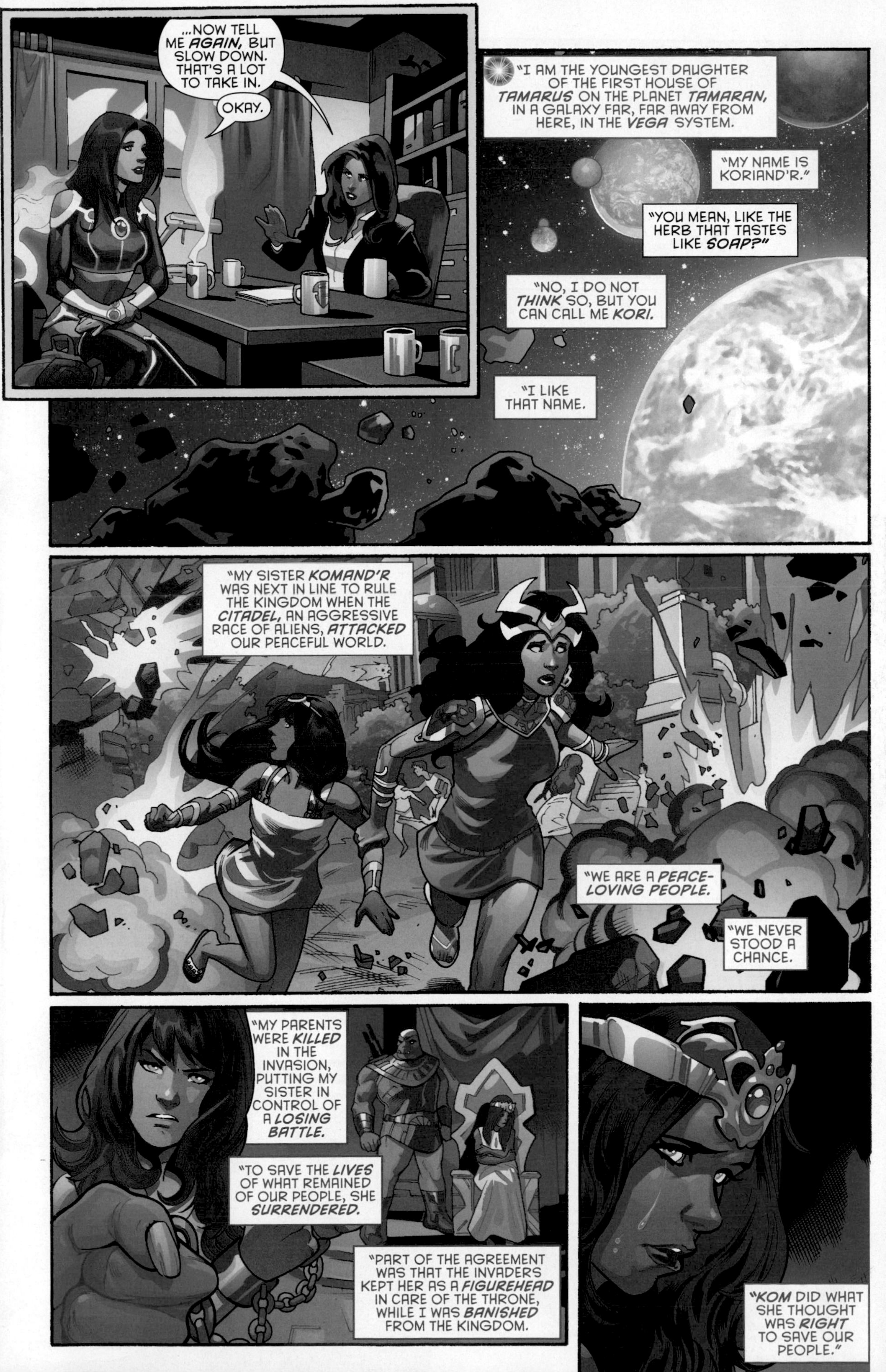
...NOW TELL ME AGAIN, BUT SLOW DOWN. THAT'S A LOT TO TAKE IN.
OKAY.
"I AM THE YOUNGEST DAUGHTER OF THE FIRST HOUSE OF TAMARUS ON THE PLANET TAMARAN, IN A GALAXY FAR, FAR AWAY FROM HERE, IN THE VEGA SYSTEM.
"MY NAME IS KORIAND'R."
"YOU MEAN, LIKE THE HERB THAT TASTES LIKE SOAP?"
"NO, I DO NOT THINK SO, BUT YOU CAN CALL ME KORI.
"I LIKE THAT NAME.
"MY SISTER KOMAND'R WAS NEXT IN LINE TO RULE THE KINGDOM WHEN THE CITADEL, AN AGGRESSIVE RACE OF ALIENS, ATTACKED OUR PEACEFUL WORLD.
"WE ARE A PEACE-LOVING PEOPLE.
"WE NEVER STOOD A CHANCE.
"MY PARENTS WERE KILLED IN THE INVASION, PUTTING MY SISTER IN CONTROL OF A LOSING BATTLE.
"TO SAVE THE LIVES OF WHAT REMAINED OF OUR PEOPLE, SHE SURRENDERED.
"PART OF THE AGREEMENT WAS THAT THE INVADERS KEPT HER AS A FIGUREHEAD IN CARE OF THE THRONE, WHILE I WAS BANISHED FROM THE KINGDOM.
"KOM DID WHAT SHE THOUGHT WAS RIGHT TO SAVE OUR PEOPLE."

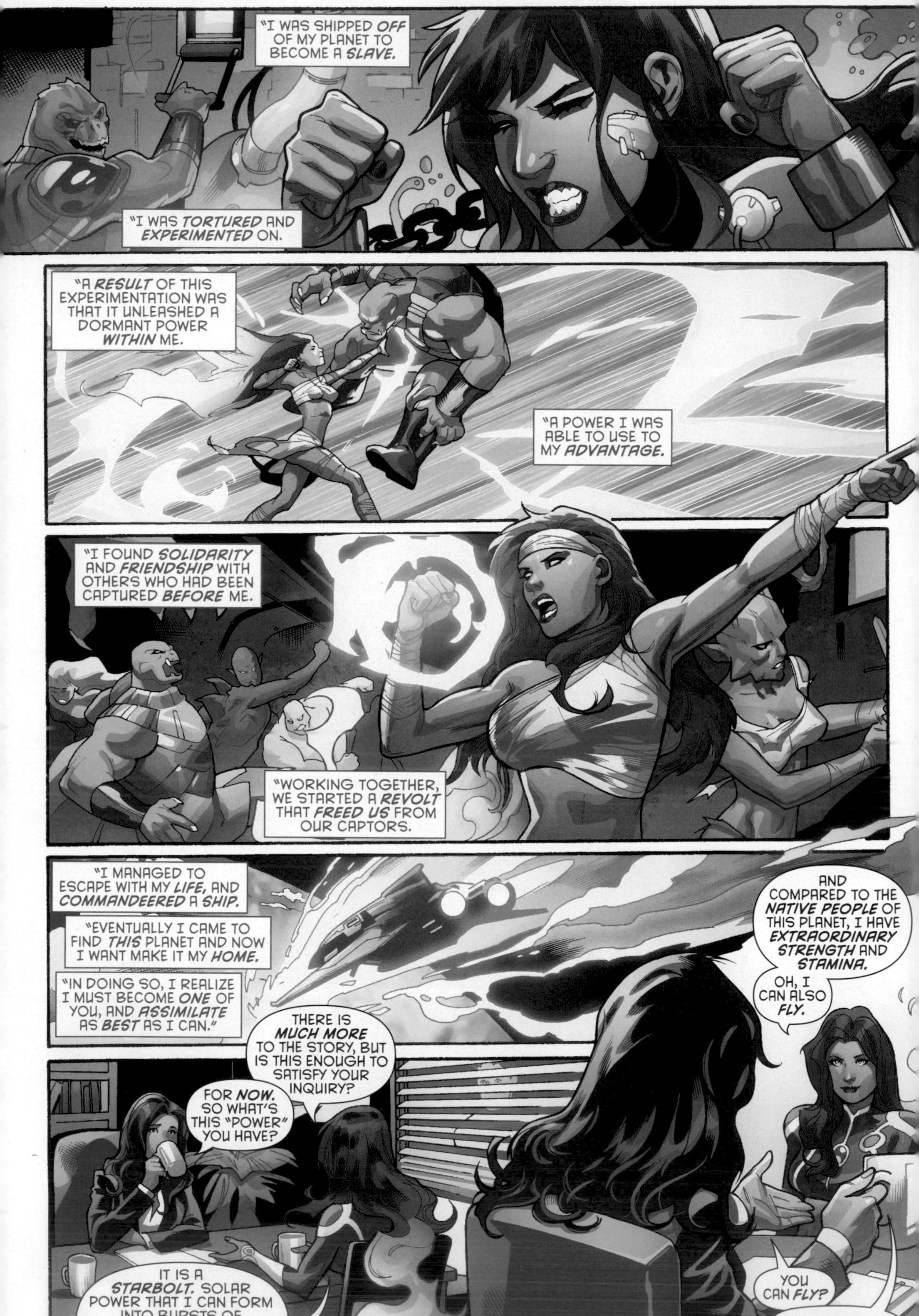
"I WAS SHIPPED OFF OF MY PLANET TO BECOME A SLAVE.
"I WAS TORTURED AND EXPERIMENTED ON.
"A RESULT OF THIS EXPERIMENTATION WAS THAT IT UNLEASHED A DORMANT POWER WITHIN ME.
"A POWER I WAS ABLE TO USE TO MY ADVANTAGE.
"I FOUND SOLIDARITY AND FRIENDSHIP WITH OTHERS WHO HAD BEEN CAPTURED BEFORE ME.
"WORKING TOGETHER, WE STARTED A REVOLT THAT FREED US FROM OUR CAPTORS.
"I MANAGED TO ESCAPE WITH MY LIFE, AND COMMANDEERED A SHIP.
"EVENTUALLY I CAME TO FIND THIS PLANET AND NOW I WANT MAKE IT MY HOME.
"IN DOING SO, I REALIZE I MUST BECOME ONE OF YOU, AND ASSIMILATE AS BEST AS I CAN."
THERE IS MUCH MORE TO THE STORY, BUT IS THIS ENOUGH TO SATISFY YOUR INQUIRY?
FOR NOW. SO WHAT'S THIS "POWER" YOU HAVE?
IT IS A STARBOLT. SOLAR POWER THAT I CAN FORM INTO BURSTS OF CONCENTRATED ENERGY.
AND COMPARED TO THE NATIVE PEOPLE OF THIS PLANET, I HAVE EXTRAORDINARY STRENGTH AND STAMINA.
OH, I CAN ALSO FLY.
YOU CAN FLY?
YES. WOULD YOU LIKE ME TO DEMONSTRATE?

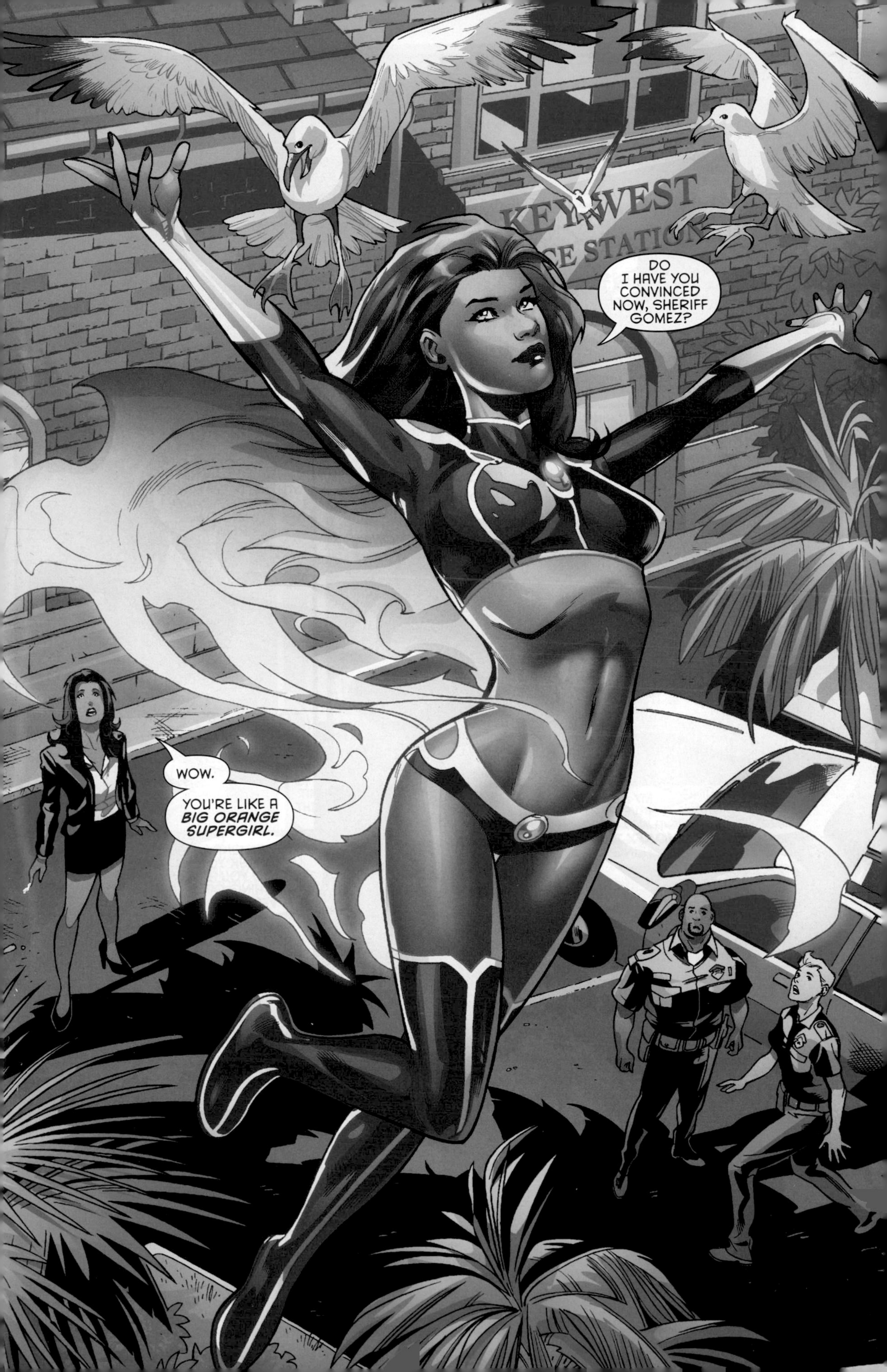
KEY WEST
DO I HAVE YOU CONVINCED NOW, SHERIFF GOMEZ?
WOW.
YOU'RE LIKE A BIG ORANGE SUPERGIRL.

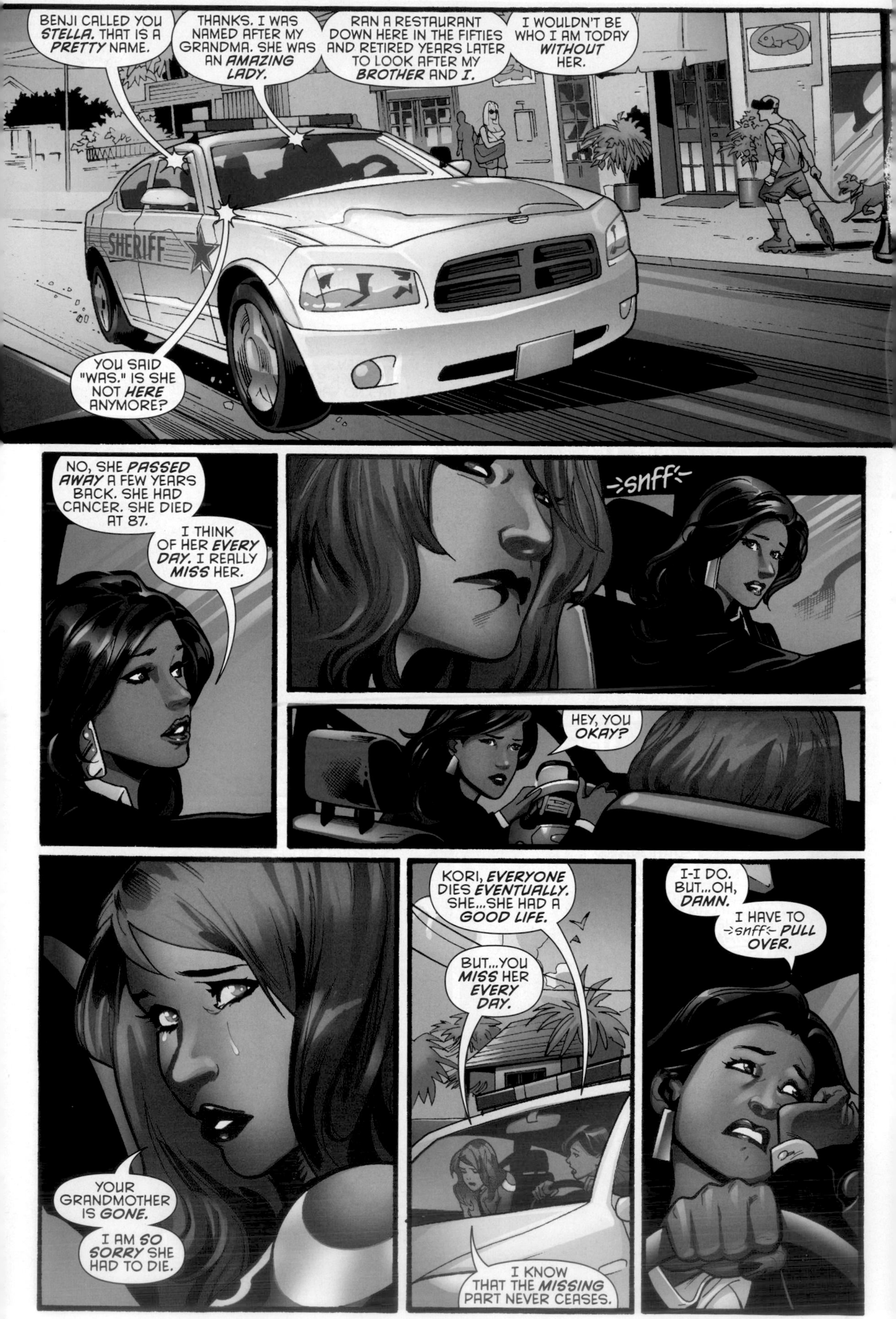

BENJI CALLED YOU STELLA. THAT IS A PRETTY NAME.
THANKS. I WAS NAMED AFTER MY GRANDMA. SHE WAS AN AMAZING LADY.
RAN A RESTAURANT DOWN HERE IN THE FIFTIES AND RETIRED YEARS LATER TO LOOK AFTER MY BROTHER AND I.
I WOULDN'T BE WHO I AM TODAY WITHOUT HER.
YOU SAID "WAS." IS SHE NOT HERE ANYMORE?
SHERIFF
NO, SHE PASSED AWAY A FEW YEARS BACK. SHE HAD CANCER. SHE DIED AT 87.
I THINK OF HER EVERY DAY. I REALLY MISS HER.
snff
HEY, YOU OKAY?
YOUR GRANDMOTHER IS GONE.
I AM SO SORRY SHE HAD TO DIE.
KORI, EVERYONE DIES EVENTUALLY. SHE...SHE HAD A GOOD LIFE.
BUT...YOU MISS HER EVERY DAY.
I KNOW THAT THE MISSING PART NEVER CEASES.
I-I DO. BUT...OH, DAMN.
I HAVE TO snff PULL OVER.

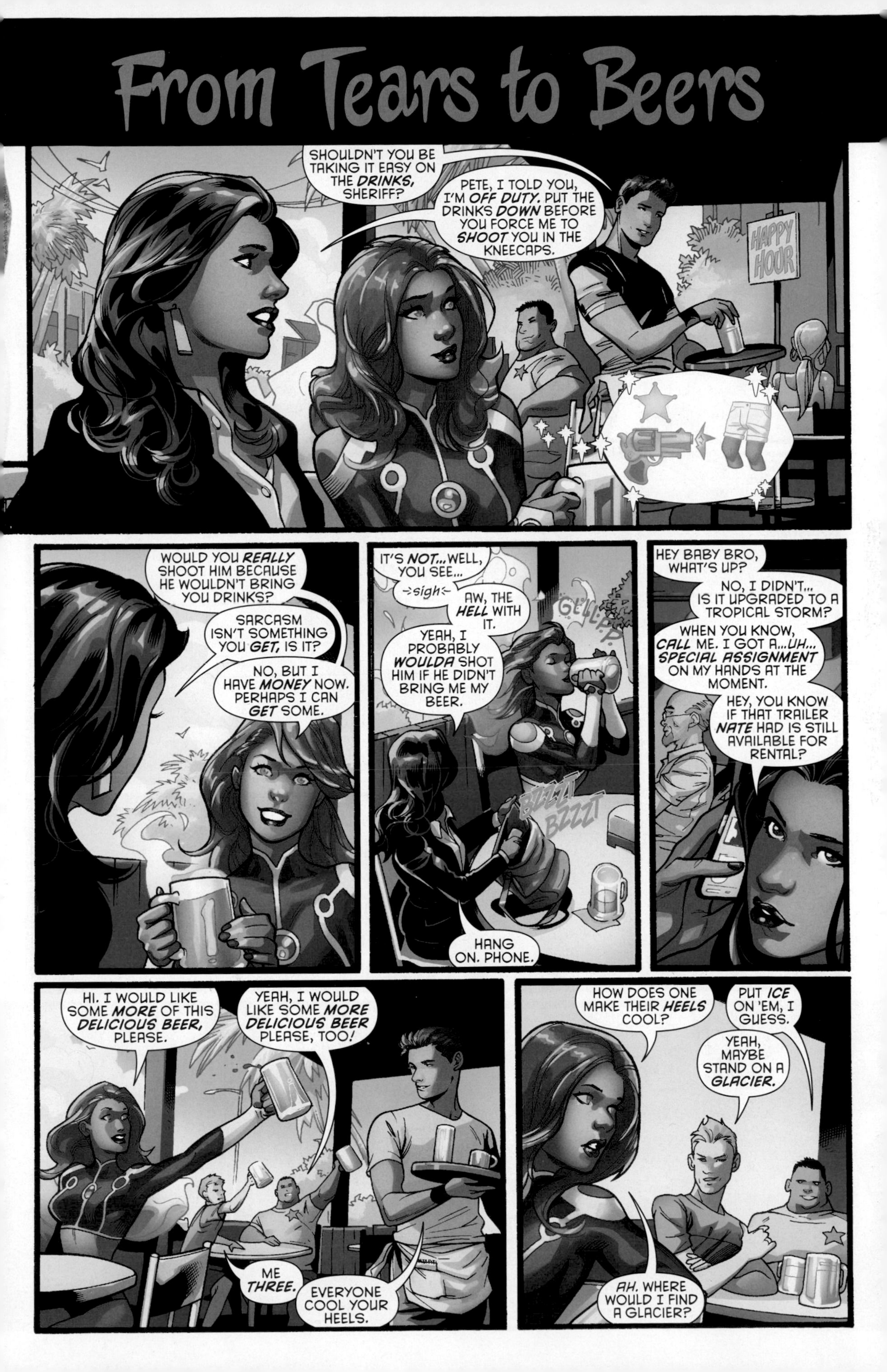
From Tears to Beers
SHOULDN'T YOU BE TAKING IT EASY ON THE DRINKS, SHERIFF?
PETE, I TOLD YOU, I'M OFF DUTY. PUT THE DRINKS DOWN BEFORE YOU FORCE ME TO SHOOT YOU IN THE KNEECAPS.
HAPPY HOUR
WOULD YOU REALLY SHOOT HIM BECAUSE HE WOULDN'T BRING YOU DRINKS?
SARCASM ISN'T SOMETHING YOU GET, IS IT?
NO, BUT I HAVE MONEY NOW. PERHAPS I CAN GET SOME.
IT'S NOT... WELL, YOU SEE...
sigh
AW, THE HELL WITH IT.
YEAH, I PROBABLY WOULDA SHOT HIM IF HE DIDN'T BRING ME MY BEER.
GLLLP
BZZZT BZZZT
HANG ON. PHONE.
HEY BABY BRO, WHAT'S UP?
NO, I DIDN'T... IS IT UPGRADED TO A TROPICAL STORM?
WHEN YOU KNOW, CALL ME. I GOT A... UH... SPECIAL ASSIGNMENT ON MY HANDS AT THE MOMENT.
HEY, YOU KNOW IF THAT TRAILER NATE HAD IS STILL AVAILABLE FOR RENTAL?
HI. I WOULD LIKE SOME MORE OF THIS DELICIOUS BEER, PLEASE.
YEAH, I WOULD LIKE SOME MORE DELICIOUS BEER PLEASE, TOO!
ME THREE.
EVERYONE COOL YOUR HEELS.
HOW DOES ONE MAKE THEIR HEELS COOL?
PUT ICE ON 'EM, I GUESS.
YEAH, MAYBE STAND ON A GLACIER.
AH. WHERE WOULD I FIND A GLACIER?

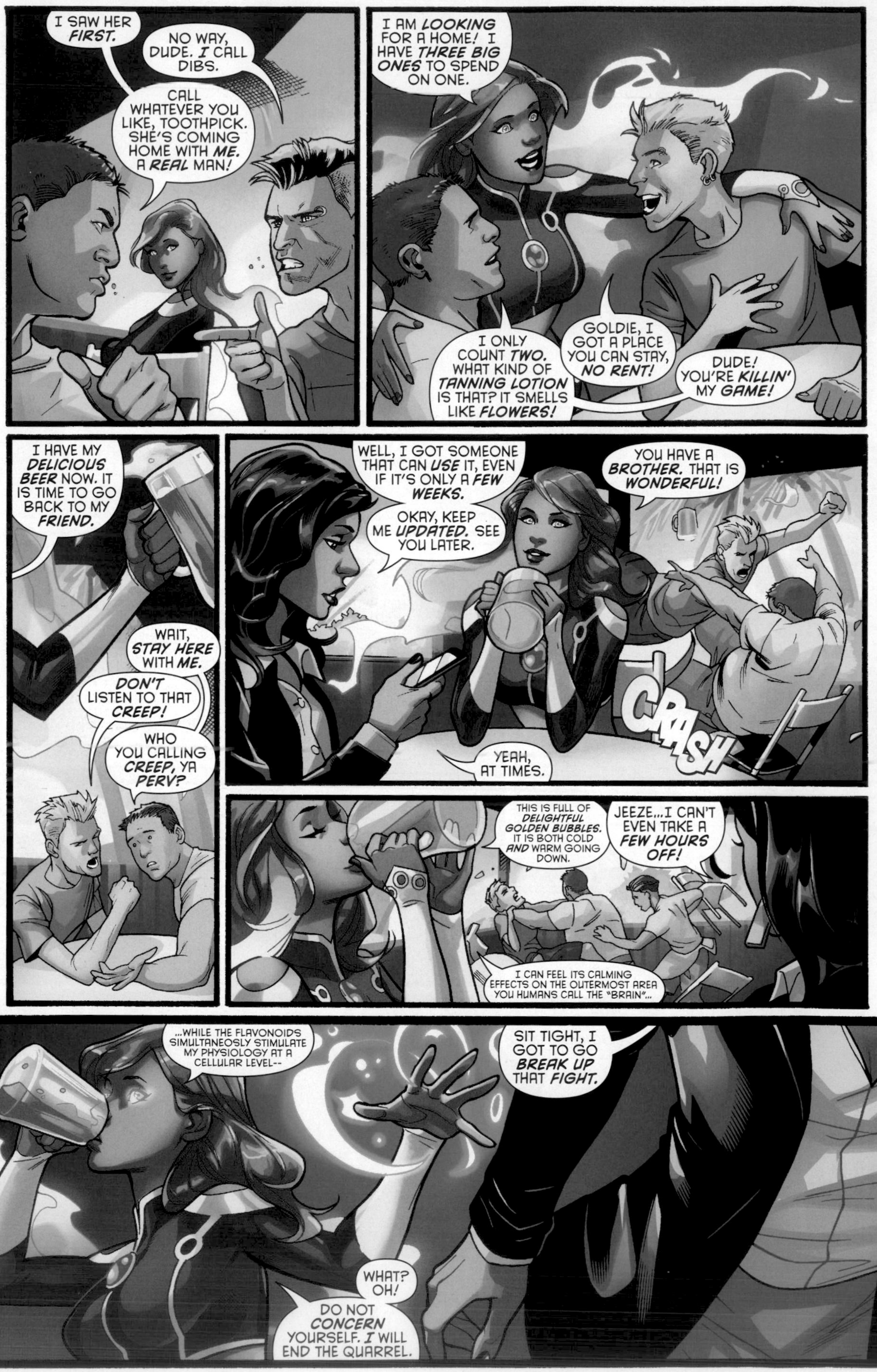
I SAW HER FIRST.
NO WAY, DUDE. I CALL DIBS.
CALL WHATEVER YOU LIKE, TOOTHPICK. SHE'S COMING HOME WITH ME. A REAL MAN!
I AM LOOKING FOR A HOME! I HAVE THREE BIG ONES TO SPEND ON ONE.
I ONLY COUNT TWO. WHAT KIND OF TANNING LOTION IS THAT? IT SMELLS LIKE FLOWERS!
GOLDIE, I GOT A PLACE YOU CAN STAY, NO RENT!
DUDE! YOU'RE KILLIN' MY GAME!
I HAVE MY DELICIOUS BEER NOW. IT IS TIME TO GO BACK TO MY FRIEND.
WAIT, STAY HERE WITH ME.
DON'T LISTEN TO THAT CREEP!
WHO YOU CALLING CREEP, YA PERV?
WELL, I GOT SOMEONE THAT CAN USE IT, EVEN IF IT'S ONLY A FEW WEEKS.
OKAY, KEEP ME UPDATED. SEE YOU LATER.
YOU HAVE A BROTHER. THAT IS WONDERFUL!
YEAH, AT TIMES.
CRASH
THIS IS FULL OF DELIGHTFUL GOLDEN BUBBLES. IT IS BOTH COLD AND WARM GOING DOWN.
I CAN FEEL ITS CALMING EFFECTS ON THE OUTERMOST AREA YOU HUMANS CALL THE "BRAIN"...
JEEZE...I CAN'T EVEN TAKE A FEW HOURS OFF!
...WHILE THE FLAVONOIDS SIMULTANEOSLY STIMULATE MY PHYSIOLOGY AT A CELLULAR LEVEL--
SIT TIGHT, I GOT TO GO BREAK UP THAT FIGHT.
WHAT? OH!
DO NOT CONCERN YOURSELF. I WILL END THE QUARREL.

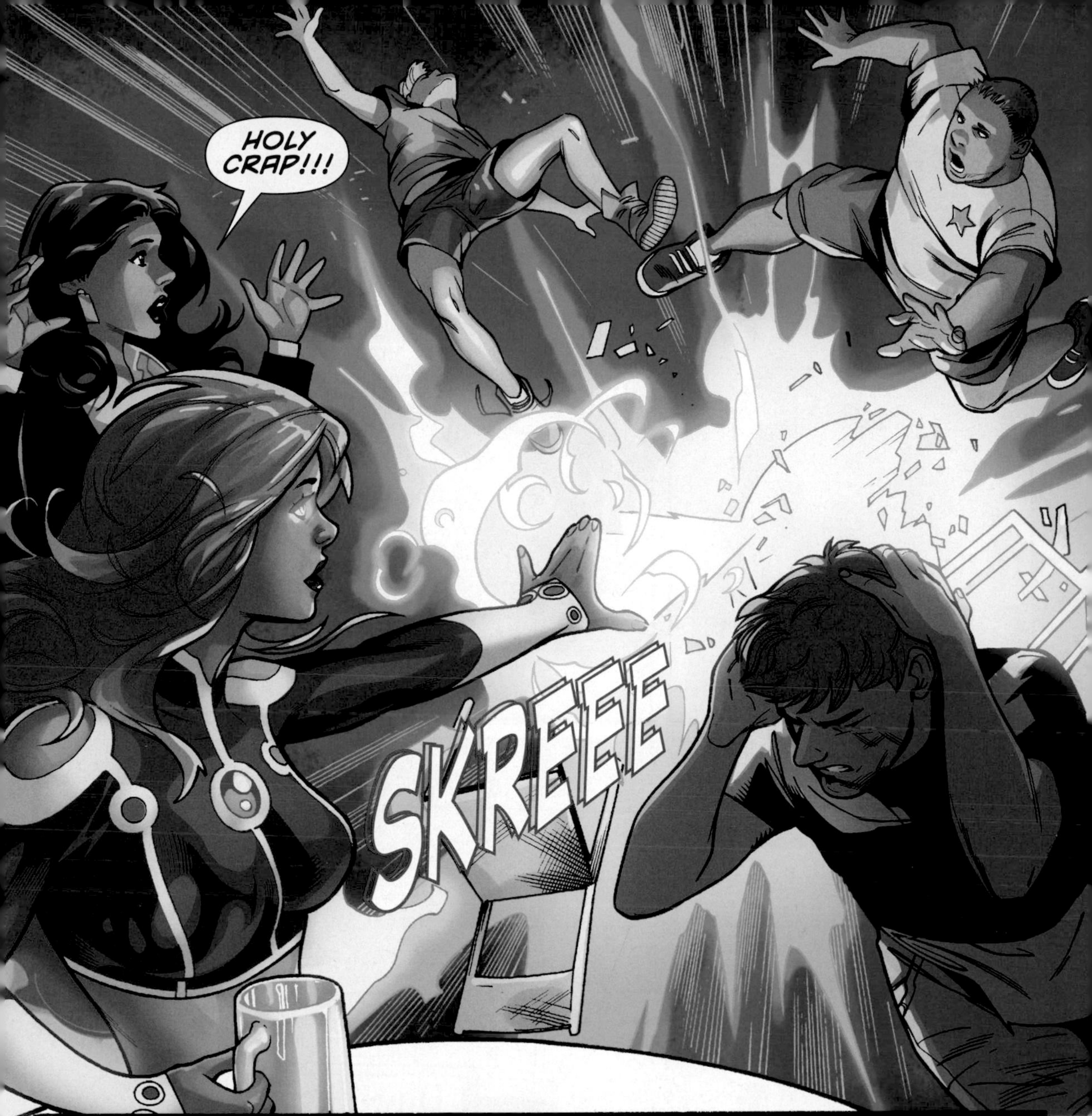
HOLY CRAP!!!
SKREEE
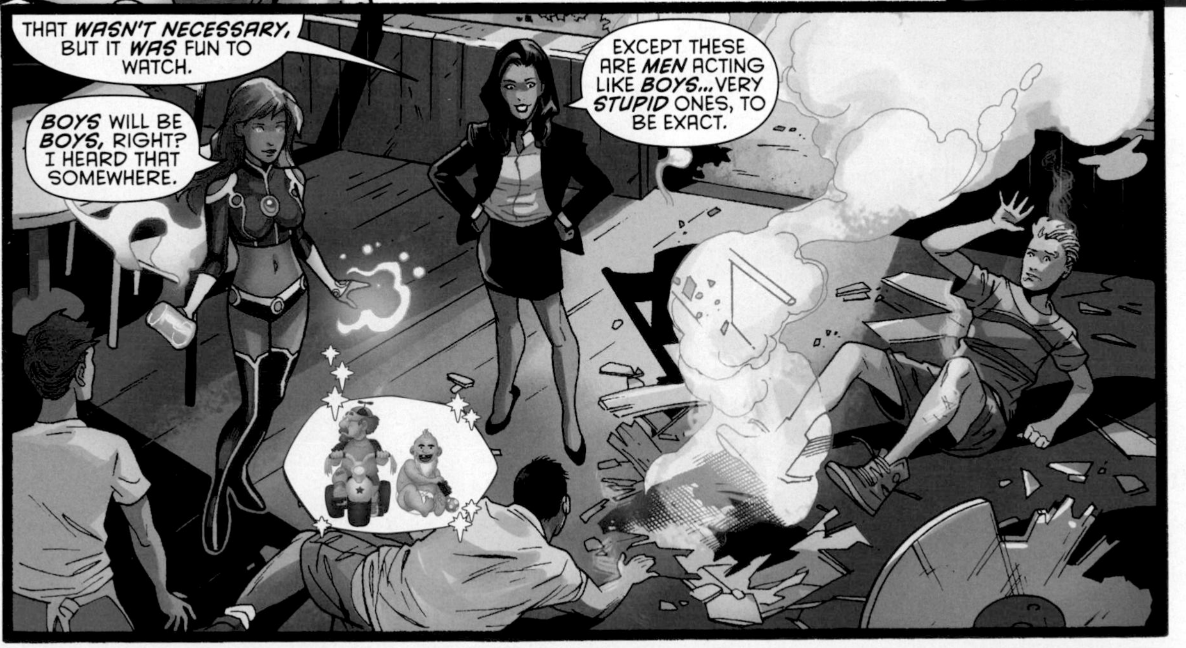
THAT WASN'T NECESSARY, BUT IT WAS FUN TO WATCH.
EXCEPT THESE ARE MEN ACTING LIKE BOYS... VERY STUPID ONES, TO BE EXACT.
BOYS WILL BE BOYS, RIGHT? I HEARD THAT SOMEWHERE.

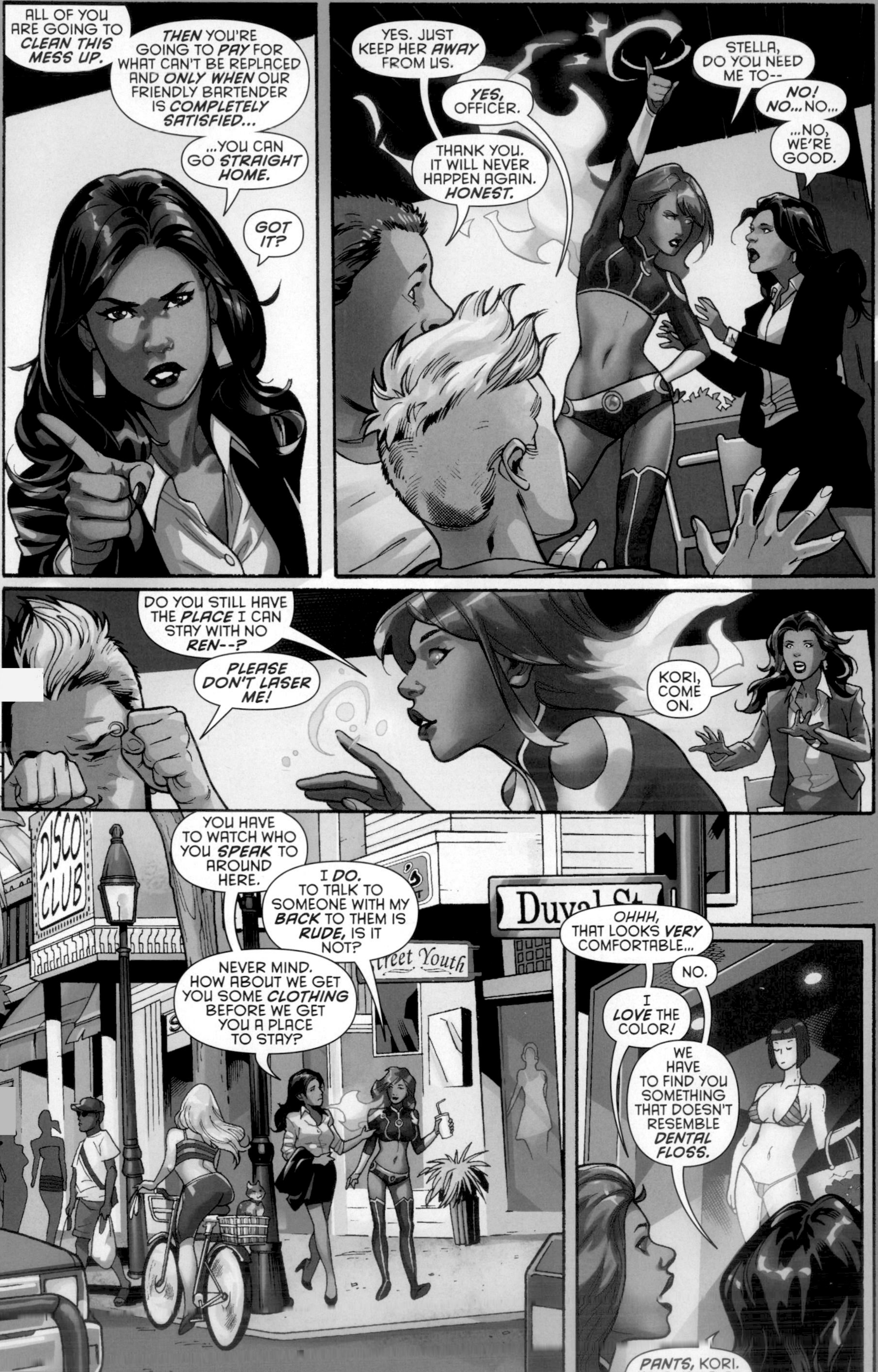
ALL OF YOU ARE GOING TO CLEAN THIS MESS UP.
THEN YOU'RE GOING TO PAY FOR WHAT CAN'T BE REPLACED AND ONLY WHEN OUR FRIENDLY BARTENDER IS COMPLETELY SATISFIED...
...YOU CAN GO STRAIGHT HOME.
GOT IT?
YES. JUST KEEP HER AWAY FROM US.
YES, OFFICER.
THANK YOU. IT WILL NEVER HAPPEN AGAIN. HONEST.
STELLA, DO YOU NEED ME TO--
NO! NO...NO...
...NO, WE'RE GOOD.
DO YOU STILL HAVE THE PLACE I CAN STAY WITH NO REN--?
PLEASE DON'T LASER ME!
KORI, COME ON.
DISCO CLUB
YOU HAVE TO WATCH WHO YOU SPEAK TO AROUND HERE.
I DO. TO TALK TO SOMEONE WITH MY BACK TO THEM IS RUDE, IS IT NOT?
NEVER MIND. HOW ABOUT WE GET YOU SOME CLOTHING BEFORE WE GET YOU A PLACE TO STAY?
Duval St
OHHH, THAT LOOKS VERY COMFORTABLE...
NO.
I LOVE THE COLOR!
WE HAVE TO FIND YOU SOMETHING THAT DOESN'T RESEMBLE DENTAL FLOSS.
PANTS, KORI. HAVE YOU EVER TRIED PANTS?

You Can Lead a Horse To Water, But...

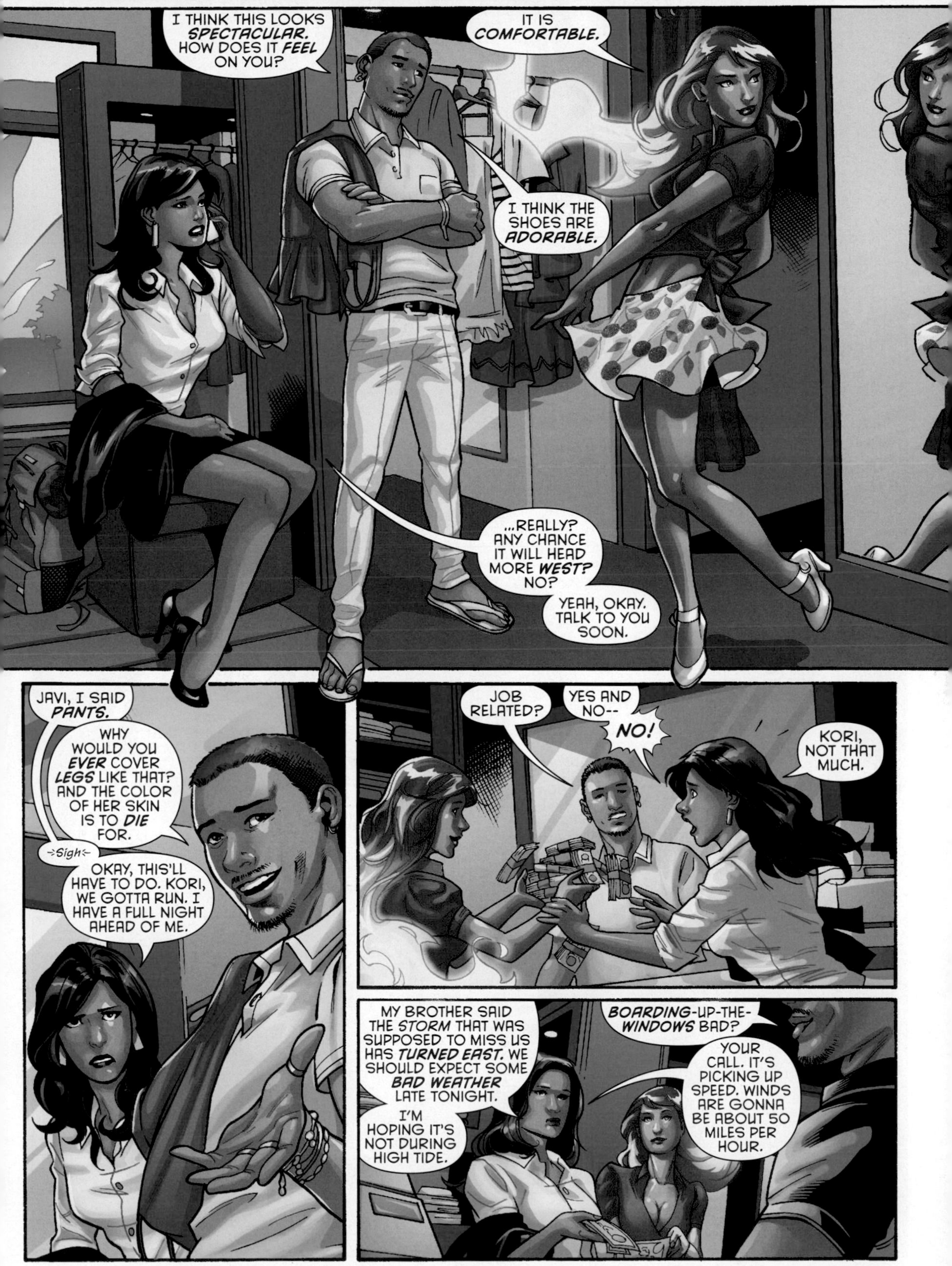
I THINK THIS LOOKS SPECTACULAR. HOW DOES IT FEEL ON YOU?
IT IS COMFORTABLE.
I THINK THE SHOES ARE ADORABLE.
...REALLY? ANY CHANCE IT WILL HEAD MORE WEST? NO?
YEAH, OKAY. TALK TO YOU SOON.
JAVI, I SAID PANTS.
WHY WOULD YOU EVER COVER LEGS LIKE THAT? AND THE COLOR OF HER SKIN IS TO DIE FOR.
Sigh
OKAY, THIS'LL HAVE TO DO. KORI, WE GOTTA RUN. I HAVE A FULL NIGHT AHEAD OF ME.
JOB RELATED?
YES AND NO--
NO!
KORI, NOT THAT MUCH.
MY BROTHER SAID THE STORM THAT WAS SUPPOSED TO MISS US HAS TURNED EAST. WE SHOULD EXPECT SOME BAD WEATHER LATE TONIGHT.
I'M HOPING IT'S NOT DURING HIGH TIDE.
BOARDING-UP-THE-WINDOWS BAD?
YOUR CALL. IT'S PICKING UP SPEED. WINDS ARE GONNA BE ABOUT 50 MILES PER HOUR.

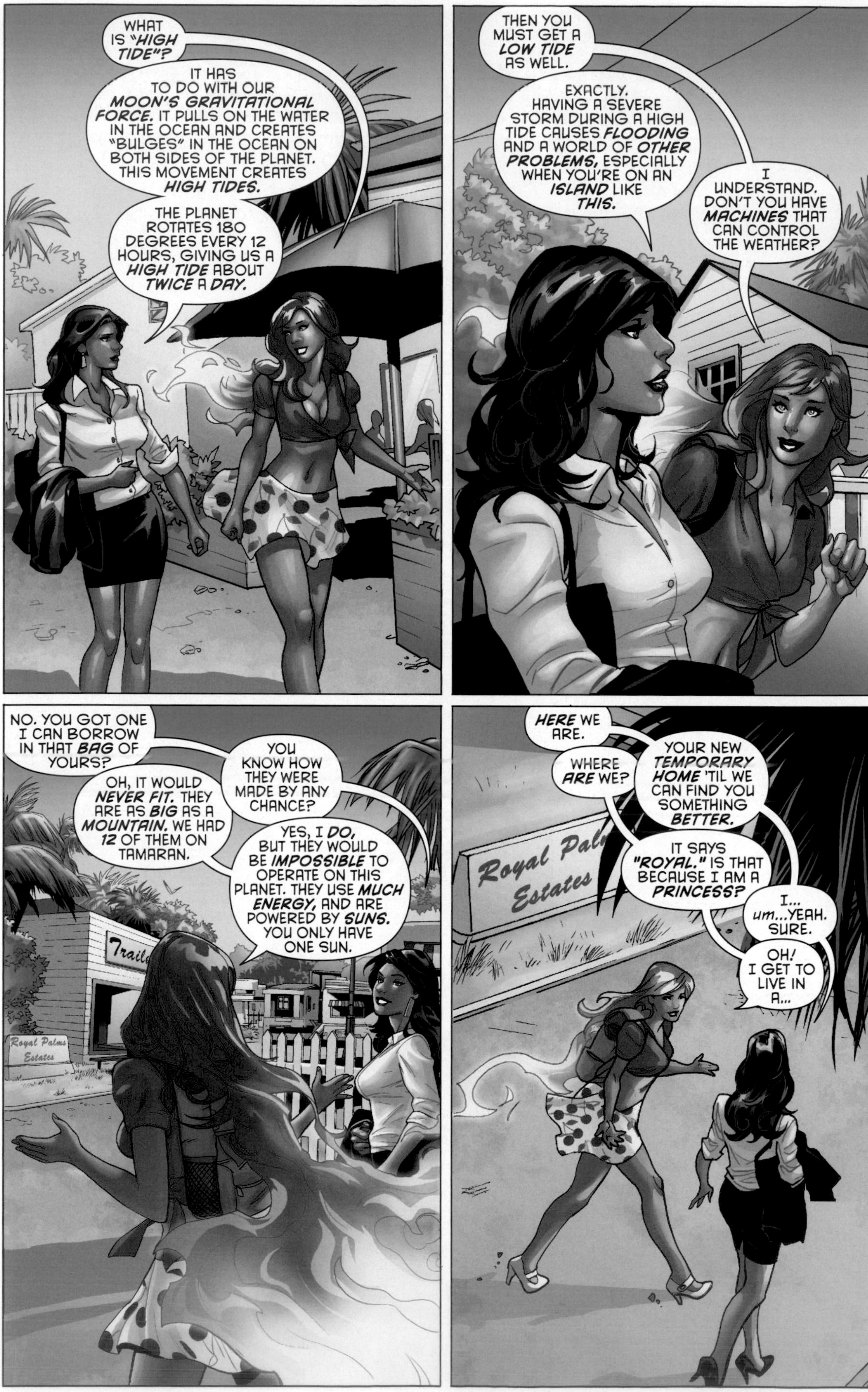
WHAT IS "HIGH TIDE"?
IT HAS TO DO WITH OUR MOON'S GRAVITATIONAL FORCE. IT PULLS ON THE WATER IN THE OCEAN AND CREATES "BULGES" IN THE OCEAN ON BOTH SIDES OF THE PLANET. THIS MOVEMENT CREATES HIGH TIDES.
THE PLANET ROTATES 180 DEGREES EVERY 12 HOURS, GIVING US A HIGH TIDE ABOUT TWICE A DAY.
THEN YOU MUST GET A LOW TIDE AS WELL.
EXACTLY. HAVING A SEVERE STORM DURING A HIGH TIDE CAUSES FLOODING AND A WORLD OF OTHER PROBLEMS, ESPECIALLY WHEN YOU'RE ON AN ISLAND LIKE THIS.
I UNDERSTAND. DON'T YOU HAVE MACHINES THAT CAN CONTROL THE WEATHER?
NO. YOU GOT ONE I CAN BORROW IN THAT BAG OF YOURS?
OH, IT WOULD NEVER FIT. THEY ARE AS BIG AS A MOUNTAIN. WE HAD 12 OF THEM ON TAMARAN.
YOU KNOW HOW THEY WERE MADE BY ANY CHANCE?
YES, I DO, BUT THEY WOULD BE IMPOSSIBLE TO OPERATE ON THIS PLANET. THEY USE MUCH ENERGY, AND ARE POWERED BY SUNS. YOU ONLY HAVE ONE SUN.
Royal Palms Estates
HERE WE ARE.
WHERE ARE WE?
YOUR NEW TEMPORARY HOME 'TIL WE CAN FIND YOU SOMETHING BETTER.
IT SAYS "ROYAL." IS THAT BECAUSE I AM A PRINCESS?
I... um...YEAH. SURE.
OH! I GET TO LIVE IN A...

Hurricane Toy

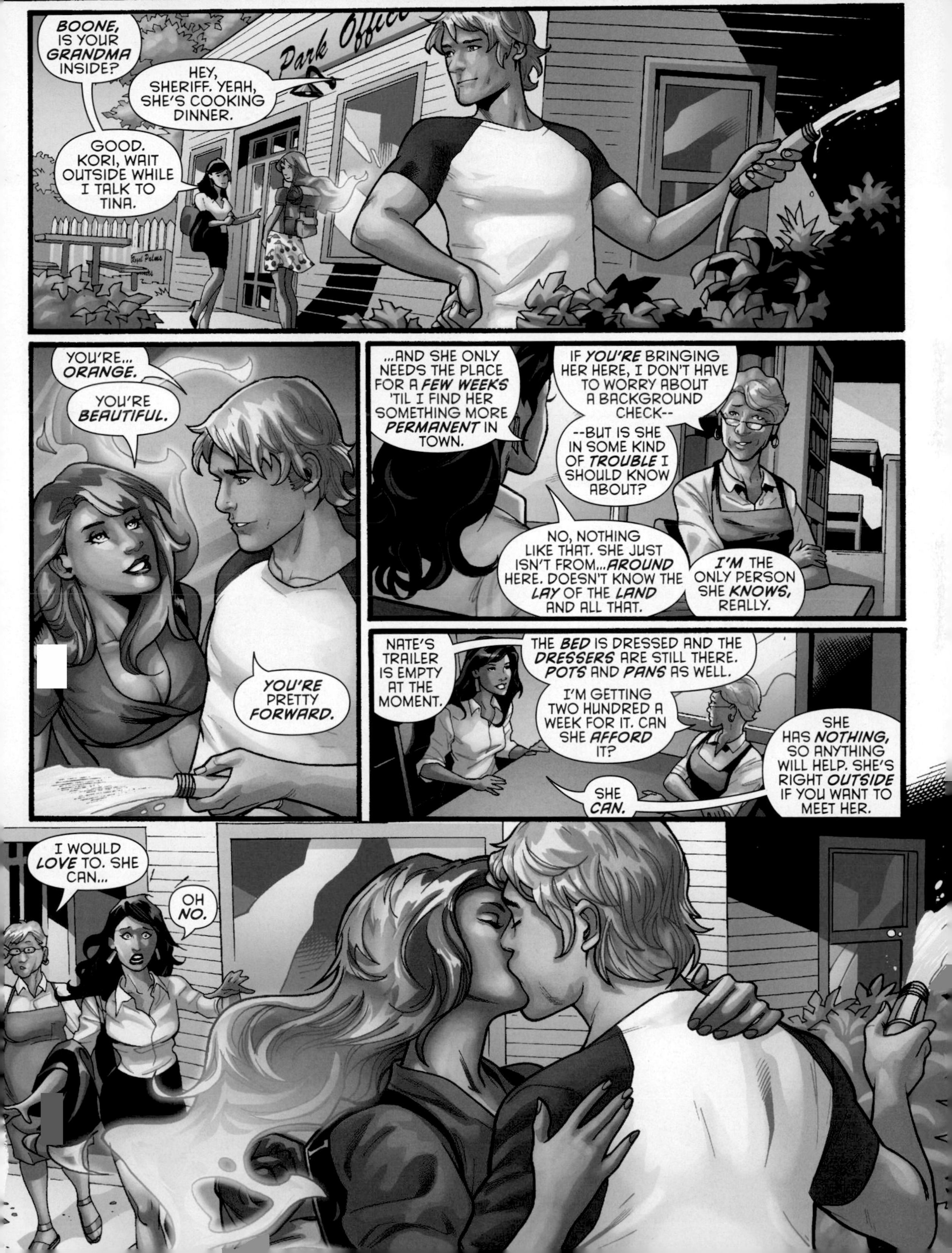
BOONE, IS YOUR GRANDMA INSIDE?
HEY, SHERIFF. YEAH, SHE'S COOKING DINNER.
GOOD. KORI, WAIT OUTSIDE WHILE I TALK TO TINA.
Park Office
YOU'RE... ORANGE.
YOU'RE BEAUTIFUL.
YOU'RE PRETTY FORWARD.
...AND SHE ONLY NEEDS THE PLACE FOR A FEW WEEKS 'TIL I FIND HER SOMETHING MORE PERMANENT IN TOWN.
IF YOU'RE BRINGING HER HERE, I DON'T HAVE TO WORRY ABOUT A BACKGROUND CHECK--
--BUT IS SHE IN SOME KIND OF TROUBLE I SHOULD KNOW ABOUT?
NO, NOTHING LIKE THAT. SHE JUST ISN'T FROM...AROUND HERE. DOESN'T KNOW THE LAY OF THE LAND AND ALL THAT.
I'M THE ONLY PERSON SHE KNOWS, REALLY.
NATE'S TRAILER IS EMPTY AT THE MOMENT.
THE BED IS DRESSED AND THE DRESSERS ARE STILL THERE. POTS AND PANS AS WELL.
I'M GETTING TWO HUNDRED A WEEK FOR IT. CAN SHE AFFORD IT?
SHE CAN.
SHE HAS NOTHING, SO ANYTHING WILL HELP. SHE'S RIGHT OUTSIDE IF YOU WANT TO MEET HER.
I WOULD LOVE TO. SHE CAN...
OH NO.

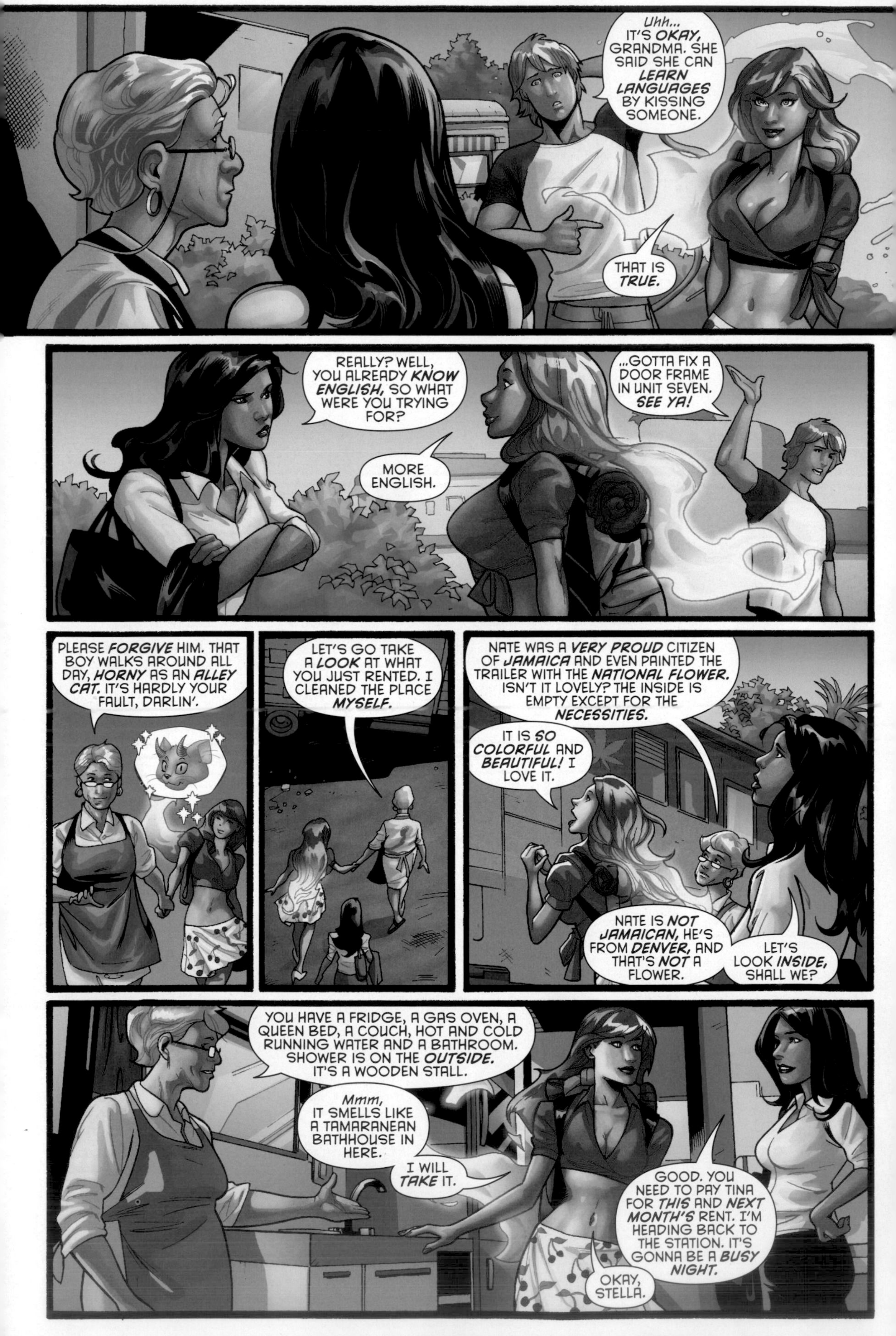
Uhh... IT'S OKAY, GRANDMA. SHE SAID SHE CAN LEARN LANGUAGES BY KISSING SOMEONE.
THAT IS TRUE.
REALLY? WELL, YOU ALREADY KNOW ENGLISH, SO WHAT WERE YOU TRYING FOR?
MORE ENGLISH.
...GOTTA FIX A DOOR FRAME IN UNIT SEVEN. SEE YA!
PLEASE FORGIVE HIM. THAT BOY WALKS AROUND ALL DAY, HORNY AS AN ALLEY CAT. IT'S HARDLY YOUR FAULT, DARLIN'.
LET'S GO TAKE A LOOK AT WHAT YOU JUST RENTED. I CLEANED THE PLACE MYSELF.
NATE WAS A VERY PROUD CITIZEN OF JAMAICA AND EVEN PAINTED THE TRAILER WITH THE NATIONAL FLOWER. ISN'T IT LOVELY? THE INSIDE IS EMPTY EXCEPT FOR THE NECESSITIES.
IT IS SO COLORFUL AND BEAUTIFUL! I LOVE IT.
NATE IS NOT JAMAICAN, HE'S FROM DENVER, AND THAT'S NOT A FLOWER.
LET'S LOOK INSIDE, SHALL WE?
YOU HAVE A FRIDGE, A GAS OVEN, A QUEEN BED, A COUCH, HOT AND COLD RUNNING WATER AND A BATHROOM. SHOWER IS ON THE OUTSIDE. IT'S A WOODEN STALL.
Mmm, IT SMELLS LIKE A TAMARANEAN BATHHOUSE IN HERE.
I WILL TAKE IT.
GOOD. YOU NEED TO PAY TINA FOR THIS AND NEXT MONTH'S RENT. I'M HEADING BACK TO THE STATION. IT'S GONNA BE A BUSY NIGHT.
OKAY, STELLA.

Tropical Depression

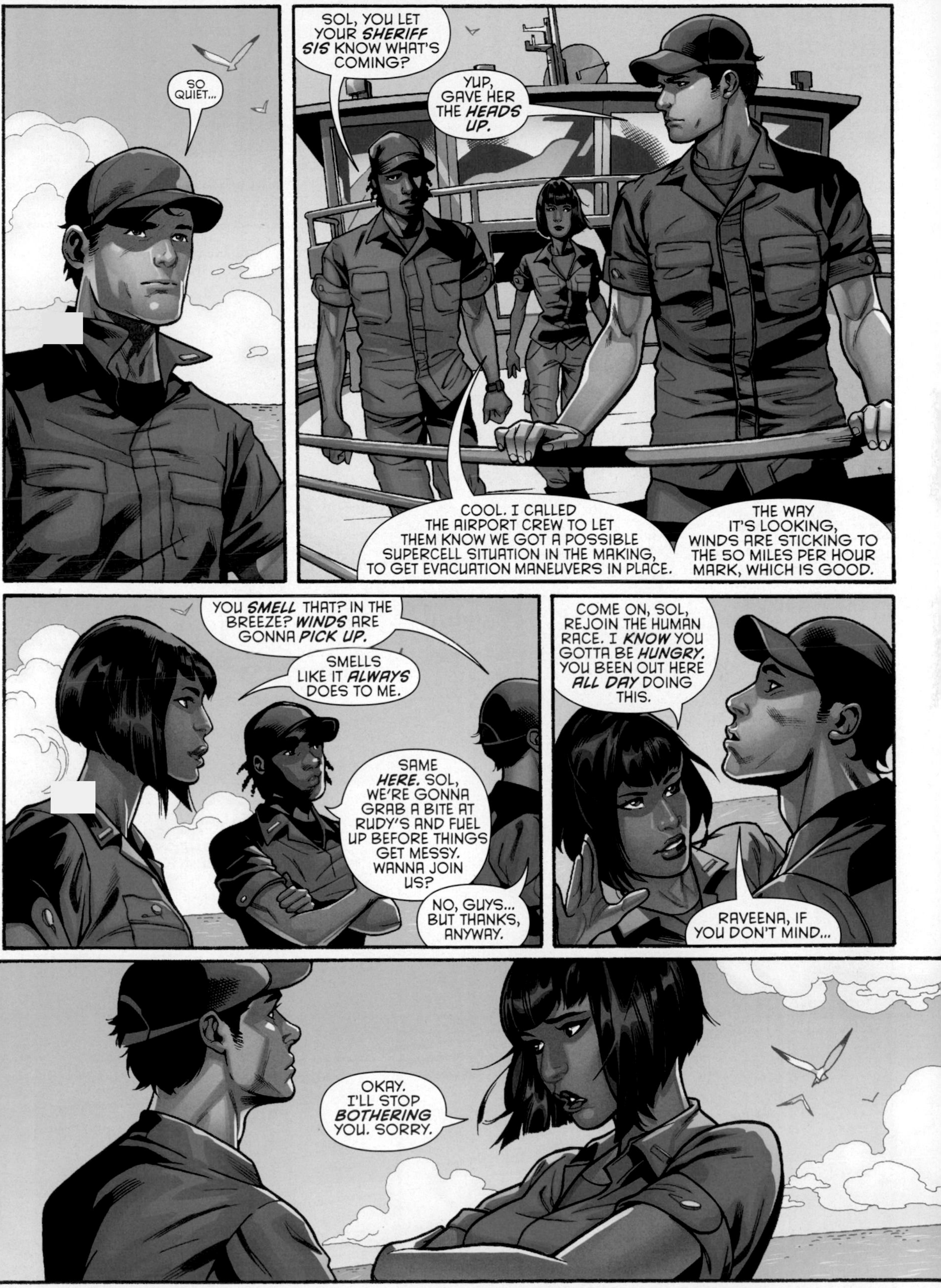

SO QUIET...
SOL, YOU LET YOUR SHERIFF SIS KNOW WHAT'S COMING?
YUP, GAVE HER THE HEADS UP.
COOL. I CALLED THE AIRPORT CREW TO LET THEM KNOW WE GOT A POSSIBLE SUPERCELL SITUATION IN THE MAKING, TO GET EVACUATION MANEUVERS IN PLACE.
THE WAY IT'S LOOKING, WINDS ARE STICKING TO THE 50 MILES PER HOUR MARK, WHICH IS GOOD.
YOU SMELL THAT? IN THE BREEZE? WINDS ARE GONNA PICK UP.
SMELLS LIKE IT ALWAYS DOES TO ME.
SAME HERE. SOL, WE'RE GONNA GRAB A BITE AT RUDY'S AND FUEL UP BEFORE THINGS GET MESSY. WANNA JOIN US?
NO, GUYS... BUT THANKS, ANYWAY.
COME ON, SOL, REJOIN THE HUMAN RACE. I KNOW YOU GOTTA BE HUNGRY. YOU BEEN OUT HERE ALL DAY DOING THIS.
RAVEENA, IF YOU DON'T MIND...
OKAY. I'LL STOP BOTHERING YOU. SORRY.

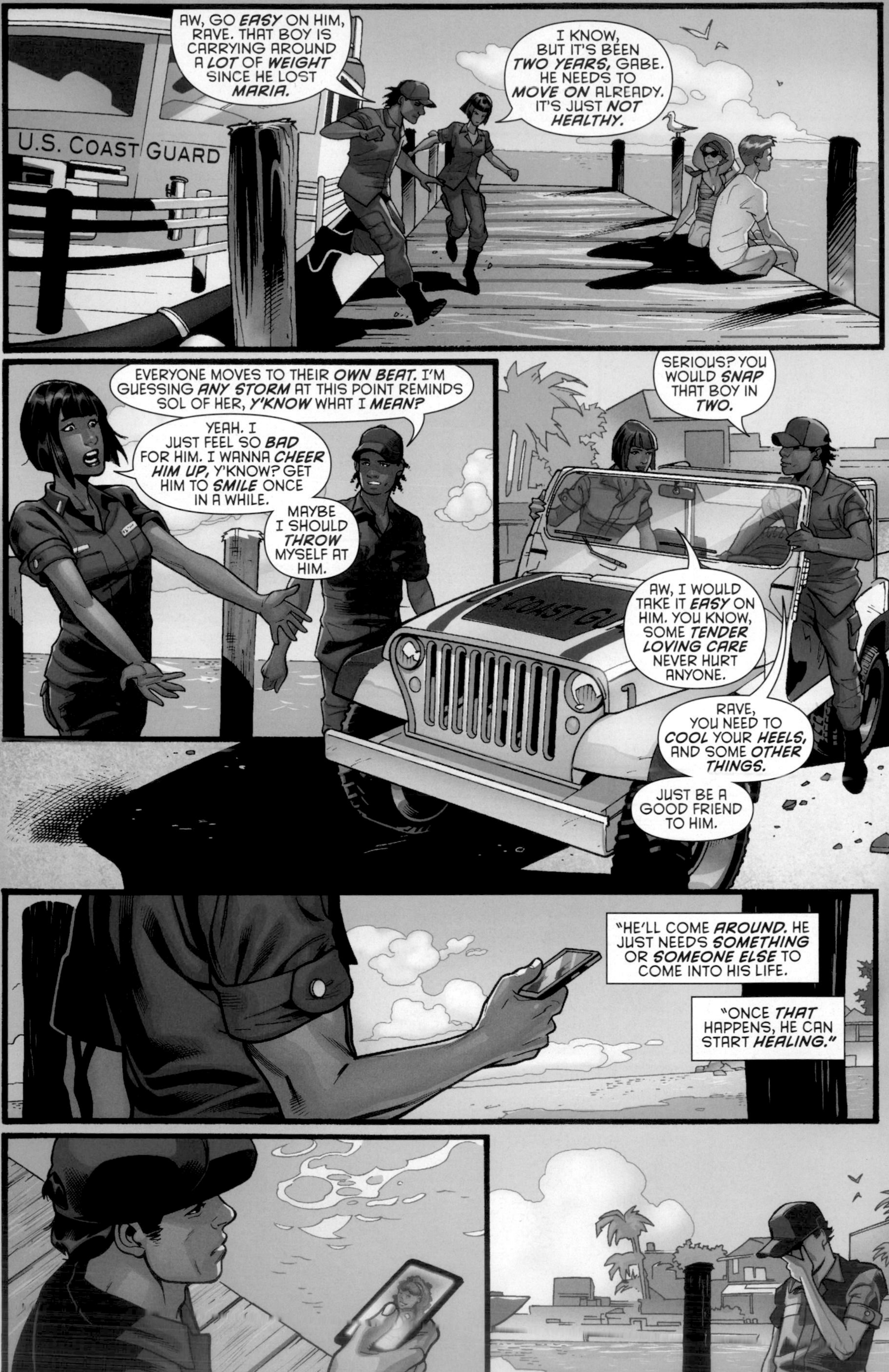

U.S. COAST GUARD
AW, GO EASY ON HIM, RAVE. THAT BOY IS CARRYING AROUND A LOT OF WEIGHT SINCE HE LOST MARIA.
I KNOW, BUT IT'S BEEN TWO YEARS, GABE. HE NEEDS TO MOVE ON ALREADY. IT'S JUST NOT HEALTHY.
EVERYONE MOVES TO THEIR OWN BEAT. I'M GUESSING ANY STORM AT THIS POINT REMINDS SOL OF HER, Y'KNOW WHAT I MEAN?
YEAH. I JUST FEEL SO BAD FOR HIM. I WANNA CHEER HIM UP, Y'KNOW? GET HIM TO SMILE ONCE IN A WHILE.
MAYBE I SHOULD THROW MYSELF AT HIM.
SERIOUS? YOU WOULD SNAP THAT BOY IN TWO.
AW, I WOULD TAKE IT EASY ON HIM. YOU KNOW, SOME TENDER LOVING CARE NEVER HURT ANYONE.
RAVE, YOU NEED TO COOL YOUR HEELS, AND SOME OTHER THINGS.
JUST BE A GOOD FRIEND TO HIM.
"HE'LL COME AROUND. HE JUST NEEDS SOMETHING OR SOMEONE ELSE TO COME INTO HIS LIFE.
"ONCE THAT HAPPENS, HE CAN START HEALING."

Wet, Then Wild.

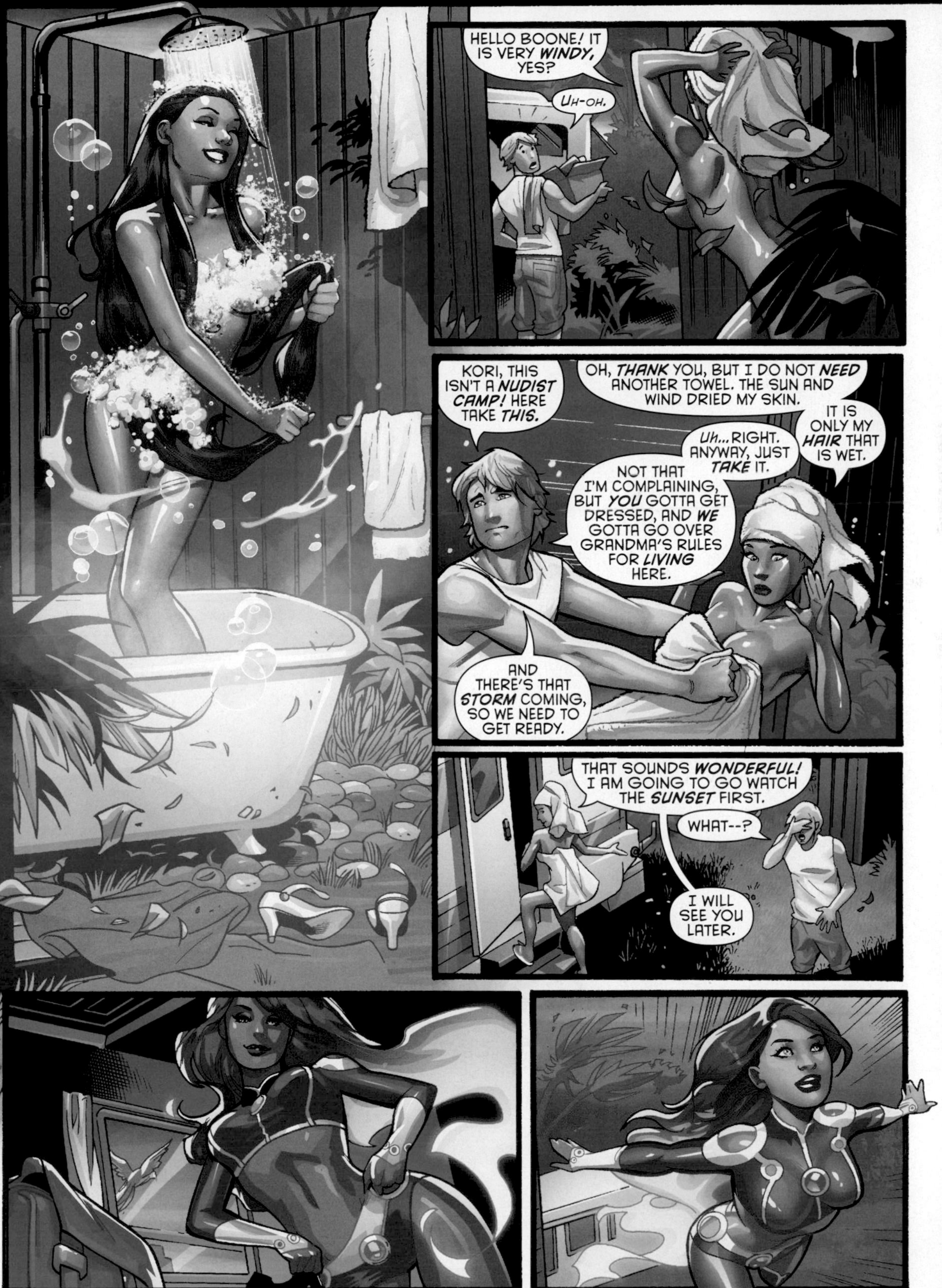
HELLO BOONE! IT IS VERY *WINDY,* YES?
UH-OH.
KORI, THIS ISN'T A *NUDIST CAMP!* HERE TAKE *THIS.*
OH, *THANK* YOU, BUT I DO NOT *NEED* ANOTHER TOWEL. THE SUN AND WIND DRIED MY SKIN.
IT IS ONLY MY *HAIR* THAT IS WET.
UH... RIGHT. ANYWAY, JUST *TAKE* IT.
NOT THAT I'M COMPLAINING, BUT *YOU* GOTTA GET DRESSED, AND *WE* GOTTA GO OVER GRANDMA'S RULES FOR *LIVING* HERE.
AND THERE'S THAT *STORM* COMING, SO WE NEED TO GET READY.
THAT SOUNDS *WONDERFUL!* I AM GOING TO GO WATCH THE *SUNSET* FIRST.
WHAT--?
I WILL SEE YOU LATER.

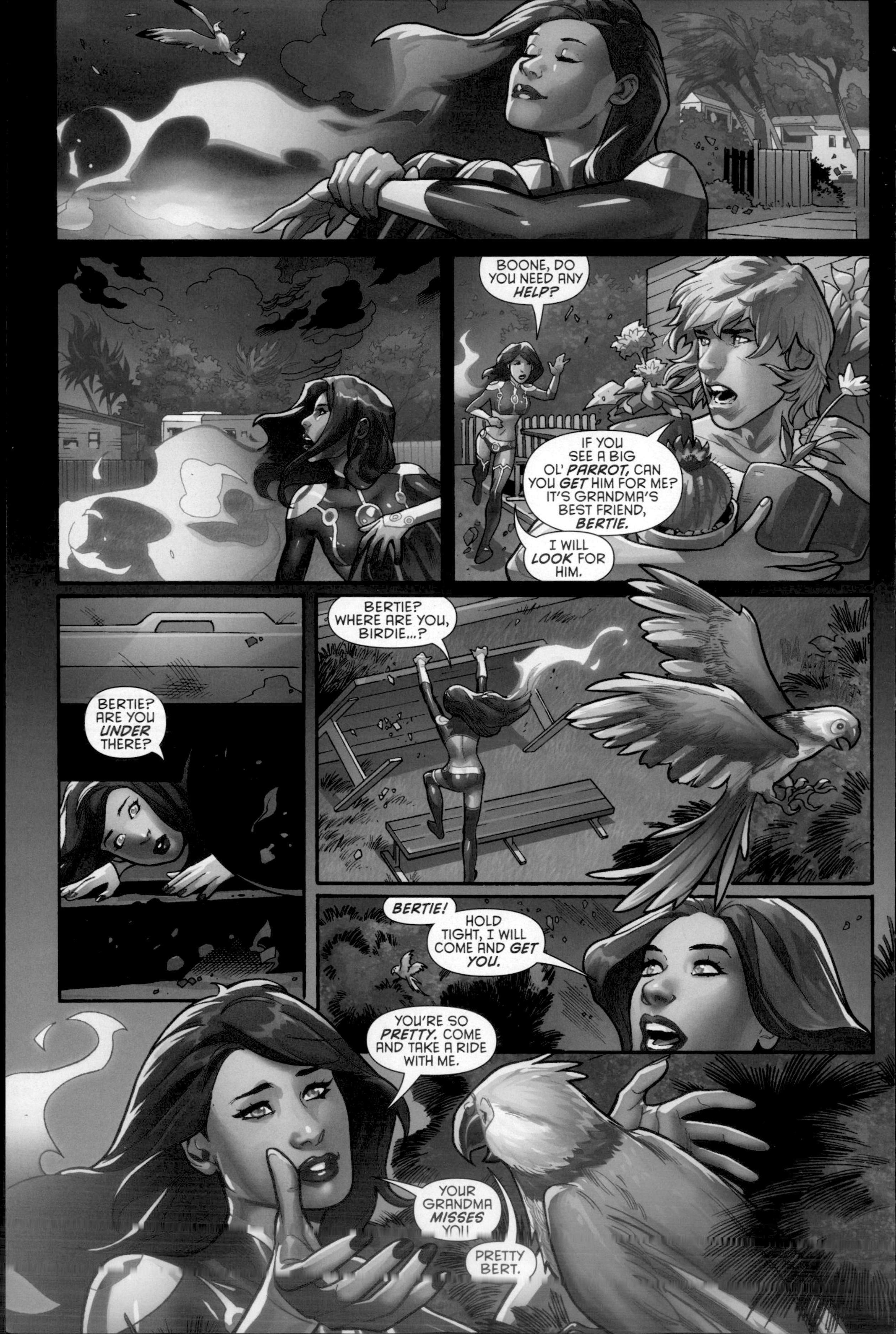
BOONE, DO YOU NEED ANY HELP?
IF YOU SEE A BIG OL' PARROT, CAN YOU GET HIM FOR ME? IT'S GRANDMA'S BEST FRIEND, BERTIE.
I WILL LOOK FOR HIM.
BERTIE? ARE YOU UNDER THERE?
BERTIE? WHERE ARE YOU, BIRDIE...?
BERTIE!
HOLD TIGHT, I WILL COME AND GET YOU.
YOU'RE SO PRETTY. COME AND TAKE A RIDE WITH ME.
YOUR GRANDMA MISSES YOU.
PRETTY BERT.

Sneak Attack!

WINDS HAVE BEEN PICKING UP BY THE MINUTE. THIS IS OFFICIALLY A HURRICANE, PEOPLE! WE NEED TO EVACUATE THE ISLAND.

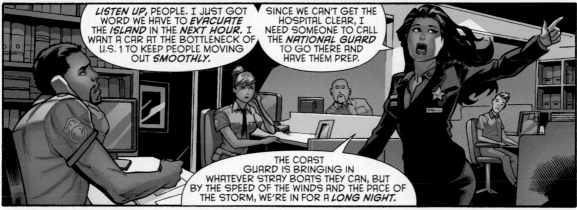

LISTEN UP, PEOPLE. I JUST GOT WORD WE HAVE TO EVACUATE THE ISLAND IN THE NEXT HOUR. I WANT A CAR AT THE BOTTLENECK OF U.S. 1 TO KEEP PEOPLE MOVING OUT SMOOTHLY.

SINCE WE CAN'T GET THE HOSPITAL CLEAR, I NEED SOMEONE TO CALL THE NATIONAL GUARD TO GO THERE AND HAVE THEM PREP.

THE COAST GUARD IS BRINGING IN WHATEVER STRAY BOATS THEY CAN, BUT BY THE SPEED OF THE WINDS AND THE PACE OF THE STORM, WE'RE IN FOR A LONG NIGHT.

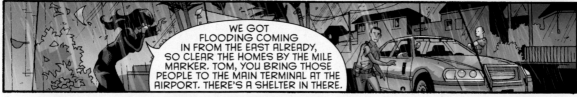

WE GOT FLOODING COMING IN FROM THE EAST ALREADY, SO CLEAR THE HOMES BY THE MILE MARKER. TOM, YOU BRING THOSE PEOPLE TO THE MAIN TERMINAL AT THE AIRPORT. THERE'S A SHELTER IN THERE.

I CAN'T THANK YOU ENOUGH, KORI.

HE IS A VERY SWEET BIRD. MAY I ASK, WHAT IS THAT ALARM FOR?

THAT'S THE SIREN FOR A STORM APPROACHING. IT ALSO MEANS TO TURN THE RADIO ON AND GET UPDATES. BEEN LISTENING FOR THE PAST 15 MINUTES AND IT'S ALL BAD NEWS.

I PUT THE BOARDS UP ON THE WINDOWS OF THE TRAILERS, GRANDMA, BUT, Y'KNOW, THEY'RE TRAILERS, SO I DUNNO WHAT GOOD IT'S GONNA DO.

GOT A FEW INCHES OF WATER ALREADY.

GET IN HERE AND CLOSE THAT DOOR.

KIDS, WE NEED TO GET TO THE SHELTER.

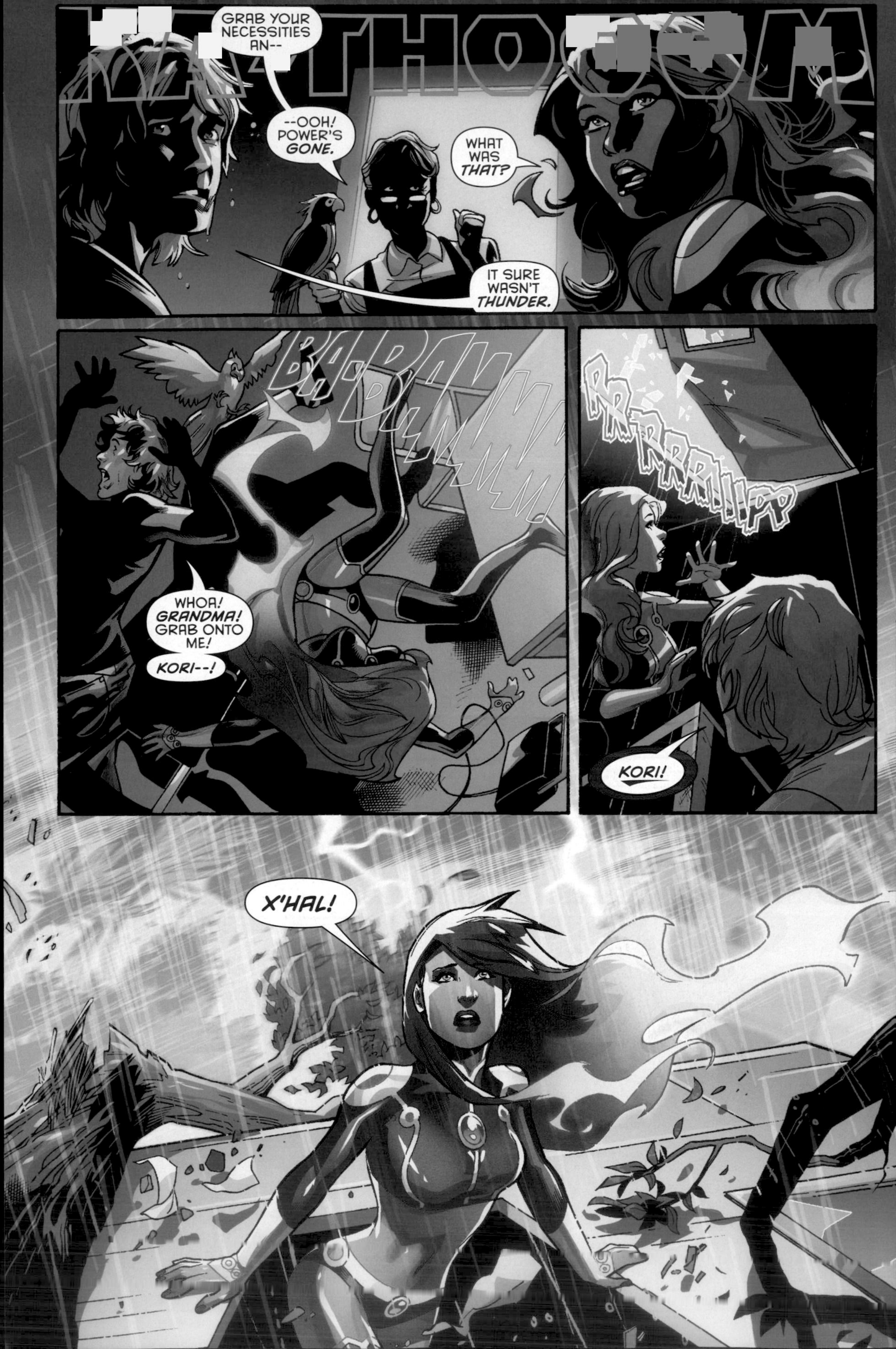
GRAB YOUR NECESSITIES AN--
--OOH! POWER'S GONE.
WHAT WAS THAT?
IT SURE WASN'T THUNDER.
WHOA! GRANDMA! GRAB ONTO ME!
KORI--!
KORI!
X'HAL!

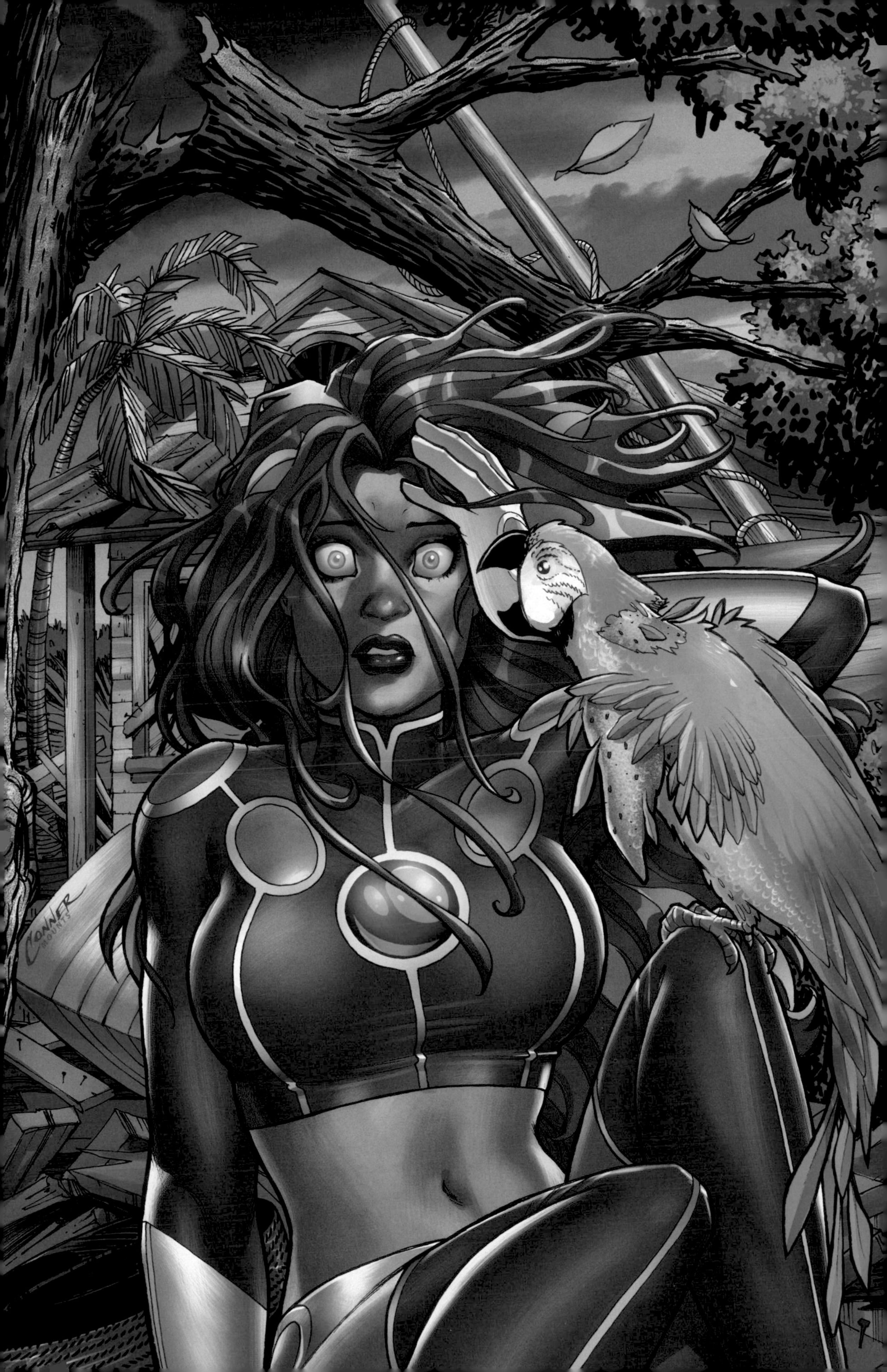
CONNER
MOUNTS

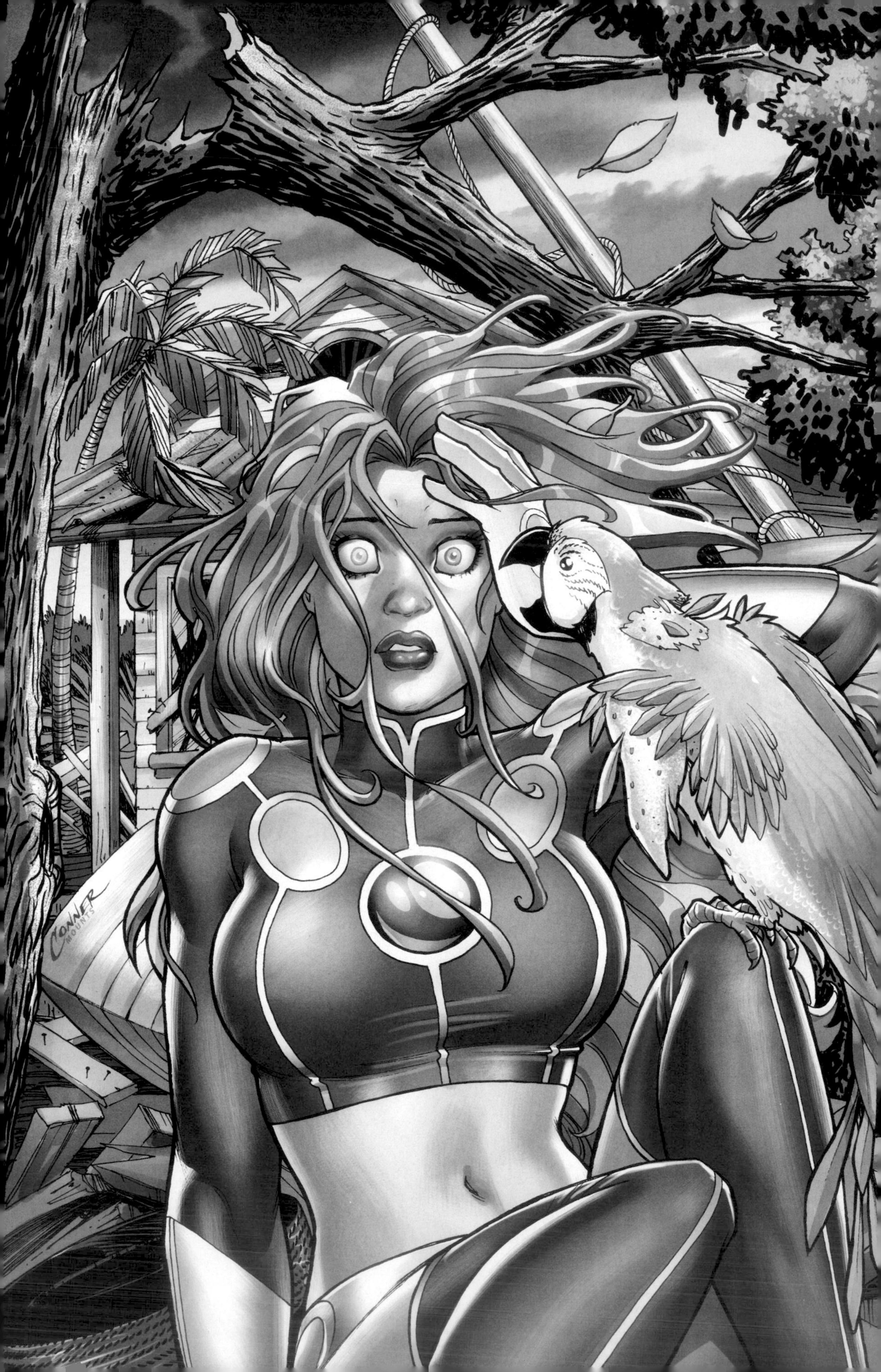
CONNER
MOUNTS

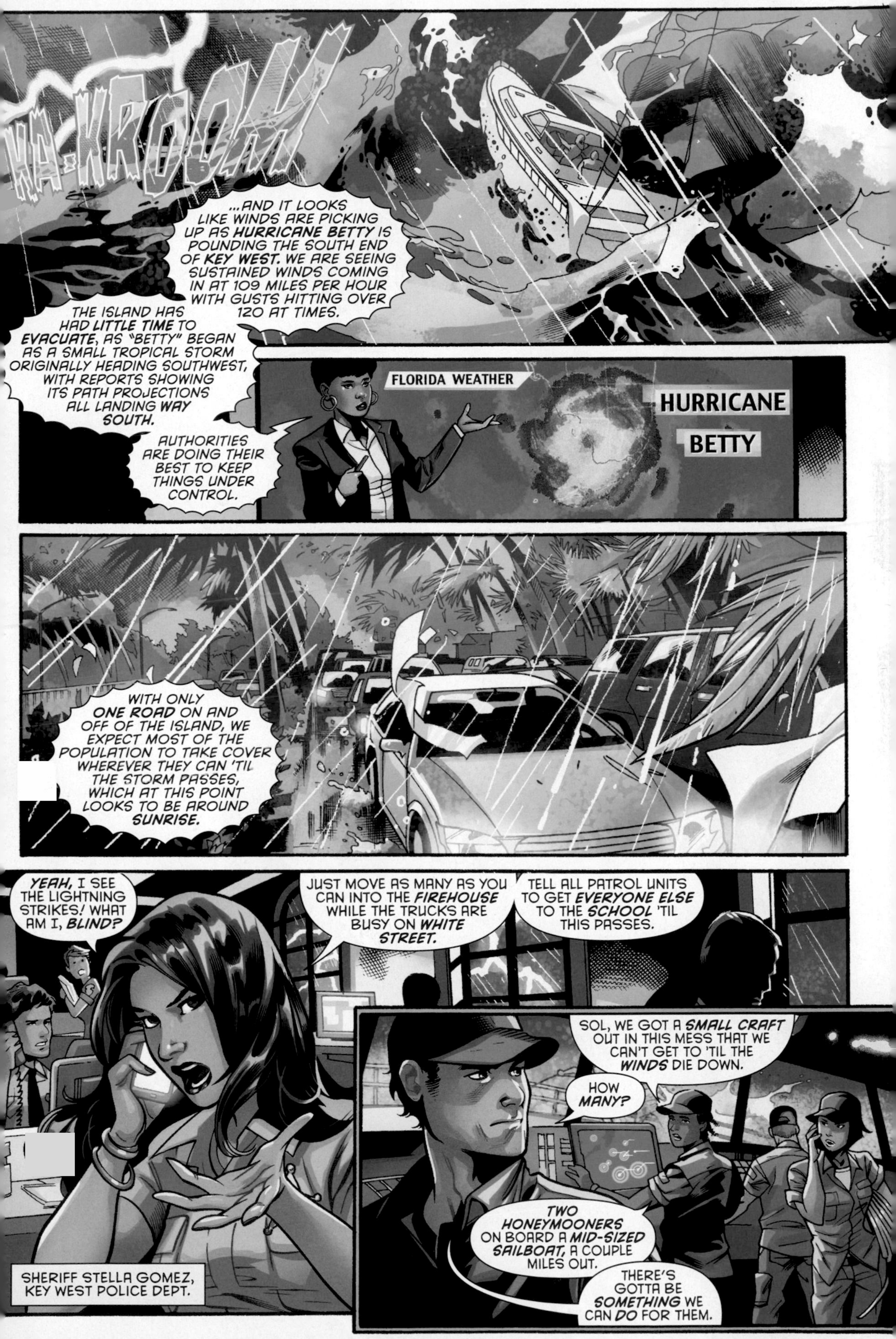
KA-KROOOM
...AND IT LOOKS LIKE WINDS ARE PICKING UP AS HURRICANE BETTY IS POUNDING THE SOUTH END OF KEY WEST. WE ARE SEEING SUSTAINED WINDS COMING IN AT 109 MILES PER HOUR WITH GUSTS HITTING OVER 120 AT TIMES.
THE ISLAND HAS HAD LITTLE TIME TO EVACUATE, AS "BETTY" BEGAN AS A SMALL TROPICAL STORM ORIGINALLY HEADING SOUTHWEST, WITH REPORTS SHOWING ITS PATH PROJECTIONS ALL LANDING WAY SOUTH.
FLORIDA WEATHER
HURRICANE
BETTY
AUTHORITIES ARE DOING THEIR BEST TO KEEP THINGS UNDER CONTROL.
WITH ONLY ONE ROAD ON AND OFF OF THE ISLAND, WE EXPECT MOST OF THE POPULATION TO TAKE COVER WHEREVER THEY CAN 'TIL THE STORM PASSES, WHICH AT THIS POINT LOOKS TO BE AROUND SUNRISE.
YEAH, I SEE THE LIGHTNING STRIKES! WHAT AM I, BLIND?
JUST MOVE AS MANY AS YOU CAN INTO THE FIREHOUSE WHILE THE TRUCKS ARE BUSY ON WHITE STREET.
TELL ALL PATROL UNITS TO GET EVERYONE ELSE TO THE SCHOOL 'TIL THIS PASSES.
SHERIFF STELLA GOMEZ, KEY WEST POLICE DEPT.
SOL, WE GOT A SMALL CRAFT OUT IN THIS MESS THAT WE CAN'T GET TO 'TIL THE WINDS DIE DOWN.
HOW MANY?
TWO HONEYMOONERS ON BOARD A MID-SIZED SAILBOAT, A COUPLE MILES OUT.
THERE'S GOTTA BE SOMETHING WE CAN DO FOR THEM.

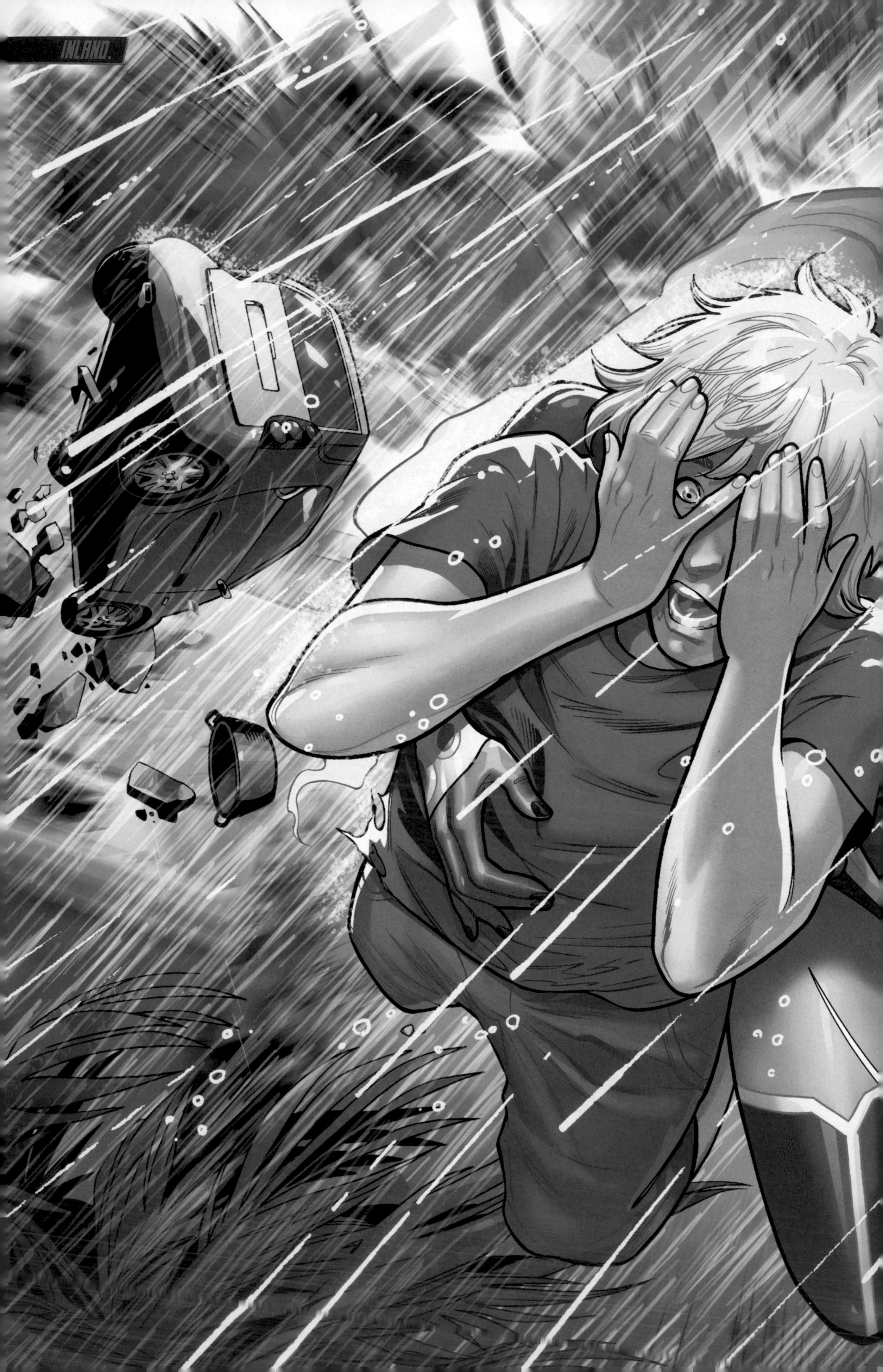
INLAND.

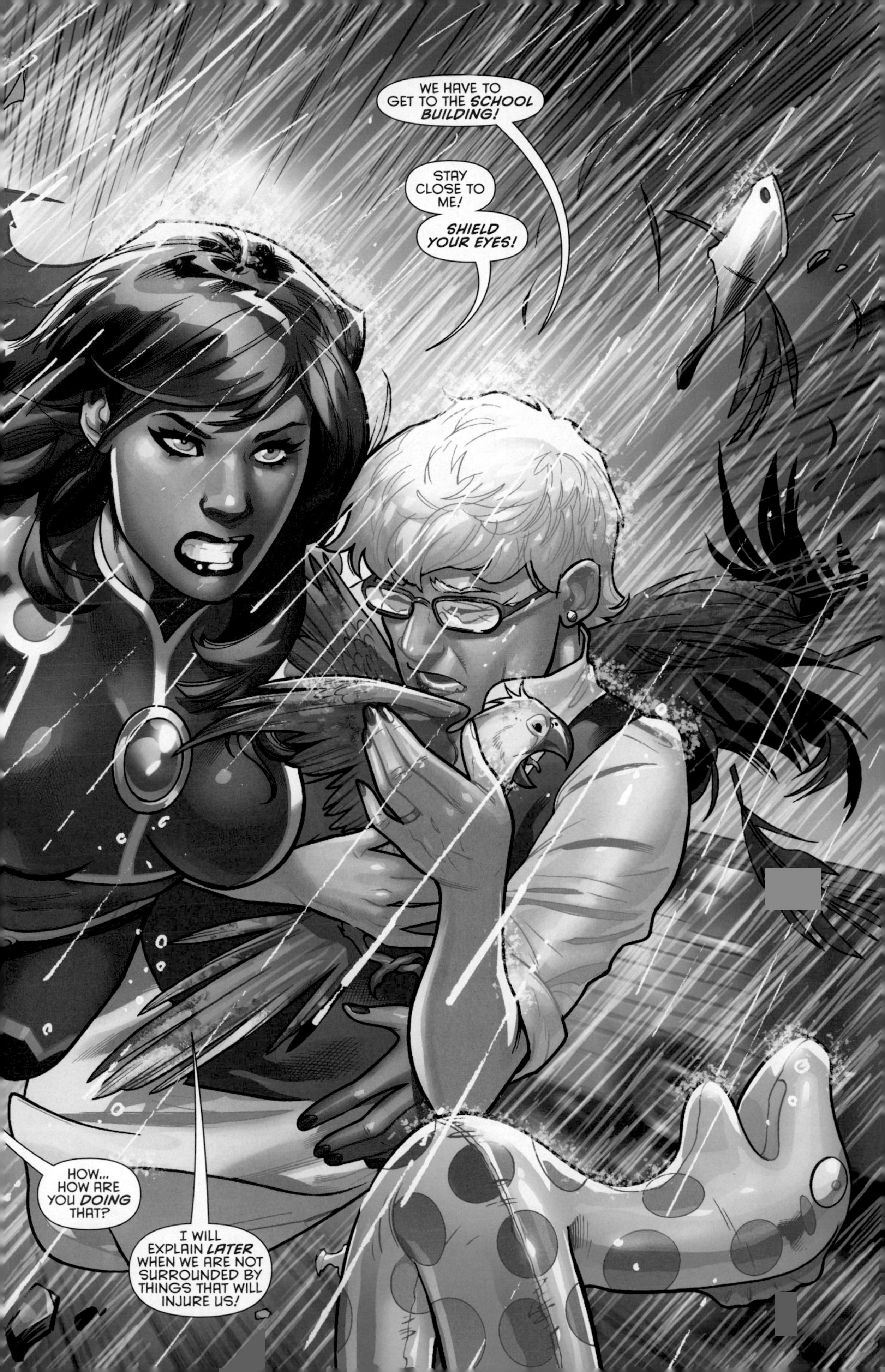
WE HAVE TO GET TO THE *SCHOOL BUILDING!*
STAY CLOSE TO ME!
SHIELD YOUR EYES!
HOW... HOW ARE YOU *DOING* THAT?
I WILL EXPLAIN *LATER* WHEN WE ARE NOT SURROUNDED BY THINGS THAT WILL INJURE US!

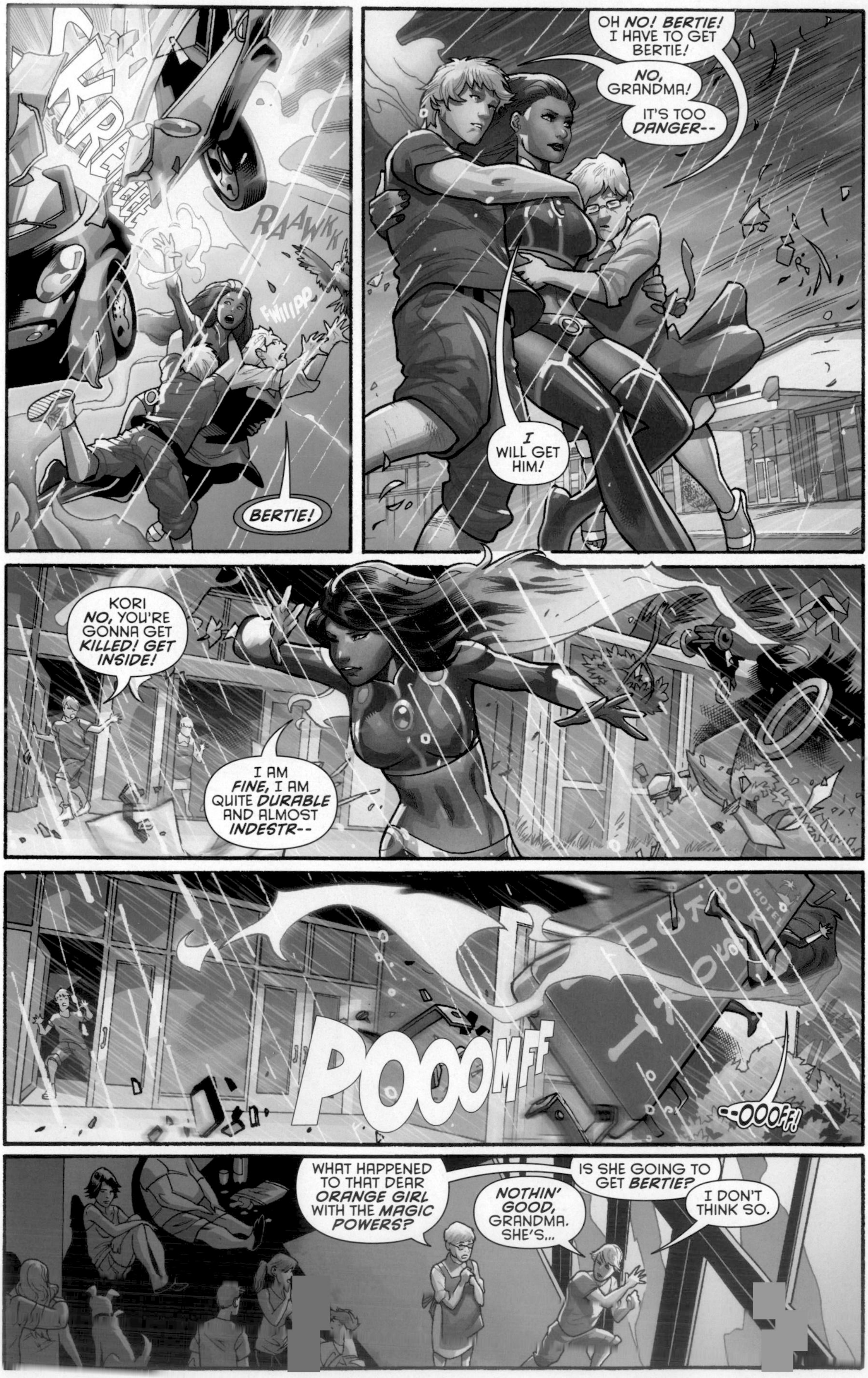
RAAWKK
FWIIIPP
BERTIE!
OH NO! BERTIE! I HAVE TO GET BERTIE!
NO, GRANDMA!
IT'S TOO DANGER--
I WILL GET HIM!
KORI NO, YOU'RE GONNA GET KILLED! GET INSIDE!
I AM FINE, I AM QUITE DURABLE AND ALMOST INDESTR--
POOOMFF
--OOOFF!
WHAT HAPPENED TO THAT DEAR ORANGE GIRL WITH THE MAGIC POWERS?
NOTHIN' GOOD, GRANDMA. SHE'S...
IS SHE GOING TO GET BERTIE?
I DON'T THINK SO.

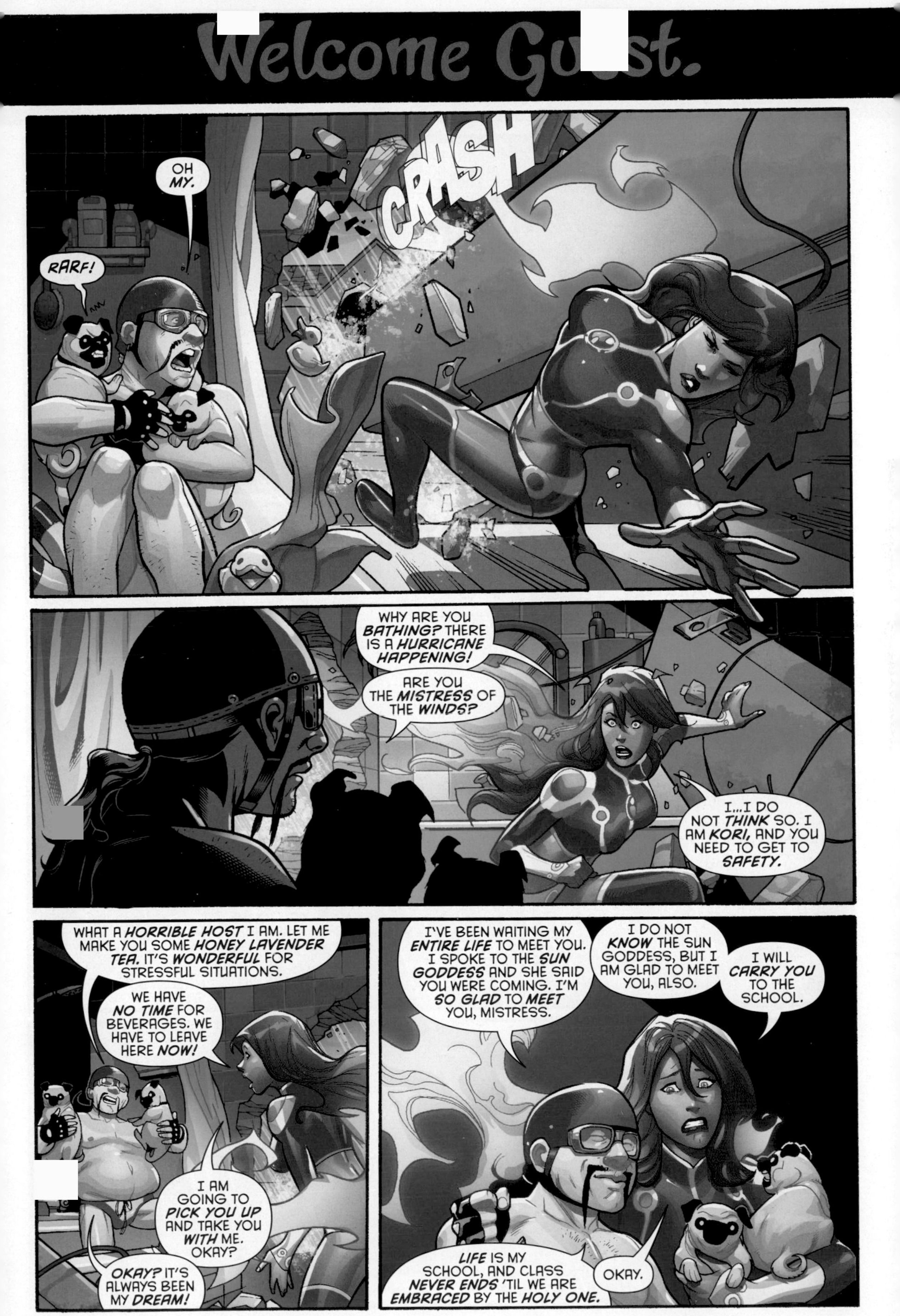
Welcome Gu st.
CRASH
OH MY.
RARF!
WHY ARE YOU BATHING? THERE IS A HURRICANE HAPPENING!
ARE YOU THE MISTRESS OF THE WINDS?
I...I DO NOT THINK SO. I AM KORI, AND YOU NEED TO GET TO SAFETY.
WHAT A HORRIBLE HOST I AM. LET ME MAKE YOU SOME HONEY LAVENDER TEA. IT'S WONDERFUL FOR STRESSFUL SITUATIONS.
WE HAVE NO TIME FOR BEVERAGES. WE HAVE TO LEAVE HERE NOW!
I AM GOING TO PICK YOU UP AND TAKE YOU WITH ME. OKAY?
OKAY? IT'S ALWAYS BEEN MY DREAM!
I'VE BEEN WAITING MY ENTIRE LIFE TO MEET YOU. I SPOKE TO THE SUN GODDESS AND SHE SAID YOU WERE COMING. I'M SO GLAD TO MEET YOU, MISTRESS.
I DO NOT KNOW THE SUN GODDESS, BUT I AM GLAD TO MEET YOU, ALSO.
I WILL CARRY YOU TO THE SCHOOL.
LIFE IS MY SCHOOL, AND CLASS NEVER ENDS 'TIL WE ARE EMBRACED BY THE HOLY ONE.
OKAY.

Jumping The Gun.

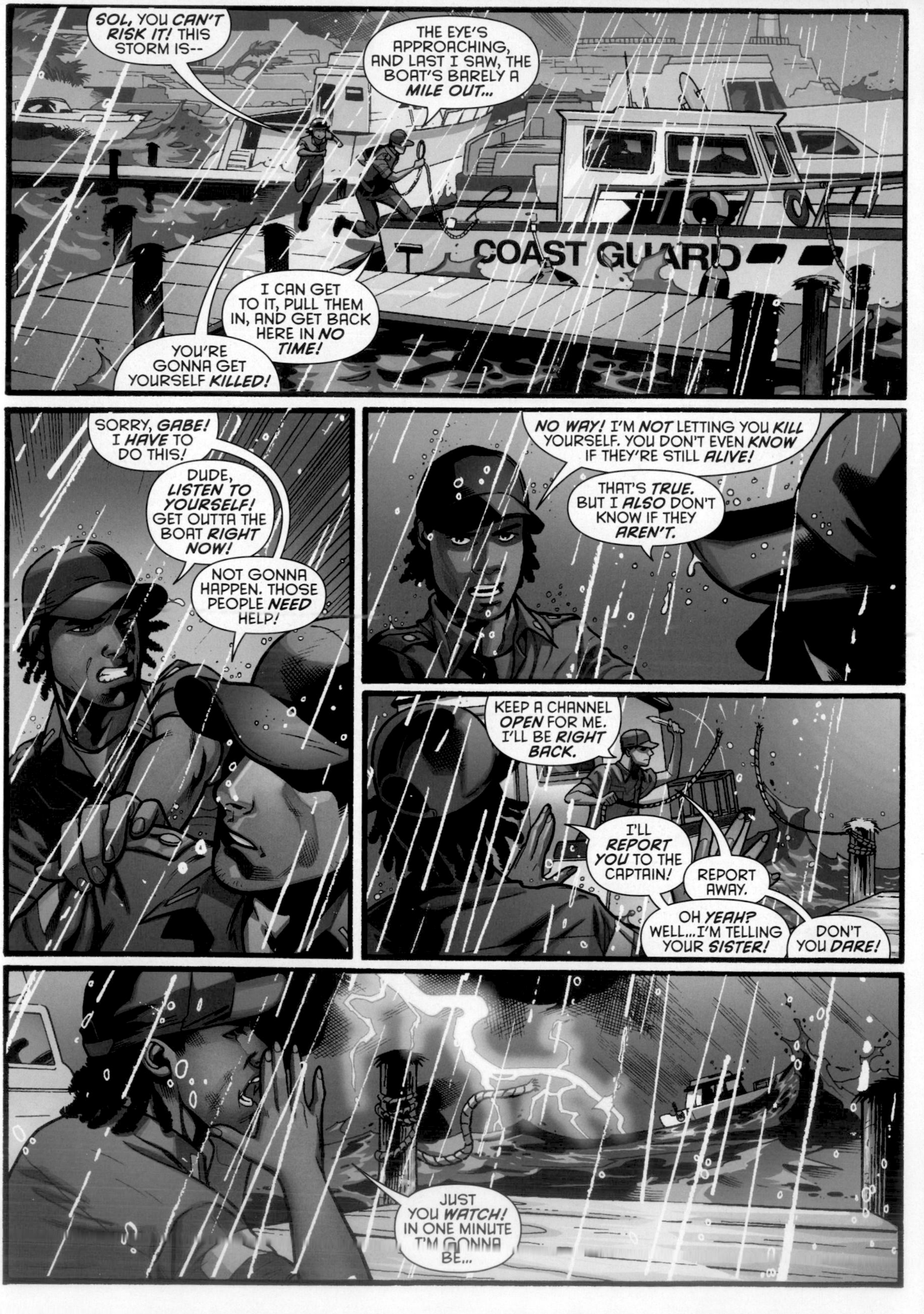

SOL, YOU CAN'T RISK IT! THIS STORM IS--
THE EYE'S APPROACHING, AND LAST I SAW, THE BOAT'S BARELY A MILE OUT...
COAST GUARD
I CAN GET TO IT, PULL THEM IN, AND GET BACK HERE IN NO TIME!
YOU'RE GONNA GET YOURSELF KILLED!
SORRY, GABE! I HAVE TO DO THIS!
DUDE, LISTEN TO YOURSELF! GET OUTTA THE BOAT RIGHT NOW!
NOT GONNA HAPPEN. THOSE PEOPLE NEED HELP!
NO WAY! I'M NOT LETTING YOU KILL YOURSELF. YOU DON'T EVEN KNOW IF THEY'RE STILL ALIVE!
THAT'S TRUE. BUT I ALSO DON'T KNOW IF THEY AREN'T.
KEEP A CHANNEL OPEN FOR ME. I'LL BE RIGHT BACK.
I'LL REPORT YOU TO THE CAPTAIN!
REPORT AWAY.
OH YEAH? WELL...I'M TELLING YOUR SISTER!
DON'T YOU DARE!
JUST YOU WATCH! IN ONE MINUTE I'M GONNA BE...

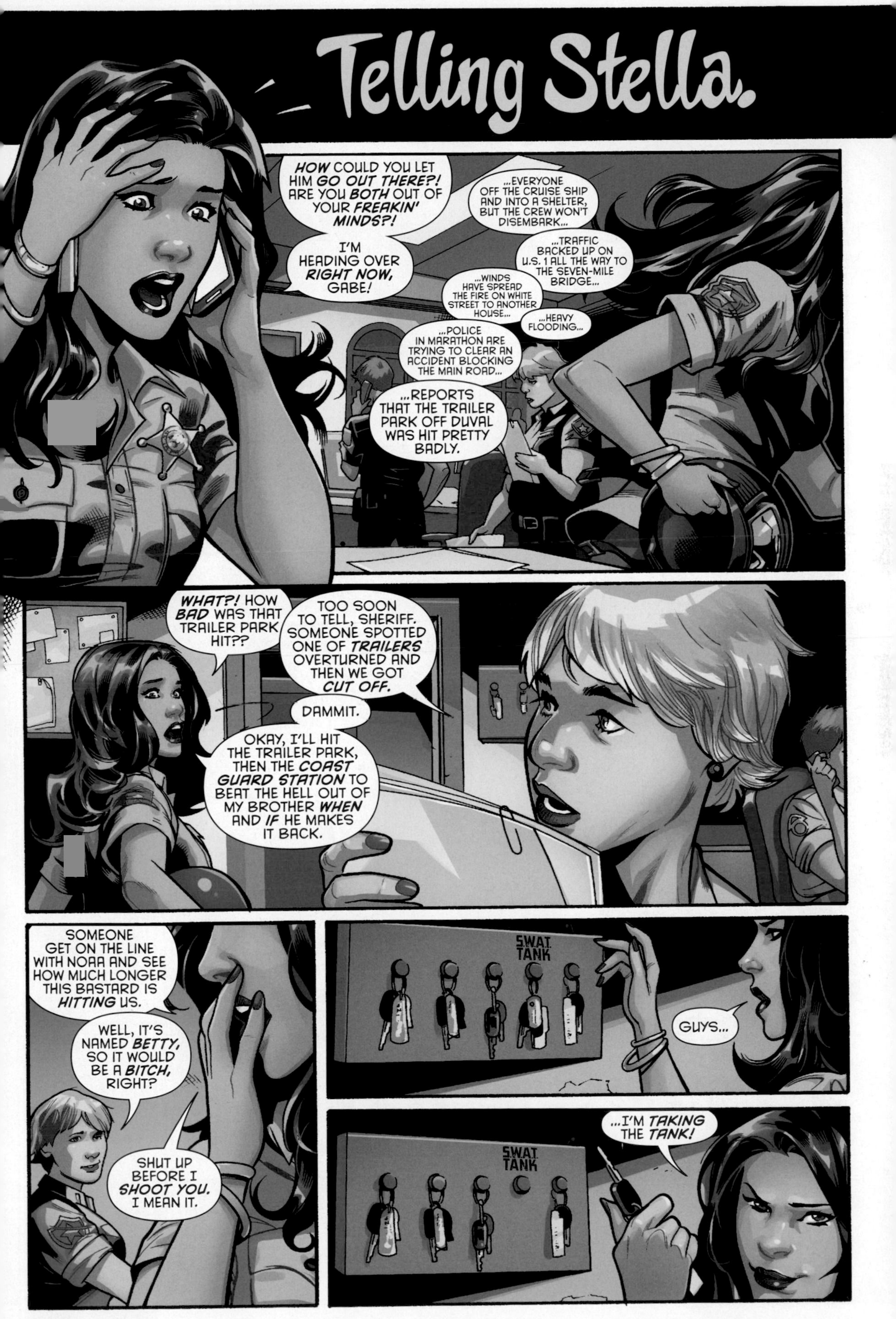
Telling Stella.
HOW COULD YOU LET HIM GO OUT THERE?! ARE YOU BOTH OUT OF YOUR FREAKIN' MINDS?!
I'M HEADING OVER RIGHT NOW, GABE!
...EVERYONE OFF THE CRUISE SHIP AND INTO A SHELTER, BUT THE CREW WON'T DISEMBARK...
...TRAFFIC BACKED UP ON U.S. 1 ALL THE WAY TO THE SEVEN-MILE BRIDGE...
...WINDS HAVE SPREAD THE FIRE ON WHITE STREET TO ANOTHER HOUSE...
...HEAVY FLOODING...
...POLICE IN MARATHON ARE TRYING TO CLEAR AN ACCIDENT BLOCKING THE MAIN ROAD...
...REPORTS THAT THE TRAILER PARK OFF DUVAL WAS HIT PRETTY BADLY.
WHAT?! HOW BAD WAS THAT TRAILER PARK HIT??
TOO SOON TO TELL, SHERIFF. SOMEONE SPOTTED ONE OF TRAILERS OVERTURNED AND THEN WE GOT CUT OFF.
DAMMIT.
OKAY, I'LL HIT THE TRAILER PARK, THEN THE COAST GUARD STATION TO BEAT THE HELL OUT OF MY BROTHER WHEN AND IF HE MAKES IT BACK.
SOMEONE GET ON THE LINE WITH NOAA AND SEE HOW MUCH LONGER THIS BASTARD IS HITTING US.
WELL, IT'S NAMED BETTY, SO IT WOULD BE A BITCH, RIGHT?
SHUT UP BEFORE I SHOOT YOU. I MEAN IT.
S.W.A.T. TANK
GUYS...
S.W.A.T. TANK
...I'M TAKING THE TANK!

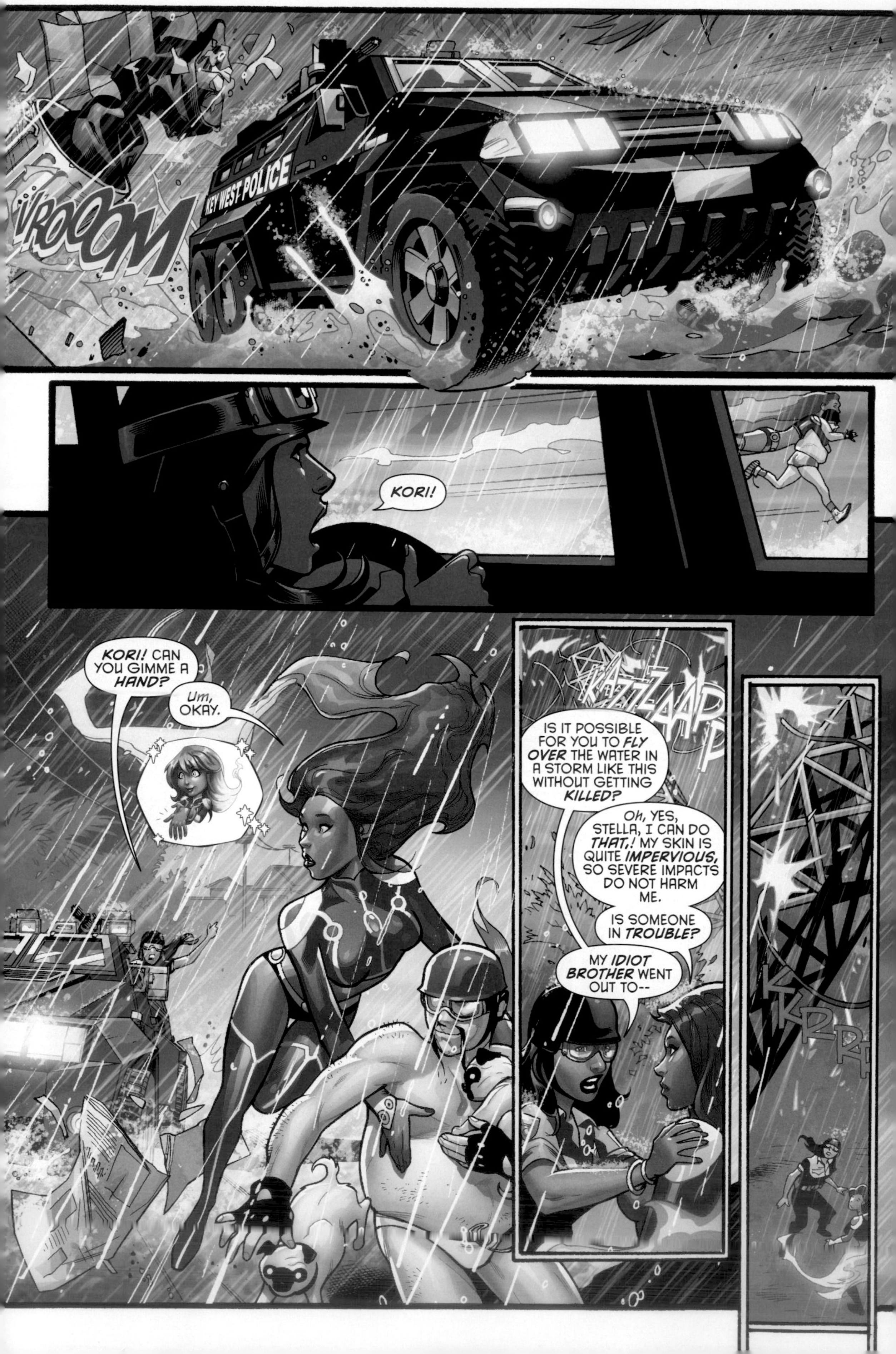
VROOOM
KEY WEST POLICE
KORI!
KORI! CAN YOU GIMME A HAND?
Um, OKAY.
KAZZZAAP
IS IT POSSIBLE FOR YOU TO FLY OVER THE WATER IN A STORM LIKE THIS WITHOUT GETTING KILLED?
Oh, YES, STELLA, I CAN DO THAT.! MY SKIN IS QUITE IMPERVIOUS, SO SEVERE IMPACTS DO NOT HARM ME.
IS SOMEONE IN TROUBLE?
MY IDIOT BROTHER WENT OUT TO--
KKRR

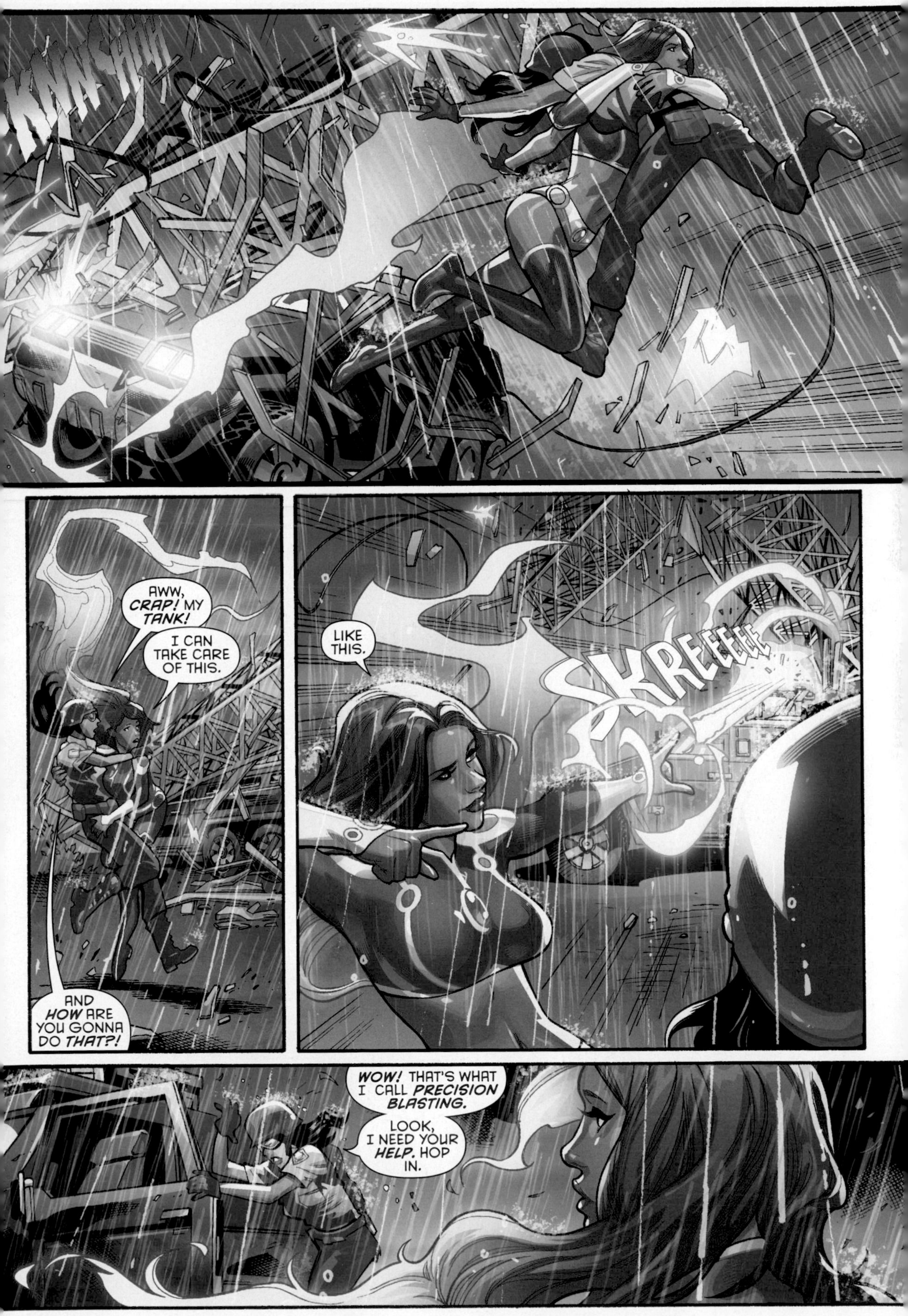
KKNNSHHH
AWW, CRAP! MY TANK!
I CAN TAKE CARE OF THIS.
AND HOW ARE YOU GONNA DO THAT?!
LIKE THIS.
SKREEEEE
WOW! THAT'S WHAT I CALL PRECISION BLASTING.
LOOK, I NEED YOUR HELP. HOP IN.

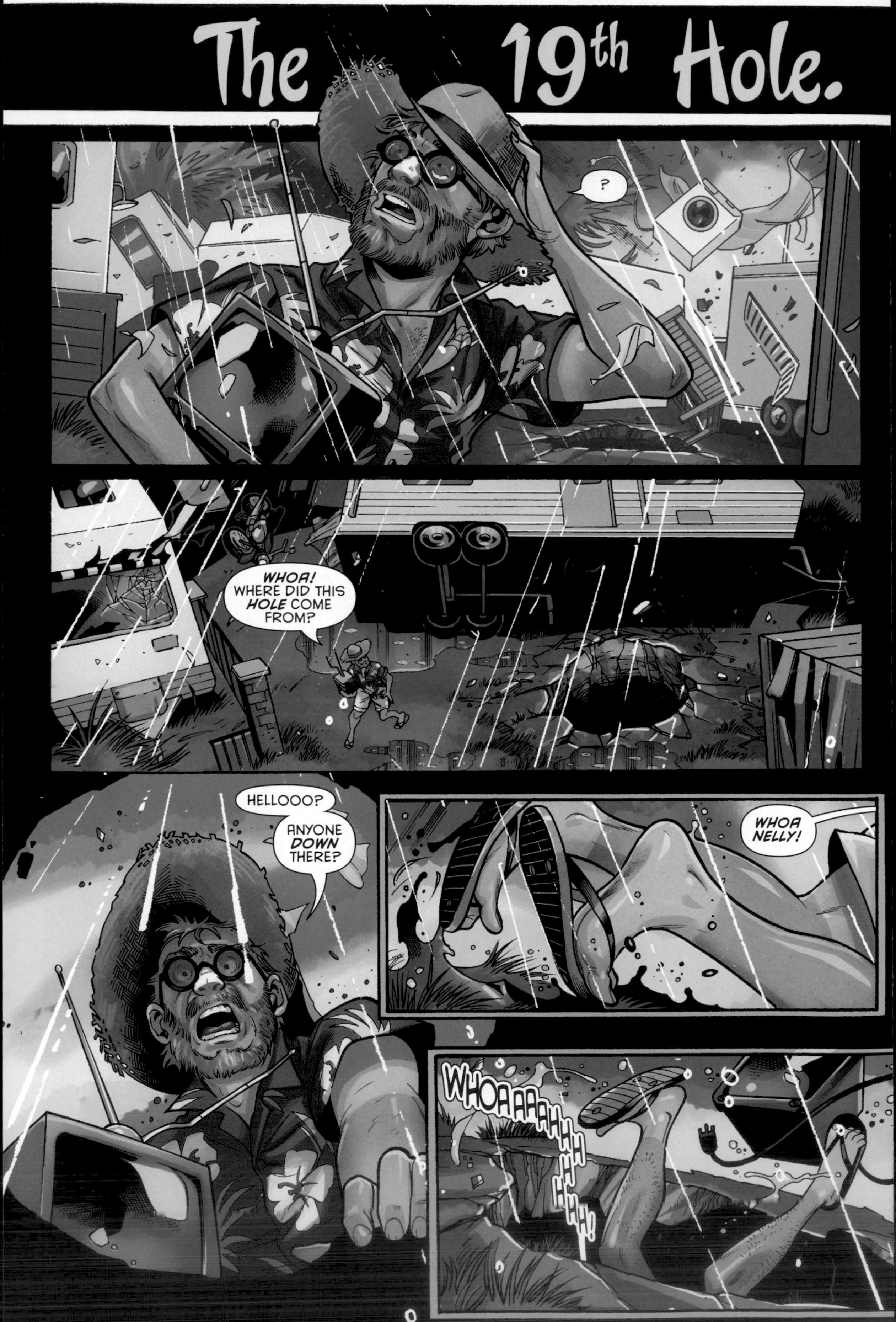

The 19th Hole.
?
WHOA! WHERE DID THIS HOLE COME FROM?
HELLOOO?
ANYONE DOWN THERE?
WHOA NELLY!
WHOAAAAAHHHHHHH!

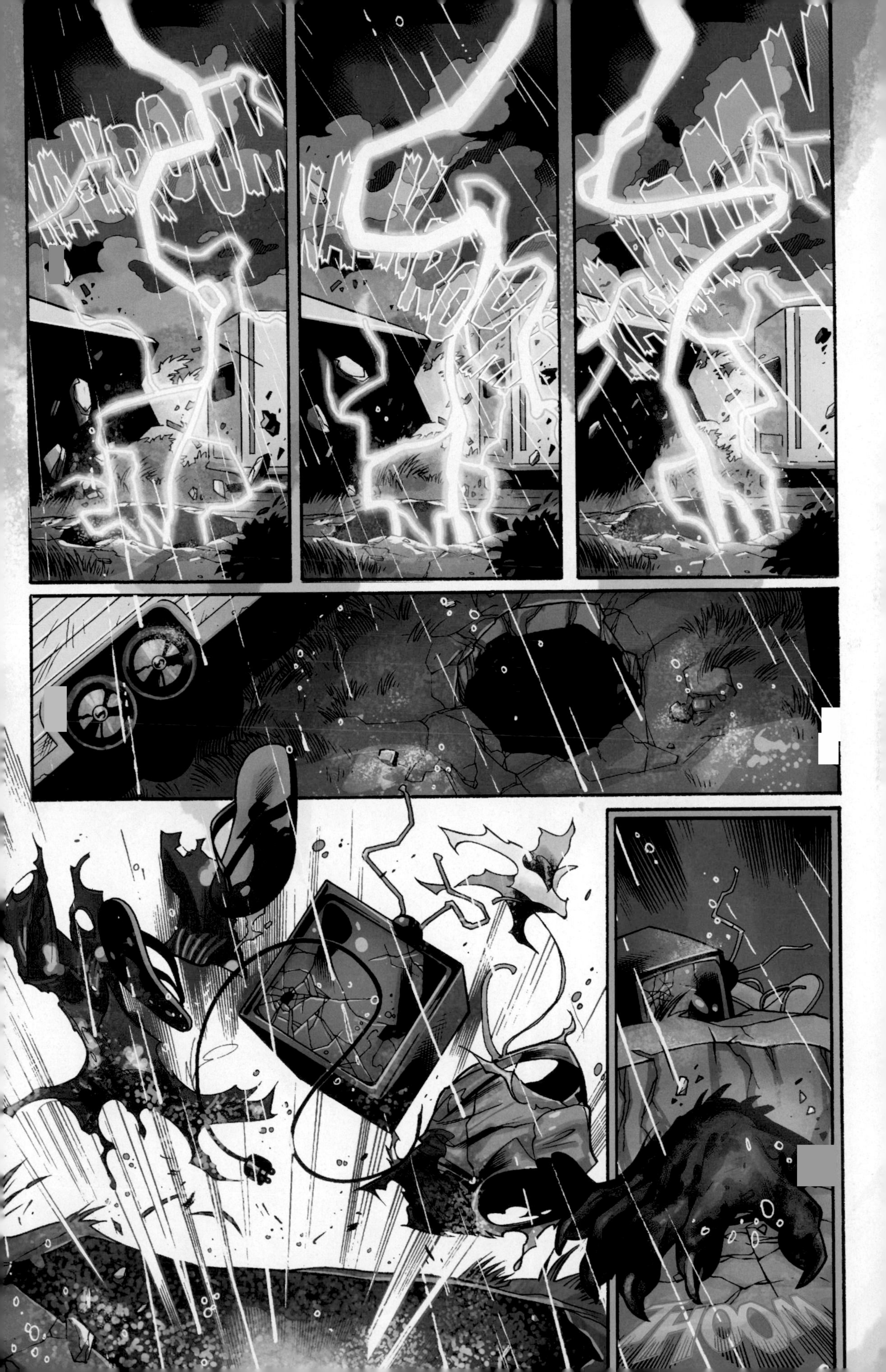

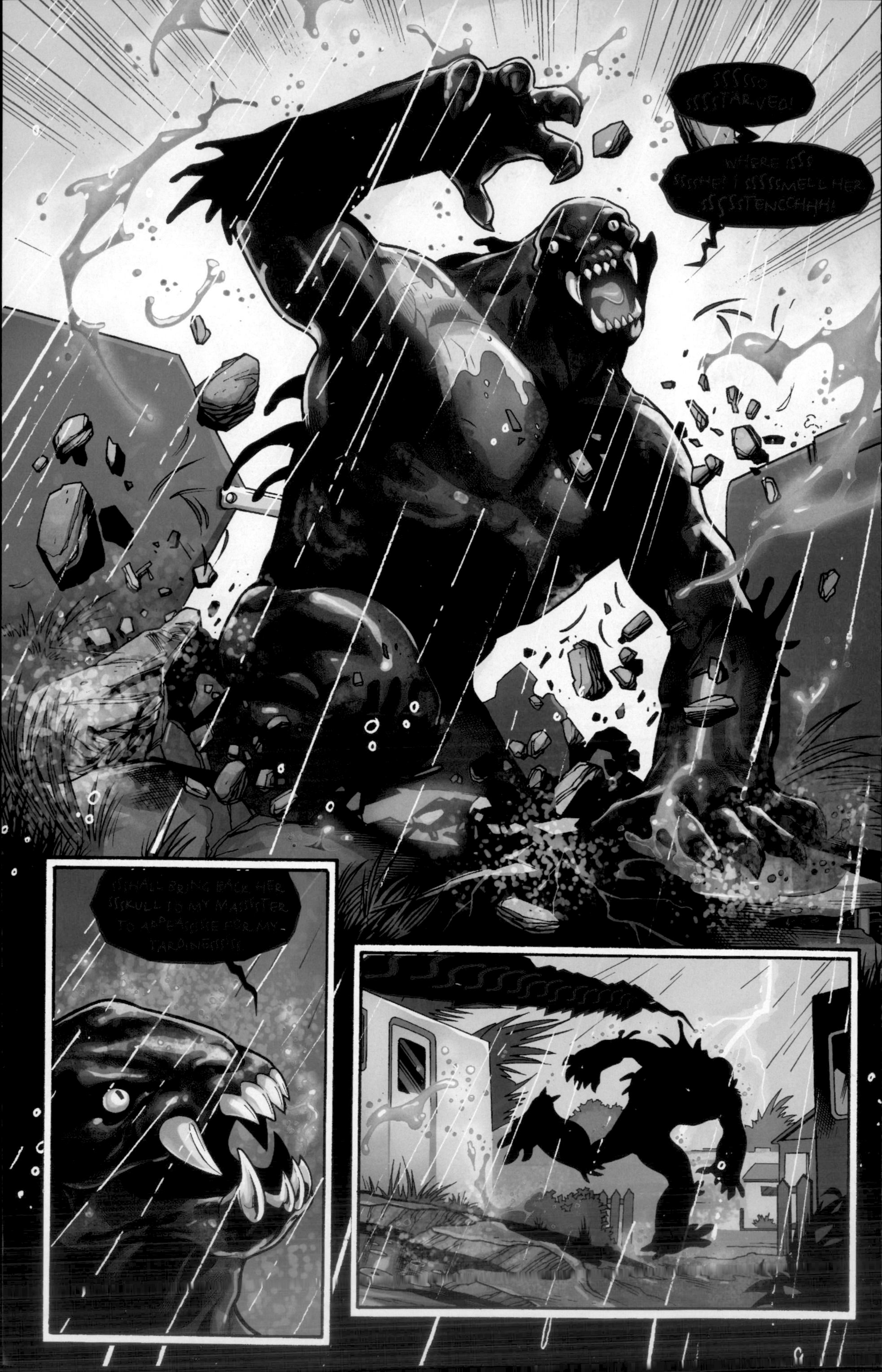
SSSSSO SSSSTARVED!
WHERE ISSS SSSHE? I SSSSSSMELL HER SSSSSTENCCHHH!
SSSHALL BRING BACK HER SSSKULL TO MY MASSSTER TO APPEASSSE FOR MY TARDINESSSSS.

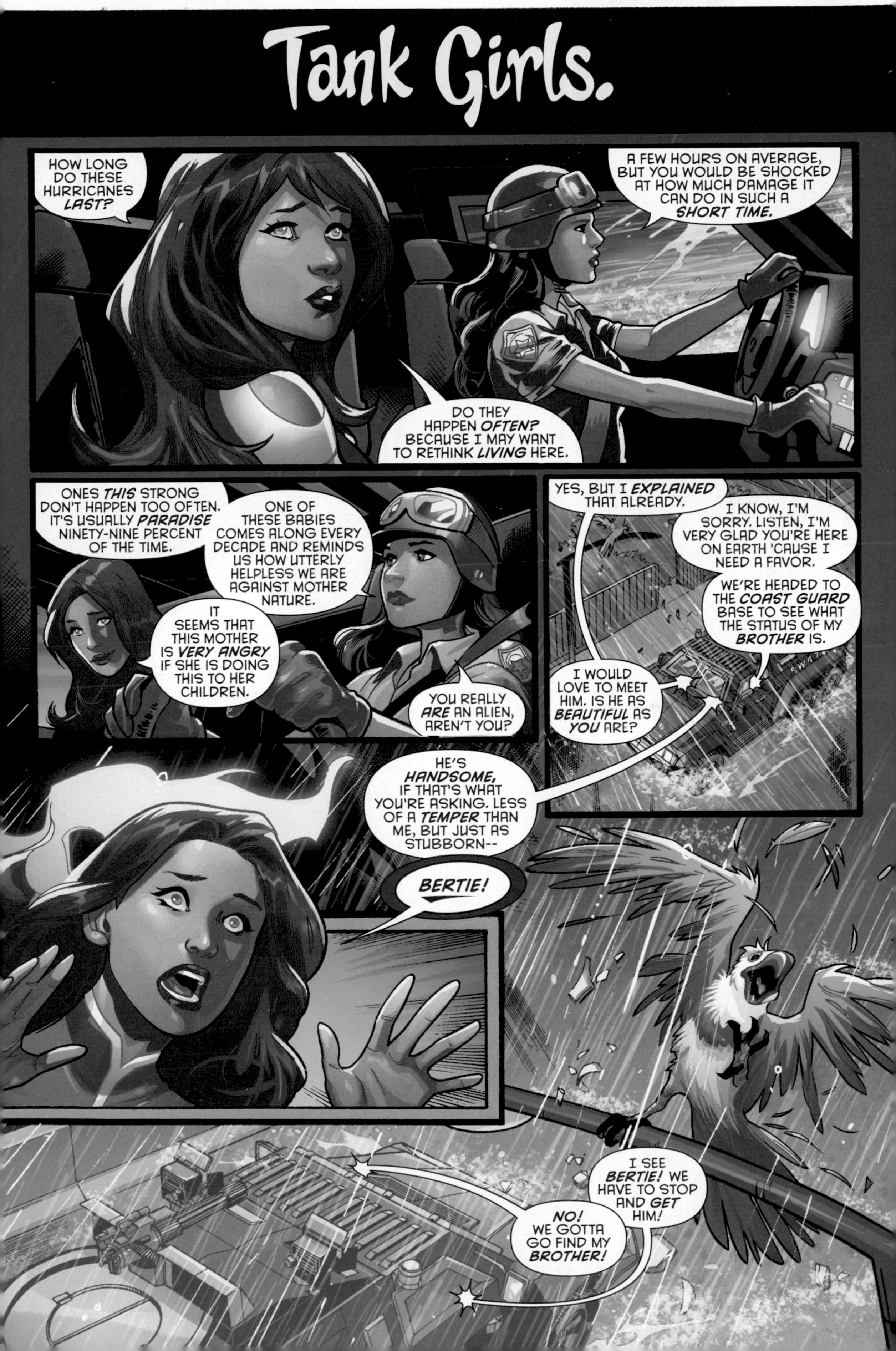
Tank Girls.
HOW LONG DO THESE HURRICANES LAST?
A FEW HOURS ON AVERAGE, BUT YOU WOULD BE SHOCKED AT HOW MUCH DAMAGE IT CAN DO IN SUCH A SHORT TIME.
DO THEY HAPPEN OFTEN? BECAUSE I MAY WANT TO RETHINK LIVING HERE.
ONES THIS STRONG DON'T HAPPEN TOO OFTEN. IT'S USUALLY PARADISE NINETY-NINE PERCENT OF THE TIME.
ONE OF THESE BABIES COMES ALONG EVERY DECADE AND REMINDS US HOW UTTERLY HELPLESS WE ARE AGAINST MOTHER NATURE.
IT SEEMS THAT THIS MOTHER IS VERY ANGRY IF SHE IS DOING THIS TO HER CHILDREN.
YOU REALLY ARE AN ALIEN, AREN'T YOU?
YES, BUT I EXPLAINED THAT ALREADY.
I KNOW, I'M SORRY. LISTEN, I'M VERY GLAD YOU'RE HERE ON EARTH 'CAUSE I NEED A FAVOR.
WE'RE HEADED TO THE COAST GUARD BASE TO SEE WHAT THE STATUS OF MY BROTHER IS.
I WOULD LOVE TO MEET HIM. IS HE AS BEAUTIFUL AS YOU ARE?
HE'S HANDSOME, IF THAT'S WHAT YOU'RE ASKING. LESS OF A TEMPER THAN ME, BUT JUST AS STUBBORN--
BERTIE!
I SEE BERTIE! WE HAVE TO STOP AND GET HIM!
NO! WE GOTTA GO FIND MY BROTHER!

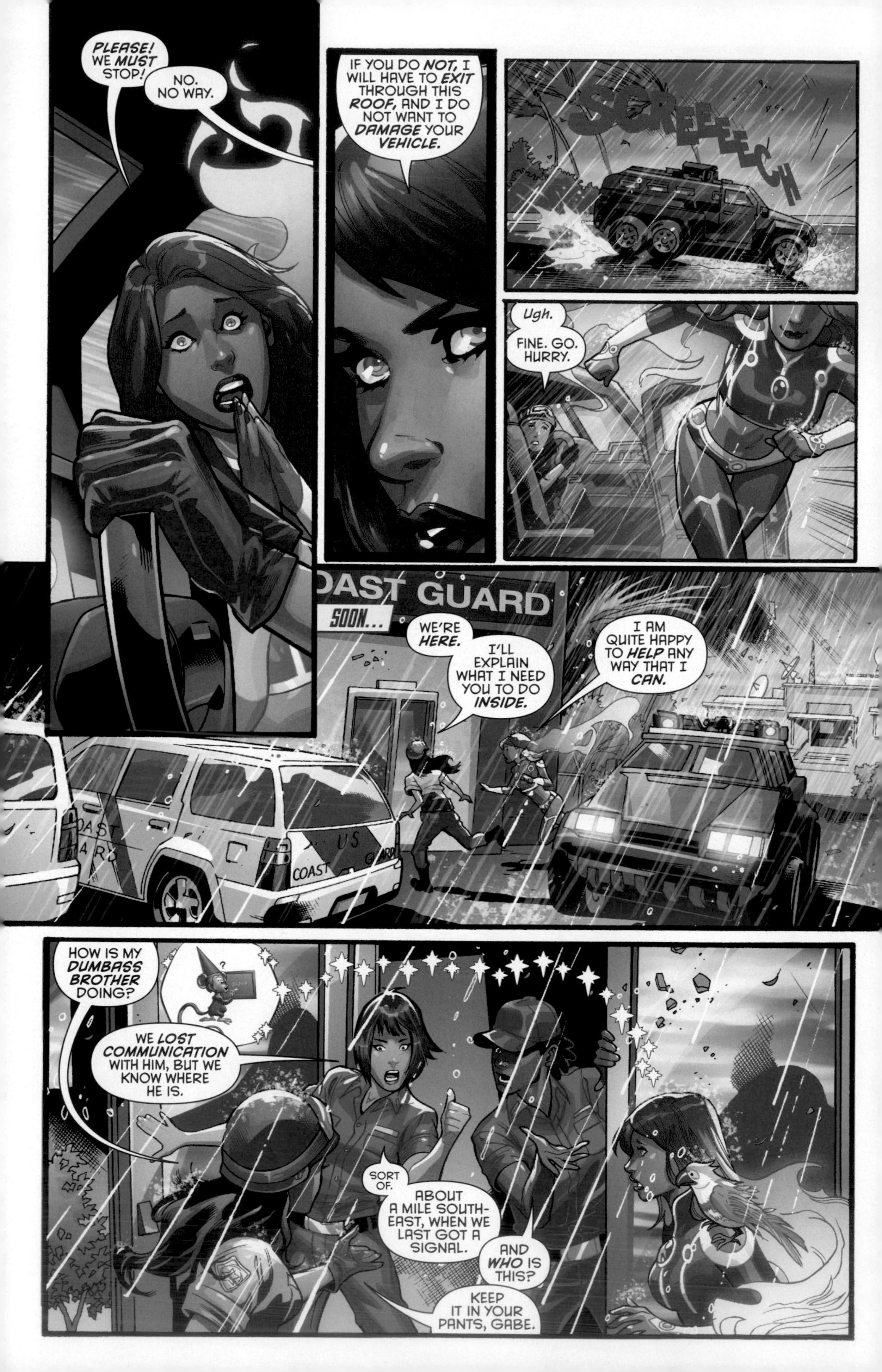
PLEASE! WE MUST STOP!
NO. NO WAY.
IF YOU DO NOT, I WILL HAVE TO EXIT THROUGH THIS ROOF, AND I DO NOT WANT TO DAMAGE YOUR VEHICLE.
SCREEEEECH
Ugh.
FINE. GO. HURRY.
COAST GUARD
SOON...
WE'RE HERE.
I'LL EXPLAIN WHAT I NEED YOU TO DO INSIDE.
I AM QUITE HAPPY TO HELP ANY WAY THAT I CAN.
US
COAST
GUARD
HOW IS MY DUMBASS BROTHER DOING?
WE LOST COMMUNICATION WITH HIM, BUT WE KNOW WHERE HE IS.
SORT OF.
ABOUT A MILE SOUTH-EAST, WHEN WE LAST GOT A SIGNAL.
AND WHO IS THIS?
KEEP IT IN YOUR PANTS, GABE.

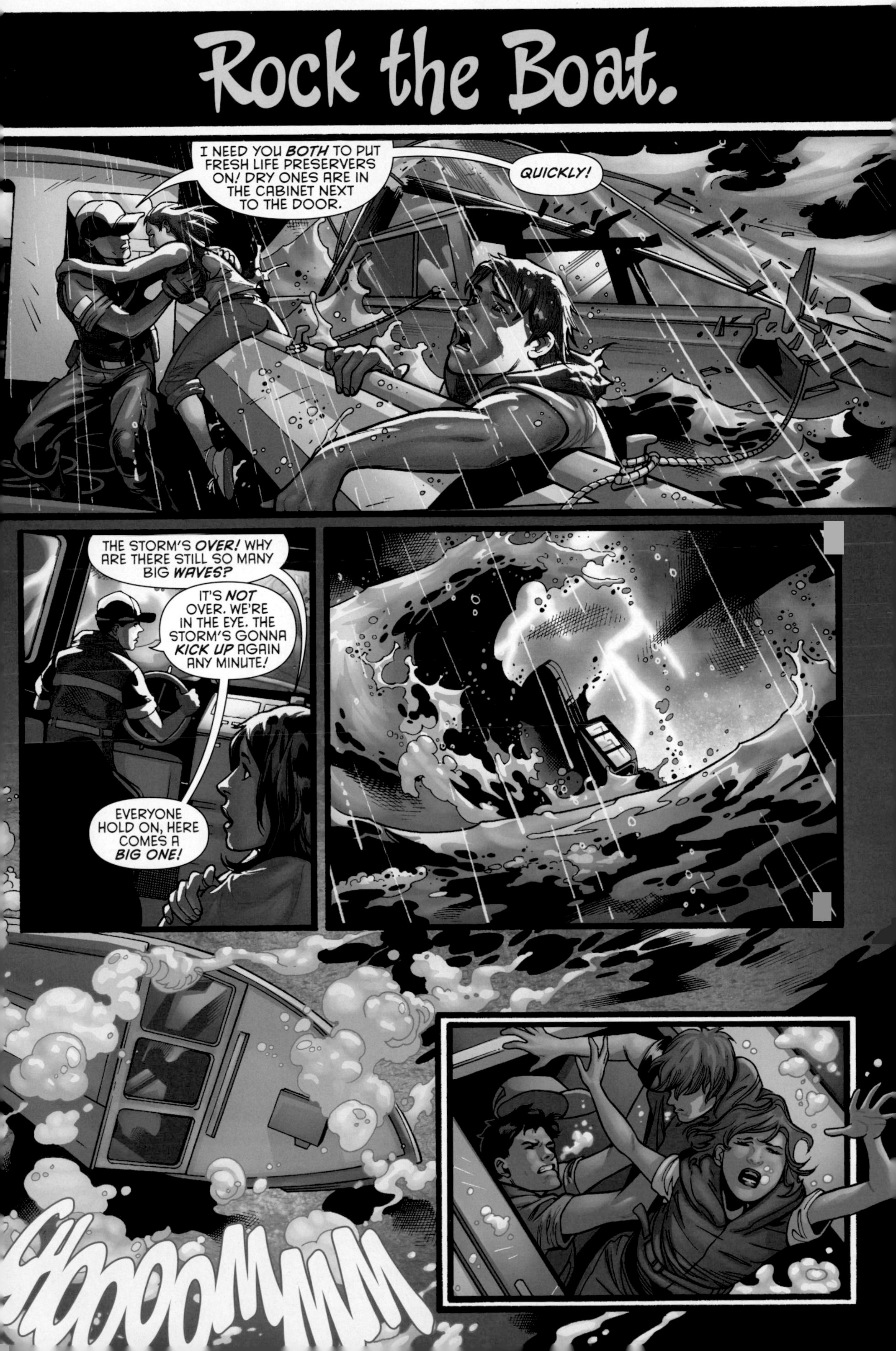
Rock the Boat.
I NEED YOU BOTH TO PUT FRESH LIFE PRESERVERS ON! DRY ONES ARE IN THE CABINET NEXT TO THE DOOR.
QUICKLY!
THE STORM'S OVER! WHY ARE THERE STILL SO MANY BIG WAVES?
IT'S NOT OVER. WE'RE IN THE EYE. THE STORM'S GONNA KICK UP AGAIN ANY MINUTE!
EVERYONE HOLD ON, HERE COMES A BIG ONE!
WHOOOMMM

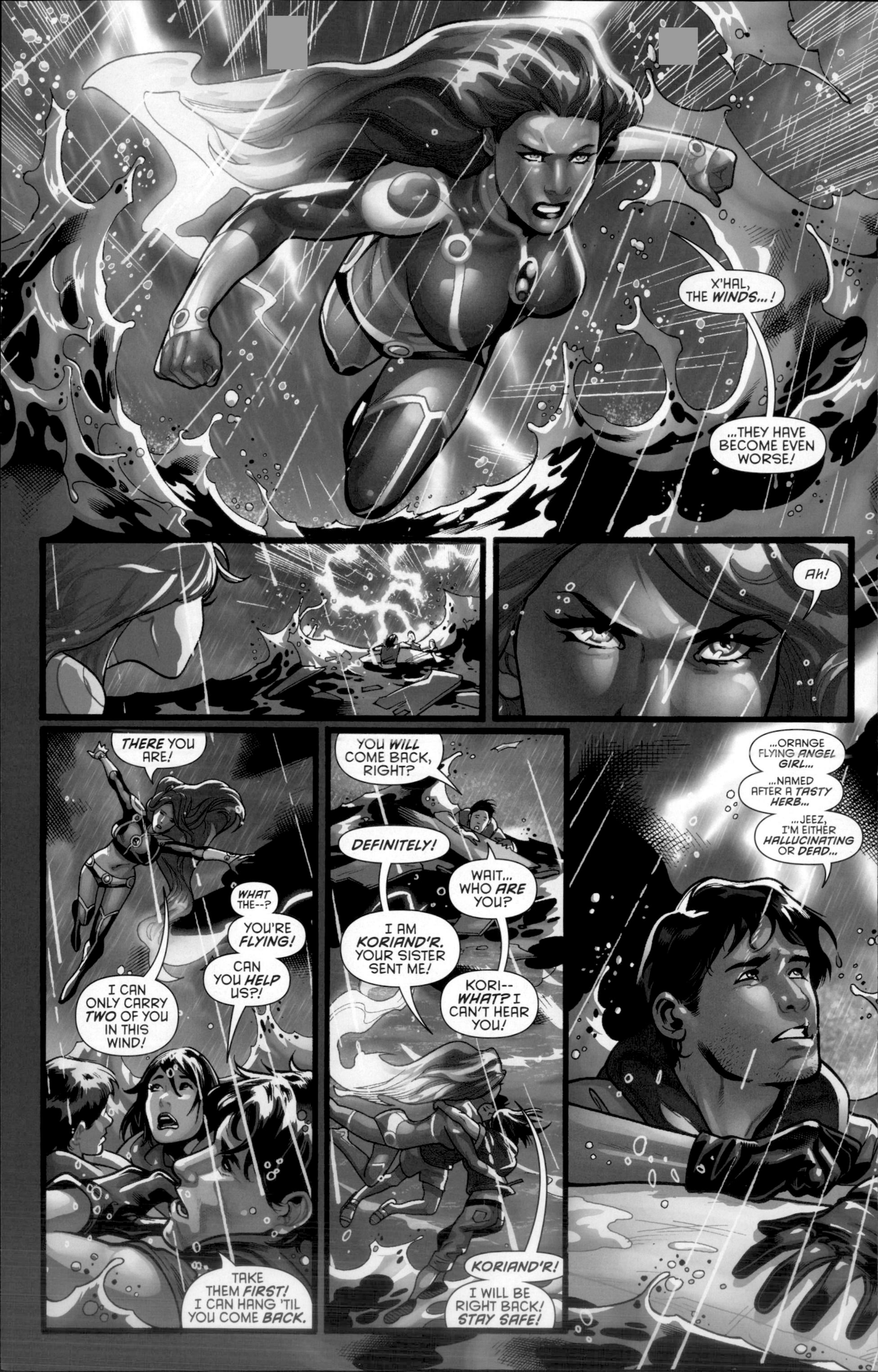
X'HAL, THE *WINDS*...!
...THEY HAVE BECOME EVEN WORSE!
Ah!
THERE YOU ARE!
WHAT THE--?
YOU'RE *FLYING!*
CAN YOU *HELP* US?!
I CAN ONLY CARRY *TWO* OF YOU IN THIS WIND!
TAKE THEM *FIRST!* I CAN HANG 'TIL YOU COME *BACK.*
YOU *WILL* COME BACK, RIGHT?
DEFINITELY!
WAIT... WHO *ARE* YOU?
I AM *KORIAND'R.* YOUR SISTER SENT ME!
KORI-- *WHAT?* I CAN'T HEAR YOU!
KORIAND'R!
I WILL BE RIGHT BACK! *STAY SAFE!*
...ORANGE FLYING *ANGEL GIRL*...
...NAMED AFTER A *TASTY HERB*...
...JEEZ, I'M EITHER *HALLUCINATING* OR *DEAD*...

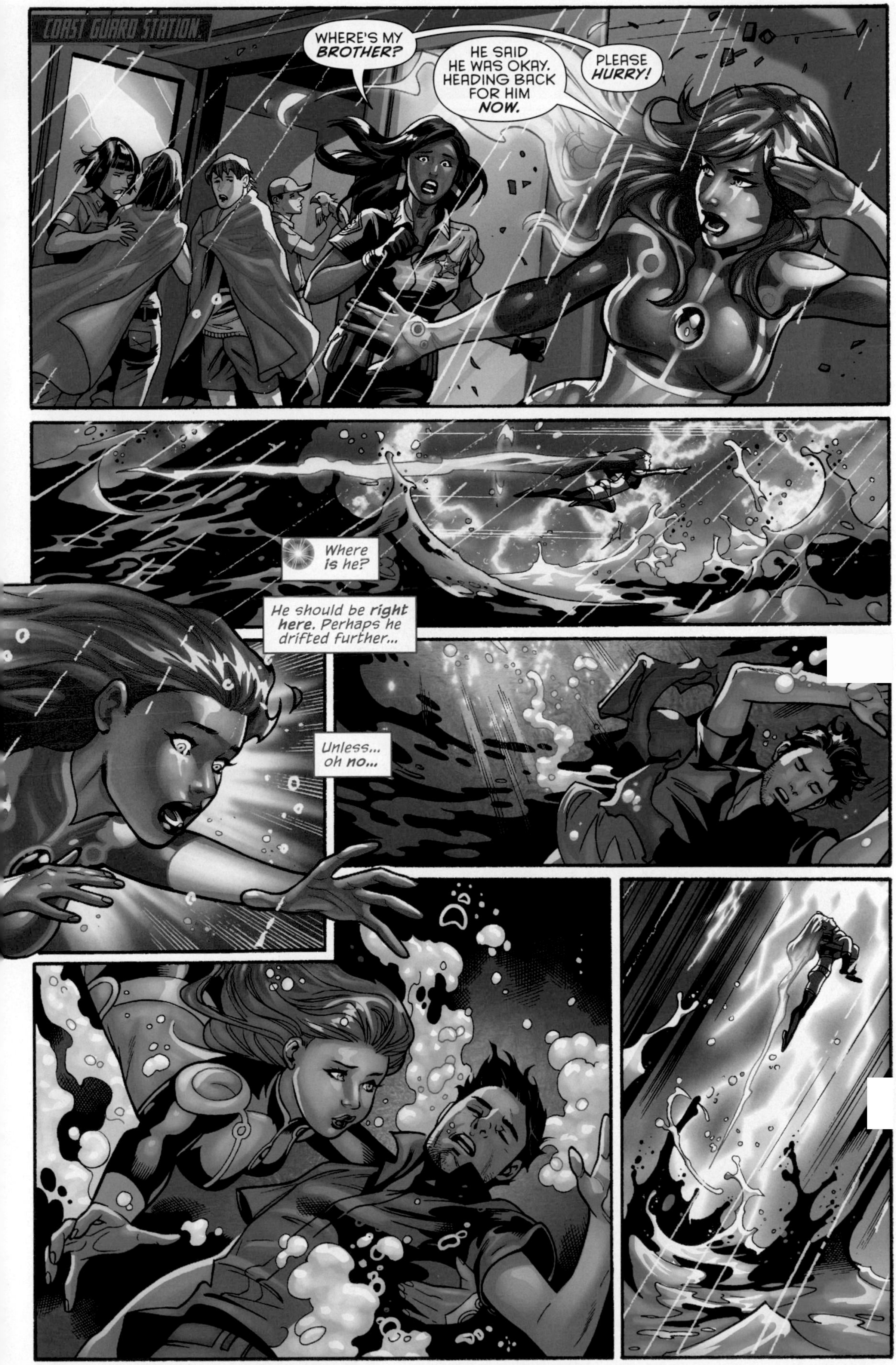
COAST GUARD STATION.
WHERE'S MY BROTHER?
HE SAID HE WAS OKAY. HEADING BACK FOR HIM NOW.
PLEASE HURRY!
Where is he?
He should be right here. Perhaps he drifted further...
Unless... oh no...

Mouth-To-Mouth

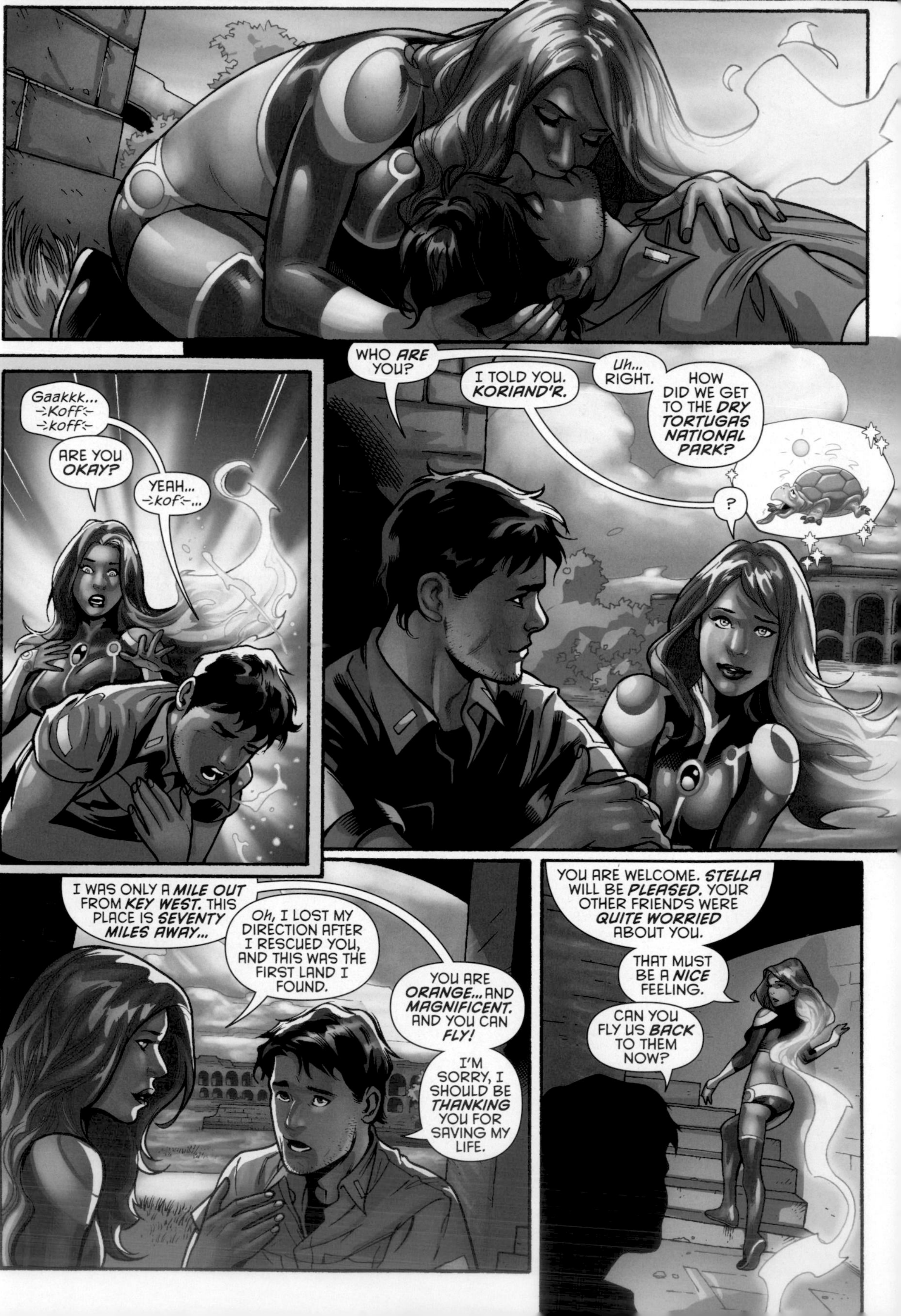
Gaakkk... -Koff- -koff-
ARE YOU OKAY?
YEAH... -kof-...
WHO ARE YOU?
I TOLD YOU. KORIAND'R.
Uh... RIGHT.
HOW DID WE GET TO THE DRY TORTUGAS NATIONAL PARK?
?
I WAS ONLY A MILE OUT FROM KEY WEST. THIS PLACE IS SEVENTY MILES AWAY...
Oh, I LOST MY DIRECTION AFTER I RESCUED YOU, AND THIS WAS THE FIRST LAND I FOUND.
YOU ARE ORANGE... AND MAGNIFICENT. AND YOU CAN FLY!
I'M SORRY, I SHOULD BE THANKING YOU FOR SAVING MY LIFE.
YOU ARE WELCOME. STELLA WILL BE PLEASED. YOUR OTHER FRIENDS WERE QUITE WORRIED ABOUT YOU.
THAT MUST BE A NICE FEELING.
CAN YOU FLY US BACK TO THEM NOW?

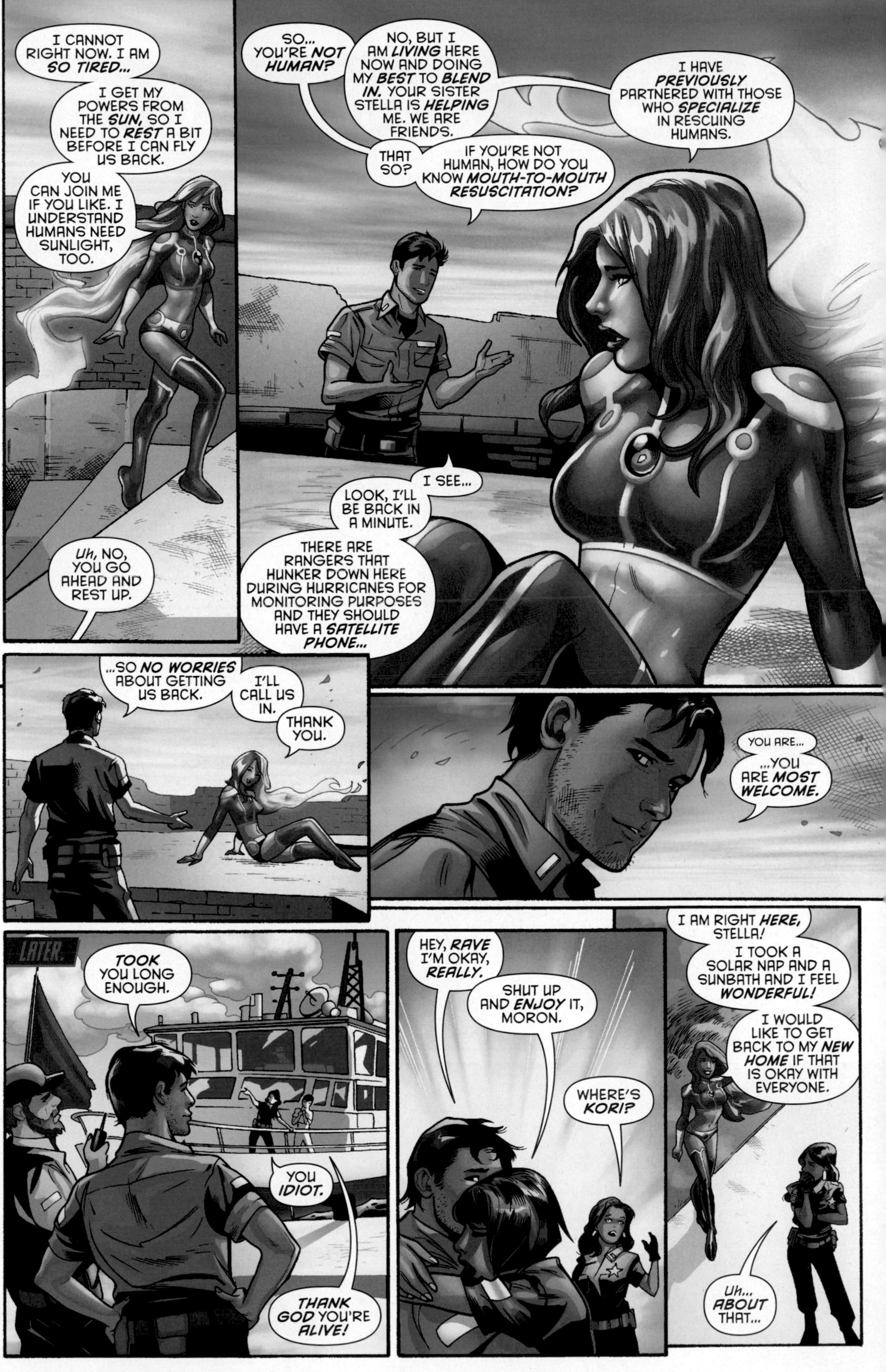

I CANNOT RIGHT NOW. I AM SO TIRED...
I GET MY POWERS FROM THE SUN, SO I NEED TO REST A BIT BEFORE I CAN FLY US BACK.
YOU CAN JOIN ME IF YOU LIKE. I UNDERSTAND HUMANS NEED SUNLIGHT, TOO.
UH, NO, YOU GO AHEAD AND REST UP.
SO... YOU'RE NOT HUMAN?
NO, BUT I AM LIVING HERE NOW AND DOING MY BEST TO BLEND IN. YOUR SISTER STELLA IS HELPING ME. WE ARE FRIENDS.
THAT SO?
IF YOU'RE NOT HUMAN, HOW DO YOU KNOW MOUTH-TO-MOUTH RESUSCITATION?
I HAVE PREVIOUSLY PARTNERED WITH THOSE WHO SPECIALIZE IN RESCUING HUMANS.
I SEE...
LOOK, I'LL BE BACK IN A MINUTE.
THERE ARE RANGERS THAT HUNKER DOWN HERE DURING HURRICANES FOR MONITORING PURPOSES AND THEY SHOULD HAVE A SATELLITE PHONE...
...SO NO WORRIES ABOUT GETTING US BACK.
I'LL CALL US IN.
THANK YOU.
YOU ARE...
...YOU ARE MOST WELCOME.
LATER.
TOOK YOU LONG ENOUGH.
YOU IDIOT.
THANK GOD YOU'RE ALIVE!
HEY, RAVE I'M OKAY, REALLY.
SHUT UP AND ENJOY IT, MORON.
WHERE'S KORI?
I AM RIGHT HERE, STELLA!
I TOOK A SOLAR NAP AND A SUNBATH AND I FEEL WONDERFUL!
I WOULD LIKE TO GET BACK TO MY NEW HOME IF THAT IS OKAY WITH EVERYONE.
UH... ABOUT THAT...

Quick Turnaround.

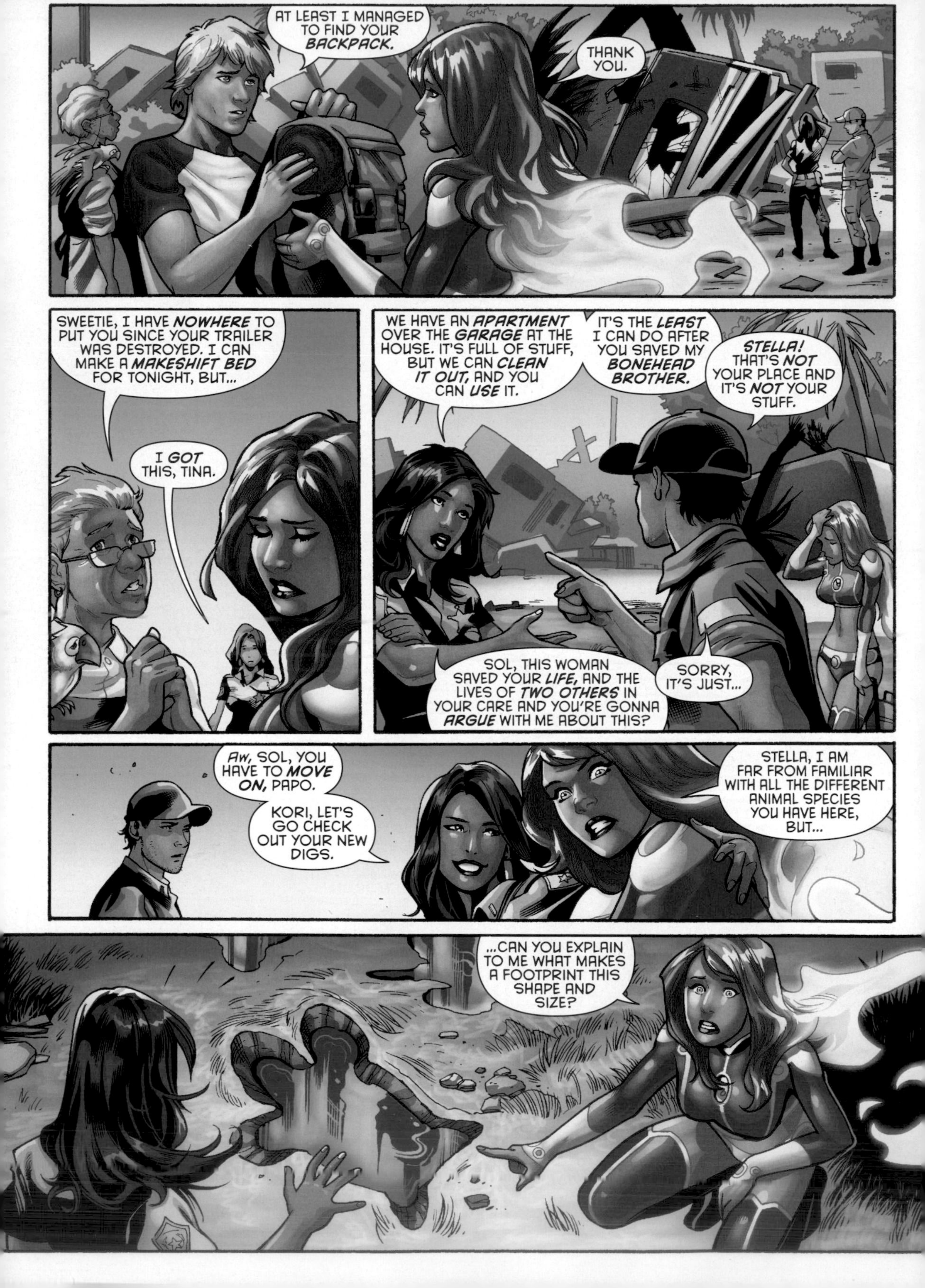
AT LEAST I MANAGED TO FIND YOUR BACKPACK.
THANK YOU.
SWEETIE, I HAVE NOWHERE TO PUT YOU SINCE YOUR TRAILER WAS DESTROYED. I CAN MAKE A MAKESHIFT BED FOR TONIGHT, BUT...
I GOT THIS, TINA.
WE HAVE AN APARTMENT OVER THE GARAGE AT THE HOUSE. IT'S FULL OF STUFF, BUT WE CAN CLEAN IT OUT, AND YOU CAN USE IT.
IT'S THE LEAST I CAN DO AFTER YOU SAVED MY BONEHEAD BROTHER.
STELLA! THAT'S NOT YOUR PLACE AND IT'S NOT YOUR STUFF.
SOL, THIS WOMAN SAVED YOUR LIFE, AND THE LIVES OF TWO OTHERS IN YOUR CARE AND YOU'RE GONNA ARGUE WITH ME ABOUT THIS?
SORRY, IT'S JUST...
AW, SOL, YOU HAVE TO MOVE ON, PAPO.
KORI, LET'S GO CHECK OUT YOUR NEW DIGS.
STELLA, I AM FAR FROM FAMILIAR WITH ALL THE DIFFERENT ANIMAL SPECIES YOU HAVE HERE, BUT...
...CAN YOU EXPLAIN TO ME WHAT MAKES A FOOTPRINT THIS SHAPE AND SIZE?

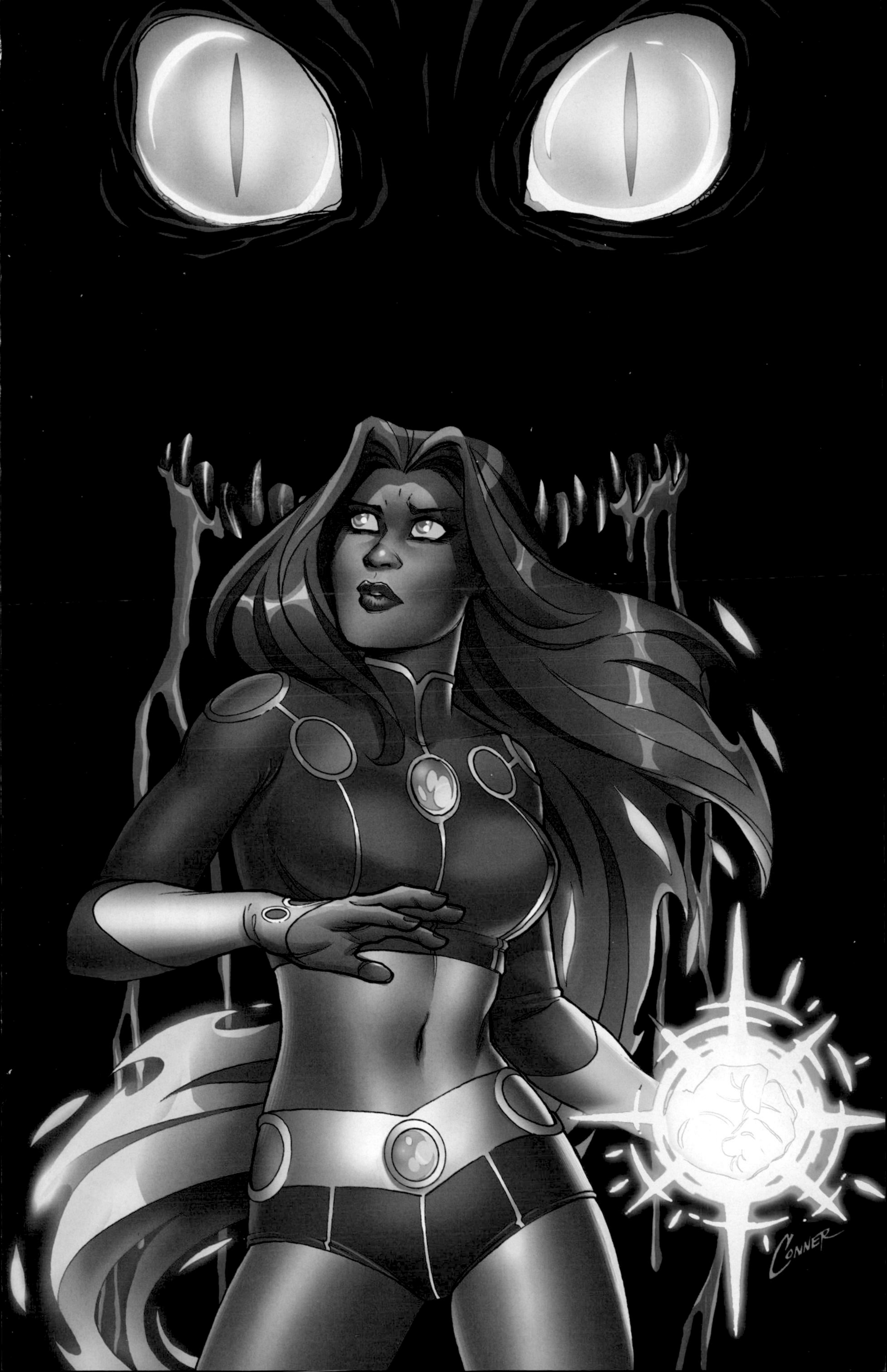
CONNER

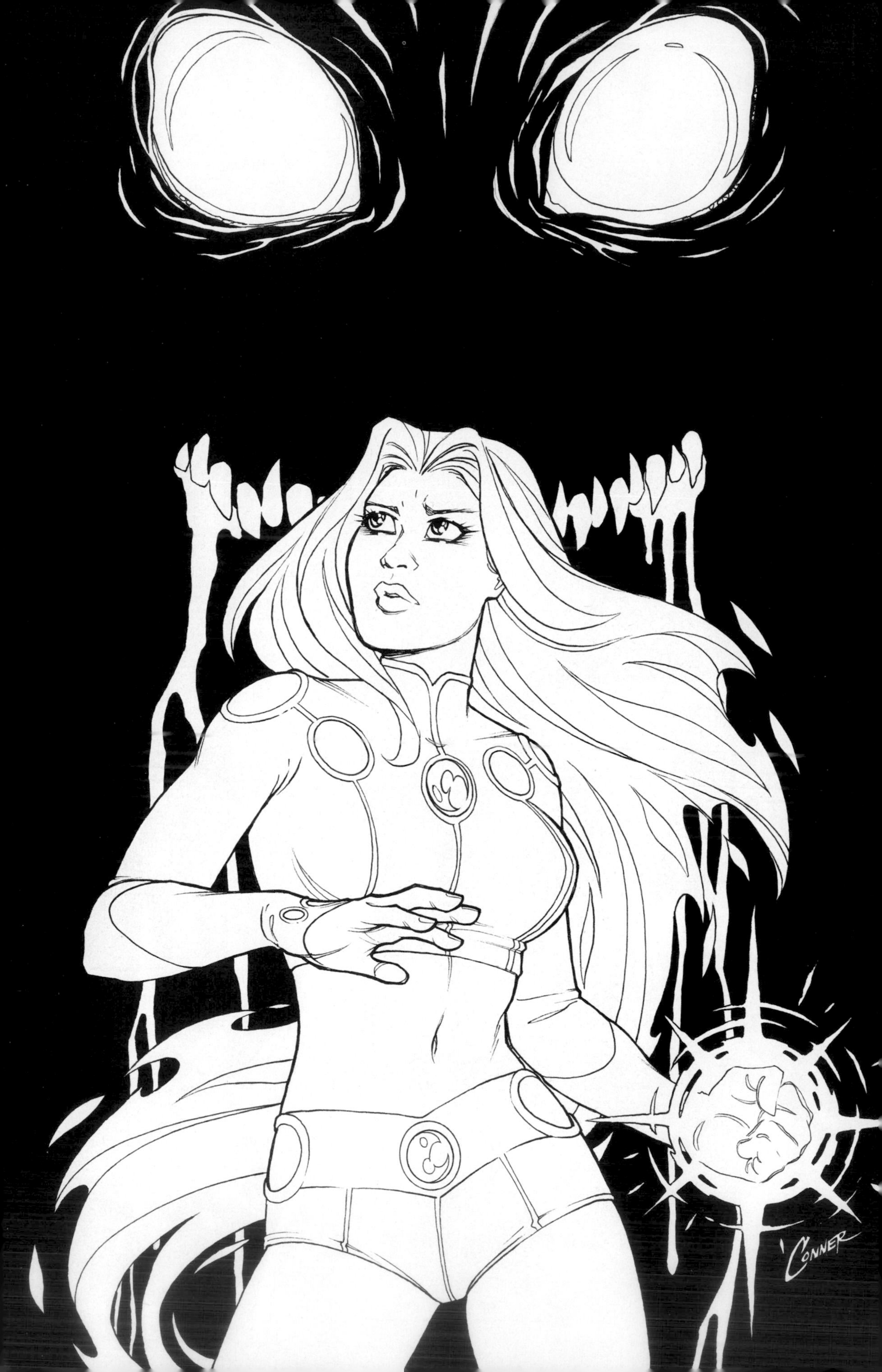

CONNER

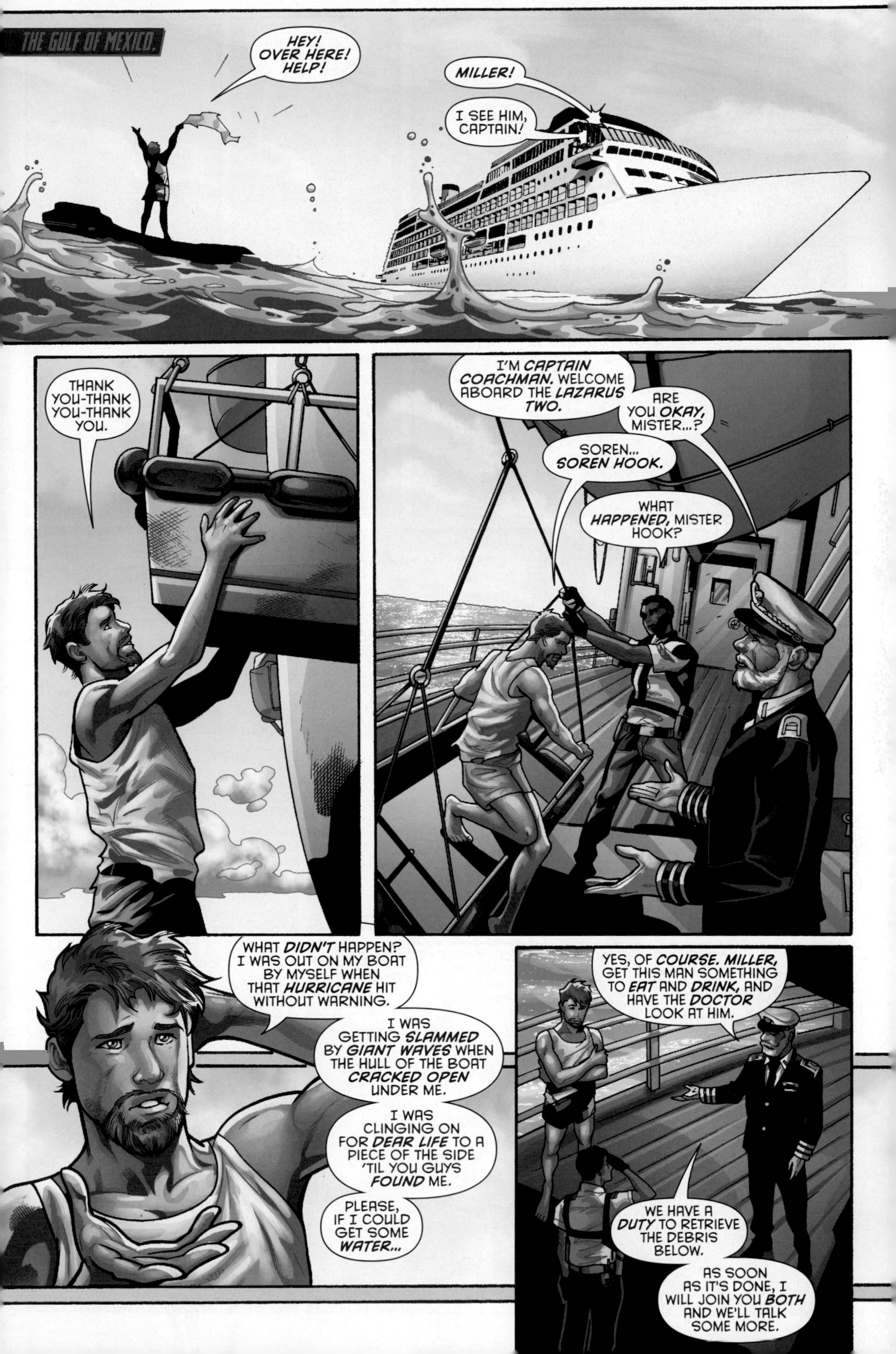

THE GULF OF MEXICO.
HEY! OVER HERE! HELP!
MILLER!
I SEE HIM, CAPTAIN!
THANK YOU-THANK YOU-THANK YOU.
I'M CAPTAIN COACHMAN. WELCOME ABOARD THE LAZARUS TWO.
ARE YOU OKAY, MISTER...?
SOREN... SOREN HOOK.
WHAT HAPPENED, MISTER HOOK?
WHAT DIDN'T HAPPEN? I WAS OUT ON MY BOAT BY MYSELF WHEN THAT HURRICANE HIT WITHOUT WARNING.
I WAS GETTING SLAMMED BY GIANT WAVES WHEN THE HULL OF THE BOAT CRACKED OPEN UNDER ME.
I WAS CLINGING ON FOR DEAR LIFE TO A PIECE OF THE SIDE 'TIL YOU GUYS FOUND ME.
PLEASE, IF I COULD GET SOME WATER...
YES, OF COURSE. MILLER, GET THIS MAN SOMETHING TO EAT AND DRINK, AND HAVE THE DOCTOR LOOK AT HIM.
WE HAVE A DUTY TO RETRIEVE THE DEBRIS BELOW.
AS SOON AS IT'S DONE, I WILL JOIN YOU BOTH AND WE'LL TALK SOME MORE.

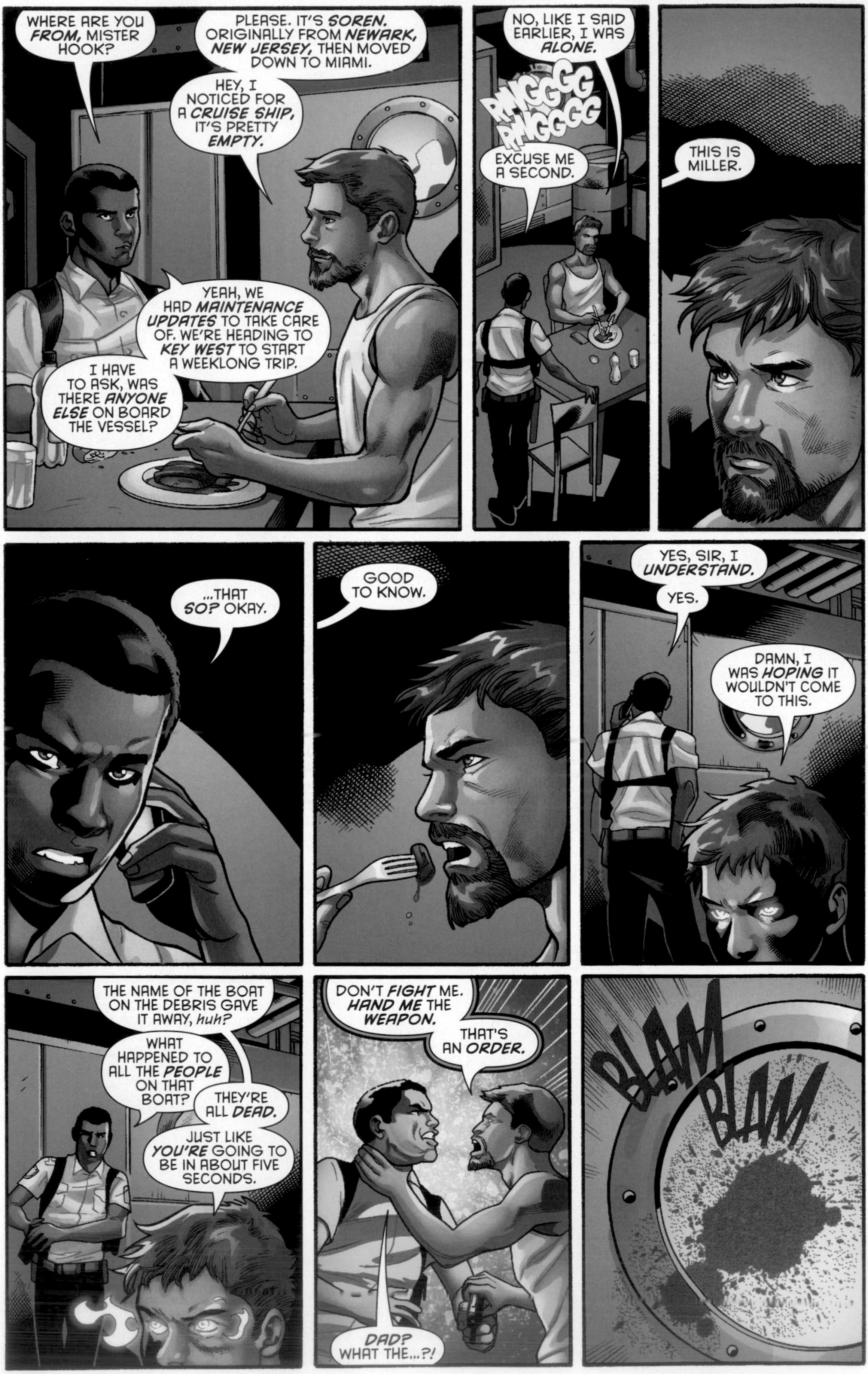
WHERE ARE YOU FROM, MISTER HOOK?
PLEASE. IT'S SOREN. ORIGINALLY FROM NEWARK, NEW JERSEY, THEN MOVED DOWN TO MIAMI.
HEY, I NOTICED FOR A CRUISE SHIP, IT'S PRETTY EMPTY.
YEAH, WE HAD MAINTENANCE UPDATES TO TAKE CARE OF. WE'RE HEADING TO KEY WEST TO START A WEEKLONG TRIP.
I HAVE TO ASK, WAS THERE ANYONE ELSE ON BOARD THE VESSEL?
NO, LIKE I SAID EARLIER, I WAS ALONE.
RMGGGG RMGGGG
EXCUSE ME A SECOND.
THIS IS MILLER.
...THAT SO? OKAY.
GOOD TO KNOW.
YES, SIR, I UNDERSTAND.
YES.
DAMN, I WAS HOPING IT WOULDN'T COME TO THIS.
THE NAME OF THE BOAT ON THE DEBRIS GAVE IT AWAY, huh?
WHAT HAPPENED TO ALL THE PEOPLE ON THAT BOAT?
THEY'RE ALL DEAD.
JUST LIKE YOU'RE GOING TO BE IN ABOUT FIVE SECONDS.
DON'T FIGHT ME. HAND ME THE WEAPON.
THAT'S AN ORDER.
DAD? WHAT THE...?!
BLAM BLAM

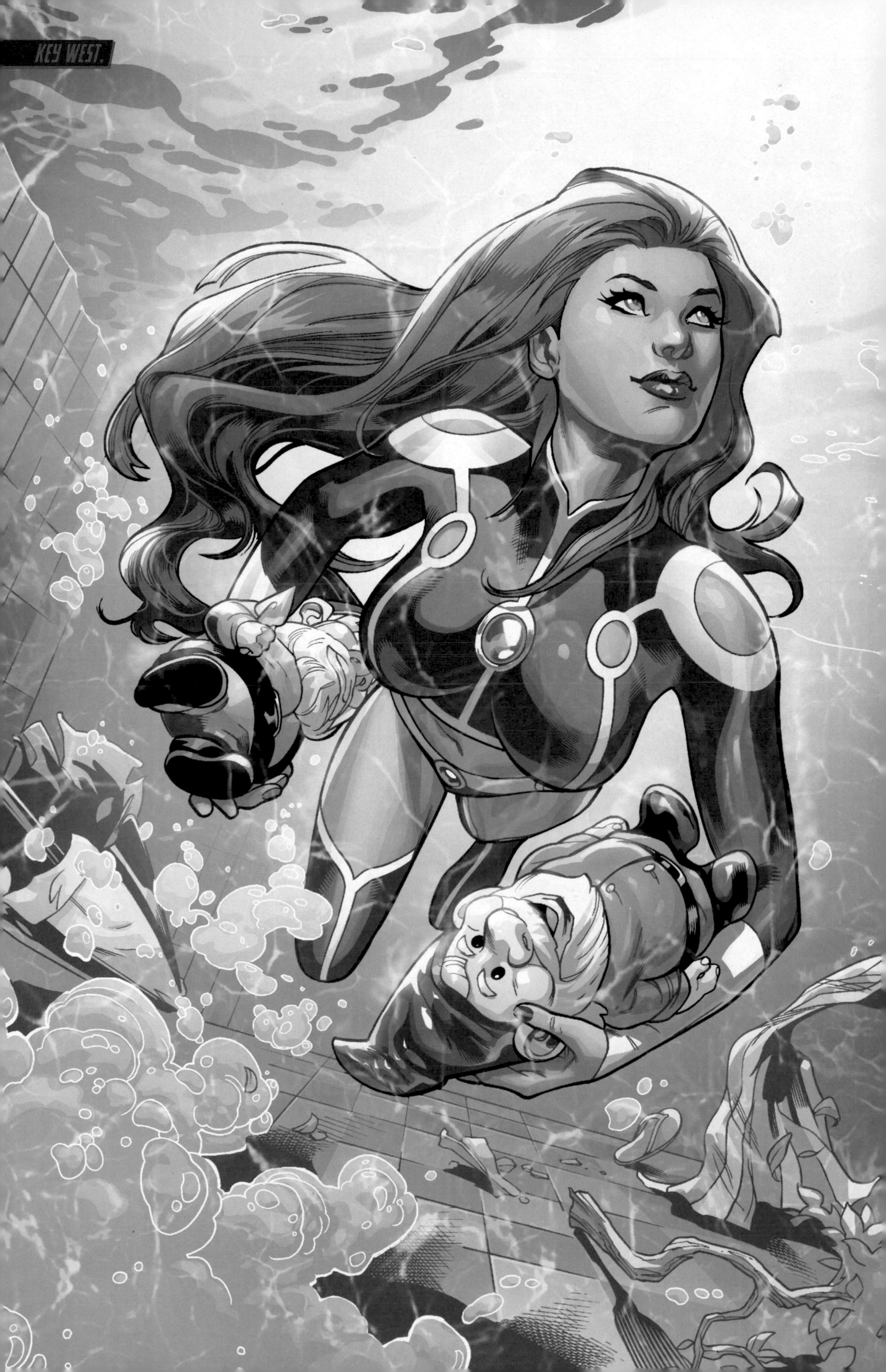
KEY WEST.

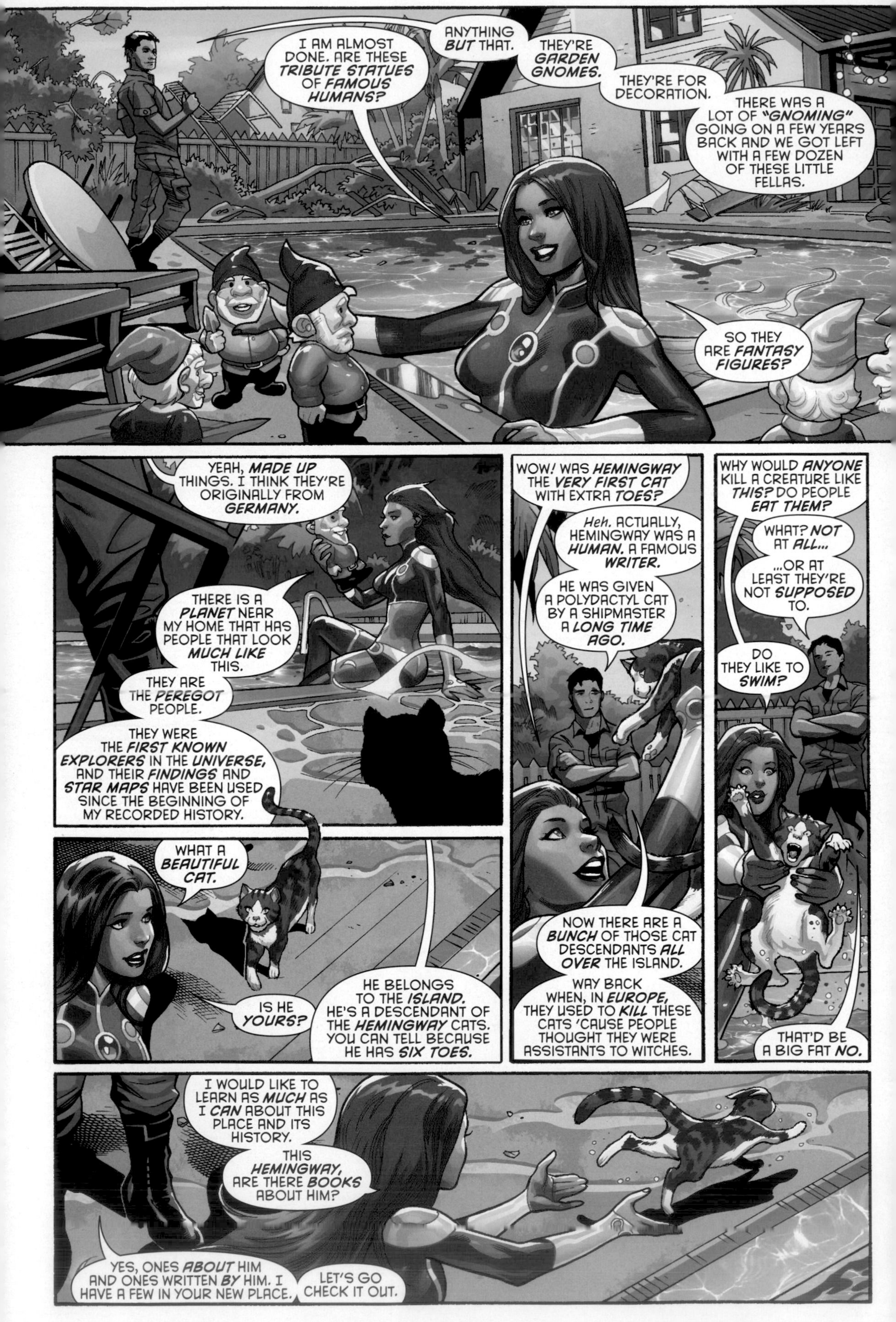

I AM ALMOST DONE. ARE THESE TRIBUTE STATUES OF FAMOUS HUMANS?
ANYTHING BUT THAT.
THEY'RE GARDEN GNOMES.
THEY'RE FOR DECORATION.
THERE WAS A LOT OF "GNOMING" GOING ON A FEW YEARS BACK AND WE GOT LEFT WITH A FEW DOZEN OF THESE LITTLE FELLAS.
SO THEY ARE FANTASY FIGURES?
YEAH, MADE UP THINGS. I THINK THEY'RE ORIGINALLY FROM GERMANY.
THERE IS A PLANET NEAR MY HOME THAT HAS PEOPLE THAT LOOK MUCH LIKE THIS.
THEY ARE THE PEREGOT PEOPLE.
THEY WERE THE FIRST KNOWN EXPLORERS IN THE UNIVERSE, AND THEIR FINDINGS AND STAR MAPS HAVE BEEN USED SINCE THE BEGINNING OF MY RECORDED HISTORY.
WHAT A BEAUTIFUL CAT.
IS HE YOURS?
HE BELONGS TO THE ISLAND. HE'S A DESCENDANT OF THE HEMINGWAY CATS. YOU CAN TELL BECAUSE HE HAS SIX TOES.
WOW! WAS HEMINGWAY THE VERY FIRST CAT WITH EXTRA TOES?
Heh. ACTUALLY, HEMINGWAY WAS A HUMAN. A FAMOUS WRITER.
HE WAS GIVEN A POLYDACTYL CAT BY A SHIPMASTER A LONG TIME AGO.
NOW THERE ARE A BUNCH OF THOSE CAT DESCENDANTS ALL OVER THE ISLAND.
WAY BACK WHEN, IN EUROPE, THEY USED TO KILL THESE CATS 'CAUSE PEOPLE THOUGHT THEY WERE ASSISTANTS TO WITCHES.
WHY WOULD ANYONE KILL A CREATURE LIKE THIS? DO PEOPLE EAT THEM?
WHAT? NOT AT ALL...
...OR AT LEAST THEY'RE NOT SUPPOSED TO.
DO THEY LIKE TO SWIM?
THAT'D BE A BIG FAT NO.
I WOULD LIKE TO LEARN AS MUCH AS I CAN ABOUT THIS PLACE AND ITS HISTORY.
THIS HEMINGWAY, ARE THERE BOOKS ABOUT HIM?
YES, ONES ABOUT HIM AND ONES WRITTEN BY HIM. I HAVE A FEW IN YOUR NEW PLACE.
LET'S GO CHECK IT OUT.

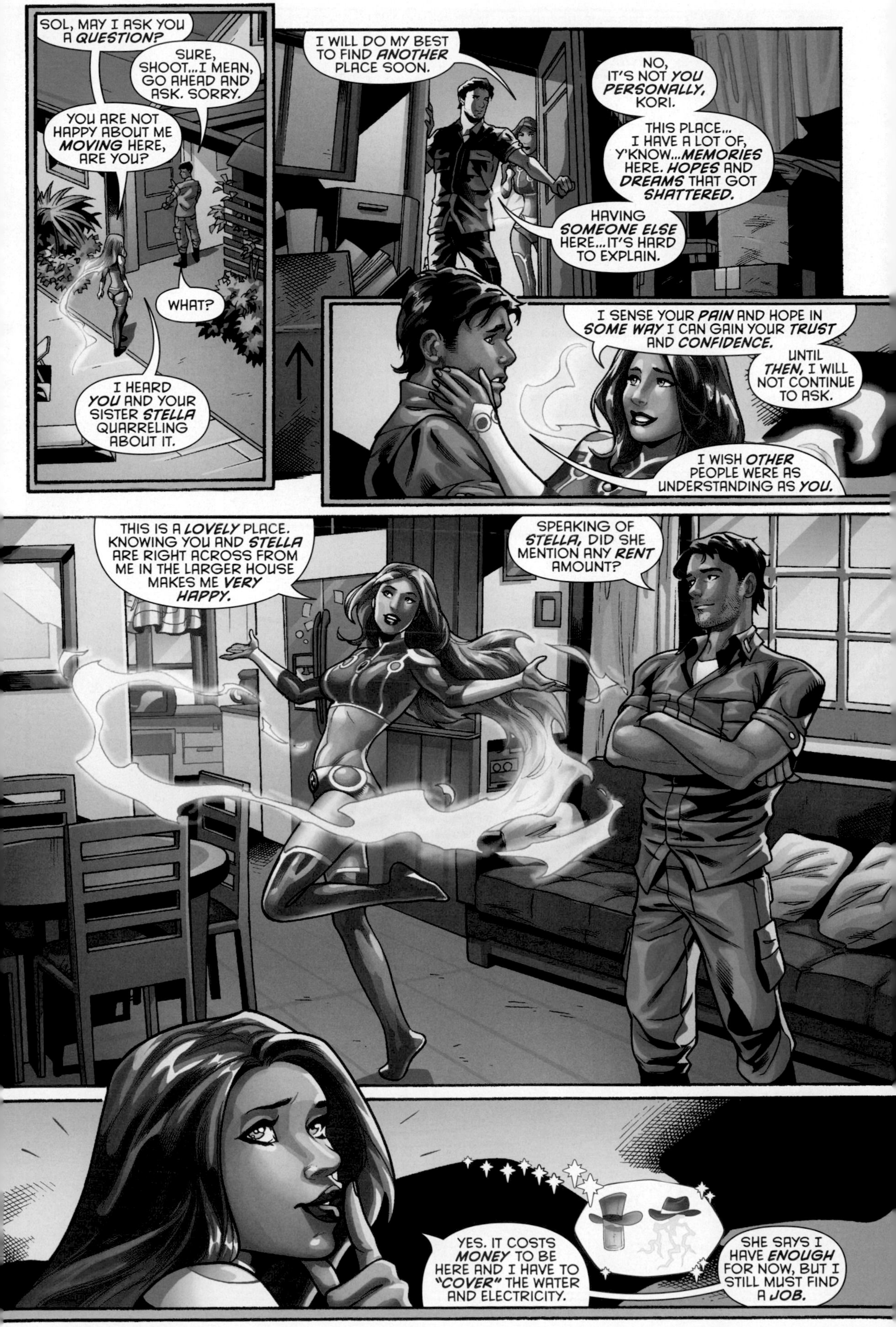
SOL, MAY I ASK YOU A QUESTION?
SURE, SHOOT...I MEAN, GO AHEAD AND ASK. SORRY.
YOU ARE NOT HAPPY ABOUT ME MOVING HERE, ARE YOU?
WHAT?
I HEARD YOU AND YOUR SISTER STELLA QUARRELING ABOUT IT.
I WILL DO MY BEST TO FIND ANOTHER PLACE SOON.
NO, IT'S NOT YOU PERSONALLY, KORI.
THIS PLACE... I HAVE A LOT OF, Y'KNOW...MEMORIES HERE. HOPES AND DREAMS THAT GOT SHATTERED.
HAVING SOMEONE ELSE HERE...IT'S HARD TO EXPLAIN.
I SENSE YOUR PAIN AND HOPE IN SOME WAY I CAN GAIN YOUR TRUST AND CONFIDENCE.
UNTIL THEN, I WILL NOT CONTINUE TO ASK.
I WISH OTHER PEOPLE WERE AS UNDERSTANDING AS YOU.
THIS IS A LOVELY PLACE. KNOWING YOU AND STELLA ARE RIGHT ACROSS FROM ME IN THE LARGER HOUSE MAKES ME VERY HAPPY.
SPEAKING OF STELLA, DID SHE MENTION ANY RENT AMOUNT?
YES. IT COSTS MONEY TO BE HERE AND I HAVE TO "COVER" THE WATER AND ELECTRICITY.
SHE SAYS I HAVE ENOUGH FOR NOW, BUT I STILL MUST FIND A JOB.

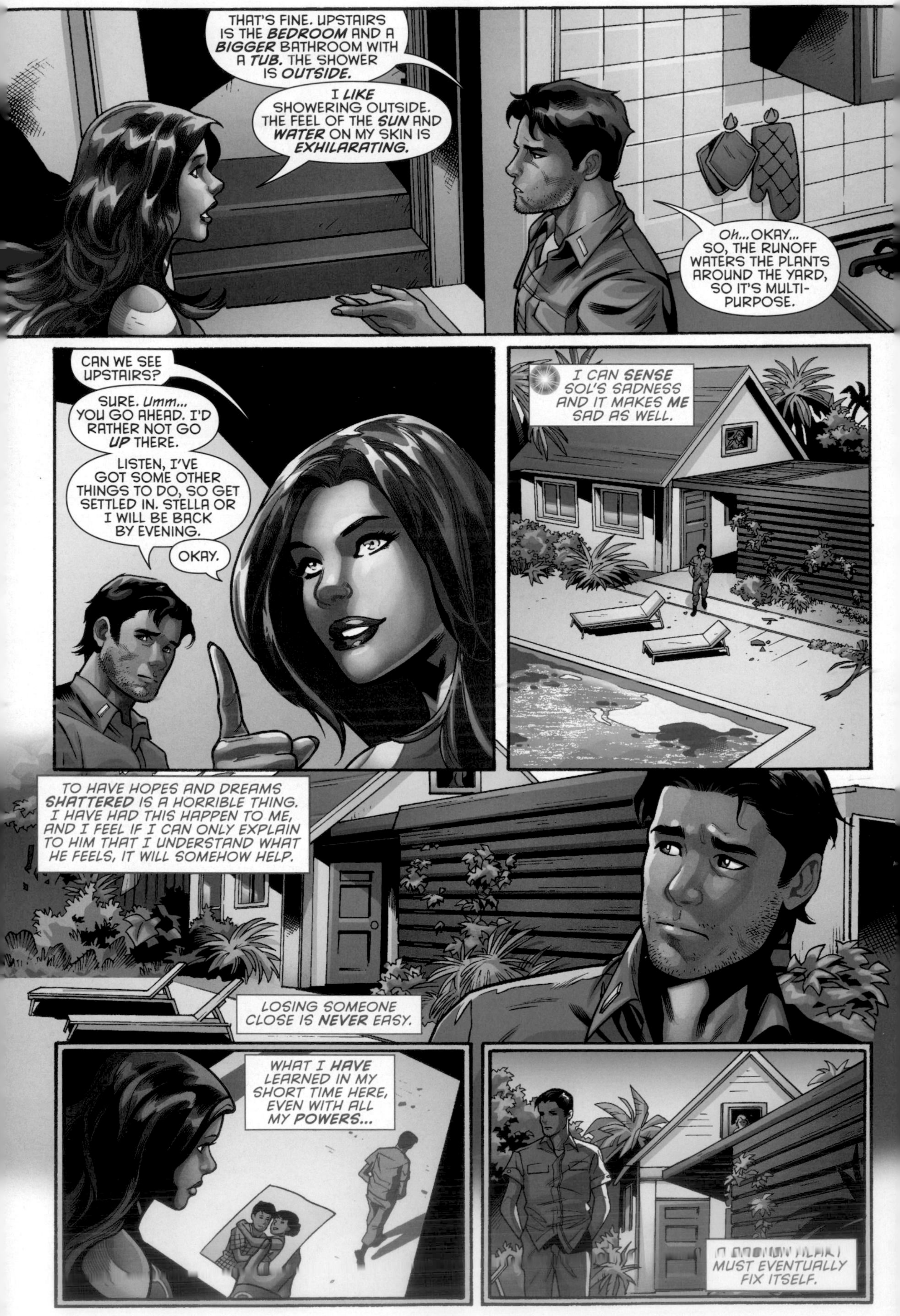
THAT'S FINE. UPSTAIRS IS THE **BEDROOM** AND A **BIGGER** BATHROOM WITH A **TUB.** THE SHOWER IS **OUTSIDE.**
I **LIKE** SHOWERING OUTSIDE. THE FEEL OF THE **SUN** AND **WATER** ON MY SKIN IS **EXHILARATING.**
Oh... OKAY... SO, THE RUNOFF WATERS THE PLANTS AROUND THE YARD, SO IT'S MULTI-PURPOSE.
CAN WE SEE UPSTAIRS?
SURE. *Umm...* YOU GO AHEAD. I'D RATHER NOT GO *UP* THERE.
LISTEN, I'VE GOT SOME OTHER THINGS TO DO, SO GET SETTLED IN. STELLA OR I WILL BE BACK BY EVENING.
OKAY.
*I CAN **SENSE** SOL'S SADNESS AND IT MAKES **ME** SAD AS WELL.*
*TO HAVE HOPES AND DREAMS **SHATTERED** IS A HORRIBLE THING. I HAVE HAD THIS HAPPEN TO ME, AND I FEEL IF I CAN ONLY EXPLAIN TO HIM THAT I UNDERSTAND WHAT HE FEELS, IT WILL SOMEHOW HELP.*
*LOSING SOMEONE CLOSE IS **NEVER** EASY.*
*WHAT I **HAVE** LEARNED IN MY SHORT TIME HERE, EVEN WITH ALL MY **POWERS...***
MUST EVENTUALLY FIX ITSELF.

Everything Must Eat.

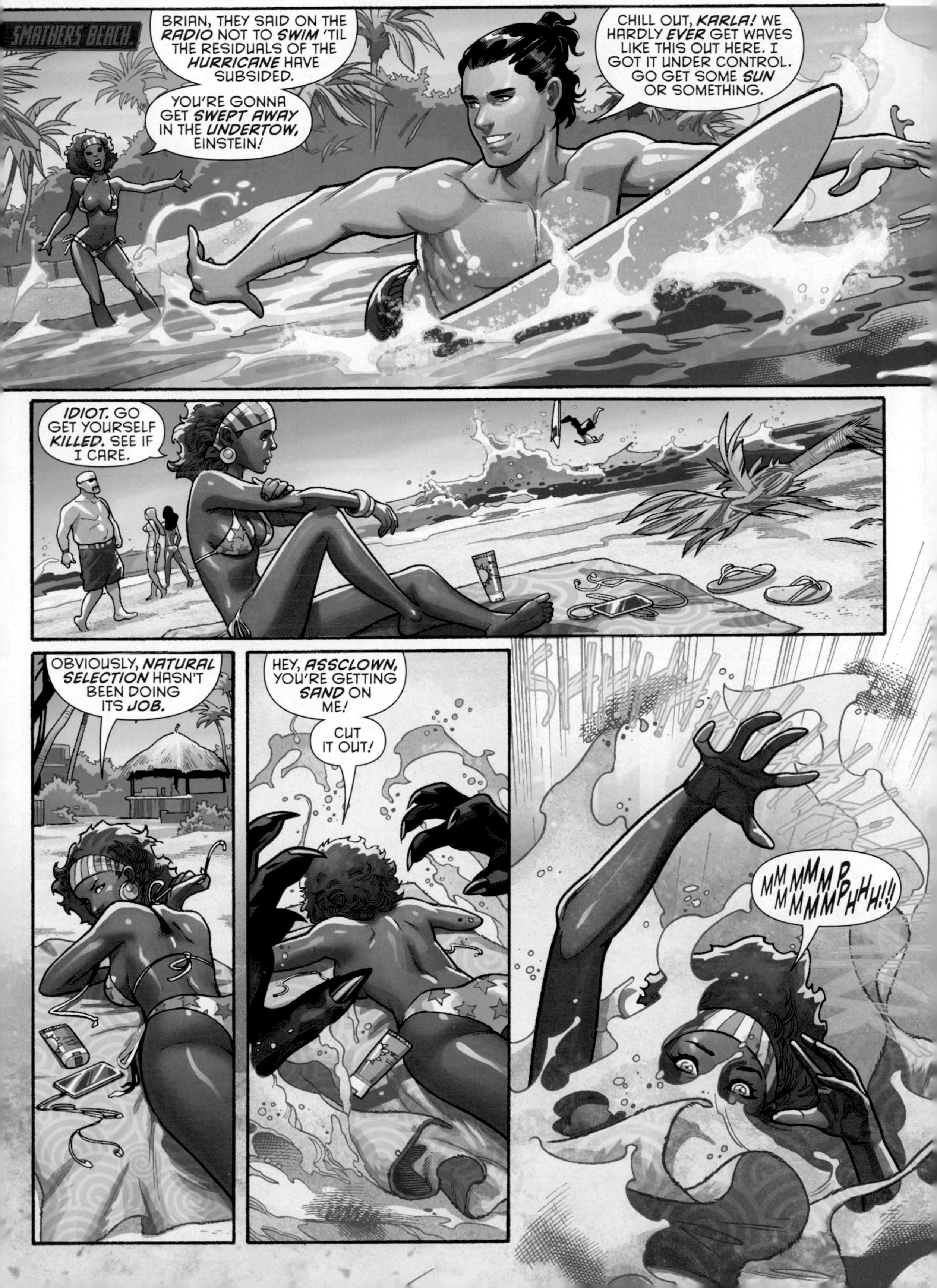
SMATHERS BEACH.
BRIAN, THEY SAID ON THE RADIO NOT TO SWIM 'TIL THE RESIDUALS OF THE HURRICANE HAVE SUBSIDED.
YOU'RE GONNA GET SWEPT AWAY IN THE UNDERTOW, EINSTEIN!
CHILL OUT, KARLA! WE HARDLY EVER GET WAVES LIKE THIS OUT HERE. I GOT IT UNDER CONTROL. GO GET SOME SUN OR SOMETHING.
IDIOT. GO GET YOURSELF KILLED. SEE IF I CARE.
OBVIOUSLY, NATURAL SELECTION HASN'T BEEN DOING ITS JOB.
HEY, ASSCLOWN, YOU'RE GETTING SAND ON ME!
CUT IT OUT!
MMMMMPH MMMMMPHHH!!!

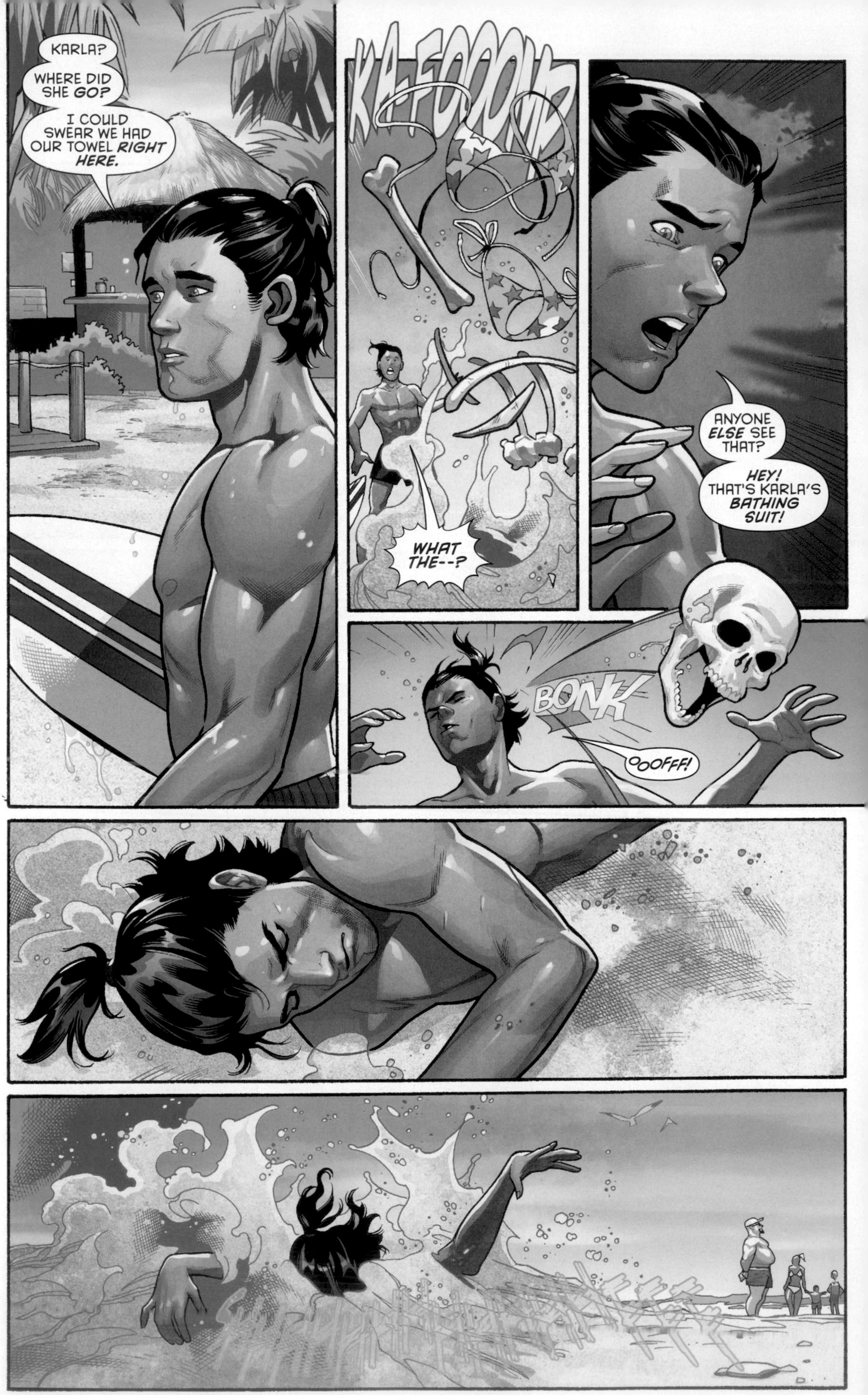
KARLA?
WHERE DID SHE GO?
I COULD SWEAR WE HAD OUR TOWEL RIGHT HERE.
KA-FOOOM!
WHAT THE--?
ANYONE ELSE SEE THAT?
HEY! THAT'S KARLA'S BATHING SUIT!
BONK!
OOOFFF!

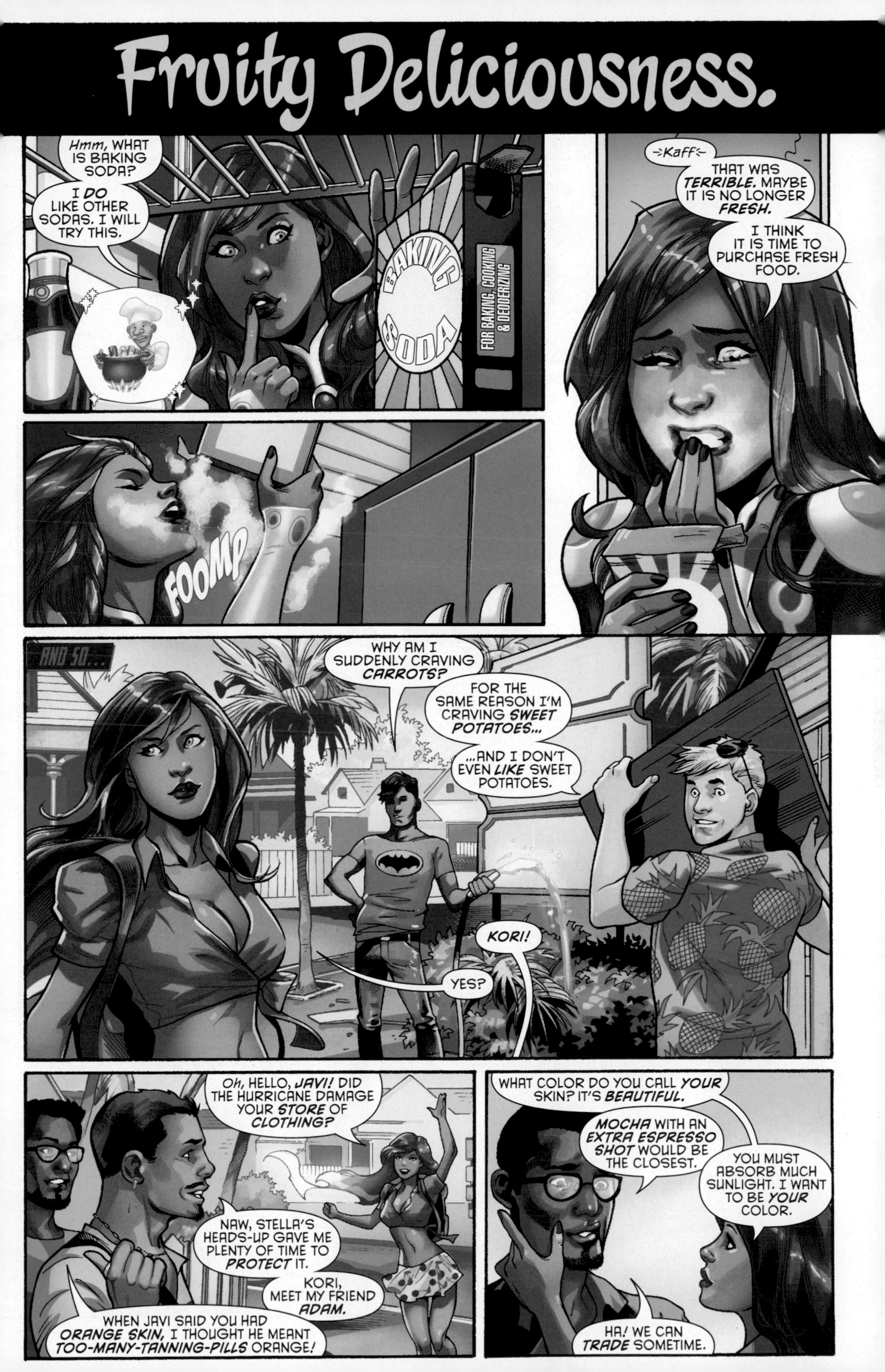
Fruity Deliciousness.
Hmm, WHAT IS BAKING SODA?
I DO LIKE OTHER SODAS. I WILL TRY THIS.
BAKING SODA
FOR BAKING, COOKING & DEODERIZING
FOOMP
Kaff
THAT WAS TERRIBLE. MAYBE IT IS NO LONGER FRESH.
I THINK IT IS TIME TO PURCHASE FRESH FOOD.
AND SO...
WHY AM I SUDDENLY CRAVING CARROTS?
FOR THE SAME REASON I'M CRAVING SWEET POTATOES...
...AND I DON'T EVEN LIKE SWEET POTATOES.
KORI!
YES?
Oh, HELLO, JAVI! DID THE HURRICANE DAMAGE YOUR STORE OF CLOTHING?
NAW, STELLA'S HEADS-UP GAVE ME PLENTY OF TIME TO PROTECT IT.
KORI, MEET MY FRIEND ADAM.
WHEN JAVI SAID YOU HAD ORANGE SKIN, I THOUGHT HE MEANT TOO-MANY-TANNING-PILLS ORANGE!
WHAT COLOR DO YOU CALL YOUR SKIN? IT'S BEAUTIFUL.
MOCHA WITH AN EXTRA ESPRESSO SHOT WOULD BE THE CLOSEST.
YOU MUST ABSORB MUCH SUNLIGHT. I WANT TO BE YOUR COLOR.
HA! WE CAN TRADE SOMETIME.

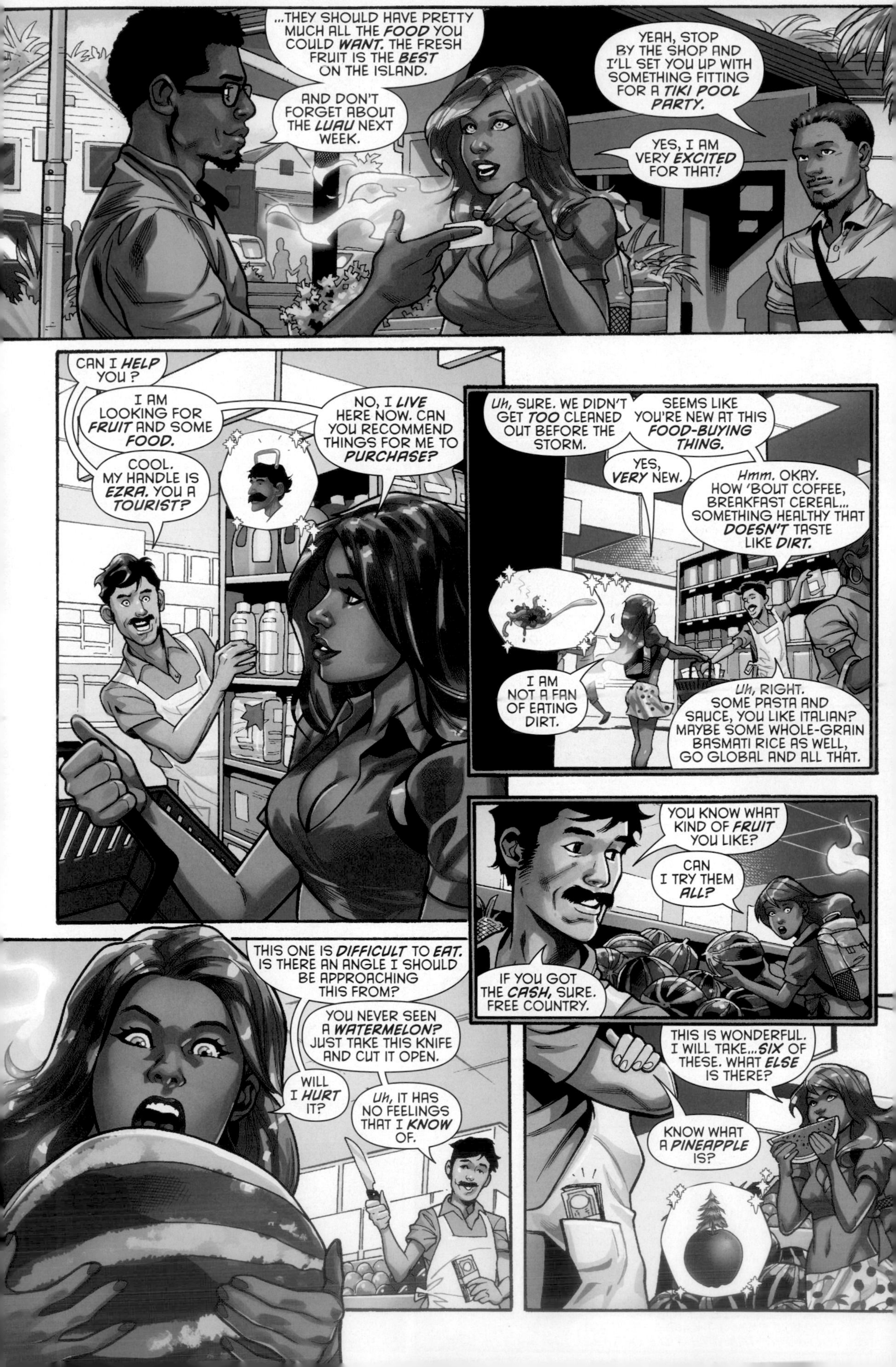

...THEY SHOULD HAVE PRETTY MUCH ALL THE FOOD YOU COULD WANT. THE FRESH FRUIT IS THE BEST ON THE ISLAND.
AND DON'T FORGET ABOUT THE LUAU NEXT WEEK.
YEAH, STOP BY THE SHOP AND I'LL SET YOU UP WITH SOMETHING FITTING FOR A TIKI POOL PARTY.
YES, I AM VERY EXCITED FOR THAT!
CAN I HELP YOU?
I AM LOOKING FOR FRUIT AND SOME FOOD.
COOL. MY HANDLE IS EZRA. YOU A TOURIST?
NO, I LIVE HERE NOW. CAN YOU RECOMMEND THINGS FOR ME TO PURCHASE?
Uh, SURE. WE DIDN'T GET TOO CLEANED OUT BEFORE THE STORM.
SEEMS LIKE YOU'RE NEW AT THIS FOOD-BUYING THING.
YES, VERY NEW.
Hmm. OKAY. HOW 'BOUT COFFEE, BREAKFAST CEREAL... SOMETHING HEALTHY THAT DOESN'T TASTE LIKE DIRT.
I AM NOT A FAN OF EATING DIRT.
Uh, RIGHT. SOME PASTA AND SAUCE, YOU LIKE ITALIAN? MAYBE SOME WHOLE-GRAIN BASMATI RICE AS WELL, GO GLOBAL AND ALL THAT.
YOU KNOW WHAT KIND OF FRUIT YOU LIKE?
CAN I TRY THEM ALL?
IF YOU GOT THE CASH, SURE. FREE COUNTRY.
THIS ONE IS DIFFICULT TO EAT. IS THERE AN ANGLE I SHOULD BE APPROACHING THIS FROM?
YOU NEVER SEEN A WATERMELON? JUST TAKE THIS KNIFE AND CUT IT OPEN.
WILL I HURT IT?
Uh, IT HAS NO FEELINGS THAT I KNOW OF.
THIS IS WONDERFUL. I WILL TAKE...SIX OF THESE. WHAT ELSE IS THERE?
KNOW WHAT A PINEAPPLE IS?

Cruise Out-Of-Control.

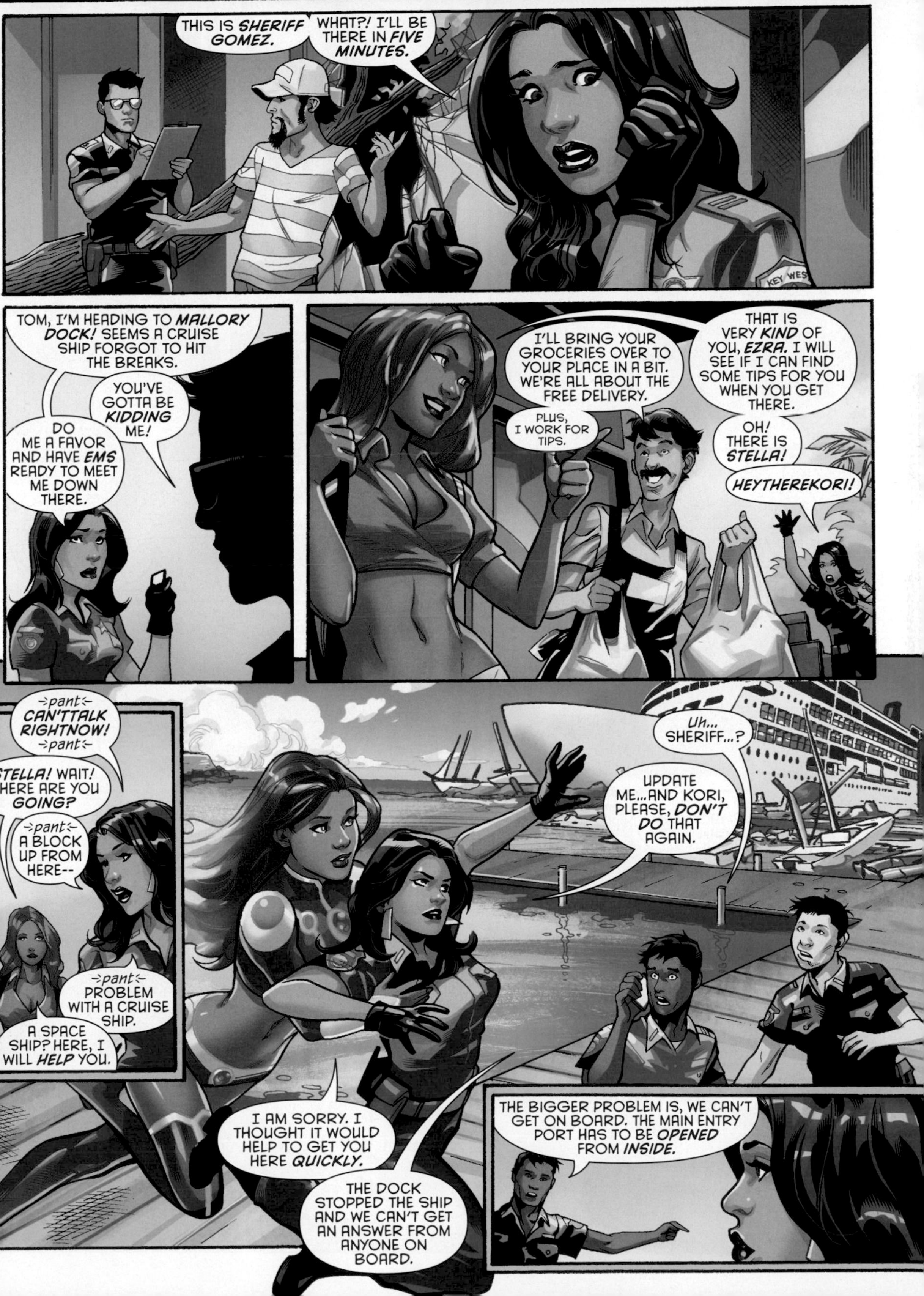
THIS IS SHERIFF GOMEZ.
WHAT?! I'LL BE THERE IN FIVE MINUTES.
KEY WEST
TOM, I'M HEADING TO MALLORY DOCK! SEEMS A CRUISE SHIP FORGOT TO HIT THE BREAKS.
YOU'VE GOTTA BE KIDDING ME!
DO ME A FAVOR AND HAVE EMS READY TO MEET ME DOWN THERE.
I'LL BRING YOUR GROCERIES OVER TO YOUR PLACE IN A BIT. WE'RE ALL ABOUT THE FREE DELIVERY.
PLUS, I WORK FOR TIPS.
THAT IS VERY KIND OF YOU, EZRA. I WILL SEE IF I CAN FIND SOME TIPS FOR YOU WHEN YOU GET THERE.
OH! THERE IS STELLA!
HEYTHEREKORI!
-pant- CAN'TTALK RIGHTNOW! -pant-
STELLA! WAIT! WHERE ARE YOU GOING?
-pant- A BLOCK UP FROM HERE--
-pant- PROBLEM WITH A CRUISE SHIP.
A SPACE SHIP? HERE, I WILL HELP YOU.
Uh... SHERIFF...?
UPDATE ME...AND KORI, PLEASE, DON'T DO THAT AGAIN.
I AM SORRY. I THOUGHT IT WOULD HELP TO GET YOU HERE QUICKLY.
THE DOCK STOPPED THE SHIP AND WE CAN'T GET AN ANSWER FROM ANYONE ON BOARD.
THE BIGGER PROBLEM IS, WE CAN'T GET ON BOARD. THE MAIN ENTRY PORT HAS TO BE OPENED FROM INSIDE.

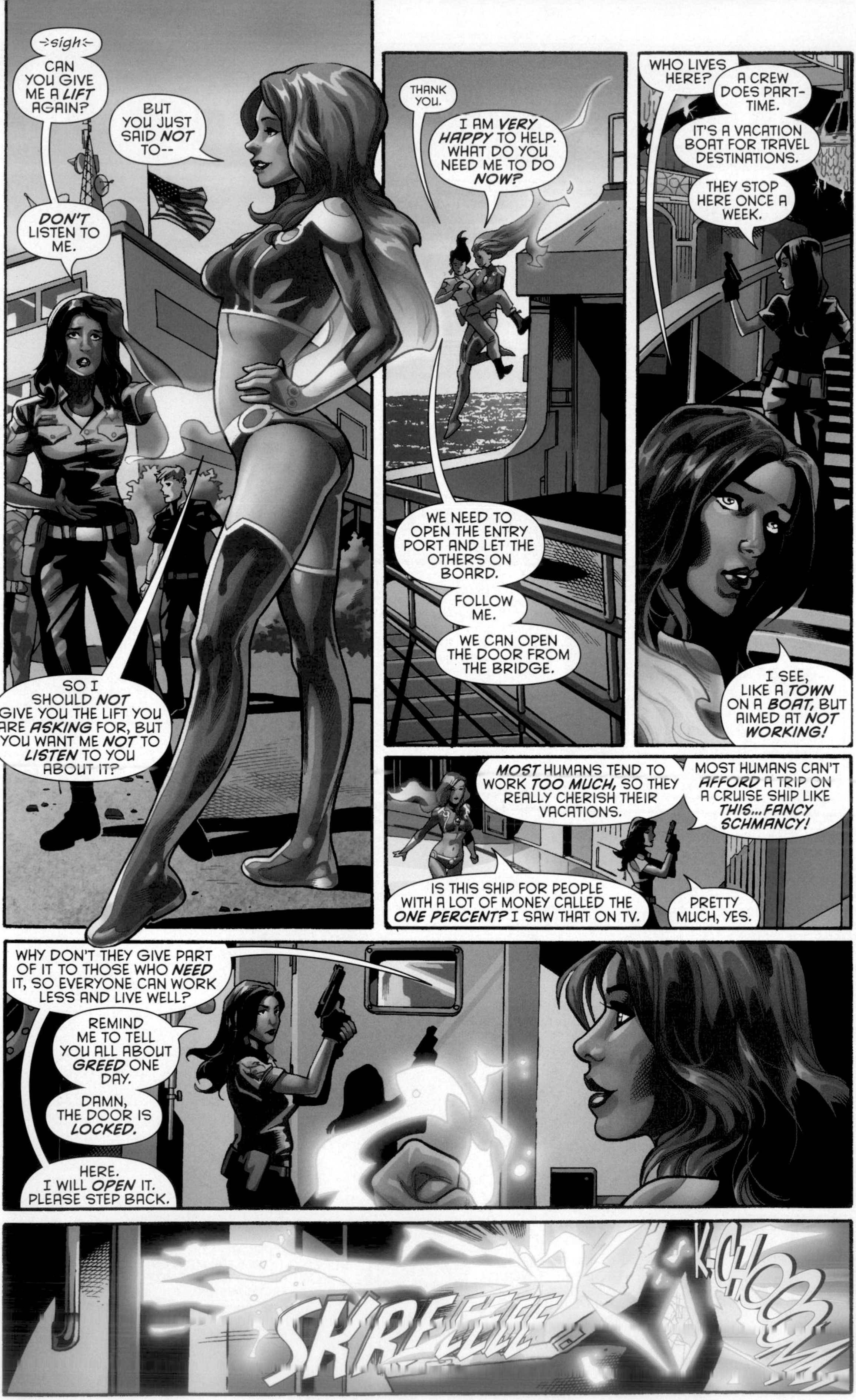
-sigh-
CAN YOU GIVE ME A LIFT AGAIN?
BUT YOU JUST SAID NOT TO--
DON'T LISTEN TO ME.
SO I SHOULD NOT GIVE YOU THE LIFT YOU ARE ASKING FOR, BUT YOU WANT ME NOT TO LISTEN TO YOU ABOUT IT?
THANK YOU.
I AM VERY HAPPY TO HELP. WHAT DO YOU NEED ME TO DO NOW?
WE NEED TO OPEN THE ENTRY PORT AND LET THE OTHERS ON BOARD.
FOLLOW ME.
WE CAN OPEN THE DOOR FROM THE BRIDGE.
WHO LIVES HERE?
A CREW DOES PART-TIME.
IT'S A VACATION BOAT FOR TRAVEL DESTINATIONS.
THEY STOP HERE ONCE A WEEK.
I SEE, LIKE A TOWN ON A BOAT, BUT AIMED AT NOT WORKING!
MOST HUMANS TEND TO WORK TOO MUCH, SO THEY REALLY CHERISH THEIR VACATIONS.
MOST HUMANS CAN'T AFFORD A TRIP ON A CRUISE SHIP LIKE THIS...FANCY SCHMANCY!
IS THIS SHIP FOR PEOPLE WITH A LOT OF MONEY CALLED THE ONE PERCENT? I SAW THAT ON TV.
PRETTY MUCH, YES.
WHY DON'T THEY GIVE PART OF IT TO THOSE WHO NEED IT, SO EVERYONE CAN WORK LESS AND LIVE WELL?
REMIND ME TO TELL YOU ALL ABOUT GREED ONE DAY.
DAMN, THE DOOR IS LOCKED.
HERE. I WILL OPEN IT. PLEASE STEP BACK.
SKREEEEE
K-CHOOOM

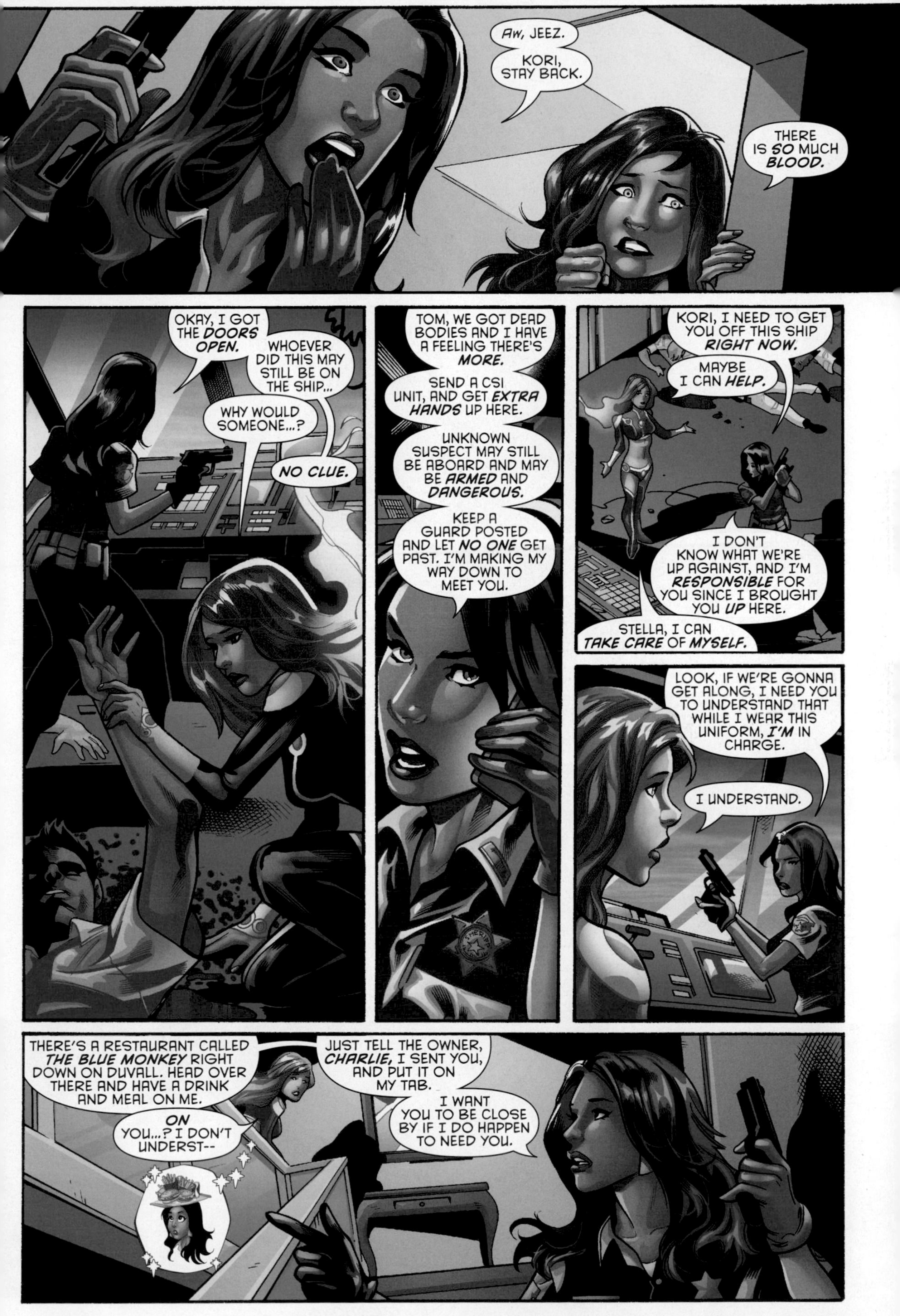
AW, JEEZ.
KORI, STAY BACK.
THERE IS SO MUCH BLOOD.
OKAY, I GOT THE DOORS OPEN.
WHOEVER DID THIS MAY STILL BE ON THE SHIP...
WHY WOULD SOMEONE...?
NO CLUE.
TOM, WE GOT DEAD BODIES AND I HAVE A FEELING THERE'S MORE.
SEND A CSI UNIT, AND GET EXTRA HANDS UP HERE.
UNKNOWN SUSPECT MAY STILL BE ABOARD AND MAY BE ARMED AND DANGEROUS.
KEEP A GUARD POSTED AND LET NO ONE GET PAST. I'M MAKING MY WAY DOWN TO MEET YOU.
KORI, I NEED TO GET YOU OFF THIS SHIP RIGHT NOW.
MAYBE I CAN HELP.
I DON'T KNOW WHAT WE'RE UP AGAINST, AND I'M RESPONSIBLE FOR YOU SINCE I BROUGHT YOU UP HERE.
STELLA, I CAN TAKE CARE OF MYSELF.
LOOK, IF WE'RE GONNA GET ALONG, I NEED YOU TO UNDERSTAND THAT WHILE I WEAR THIS UNIFORM, I'M IN CHARGE.
I UNDERSTAND.
THERE'S A RESTAURANT CALLED THE BLUE MONKEY RIGHT DOWN ON DUVALL. HEAD OVER THERE AND HAVE A DRINK AND MEAL ON ME.
ON YOU...? I DON'T UNDERST--
JUST TELL THE OWNER, CHARLIE, I SENT YOU, AND PUT IT ON MY TAB.
I WANT YOU TO BE CLOSE BY IF I DO HAPPEN TO NEED YOU.

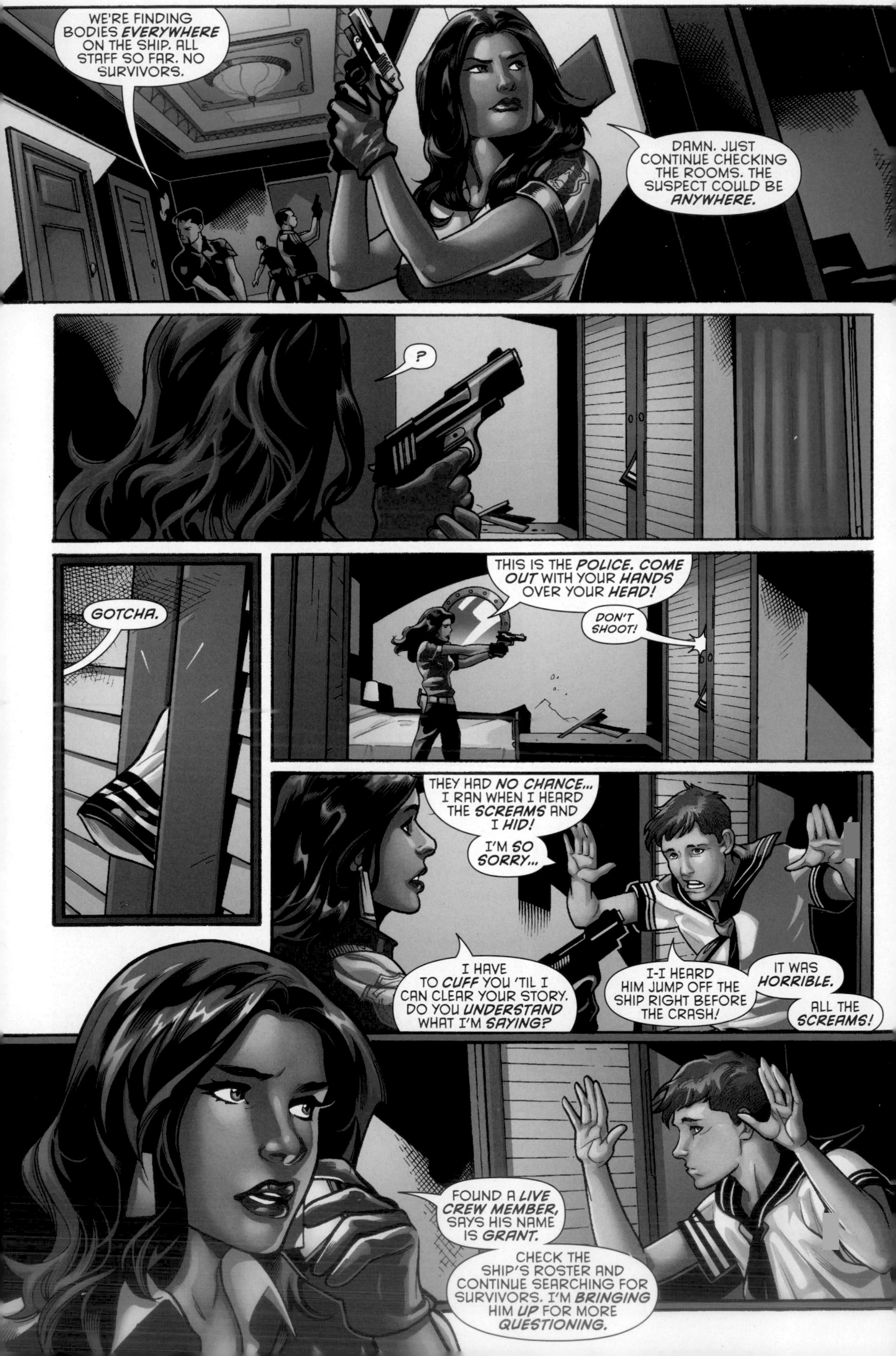
WE'RE FINDING BODIES EVERYWHERE ON THE SHIP. ALL STAFF SO FAR. NO SURVIVORS.
DAMN. JUST CONTINUE CHECKING THE ROOMS. THE SUSPECT COULD BE ANYWHERE.
?
GOTCHA.
THIS IS THE POLICE. COME OUT WITH YOUR HANDS OVER YOUR HEAD!
DON'T SHOOT!
THEY HAD NO CHANCE... I RAN WHEN I HEARD THE SCREAMS AND I HID!
I'M SO SORRY...
I HAVE TO CUFF YOU 'TIL I CAN CLEAR YOUR STORY. DO YOU UNDERSTAND WHAT I'M SAYING?
I-I HEARD HIM JUMP OFF THE SHIP RIGHT BEFORE THE CRASH!
IT WAS HORRIBLE.
ALL THE SCREAMS!
FOUND A LIVE CREW MEMBER, SAYS HIS NAME IS GRANT.
CHECK THE SHIP'S ROSTER AND CONTINUE SEARCHING FOR SURVIVORS. I'M BRINGING HIM UP FOR MORE QUESTIONING.

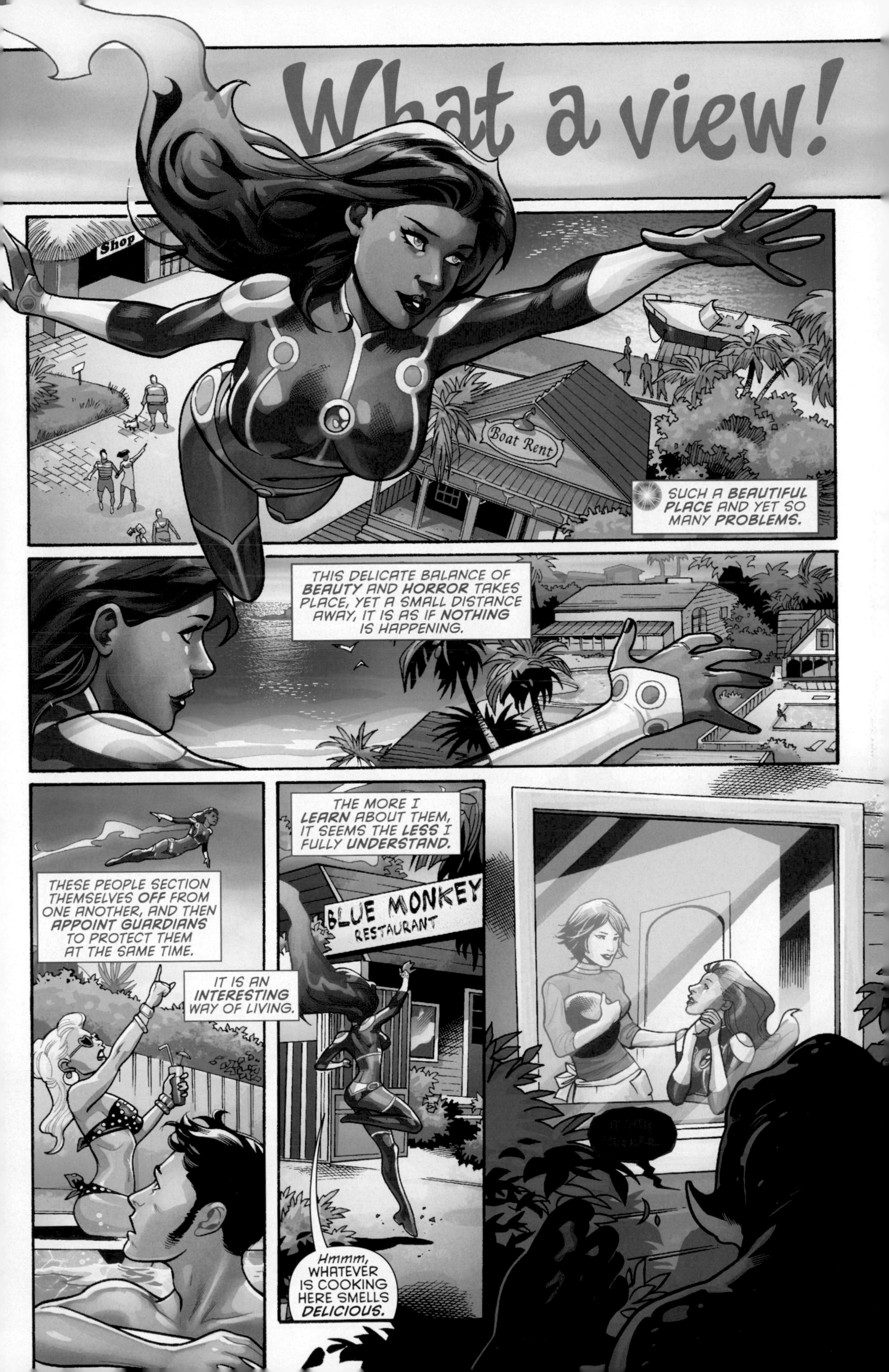
What a view!
Shop
Boat Rent
SUCH A BEAUTIFUL PLACE AND YET SO MANY PROBLEMS.
THIS DELICATE BALANCE OF BEAUTY AND HORROR TAKES PLACE, YET A SMALL DISTANCE AWAY, IT IS AS IF NOTHING IS HAPPENING.
THESE PEOPLE SECTION THEMSELVES OFF FROM ONE ANOTHER, AND THEN APPOINT GUARDIANS TO PROTECT THEM AT THE SAME TIME.
IT IS AN INTERESTING WAY OF LIVING.
THE MORE I LEARN ABOUT THEM, IT SEEMS THE LESS I FULLY UNDERSTAND.
BLUE MONKEY RESTAURANT
Hmmm, WHATEVER IS COOKING HERE SMELLS DELICIOUS.

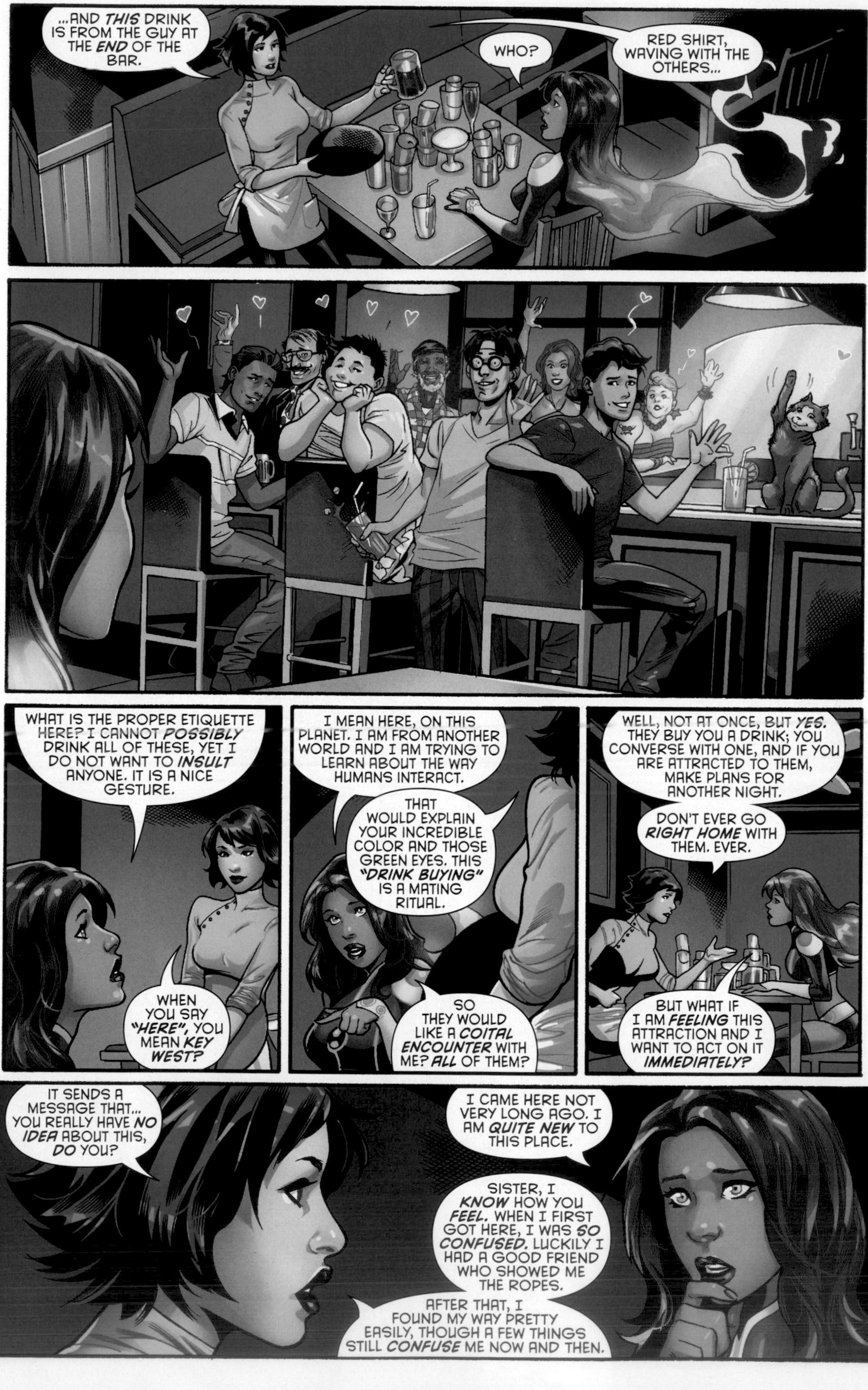
...AND THIS DRINK IS FROM THE GUY AT THE END OF THE BAR.
WHO?
RED SHIRT, WAVING WITH THE OTHERS...
WHAT IS THE PROPER ETIQUETTE HERE? I CANNOT POSSIBLY DRINK ALL OF THESE, YET I DO NOT WANT TO INSULT ANYONE. IT IS A NICE GESTURE.
WHEN YOU SAY "HERE", YOU MEAN KEY WEST?
I MEAN HERE, ON THIS PLANET. I AM FROM ANOTHER WORLD AND I AM TRYING TO LEARN ABOUT THE WAY HUMANS INTERACT.
THAT WOULD EXPLAIN YOUR INCREDIBLE COLOR AND THOSE GREEN EYES. THIS "DRINK BUYING" IS A MATING RITUAL.
SO THEY WOULD LIKE A COITAL ENCOUNTER WITH ME? ALL OF THEM?
WELL, NOT AT ONCE, BUT YES. THEY BUY YOU A DRINK; YOU CONVERSE WITH ONE, AND IF YOU ARE ATTRACTED TO THEM, MAKE PLANS FOR ANOTHER NIGHT.
DON'T EVER GO RIGHT HOME WITH THEM. EVER.
BUT WHAT IF I AM FEELING THIS ATTRACTION AND I WANT TO ACT ON IT IMMEDIATELY?
IT SENDS A MESSAGE THAT... YOU REALLY HAVE NO IDEA ABOUT THIS, DO YOU?
I CAME HERE NOT VERY LONG AGO. I AM QUITE NEW TO THIS PLACE.
SISTER, I KNOW HOW YOU FEEL. WHEN I FIRST GOT HERE, I WAS SO CONFUSED. LUCKILY I HAD A GOOD FRIEND WHO SHOWED ME THE ROPES.
AFTER THAT, I FOUND MY WAY PRETTY EASILY, THOUGH A FEW THINGS STILL CONFUSE ME NOW AND THEN.

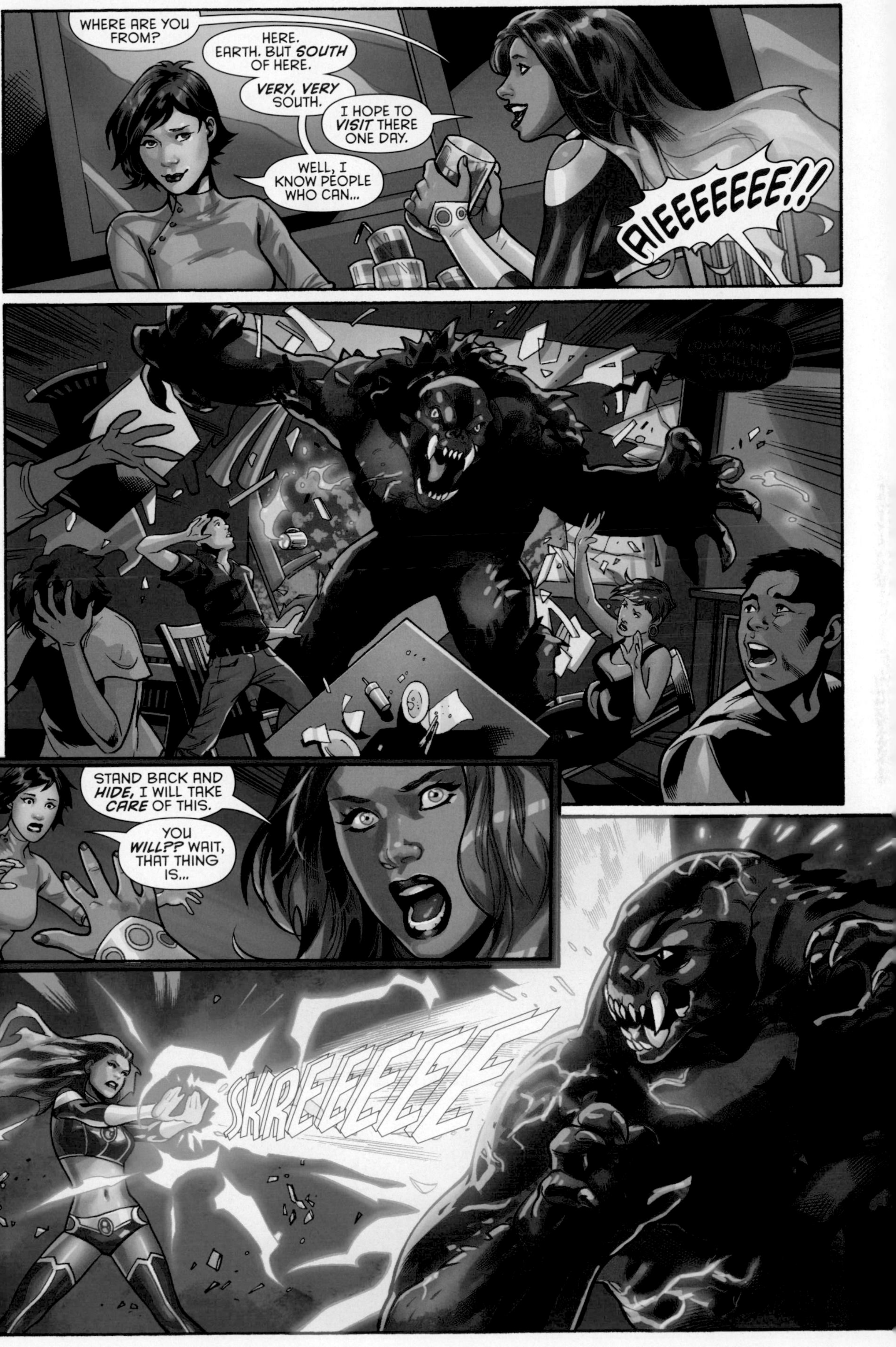
WHERE ARE YOU FROM?
HERE. EARTH. BUT SOUTH OF HERE.
VERY, VERY SOUTH.
I HOPE TO VISIT THERE ONE DAY.
WELL, I KNOW PEOPLE WHO CAN...
AIEEEEEEEE!!
STAND BACK AND HIDE, I WILL TAKE CARE OF THIS.
YOU WILL?? WAIT, THAT THING IS...
SKREEEEEZ

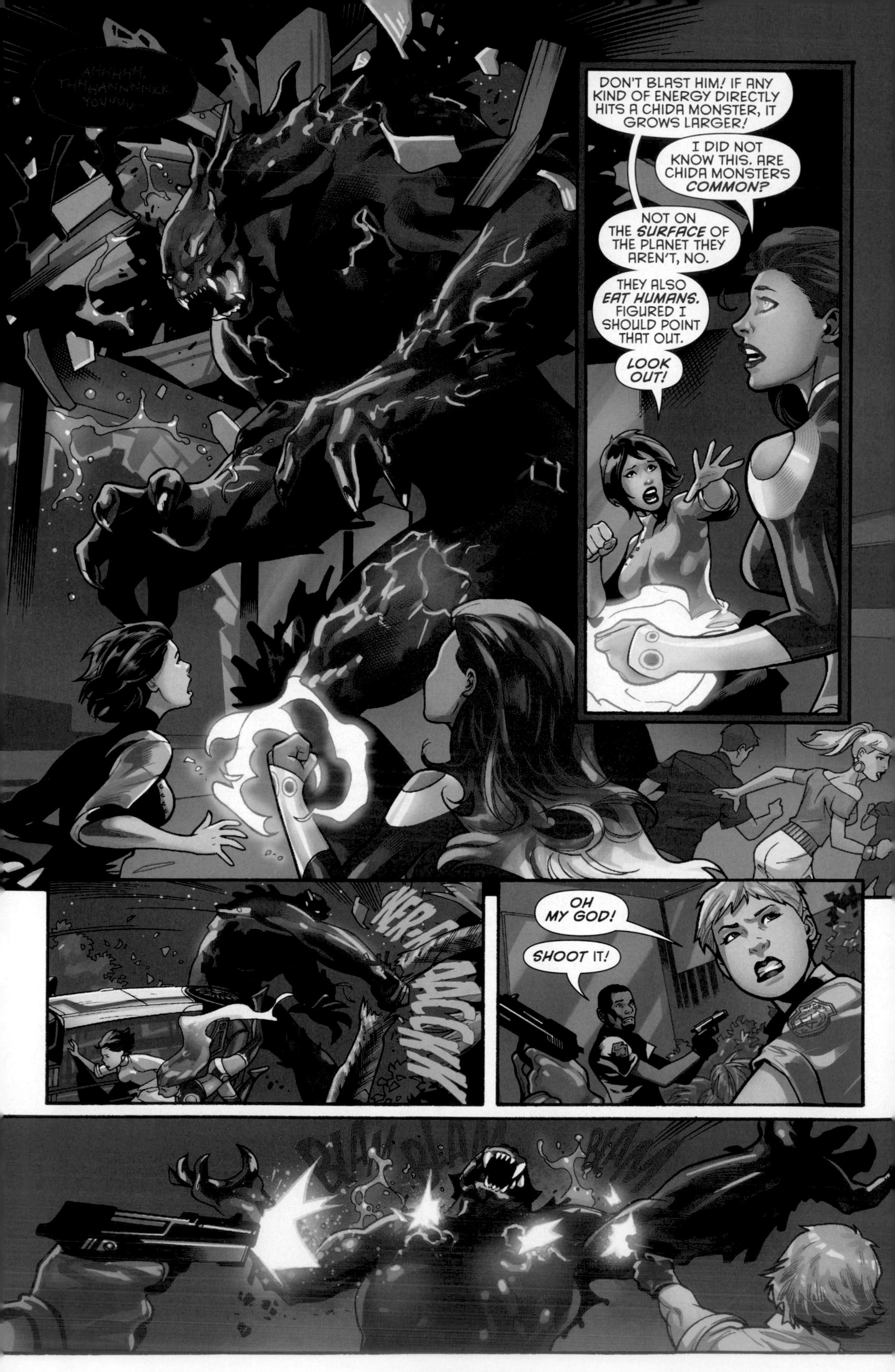
AHHHHH, THHHAANNNNKK YOUUUU...
DON'T BLAST HIM! IF ANY KIND OF ENERGY DIRECTLY HITS A CHIDA MONSTER, IT GROWS LARGER!
I DID NOT KNOW THIS. ARE CHIDA MONSTERS *COMMON?*
NOT ON THE *SURFACE* OF THE PLANET THEY AREN'T, NO.
THEY ALSO *EAT HUMANS.* FIGURED I SHOULD POINT THAT OUT.
LOOK OUT!
OH MY GOD!
SHOOT IT!

HA HA HHA
HUMAN YOU ARE
DOOOOOOMED, LITTLE
GREK HUUU

THE DOCK.

I HEARD *GUNSHOTS!*

WELL, I *SEE* SOMETHING, BUT I'M NOT SURE I *BELIEVE* IT.

YOU MEAN THAT *BIG RED MONSTER* THE SIZE OF A *SMALL HOUSE?*

YOU SEE IT, *TOO?*

DAMN, I WAS HOPING IT WAS JUST THE *HEAT* GETTING TO ME.

THE BLUE MONKEY.

I BELIEVE HE IS AFTER ME! I WILL FLY *ELSEWHERE* AND HAVE HIM *FOLLOW.*

HE'S ACTUALLY AFTER *ME.* HE'S PISSED THAT I BURIED HIM IN THE GROUND A WHILE BACK.

YOU DID *WHAT?* WHO *ARE* YOU?

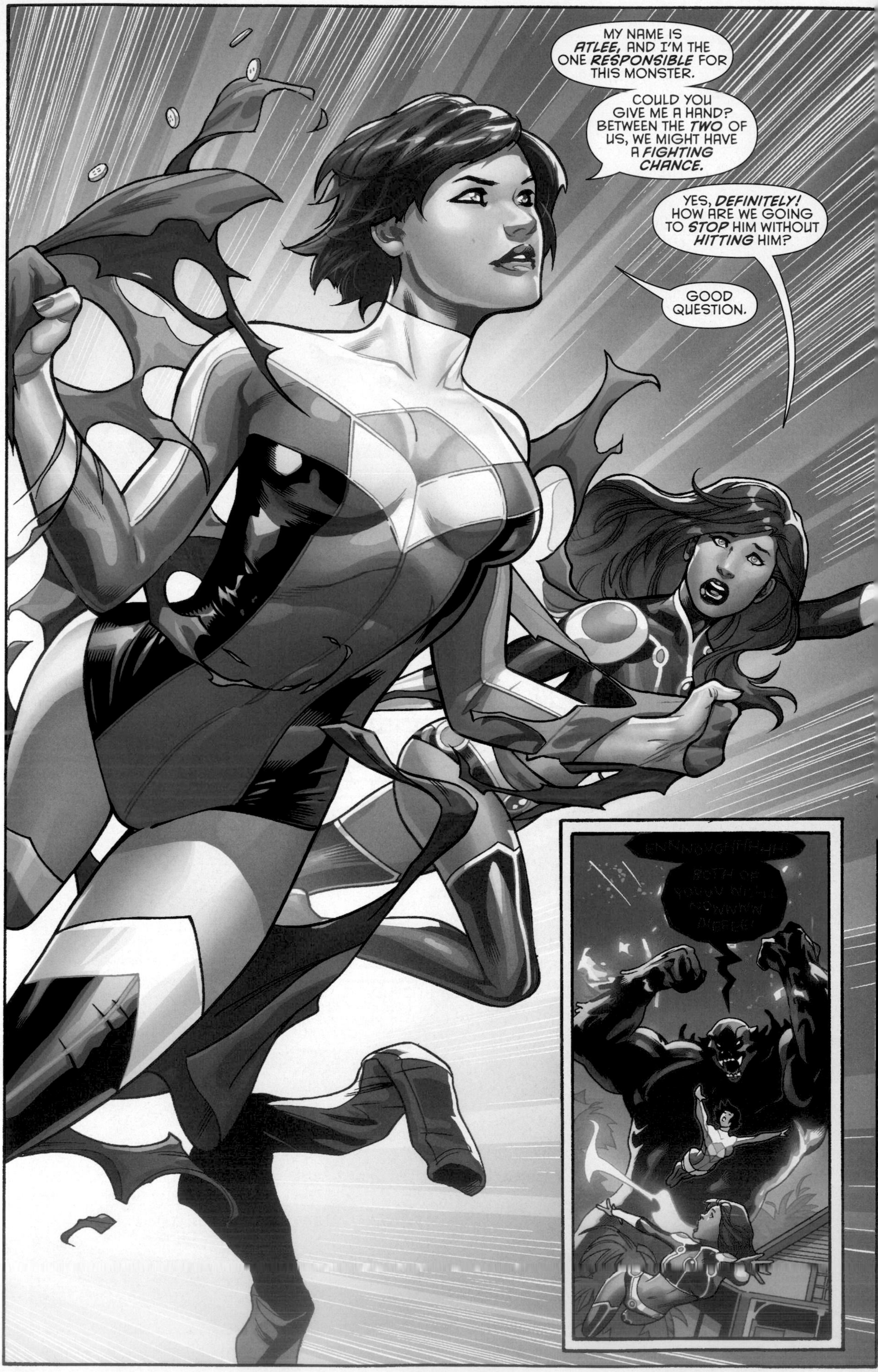
MY NAME IS ATLEE, AND I'M THE ONE RESPONSIBLE FOR THIS MONSTER.
COULD YOU GIVE ME A HAND? BETWEEN THE TWO OF US, WE MIGHT HAVE A FIGHTING CHANCE.
YES, DEFINITELY! HOW ARE WE GOING TO STOP HIM WITHOUT HITTING HIM?
GOOD QUESTION.

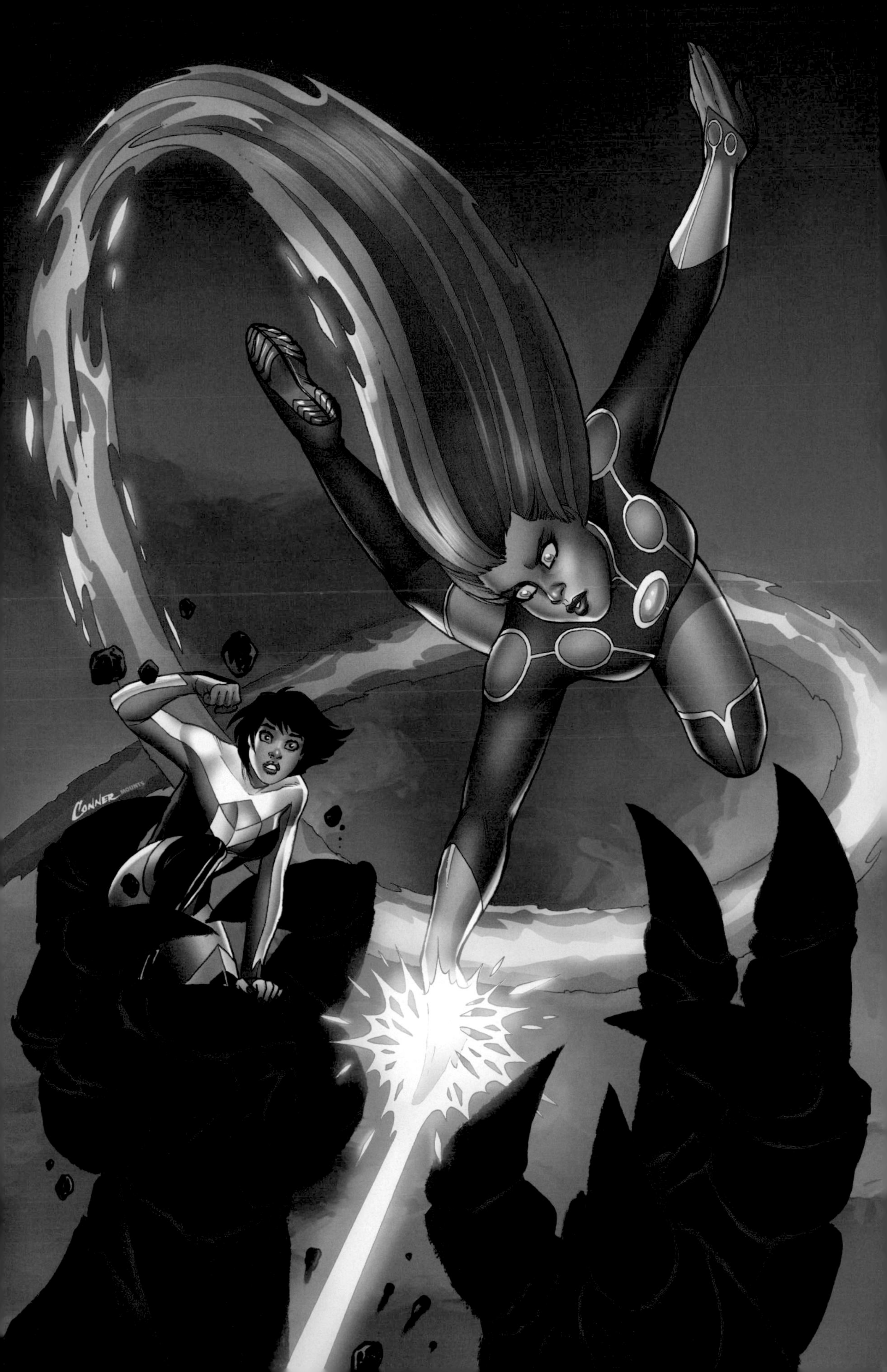
CONNER MOUNTS

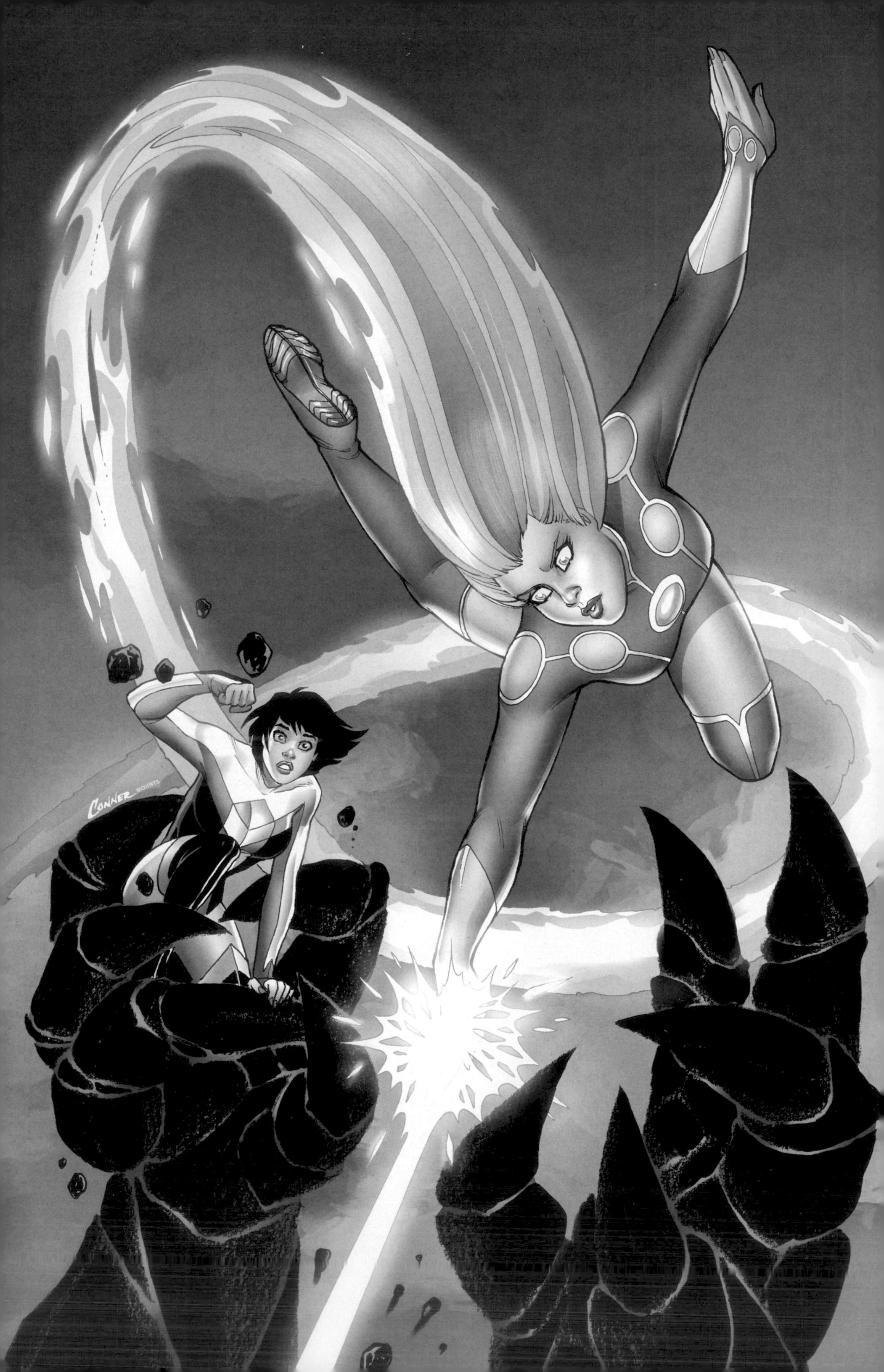
CONNER MOUNTS

KEY WEST.

SPREAD OUT! GET THE CIVILIANS TO **SAFETY!**

THE REST OF YOU, **FOLLOW ME.** WE'RE DEALING WITH SOMETHING I'VE **NEVER SEEN** BEFORE.

HEADS UP!

LITERALLY!

Whoa.

BULLETS DON'T SEEM TO BE HURTING IT, SHERIFF!

Oh, NOT GOOD.

GO BACK! GET **EVERYONE BACK!** DO **NOT** SHOOT AT IT!

WHY **NOT?**

IT MAKES HIM **BIGGER** EACH TIME HE IS HIT.

GREAT.

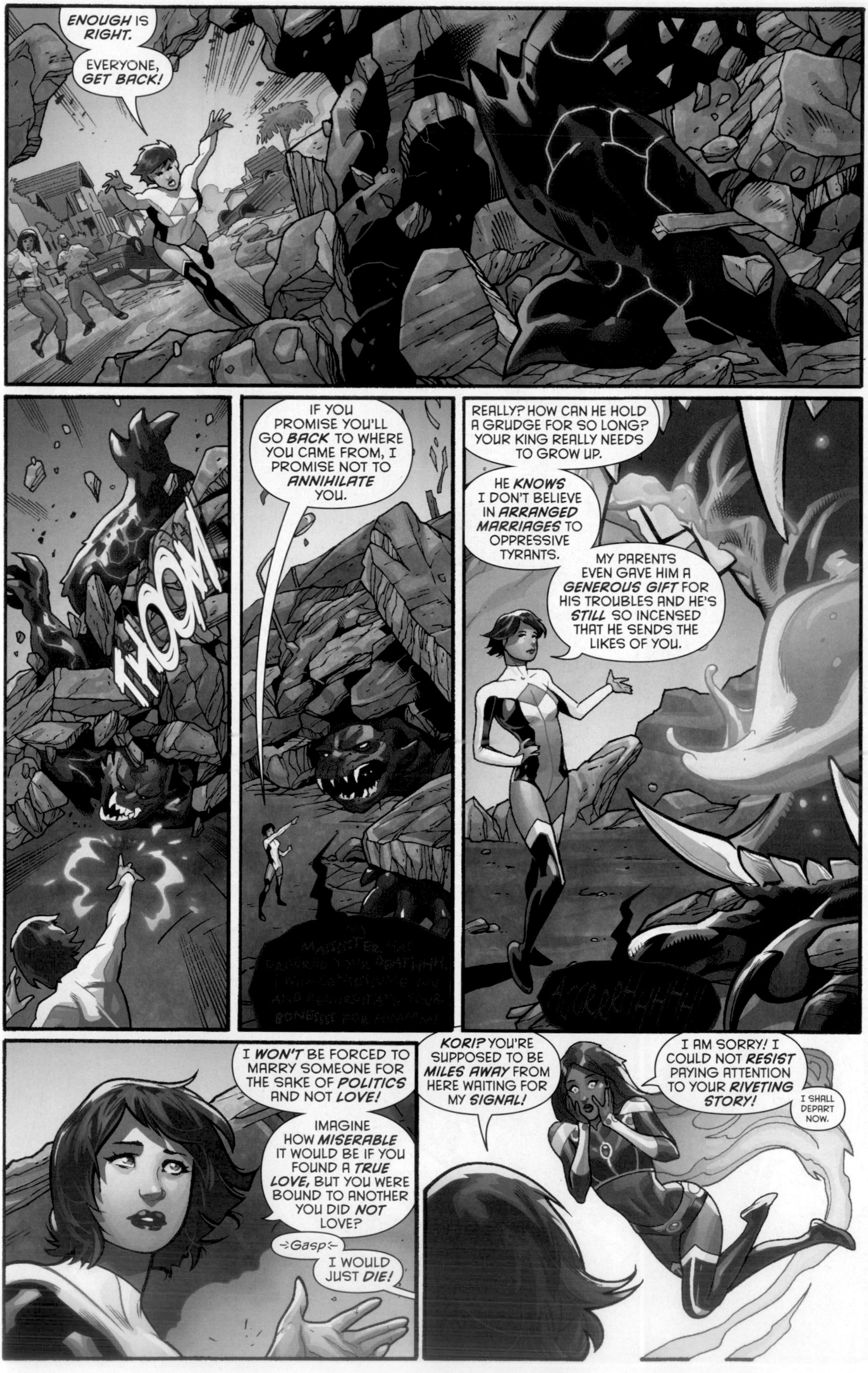
ENOUGH IS RIGHT.
EVERYONE, GET BACK!
THOOM
IF YOU PROMISE YOU'LL GO BACK TO WHERE YOU CAME FROM, I PROMISE NOT TO ANNIHILATE YOU.
REALLY? HOW CAN HE HOLD A GRUDGE FOR SO LONG? YOUR KING REALLY NEEDS TO GROW UP.
HE KNOWS I DON'T BELIEVE IN ARRANGED MARRIAGES TO OPPRESSIVE TYRANTS.
MY PARENTS EVEN GAVE HIM A GENEROUS GIFT FOR HIS TROUBLES AND HE'S STILL SO INCENSED THAT HE SENDS THE LIKES OF YOU.
I WON'T BE FORCED TO MARRY SOMEONE FOR THE SAKE OF POLITICS AND NOT LOVE!
IMAGINE HOW MISERABLE IT WOULD BE IF YOU FOUND A TRUE LOVE, BUT YOU WERE BOUND TO ANOTHER YOU DID NOT LOVE?
Gasp
I WOULD JUST DIE!
KORI? YOU'RE SUPPOSED TO BE MILES AWAY FROM HERE WAITING FOR MY SIGNAL!
I AM SORRY! I COULD NOT RESIST PAYING ATTENTION TO YOUR RIVETING STORY!
I SHALL DEPART NOW.

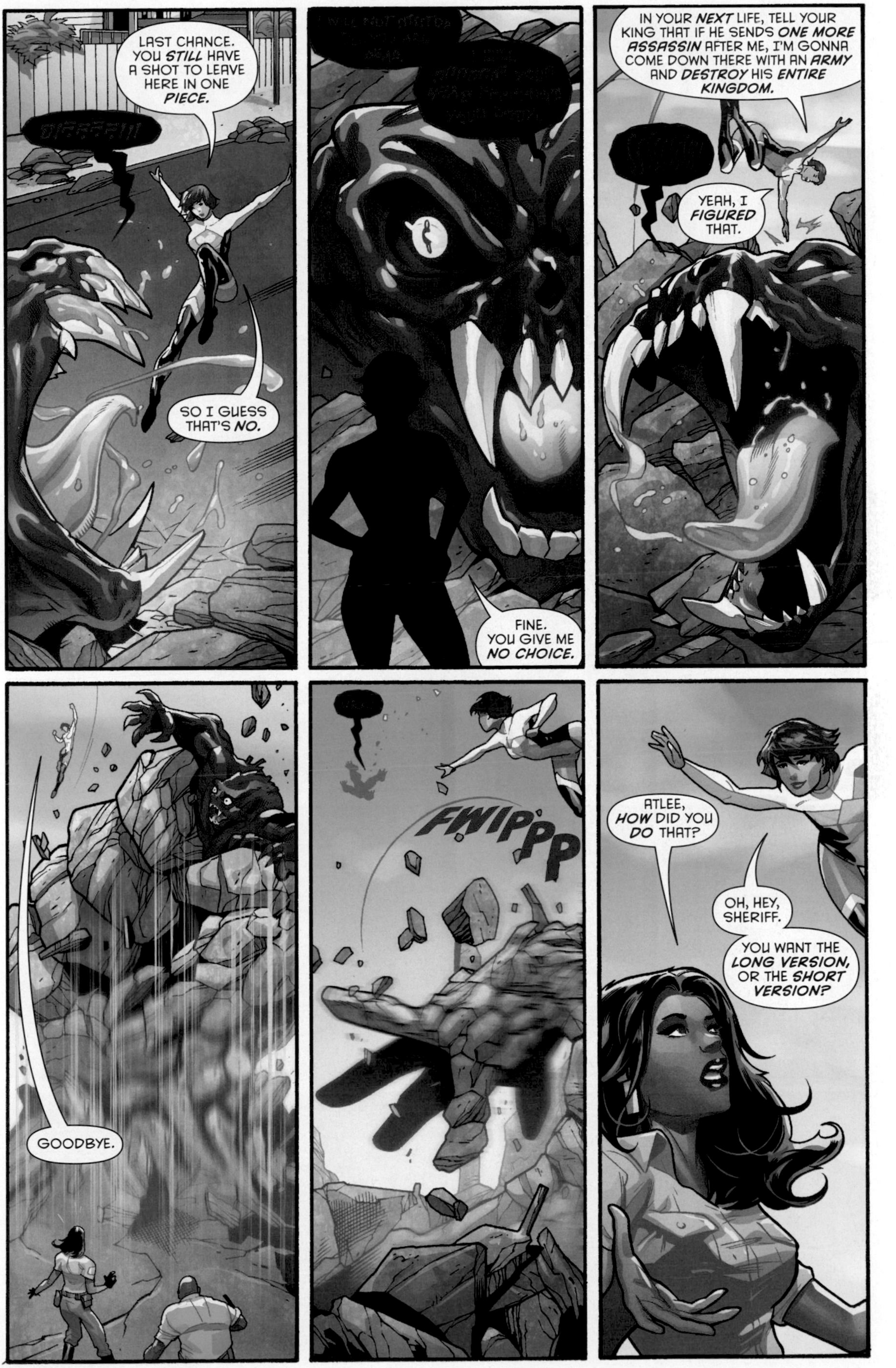
LAST CHANCE. YOU STILL HAVE A SHOT TO LEAVE HERE IN ONE PIECE.
SO I GUESS THAT'S NO.
FINE. YOU GIVE ME NO CHOICE.
IN YOUR NEXT LIFE, TELL YOUR KING THAT IF HE SENDS ONE MORE ASSASSIN AFTER ME, I'M GONNA COME DOWN THERE WITH AN ARMY AND DESTROY HIS ENTIRE KINGDOM.
YEAH, I FIGURED THAT.
GOODBYE.
FWIPPP
ATLEE, HOW DID YOU DO THAT?
OH, HEY, SHERIFF.
YOU WANT THE LONG VERSION, OR THE SHORT VERSION?

The Short Version.

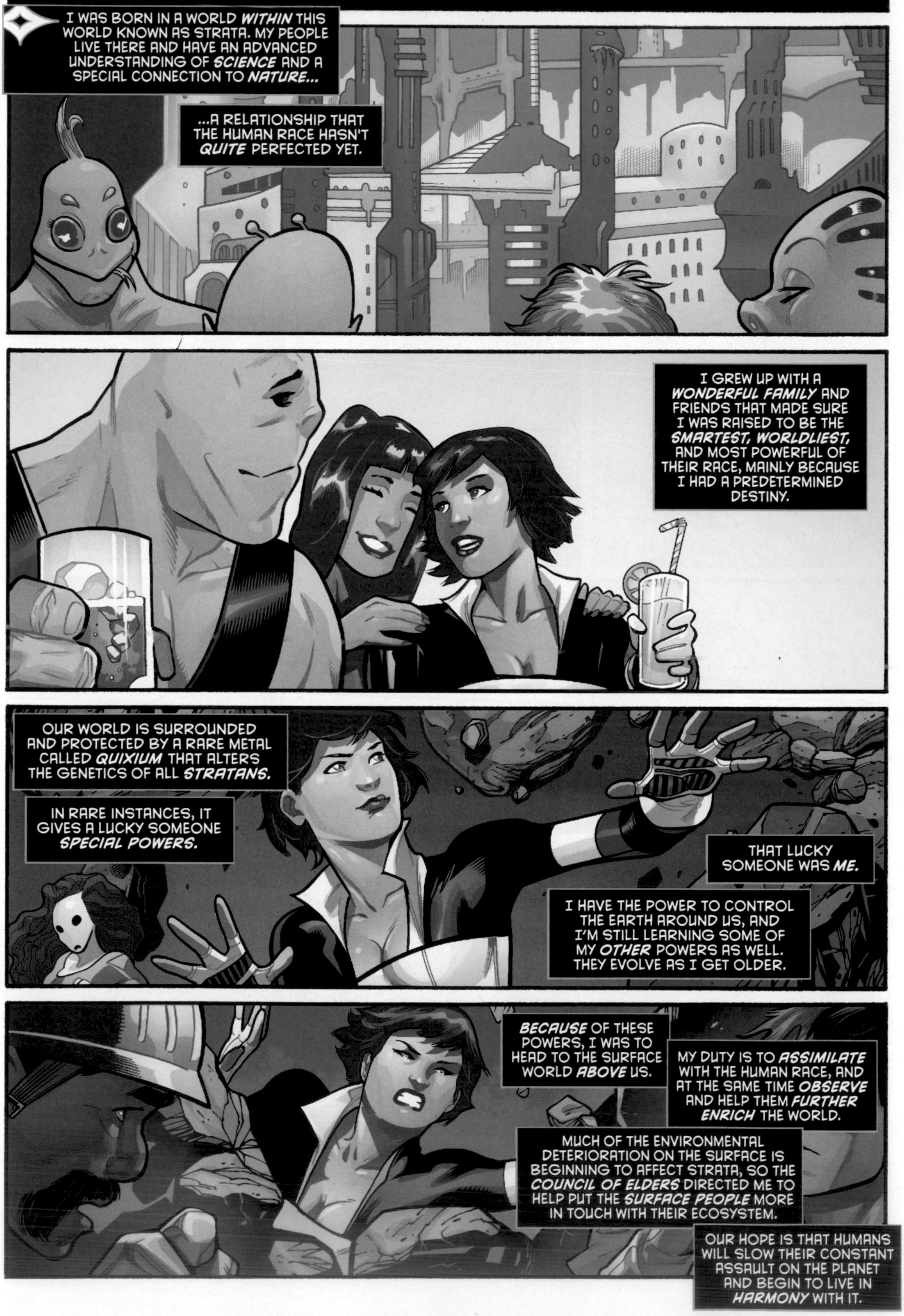
I WAS BORN IN A WORLD WITHIN THIS WORLD KNOWN AS STRATA. MY PEOPLE LIVE THERE AND HAVE AN ADVANCED UNDERSTANDING OF SCIENCE AND A SPECIAL CONNECTION TO NATURE...
...A RELATIONSHIP THAT THE HUMAN RACE HASN'T QUITE PERFECTED YET.
I GREW UP WITH A WONDERFUL FAMILY AND FRIENDS THAT MADE SURE I WAS RAISED TO BE THE SMARTEST, WORLDLIEST, AND MOST POWERFUL OF THEIR RACE, MAINLY BECAUSE I HAD A PREDETERMINED DESTINY.
OUR WORLD IS SURROUNDED AND PROTECTED BY A RARE METAL CALLED QUIXIUM THAT ALTERS THE GENETICS OF ALL STRATANS.
IN RARE INSTANCES, IT GIVES A LUCKY SOMEONE SPECIAL POWERS.
THAT LUCKY SOMEONE WAS ME.
I HAVE THE POWER TO CONTROL THE EARTH AROUND US, AND I'M STILL LEARNING SOME OF MY OTHER POWERS AS WELL. THEY EVOLVE AS I GET OLDER.
BECAUSE OF THESE POWERS, I WAS TO HEAD TO THE SURFACE WORLD ABOVE US.
MY DUTY IS TO ASSIMILATE WITH THE HUMAN RACE, AND AT THE SAME TIME OBSERVE AND HELP THEM FURTHER ENRICH THE WORLD.
MUCH OF THE ENVIRONMENTAL DETERIORATION ON THE SURFACE IS BEGINNING TO AFFECT STRATA, SO THE COUNCIL OF ELDERS DIRECTED ME TO HELP PUT THE SURFACE PEOPLE MORE IN TOUCH WITH THEIR ECOSYSTEM.
OUR HOPE IS THAT HUMANS WILL SLOW THEIR CONSTANT ASSAULT ON THE PLANET AND BEGIN TO LIVE IN HARMONY WITH IT.

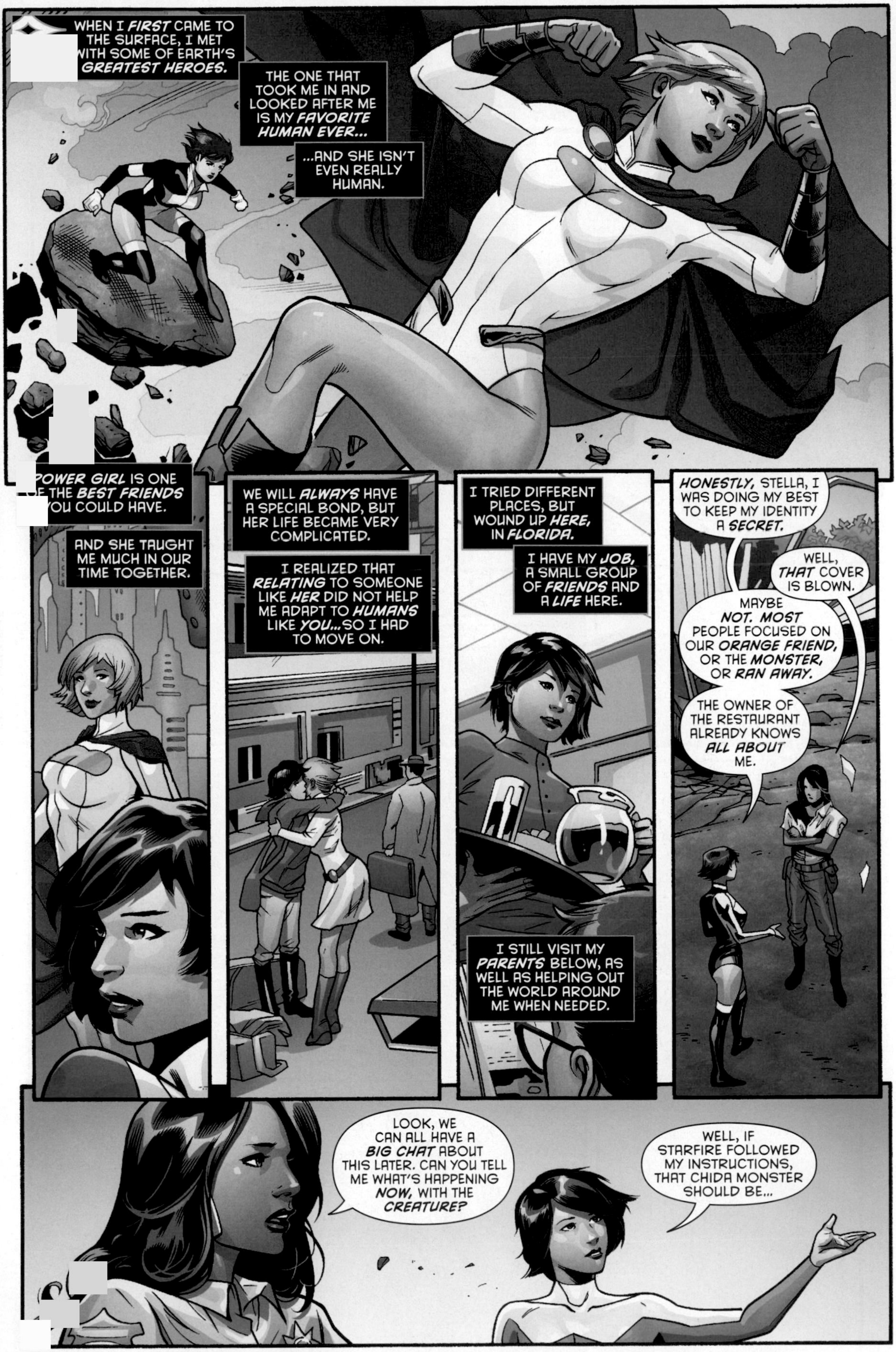

WHEN I FIRST CAME TO THE SURFACE, I MET WITH SOME OF EARTH'S GREATEST HEROES.
THE ONE THAT TOOK ME IN AND LOOKED AFTER ME IS MY FAVORITE HUMAN EVER...
...AND SHE ISN'T EVEN REALLY HUMAN.
OWER GIRL IS ONE F THE BEST FRIENDS OU COULD HAVE.
AND SHE TAUGHT ME MUCH IN OUR TIME TOGETHER.
WE WILL ALWAYS HAVE A SPECIAL BOND, BUT HER LIFE BECAME VERY COMPLICATED.
I REALIZED THAT RELATING TO SOMEONE LIKE HER DID NOT HELP ME ADAPT TO HUMANS LIKE YOU...SO I HAD TO MOVE ON.
I TRIED DIFFERENT PLACES, BUT WOUND UP HERE, IN FLORIDA.
I HAVE MY JOB, A SMALL GROUP OF FRIENDS AND A LIFE HERE.
I STILL VISIT MY PARENTS BELOW, AS WELL AS HELPING OUT THE WORLD AROUND ME WHEN NEEDED.
HONESTLY, STELLA, I WAS DOING MY BEST TO KEEP MY IDENTITY A SECRET.
WELL, THAT COVER IS BLOWN.
MAYBE NOT. MOST PEOPLE FOCUSED ON OUR ORANGE FRIEND, OR THE MONSTER, OR RAN AWAY.
THE OWNER OF THE RESTAURANT ALREADY KNOWS ALL ABOUT ME.
LOOK, WE CAN ALL HAVE A BIG CHAT ABOUT THIS LATER. CAN YOU TELL ME WHAT'S HAPPENING NOW, WITH THE CREATURE?
WELL, IF STARFIRE FOLLOWED MY INSTRUCTIONS, THAT CHIDA MONSTER SHOULD BE...

Ten Thousand Feet Under.

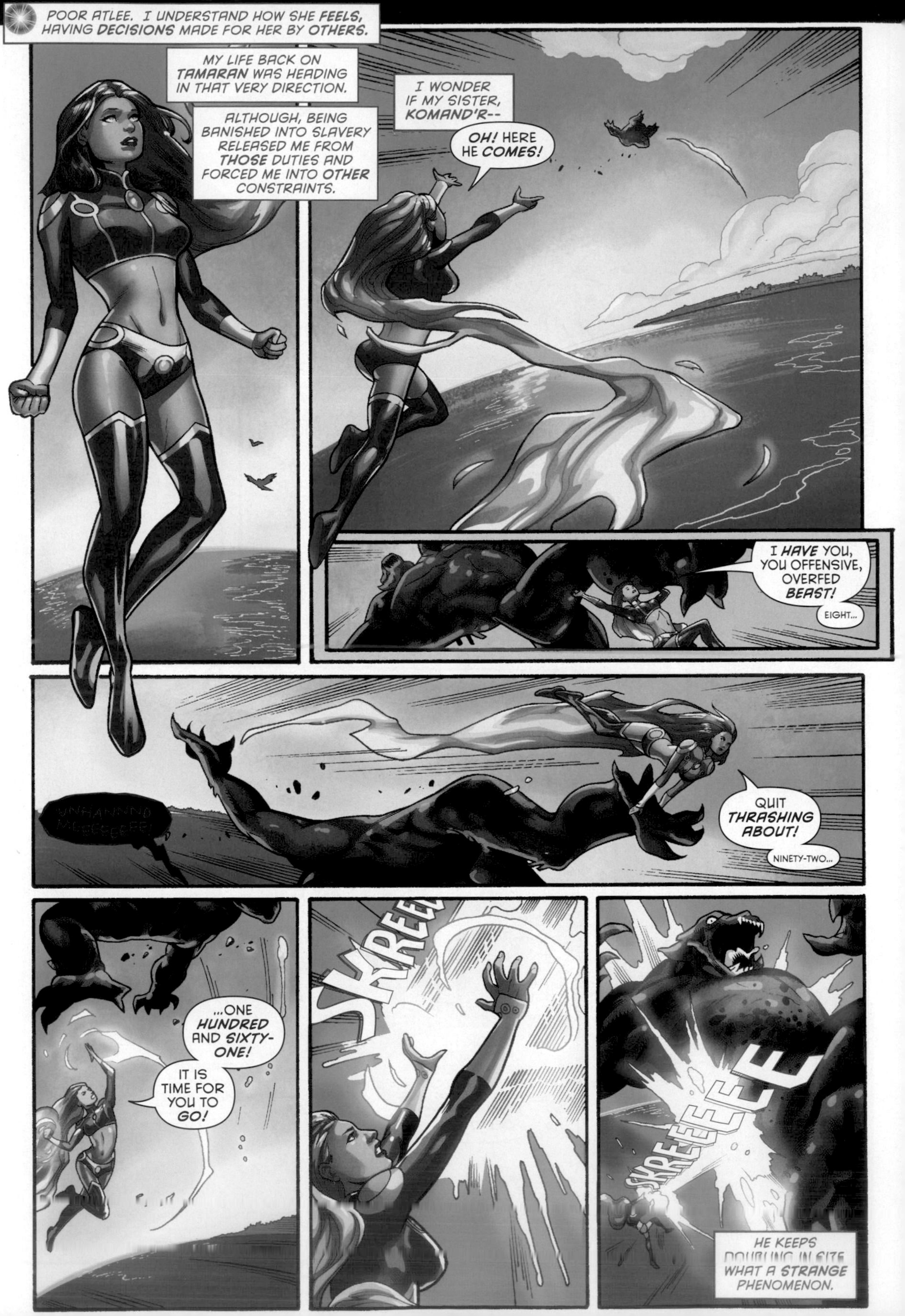
POOR ATLEE. I UNDERSTAND HOW SHE FEELS, HAVING DECISIONS MADE FOR HER BY OTHERS.
MY LIFE BACK ON TAMARAN WAS HEADING IN THAT VERY DIRECTION.
ALTHOUGH, BEING BANISHED INTO SLAVERY RELEASED ME FROM THOSE DUTIES AND FORCED ME INTO OTHER CONSTRAINTS.
I WONDER IF MY SISTER, KOMAND'R--
OH! HERE HE COMES!
I HAVE YOU, YOU OFFENSIVE, OVERFED BEAST!
EIGHT...
QUIT THRASHING ABOUT!
NINETY-TWO...
...ONE HUNDRED AND SIXTY-ONE!
IT IS TIME FOR YOU TO GO!
HE KEEPS DOUBLING IN SIZE
WHAT A STRANGE PHENOMENON.

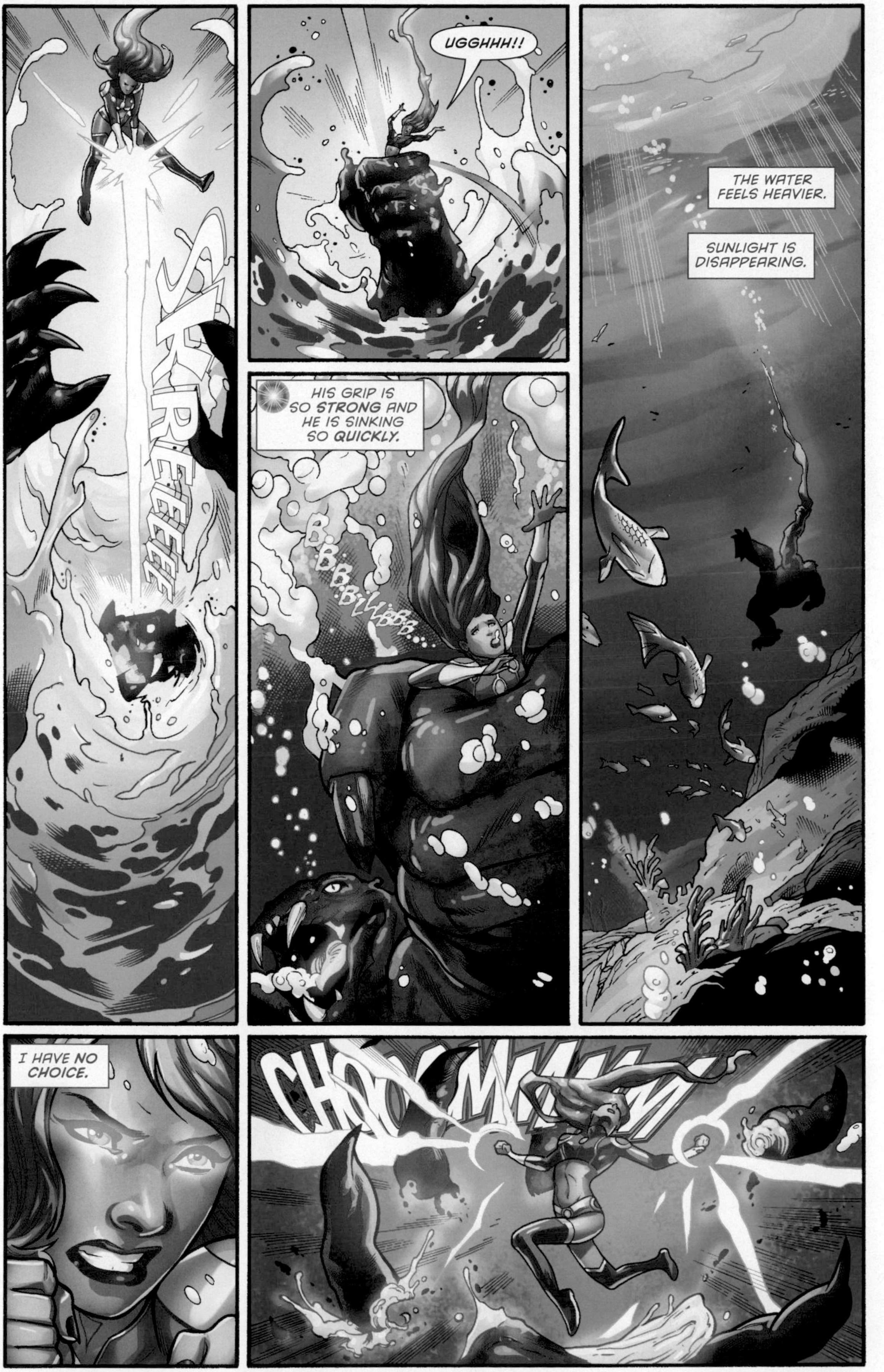
SKREEEEEE
UGGHHH!!
THE WATER FEELS HEAVIER.
SUNLIGHT IS DISAPPEARING.
HIS GRIP IS SO STRONG AND HE IS SINKING SO QUICKLY.
BBBBLLBBB
I HAVE NO CHOICE.
CHOOMMMM

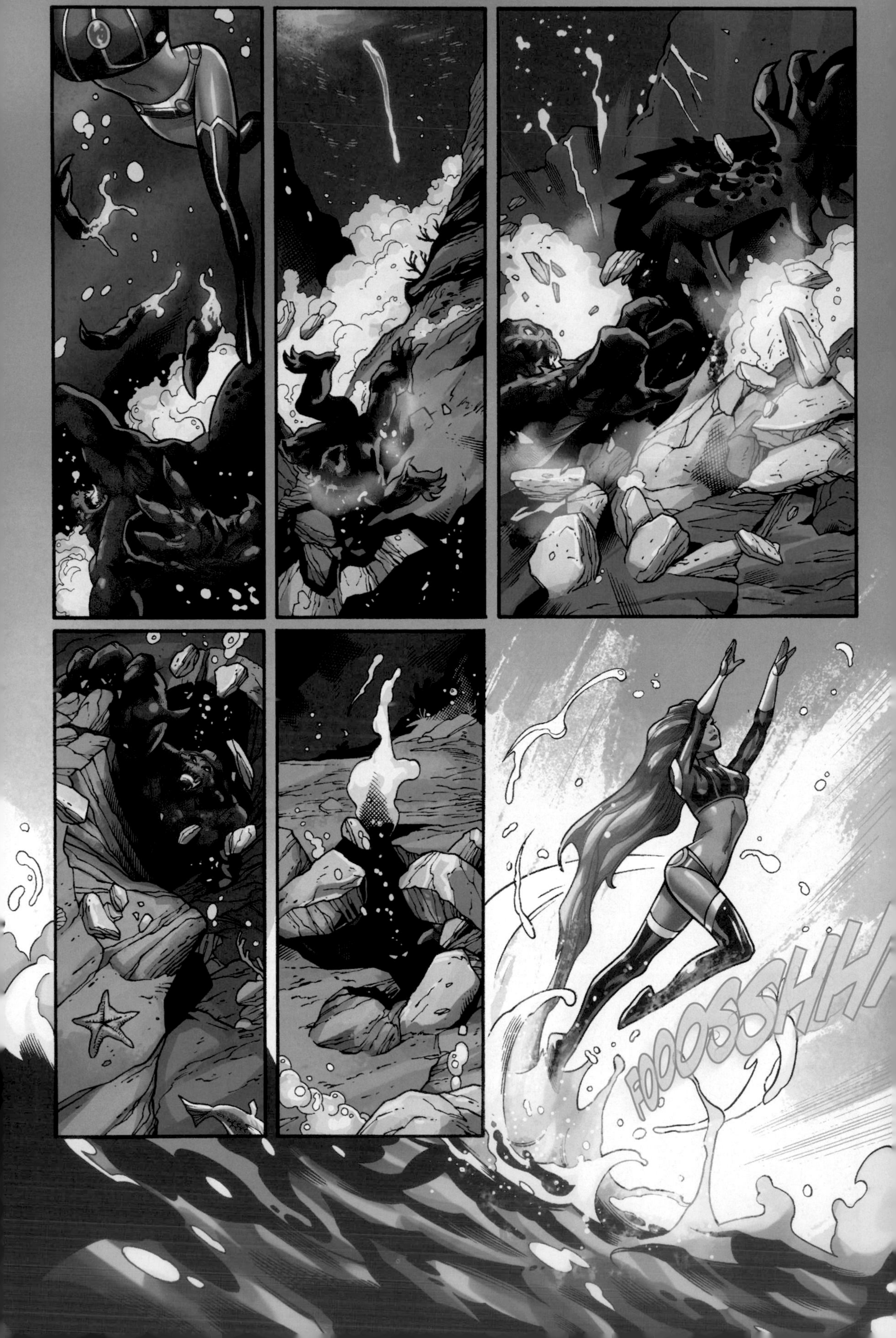
FOOOSSHHH

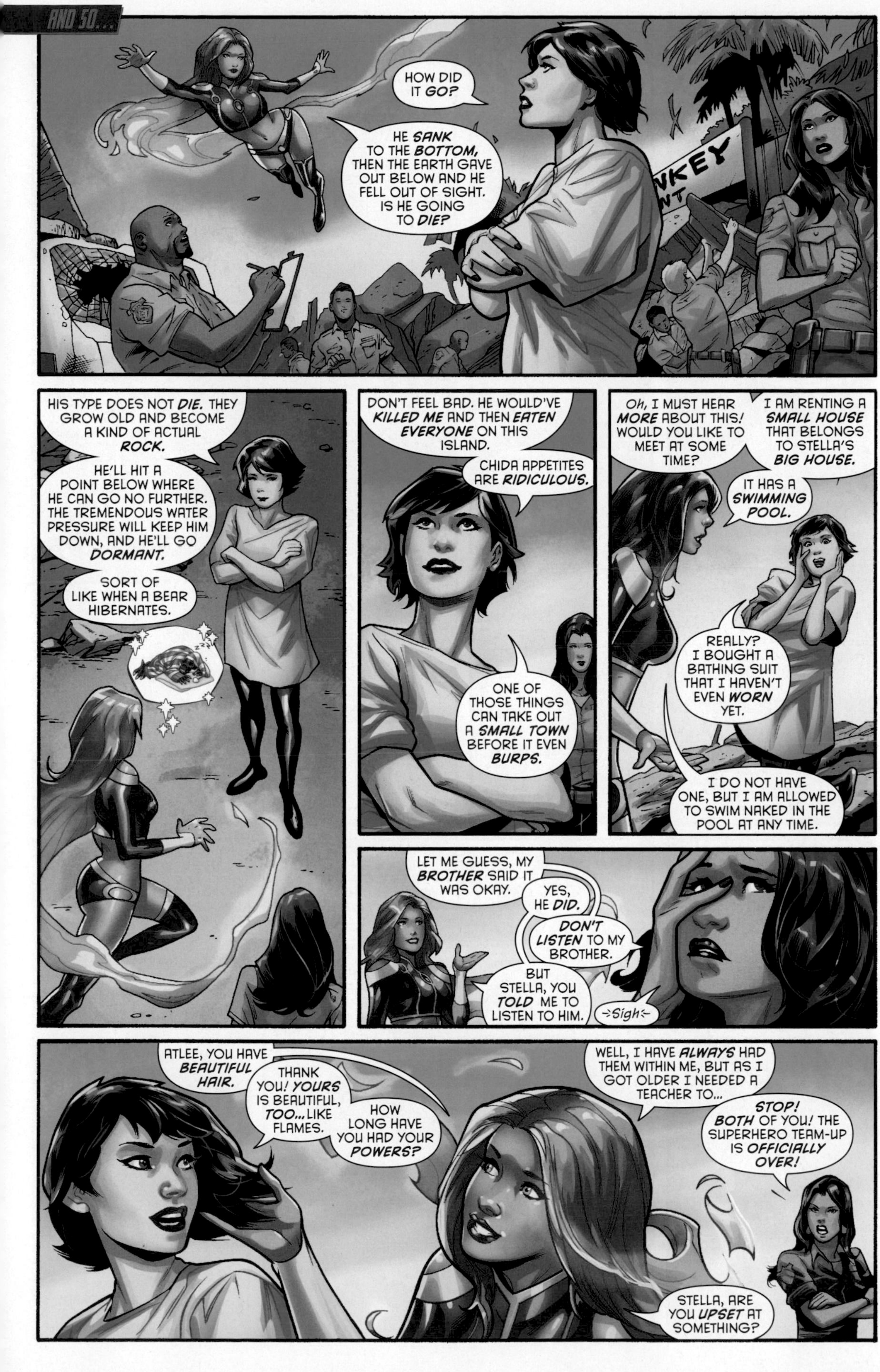
AND SO...
HOW DID IT GO?
HE SANK TO THE BOTTOM, THEN THE EARTH GAVE OUT BELOW AND HE FELL OUT OF SIGHT. IS HE GOING TO DIE?
HIS TYPE DOES NOT DIE. THEY GROW OLD AND BECOME A KIND OF ACTUAL ROCK.
HE'LL HIT A POINT BELOW WHERE HE CAN GO NO FURTHER. THE TREMENDOUS WATER PRESSURE WILL KEEP HIM DOWN, AND HE'LL GO DORMANT.
SORT OF LIKE WHEN A BEAR HIBERNATES.
DON'T FEEL BAD. HE WOULD'VE KILLED ME AND THEN EATEN EVERYONE ON THIS ISLAND.
CHIDA APPETITES ARE RIDICULOUS.
ONE OF THOSE THINGS CAN TAKE OUT A SMALL TOWN BEFORE IT EVEN BURPS.
Oh, I MUST HEAR MORE ABOUT THIS! WOULD YOU LIKE TO MEET AT SOME TIME?
I AM RENTING A SMALL HOUSE THAT BELONGS TO STELLA'S BIG HOUSE.
IT HAS A SWIMMING POOL.
REALLY? I BOUGHT A BATHING SUIT THAT I HAVEN'T EVEN WORN YET.
I DO NOT HAVE ONE, BUT I AM ALLOWED TO SWIM NAKED IN THE POOL AT ANY TIME.
LET ME GUESS, MY BROTHER SAID IT WAS OKAY.
YES, HE DID.
DON'T LISTEN TO MY BROTHER.
BUT STELLA, YOU TOLD ME TO LISTEN TO HIM.
Sigh
ATLEE, YOU HAVE BEAUTIFUL HAIR.
THANK YOU! YOURS IS BEAUTIFUL, TOO... LIKE FLAMES.
HOW LONG HAVE YOU HAD YOUR POWERS?
WELL, I HAVE ALWAYS HAD THEM WITHIN ME, BUT AS I GOT OLDER I NEEDED A TEACHER TO...
STOP! BOTH OF YOU! THE SUPERHERO TEAM-UP IS OFFICIALLY OVER!
STELLA, ARE YOU UPSET AT SOMETHING?

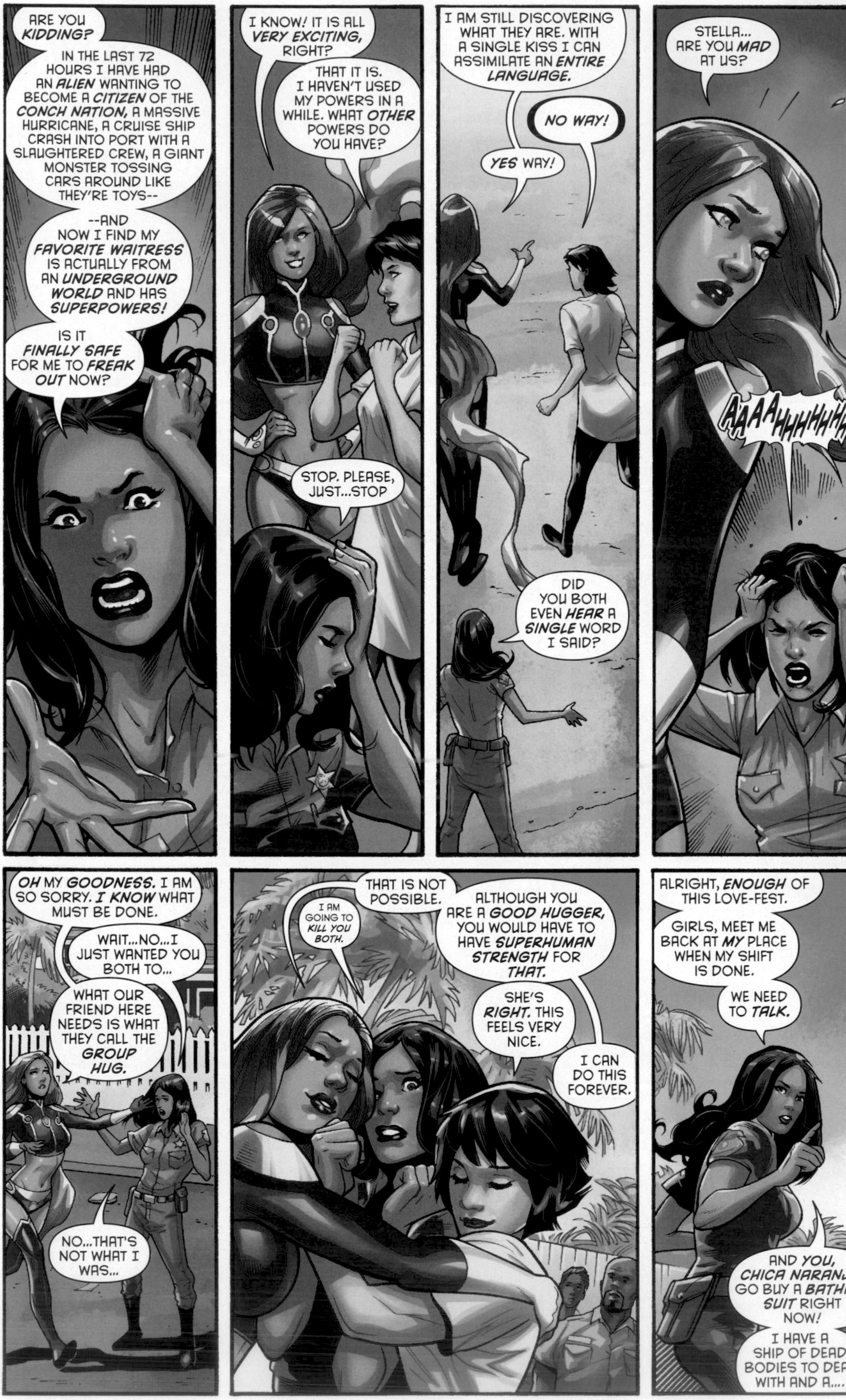
ARE YOU KIDDING?
IN THE LAST 72 HOURS I HAVE HAD AN ALIEN WANTING TO BECOME A CITIZEN OF THE CONCH NATION, A MASSIVE HURRICANE, A CRUISE SHIP CRASH INTO PORT WITH A SLAUGHTERED CREW, A GIANT MONSTER TOSSING CARS AROUND LIKE THEY'RE TOYS--
--AND NOW I FIND MY FAVORITE WAITRESS IS ACTUALLY FROM AN UNDERGROUND WORLD AND HAS SUPERPOWERS!
IS IT FINALLY SAFE FOR ME TO FREAK OUT NOW?
I KNOW! IT IS ALL VERY EXCITING, RIGHT?
THAT IT IS. I HAVEN'T USED MY POWERS IN A WHILE. WHAT OTHER POWERS DO YOU HAVE?
STOP. PLEASE, JUST...STOP
I AM STILL DISCOVERING WHAT THEY ARE. WITH A SINGLE KISS I CAN ASSIMILATE AN ENTIRE LANGUAGE.
NO WAY!
YES WAY!
DID YOU BOTH EVEN HEAR A SINGLE WORD I SAID?
STELLA... ARE YOU MAD AT US?
AAAAHHHHHHH!!!
OH MY GOODNESS. I AM SO SORRY. I KNOW WHAT MUST BE DONE.
WAIT...NO...I JUST WANTED YOU BOTH TO...
WHAT OUR FRIEND HERE NEEDS IS WHAT THEY CALL THE GROUP HUG.
NO...THAT'S NOT WHAT I WAS...
I AM GOING TO KILL YOU BOTH.
THAT IS NOT POSSIBLE.
ALTHOUGH YOU ARE A GOOD HUGGER, YOU WOULD HAVE TO HAVE SUPERHUMAN STRENGTH FOR THAT.
SHE'S RIGHT. THIS FEELS VERY NICE.
I CAN DO THIS FOREVER.
ALRIGHT, ENOUGH OF THIS LOVE-FEST.
GIRLS, MEET ME BACK AT MY PLACE WHEN MY SHIFT IS DONE.
WE NEED TO TALK.
AND YOU, CHICA NARANJA, GO BUY A BATHING SUIT RIGHT NOW!
I HAVE A SHIP OF DEAD BODIES TO DEAL WITH AND A....

Killer On The Loose.

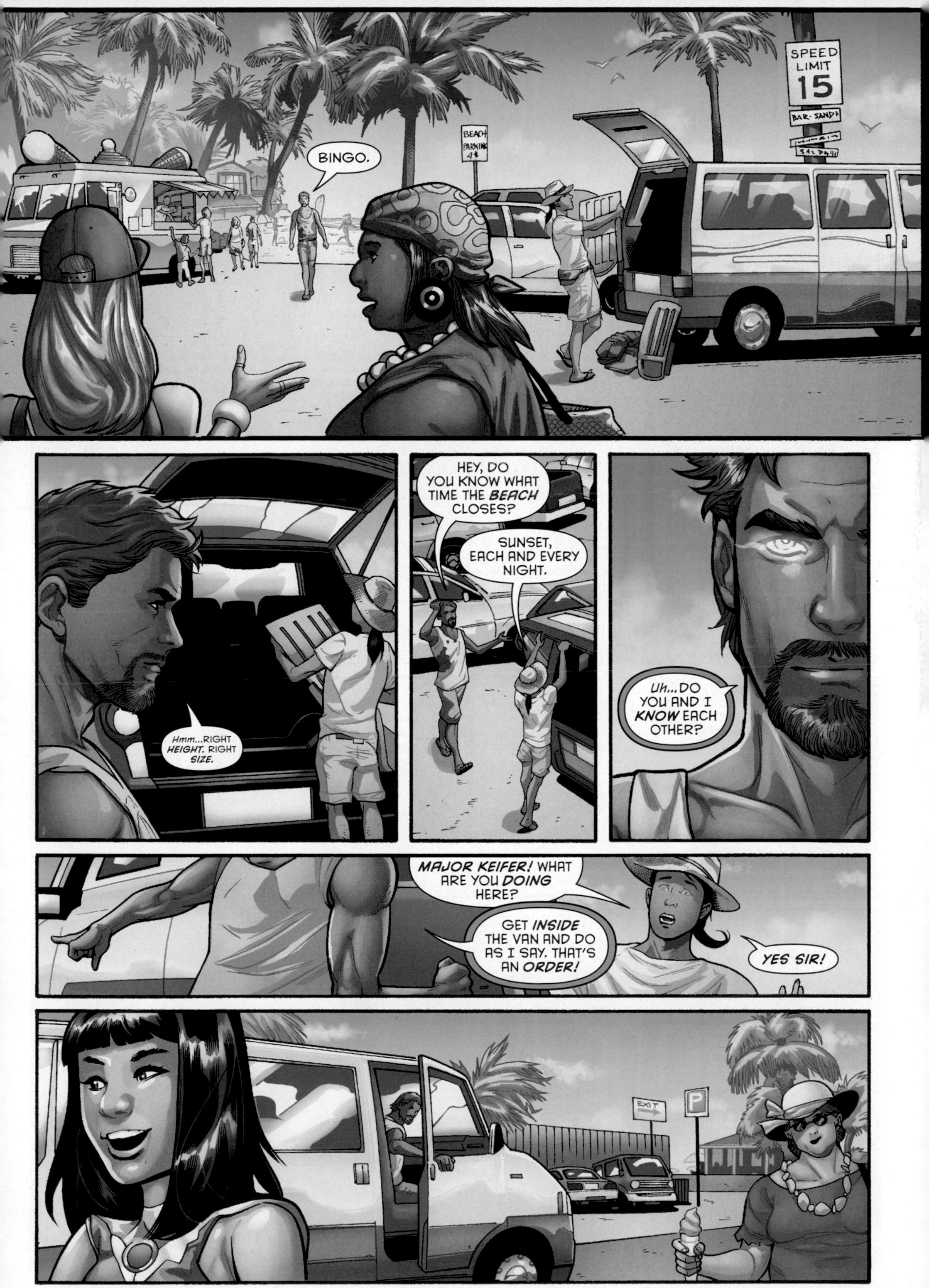

SPEED LIMIT 15
BINGO.
Hmm...RIGHT HEIGHT. RIGHT SIZE.
HEY, DO YOU KNOW WHAT TIME THE BEACH CLOSES?
SUNSET, EACH AND EVERY NIGHT.
Uh...DO YOU AND I KNOW EACH OTHER?
MAJOR KEIFER! WHAT ARE YOU DOING HERE?
GET INSIDE THE VAN AND DO AS I SAY. THAT'S AN ORDER!
YES SIR!
EXIT
P

Hugged Out.

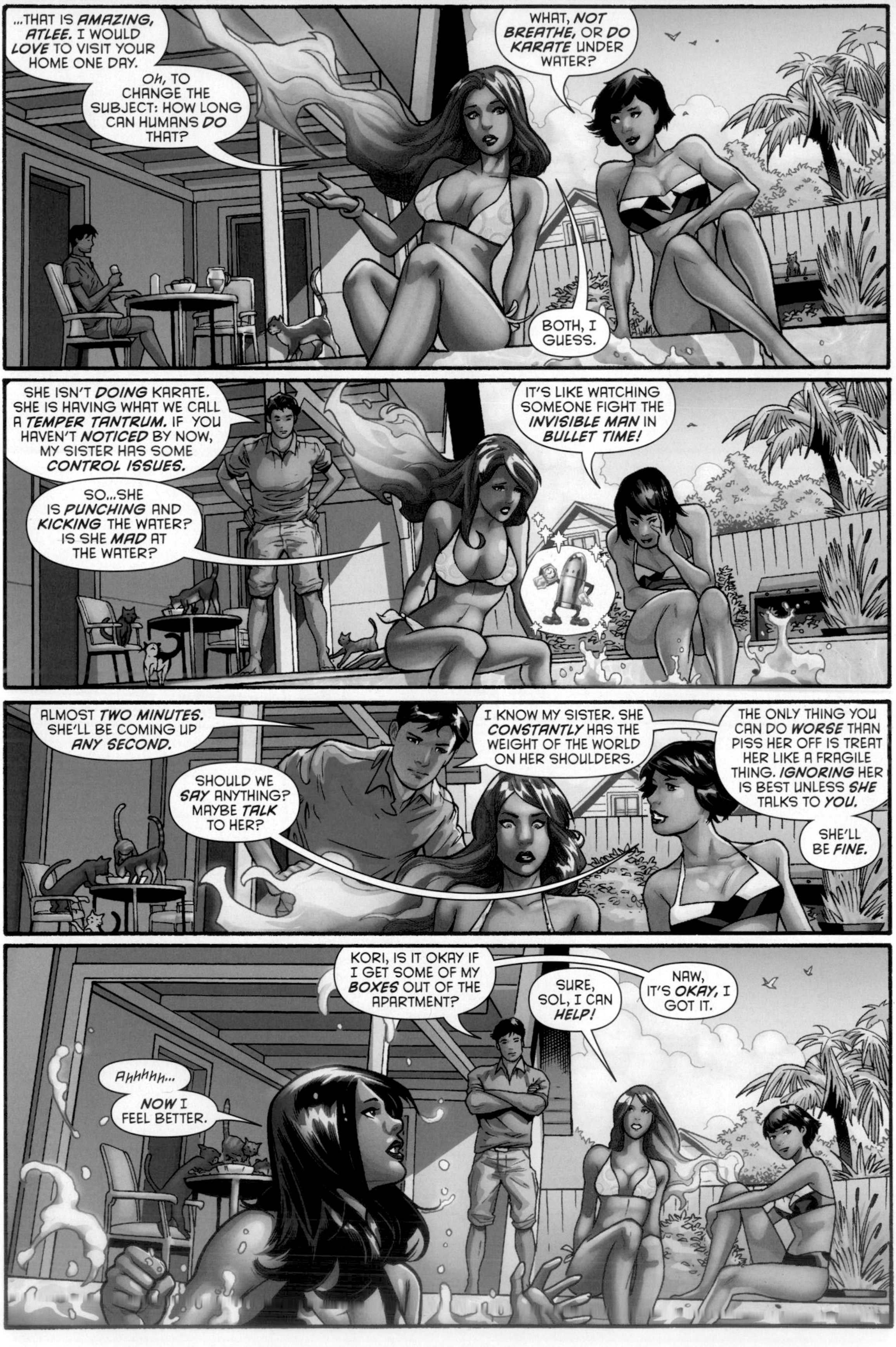
...THAT IS AMAZING, ATLEE. I WOULD LOVE TO VISIT YOUR HOME ONE DAY.
OH, TO CHANGE THE SUBJECT: HOW LONG CAN HUMANS DO THAT?
WHAT, NOT BREATHE, OR DO KARATE UNDER WATER?
BOTH, I GUESS.
SHE ISN'T DOING KARATE. SHE IS HAVING WHAT WE CALL A TEMPER TANTRUM. IF YOU HAVEN'T NOTICED BY NOW, MY SISTER HAS SOME CONTROL ISSUES.
SO...SHE IS PUNCHING AND KICKING THE WATER? IS SHE MAD AT THE WATER?
IT'S LIKE WATCHING SOMEONE FIGHT THE INVISIBLE MAN IN BULLET TIME!
ALMOST TWO MINUTES. SHE'LL BE COMING UP ANY SECOND.
SHOULD WE SAY ANYTHING? MAYBE TALK TO HER?
I KNOW MY SISTER. SHE CONSTANTLY HAS THE WEIGHT OF THE WORLD ON HER SHOULDERS.
THE ONLY THING YOU CAN DO WORSE THAN PISS HER OFF IS TREAT HER LIKE A FRAGILE THING. IGNORING HER IS BEST UNLESS SHE TALKS TO YOU.
SHE'LL BE FINE.
AHHHHH... NOW I FEEL BETTER.
KORI, IS IT OKAY IF I GET SOME OF MY BOXES OUT OF THE APARTMENT?
SURE, SOL, I CAN HELP!
NAW, IT'S OKAY, I GOT IT.

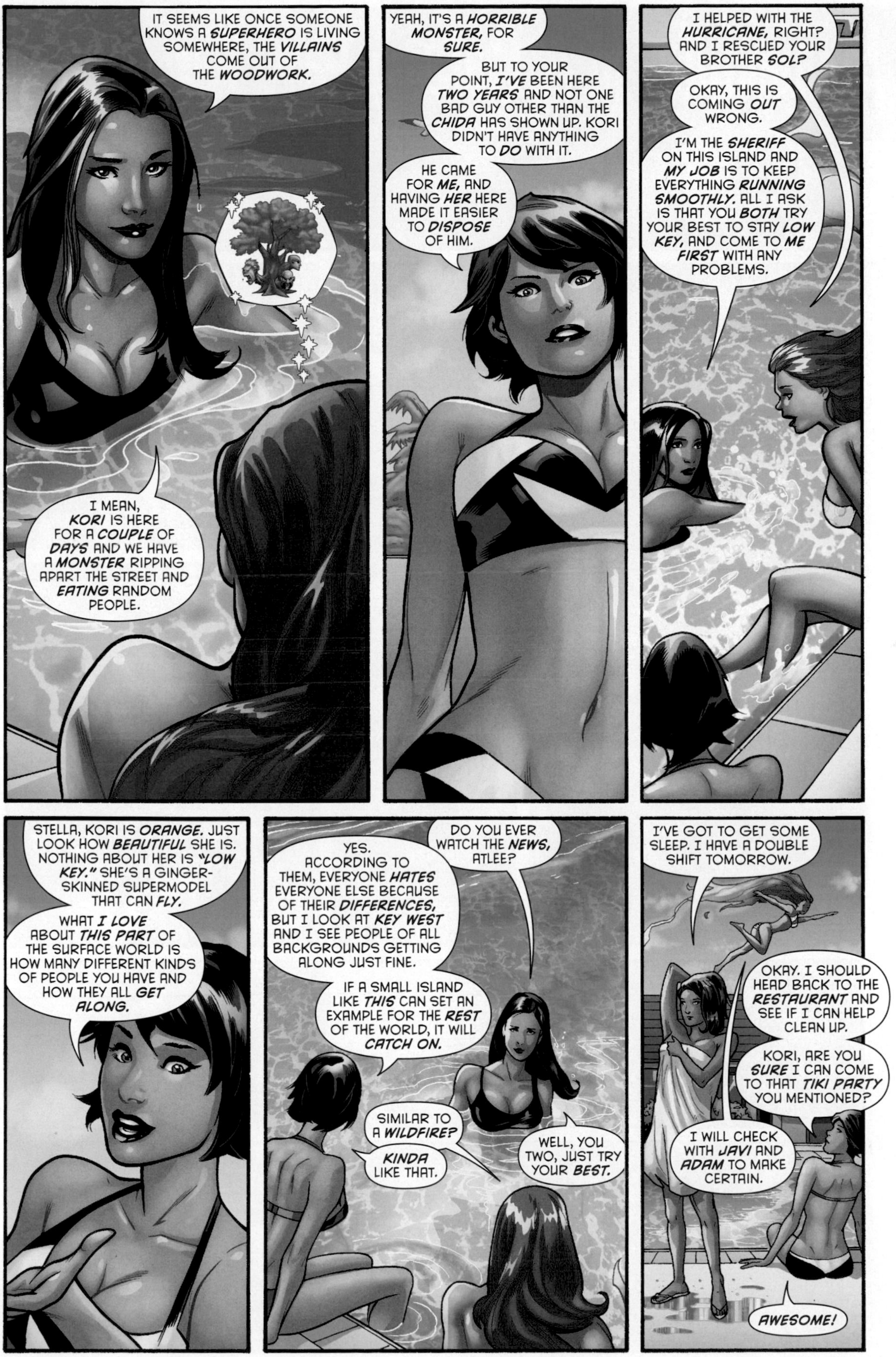
IT SEEMS LIKE ONCE SOMEONE KNOWS A SUPERHERO IS LIVING SOMEWHERE, THE VILLAINS COME OUT OF THE WOODWORK.
I MEAN, KORI IS HERE FOR A COUPLE OF DAYS AND WE HAVE A MONSTER RIPPING APART THE STREET AND EATING RANDOM PEOPLE.
YEAH, IT'S A HORRIBLE MONSTER, FOR SURE.
BUT TO YOUR POINT, I'VE BEEN HERE TWO YEARS AND NOT ONE BAD GUY OTHER THAN THE CHIDA HAS SHOWN UP. KORI DIDN'T HAVE ANYTHING TO DO WITH IT.
HE CAME FOR ME, AND HAVING HER HERE MADE IT EASIER TO DISPOSE OF HIM.
I HELPED WITH THE HURRICANE, RIGHT? AND I RESCUED YOUR BROTHER SOL?
OKAY, THIS IS COMING OUT WRONG.
I'M THE SHERIFF ON THIS ISLAND AND MY JOB IS TO KEEP EVERYTHING RUNNING SMOOTHLY. ALL I ASK IS THAT YOU BOTH TRY YOUR BEST TO STAY LOW KEY, AND COME TO ME FIRST WITH ANY PROBLEMS.
STELLA, KORI IS ORANGE. JUST LOOK HOW BEAUTIFUL SHE IS. NOTHING ABOUT HER IS "LOW KEY." SHE'S A GINGER-SKINNED SUPERMODEL THAT CAN FLY.
WHAT I LOVE ABOUT THIS PART OF THE SURFACE WORLD IS HOW MANY DIFFERENT KINDS OF PEOPLE YOU HAVE AND HOW THEY ALL GET ALONG.
DO YOU EVER WATCH THE NEWS, ATLEE?
YES. ACCORDING TO THEM, EVERYONE HATES EVERYONE ELSE BECAUSE OF THEIR DIFFERENCES, BUT I LOOK AT KEY WEST AND I SEE PEOPLE OF ALL BACKGROUNDS GETTING ALONG JUST FINE.
IF A SMALL ISLAND LIKE THIS CAN SET AN EXAMPLE FOR THE REST OF THE WORLD, IT WILL CATCH ON.
SIMILAR TO A WILDFIRE?
KINDA LIKE THAT.
WELL, YOU TWO, JUST TRY YOUR BEST.
I'VE GOT TO GET SOME SLEEP. I HAVE A DOUBLE SHIFT TOMORROW.
OKAY. I SHOULD HEAD BACK TO THE RESTAURANT AND SEE IF I CAN HELP CLEAN UP.
KORI, ARE YOU SURE I CAN COME TO THAT TIKI PARTY YOU MENTIONED?
I WILL CHECK WITH JAVI AND ADAM TO MAKE CERTAIN.
AWESOME!

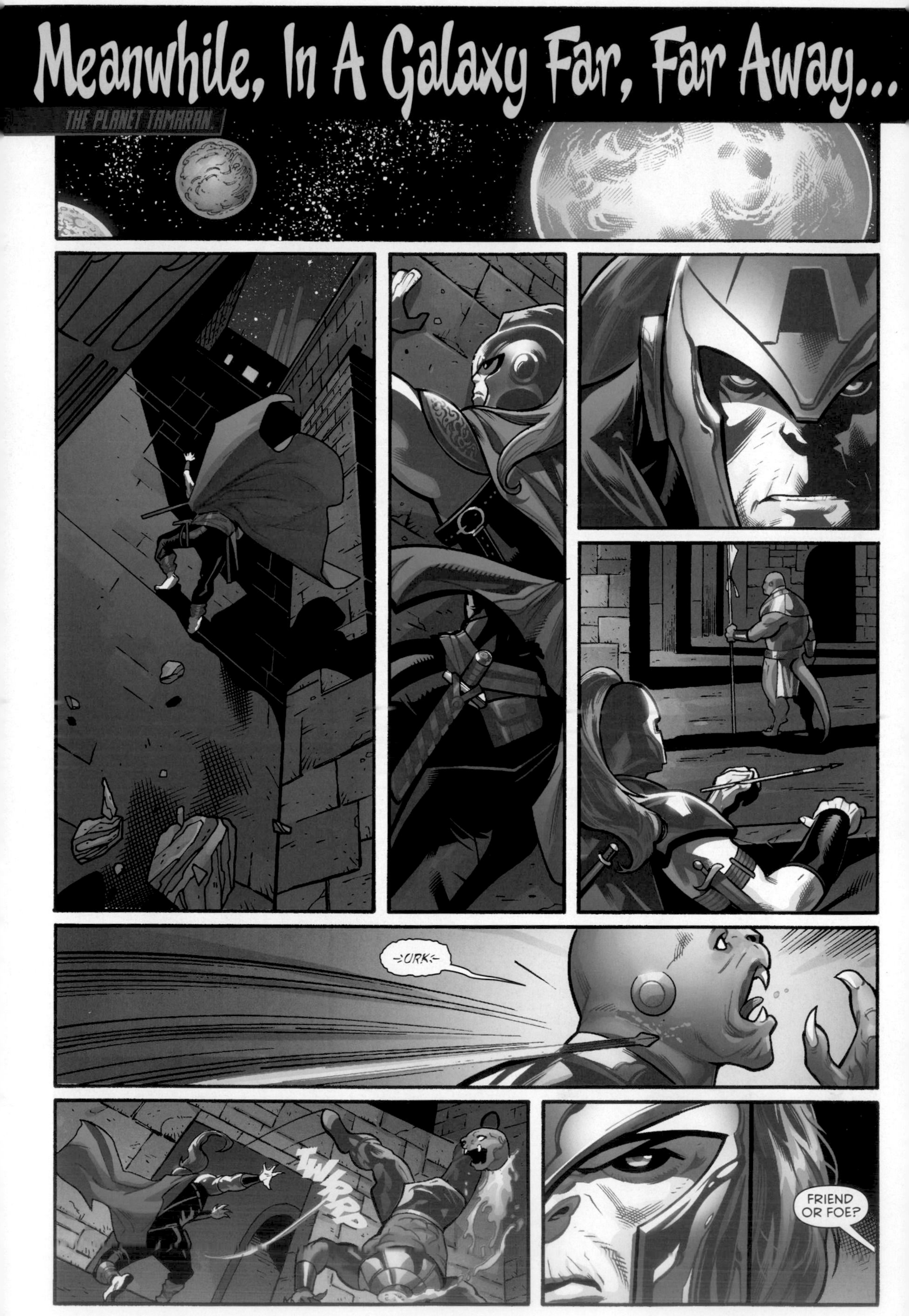
Meanwhile, In A Galaxy Far, Far Away...
THE PLANET TAMARAN.
-URK-
TWIRRP
FRIEND OR FOE?

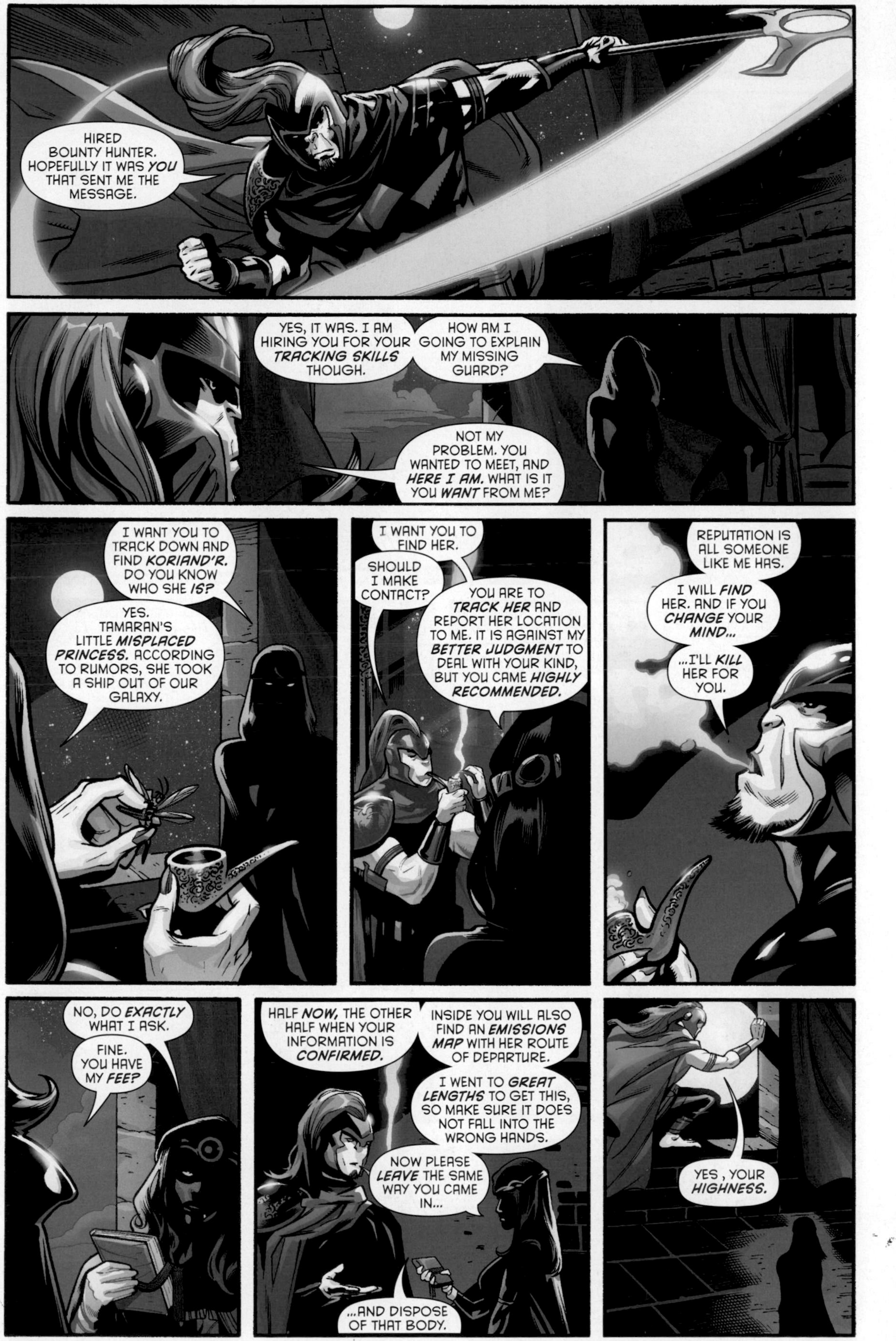
HIRED BOUNTY HUNTER. HOPEFULLY IT WAS *YOU* THAT SENT ME THE MESSAGE.
YES, IT WAS. I AM HIRING YOU FOR YOUR *TRACKING SKILLS* THOUGH.
HOW AM I GOING TO EXPLAIN MY MISSING GUARD?
NOT MY PROBLEM. YOU WANTED TO MEET, AND *HERE I AM.* WHAT IS IT YOU *WANT* FROM ME?
I WANT YOU TO TRACK DOWN AND FIND *KORIAND'R.* DO YOU KNOW WHO SHE *IS?*
YES. TAMARAN'S LITTLE *MISPLACED PRINCESS.* ACCORDING TO RUMORS, SHE TOOK A SHIP OUT OF OUR GALAXY.
I WANT YOU TO FIND HER.
SHOULD I MAKE CONTACT?
YOU ARE TO *TRACK HER* AND REPORT HER LOCATION TO ME. IT IS AGAINST MY *BETTER JUDGMENT* TO DEAL WITH YOUR KIND, BUT YOU CAME *HIGHLY RECOMMENDED.*
REPUTATION IS ALL SOMEONE LIKE ME HAS.
I WILL *FIND* HER. AND IF YOU *CHANGE* YOUR *MIND...*
...I'LL *KILL* HER FOR YOU.
NO, DO *EXACTLY* WHAT I ASK.
FINE. YOU HAVE MY *FEE?*
HALF *NOW,* THE OTHER HALF WHEN YOUR INFORMATION IS *CONFIRMED.*
INSIDE YOU WILL ALSO FIND AN *EMISSIONS MAP* WITH HER ROUTE OF DEPARTURE.
I WENT TO *GREAT LENGTHS* TO GET THIS, SO MAKE SURE IT DOES NOT FALL INTO THE WRONG HANDS.
NOW PLEASE *LEAVE* THE SAME WAY YOU CAME IN...
...AND DISPOSE OF THAT BODY.
YES , YOUR *HIGHNESS.*

Orange Crush.

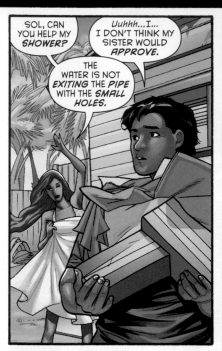

SOL, CAN YOU HELP MY *SHOWER*?

Uuhhh...I... I DON'T THINK MY SISTER WOULD APPROVE.

THE WATER IS NOT *EXITING* THE *PIPE* WITH THE *SMALL HOLES.*

Oh...YOU MEAN THE *SHOWER-HEAD.* I THINK I CAN HELP.

Ah, THE MAIN WATER LINE FOR OUTSIDE WAS TURNED *OFF.* IF IT EVER HAPPENS AGAIN, JUST TURN THIS *CLOCKWISE* AND YOU SHOULD BE *FINE.*

I SAW ON THE TV THAT THERE ARE *DROUGHTS* ON THE WEST COAST.

PEOPLE ARE TRYING TO *CONSERVE* FRESH WATER *EVERYWHERE.*

WHOOPS...Uh...YEAH, IT'S NOT MUCH OF A PROBLEM ON *THIS* COAST, BUT SOMETIMES WEATHER PATTERNS *CHANGE.*

IT HAPPENS A LOT.

FWUMP

I HAVE TO MONITOR STUFF LIKE THAT WHEN I'M WORKING AT THE *COAST GUARD STATION.*

Hmm, THE WATER FEELS SO *REFRESHING* IN HERE. YOU SHOULD *FEEL* IT. WE COULD *CONSERVE* THE *WATER* TOGETHER!

FWAP

Ooof!

HEY! KORI, YOU'RE *KILLIN'* ME, HERE!

THAT IS *NOT* TRUE.

FWIP

I CAN'T BELIEVE FOR A *SECOND* THAT YOU DON'T KNOW WHAT YOU'RE DOING TO ME RIGHT NOW.

I DO NOT UNDERSTAND.

WELL, MAYBE YOU *DO,* AND MAYBE YOU *DON'T.*

AND I HATE TO BE *ANOTHER* WET RAG... THAT JOB INTERVIEW WE SPOKE ABOUT? IT'S TOMORROW AT 9 A.M.

DON'T BE LATE. I WENT OUT OF MY WAY TO TALK YOU UP.

I GOTTA HEAD BACK TO WORK. I'LL CATCH YOU LATER.

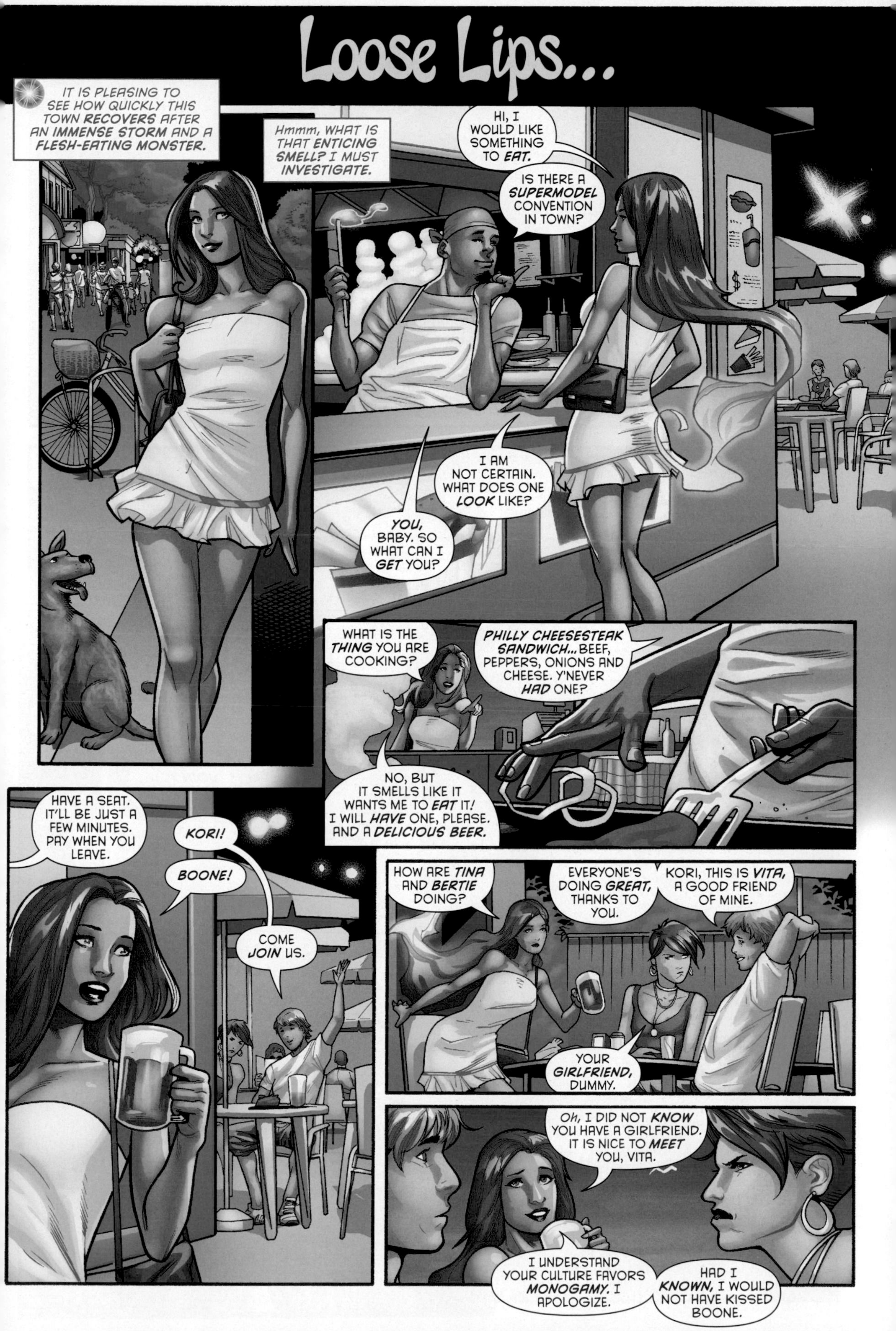
Loose Lips...
IT IS PLEASING TO SEE HOW QUICKLY THIS TOWN RECOVERS AFTER AN IMMENSE STORM AND A FLESH-EATING MONSTER.
Hmmm, WHAT IS THAT ENTICING SMELL? I MUST INVESTIGATE.
HI, I WOULD LIKE SOMETHING TO EAT.
IS THERE A SUPERMODEL CONVENTION IN TOWN?
I AM NOT CERTAIN. WHAT DOES ONE LOOK LIKE?
YOU, BABY. SO WHAT CAN I GET YOU?
WHAT IS THE THING YOU ARE COOKING?
PHILLY CHEESESTEAK SANDWICH... BEEF, PEPPERS, ONIONS AND CHEESE. Y'NEVER HAD ONE?
NO, BUT IT SMELLS LIKE IT WANTS ME TO EAT IT! I WILL HAVE ONE, PLEASE. AND A DELICIOUS BEER.
HAVE A SEAT. IT'LL BE JUST A FEW MINUTES. PAY WHEN YOU LEAVE.
KORI!
BOONE!
COME JOIN US.
HOW ARE TINA AND BERTIE DOING?
EVERYONE'S DOING GREAT, THANKS TO YOU.
KORI, THIS IS VITA, A GOOD FRIEND OF MINE.
YOUR GIRLFRIEND, DUMMY.
Oh, I DID NOT KNOW YOU HAVE A GIRLFRIEND. IT IS NICE TO MEET YOU, VITA.
I UNDERSTAND YOUR CULTURE FAVORS MONOGAMY. I APOLOGIZE.
HAD I KNOWN, I WOULD NOT HAVE KISSED BOONE.

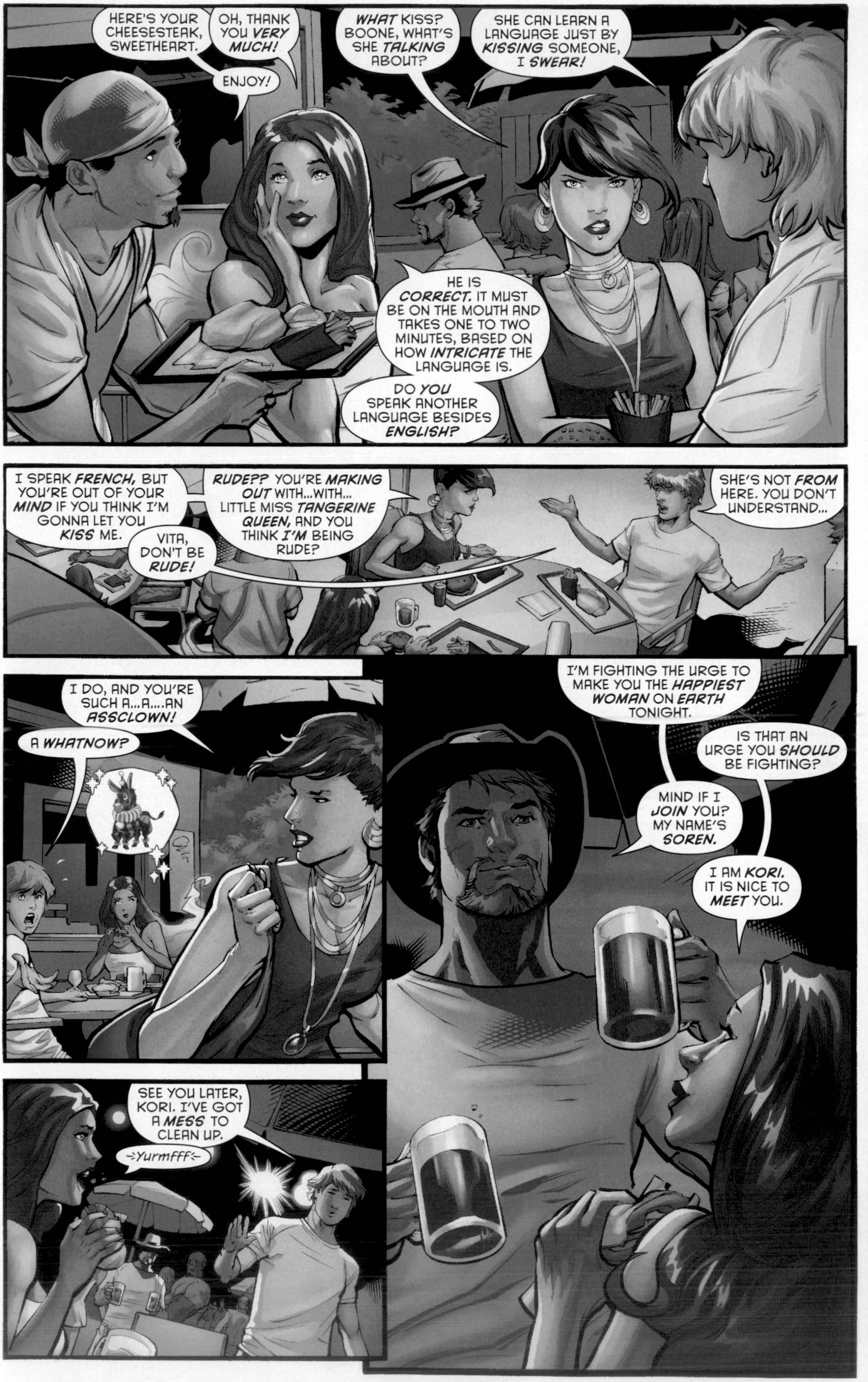

HERE'S YOUR CHEESESTEAK, SWEETHEART.
OH, THANK YOU VERY MUCH!
ENJOY!
WHAT KISS? BOONE, WHAT'S SHE TALKING ABOUT?
SHE CAN LEARN A LANGUAGE JUST BY KISSING SOMEONE, I SWEAR!
HE IS CORRECT. IT MUST BE ON THE MOUTH AND TAKES ONE TO TWO MINUTES, BASED ON HOW INTRICATE THE LANGUAGE IS.
DO YOU SPEAK ANOTHER LANGUAGE BESIDES ENGLISH?
I SPEAK FRENCH, BUT YOU'RE OUT OF YOUR MIND IF YOU THINK I'M GONNA LET YOU KISS ME.
VITA, DON'T BE RUDE!
RUDE?? YOU'RE MAKING OUT WITH...WITH... LITTLE MISS TANGERINE QUEEN, AND YOU THINK I'M BEING RUDE?
SHE'S NOT FROM HERE. YOU DON'T UNDERSTAND...
I DO, AND YOU'RE SUCH A...A...AN ASSCLOWN!
A WHATNOW?
I'M FIGHTING THE URGE TO MAKE YOU THE HAPPIEST WOMAN ON EARTH TONIGHT.
IS THAT AN URGE YOU SHOULD BE FIGHTING?
MIND IF I JOIN YOU? MY NAME'S SOREN.
I AM KORI. IT IS NICE TO MEET YOU.
SEE YOU LATER, KORI. I'VE GOT A MESS TO CLEAN UP.
~Yurmfff~

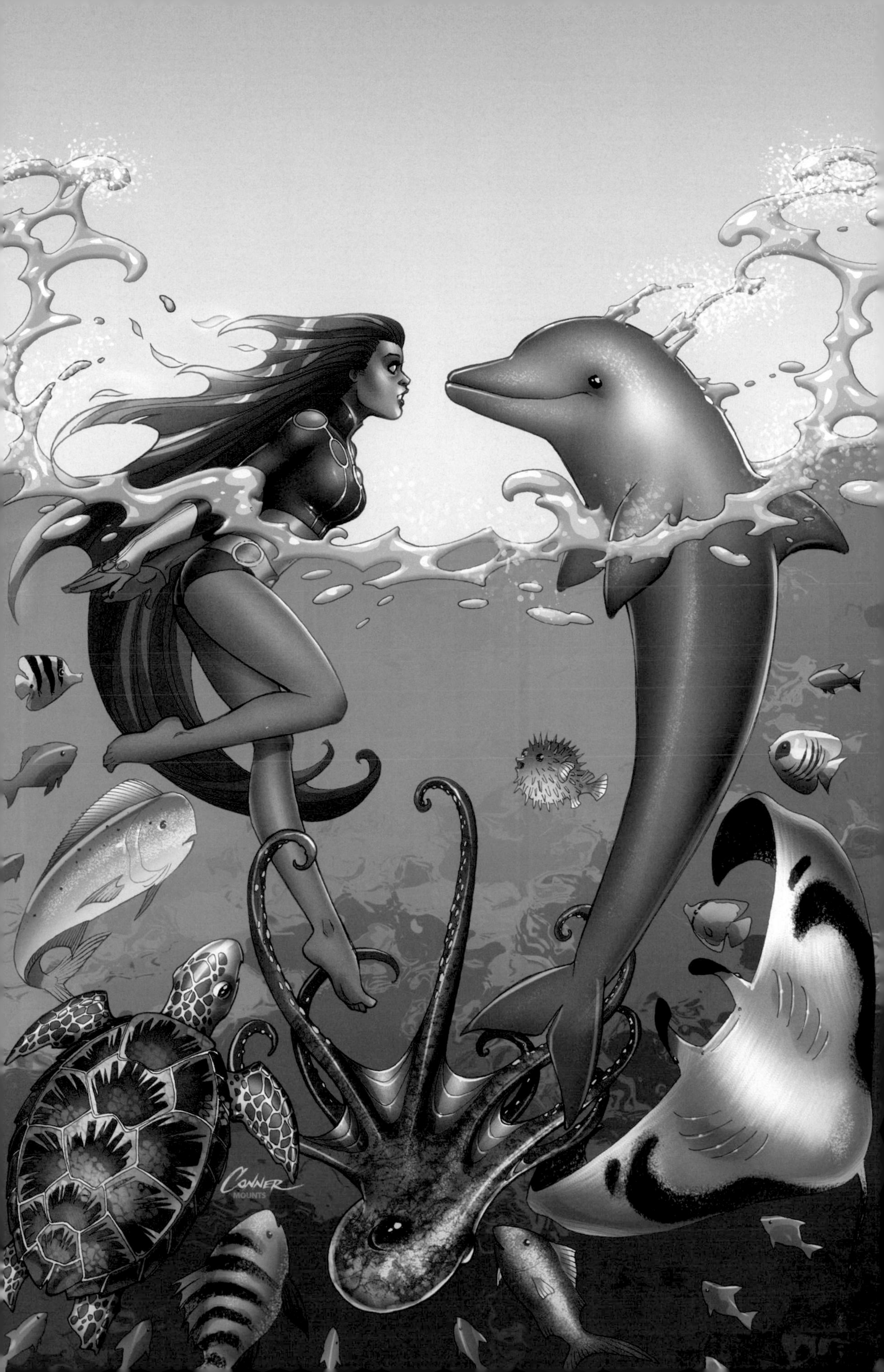
CONNER
MOUNTS

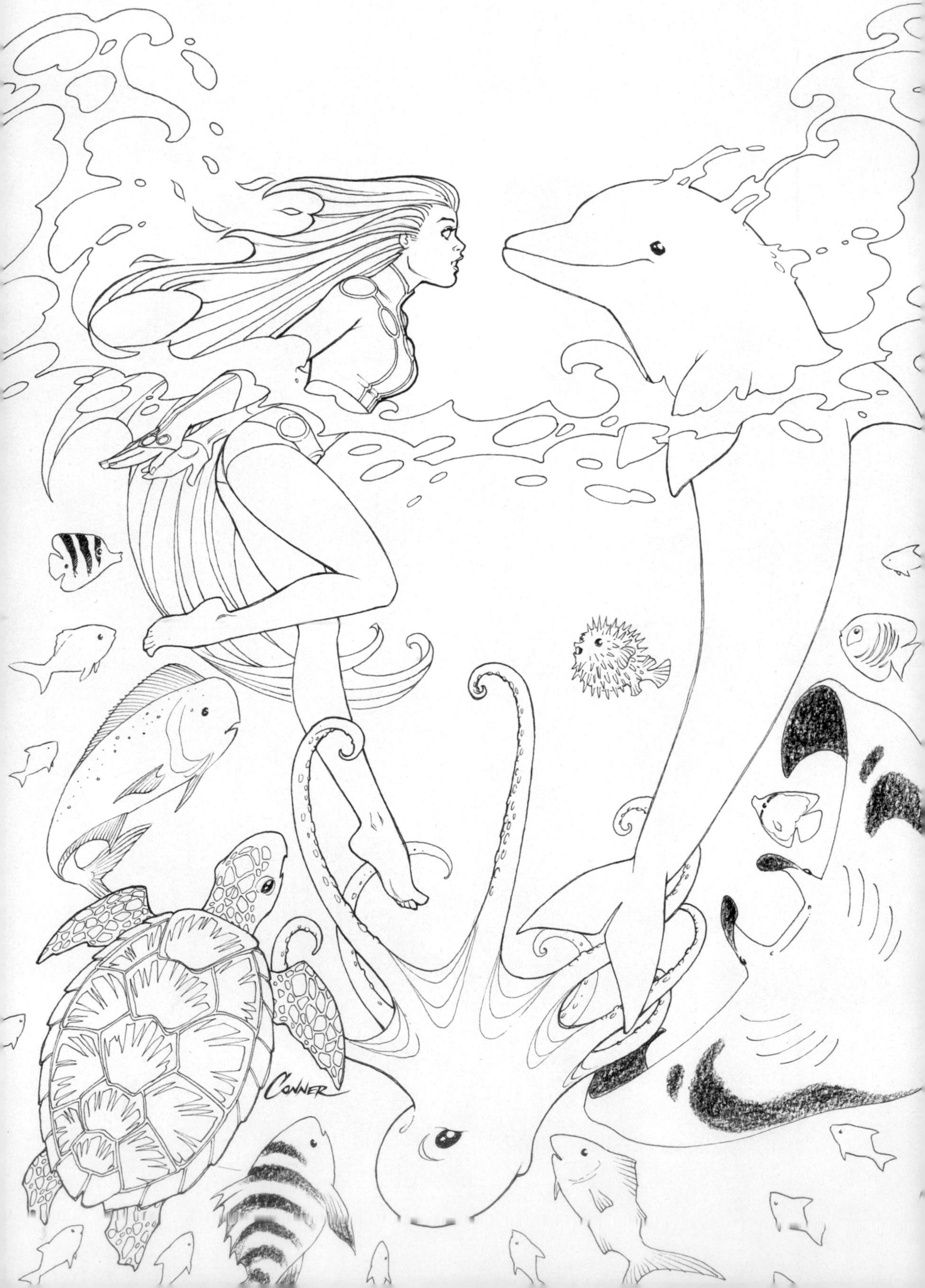
CONNER

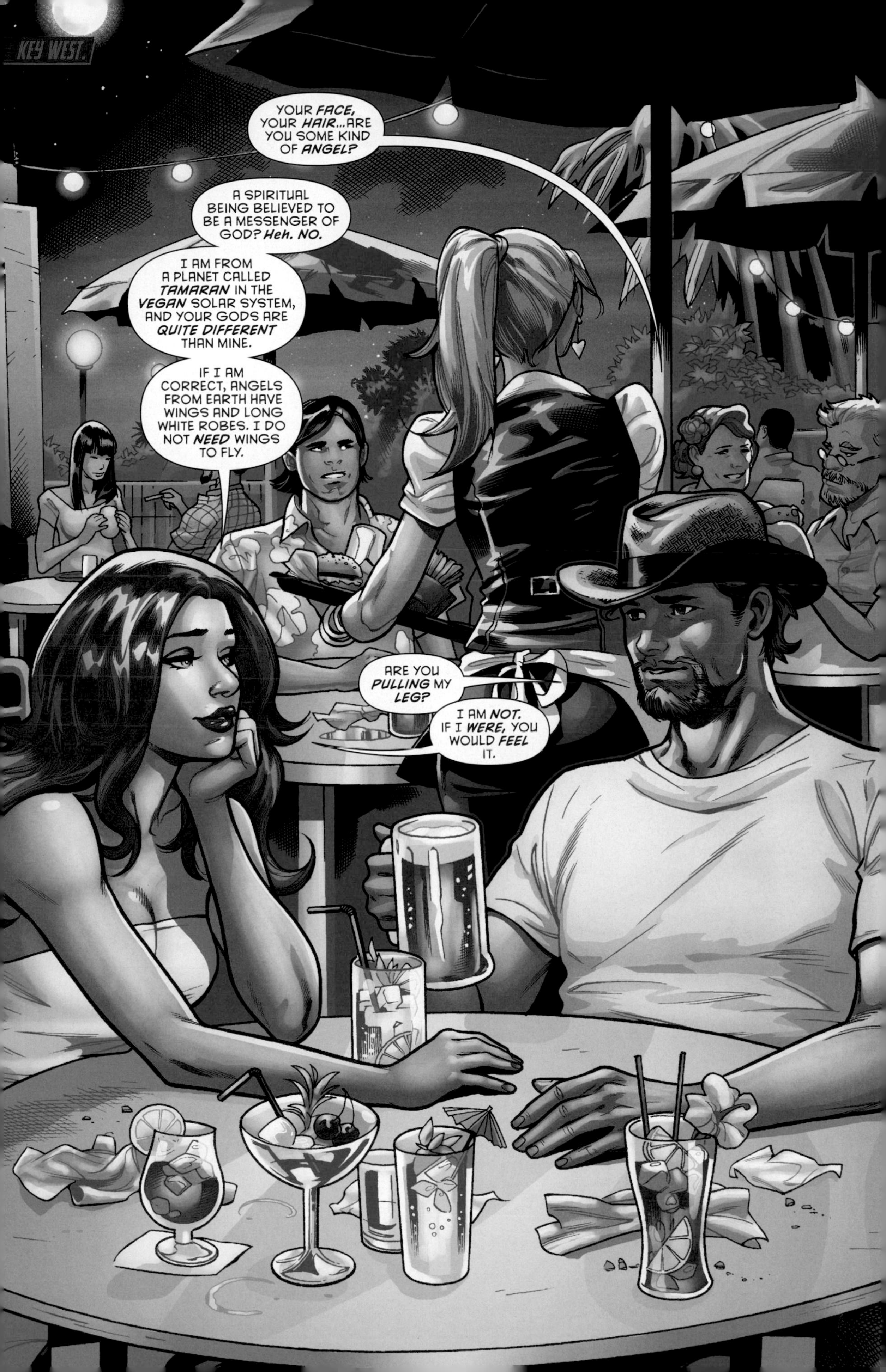
KEY WEST.
YOUR FACE, YOUR HAIR...ARE YOU SOME KIND OF ANGEL?
A SPIRITUAL BEING BELIEVED TO BE A MESSENGER OF GOD? Heh. NO.
I AM FROM A PLANET CALLED TAMARAN IN THE VEGAN SOLAR SYSTEM, AND YOUR GODS ARE QUITE DIFFERENT THAN MINE.
IF I AM CORRECT, ANGELS FROM EARTH HAVE WINGS AND LONG WHITE ROBES. I DO NOT NEED WINGS TO FLY.
ARE YOU PULLING MY LEG?
I AM NOT. IF I WERE, YOU WOULD FEEL IT.

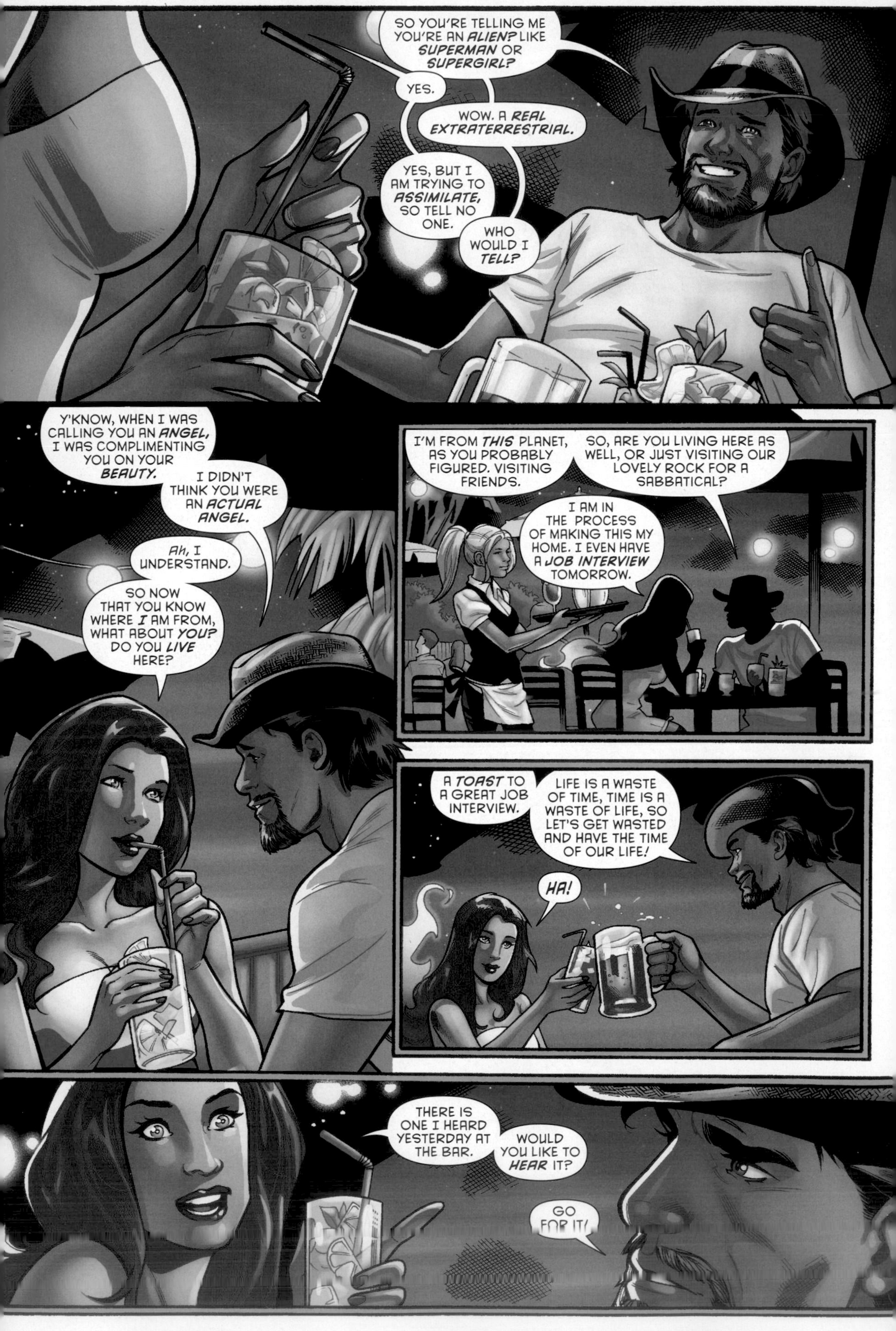
SO YOU'RE TELLING ME YOU'RE AN ALIEN? LIKE SUPERMAN OR SUPERGIRL?
YES.
WOW. A REAL EXTRATERRESTRIAL.
YES, BUT I AM TRYING TO ASSIMILATE, SO TELL NO ONE.
WHO WOULD I TELL?
Y'KNOW, WHEN I WAS CALLING YOU AN ANGEL, I WAS COMPLIMENTING YOU ON YOUR BEAUTY.
I DIDN'T THINK YOU WERE AN ACTUAL ANGEL.
Ah, I UNDERSTAND.
SO NOW THAT YOU KNOW WHERE I AM FROM, WHAT ABOUT YOU? DO YOU LIVE HERE?
I'M FROM THIS PLANET, AS YOU PROBABLY FIGURED. VISITING FRIENDS.
SO, ARE YOU LIVING HERE AS WELL, OR JUST VISITING OUR LOVELY ROCK FOR A SABBATICAL?
I AM IN THE PROCESS OF MAKING THIS MY HOME. I EVEN HAVE A JOB INTERVIEW TOMORROW.
A TOAST TO A GREAT JOB INTERVIEW.
LIFE IS A WASTE OF TIME, TIME IS A WASTE OF LIFE, SO LET'S GET WASTED AND HAVE THE TIME OF OUR LIFE!
HA!
THERE IS ONE I HEARD YESTERDAY AT THE BAR.
WOULD YOU LIKE TO HEAR IT?
GO FOR IT!

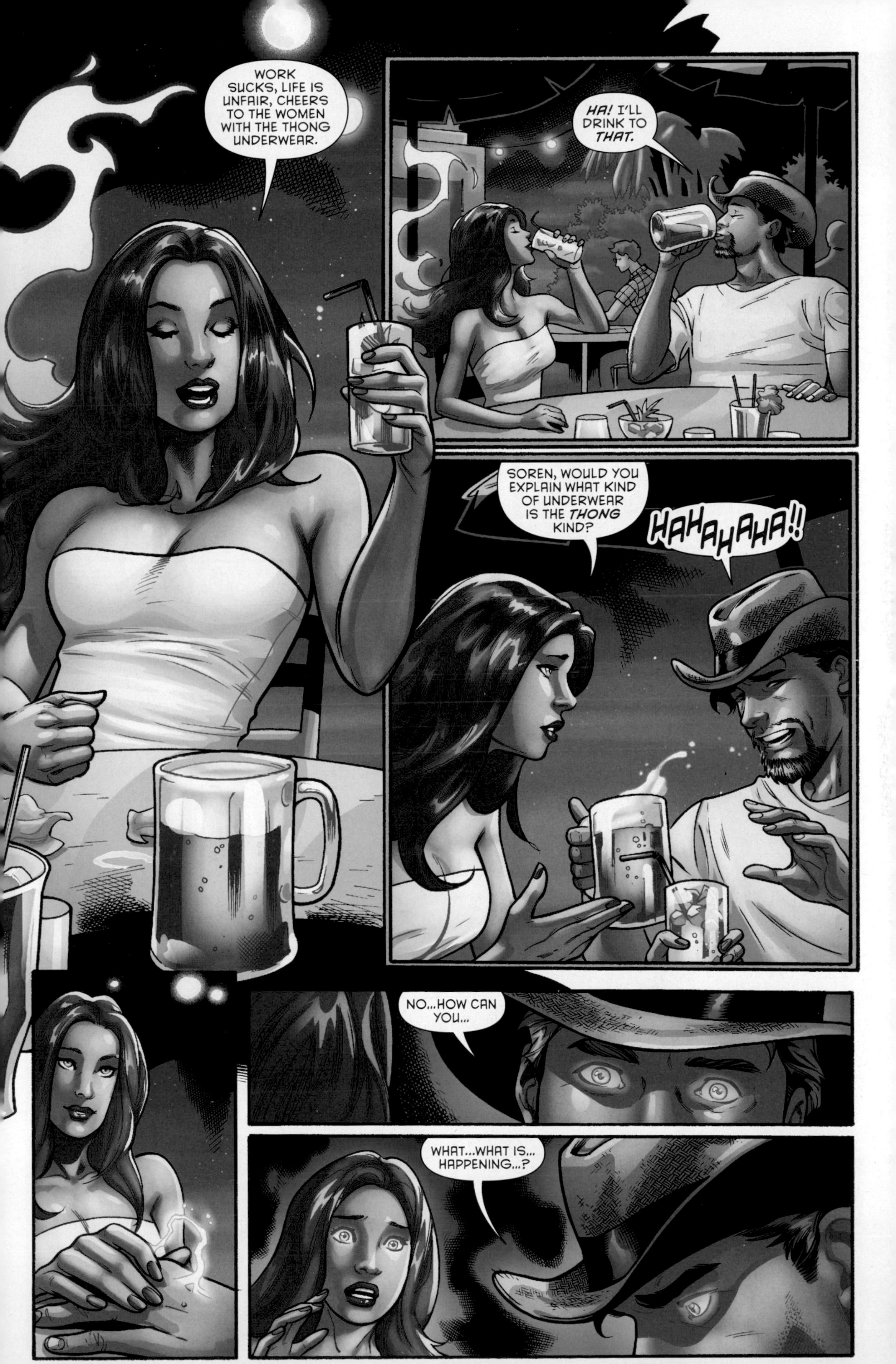
WORK SUCKS, LIFE IS UNFAIR, CHEERS TO THE WOMEN WITH THE THONG UNDERWEAR.
HA! I'LL DRINK TO *THAT.*
SOREN, WOULD YOU EXPLAIN WHAT KIND OF UNDERWEAR IS THE *THONG* KIND?
HAHAHAHA!!
NO...HOW CAN YOU...
WHAT...WHAT IS... HAPPENING...?

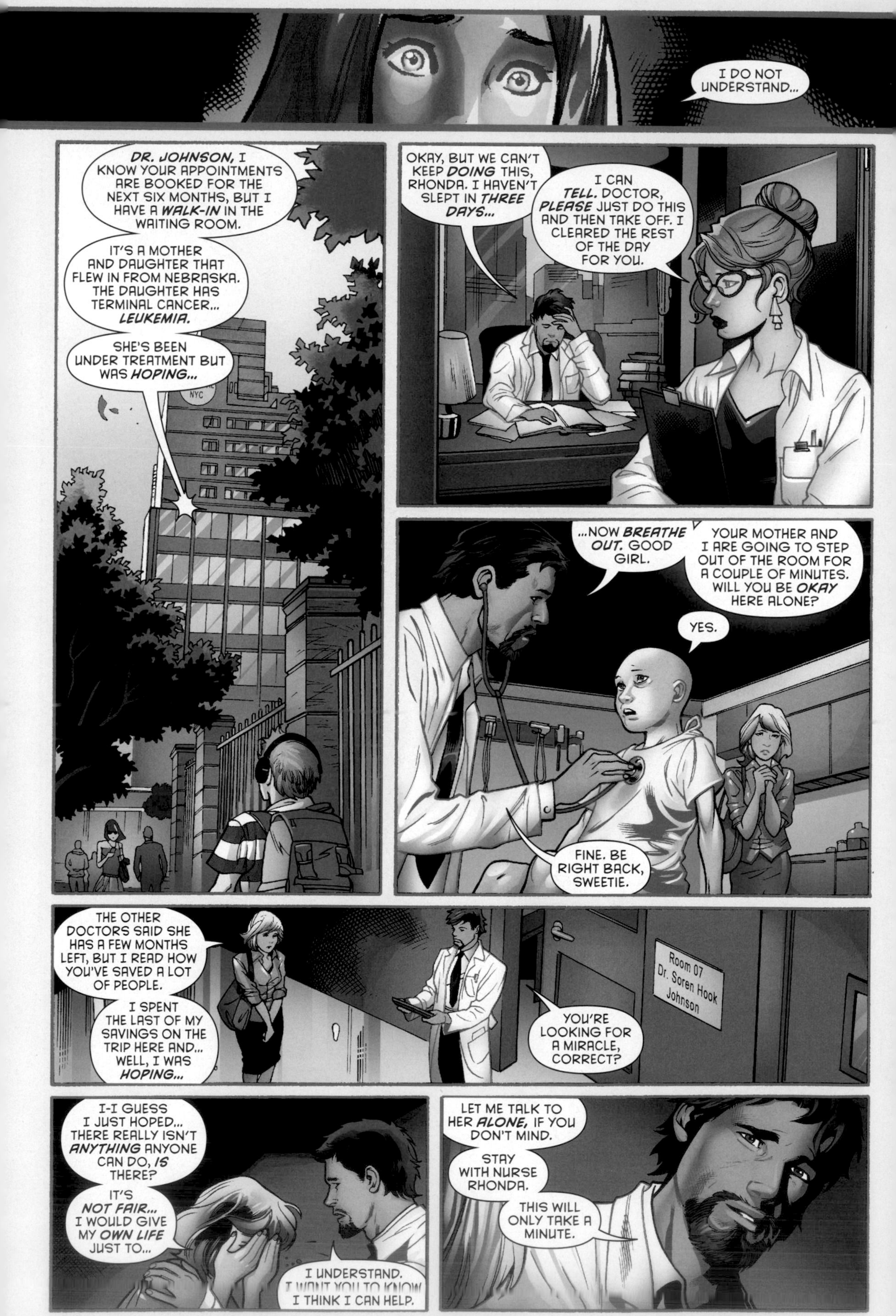
I DO NOT UNDERSTAND...
DR. JOHNSON, I KNOW YOUR APPOINTMENTS ARE BOOKED FOR THE NEXT SIX MONTHS, BUT I HAVE A WALK-IN IN THE WAITING ROOM.
IT'S A MOTHER AND DAUGHTER THAT FLEW IN FROM NEBRASKA. THE DAUGHTER HAS TERMINAL CANCER... LEUKEMIA.
SHE'S BEEN UNDER TREATMENT BUT WAS HOPING...
NYC
OKAY, BUT WE CAN'T KEEP DOING THIS, RHONDA. I HAVEN'T SLEPT IN THREE DAYS...
I CAN TELL. DOCTOR, PLEASE JUST DO THIS AND THEN TAKE OFF. I CLEARED THE REST OF THE DAY FOR YOU.
...NOW BREATHE OUT. GOOD GIRL.
YOUR MOTHER AND I ARE GOING TO STEP OUT OF THE ROOM FOR A COUPLE OF MINUTES. WILL YOU BE OKAY HERE ALONE?
YES.
FINE. BE RIGHT BACK, SWEETIE.
THE OTHER DOCTORS SAID SHE HAS A FEW MONTHS LEFT, BUT I READ HOW YOU'VE SAVED A LOT OF PEOPLE.
I SPENT THE LAST OF MY SAVINGS ON THE TRIP HERE AND... WELL, I WAS HOPING...
Room 07 Dr. Soren Hook Johnson
YOU'RE LOOKING FOR A MIRACLE, CORRECT?
I-I GUESS I JUST HOPED... THERE REALLY ISN'T ANYTHING ANYONE CAN DO, IS THERE?
IT'S NOT FAIR... I WOULD GIVE MY OWN LIFE JUST TO...
I UNDERSTAND. I WANT YOU TO KNOW I THINK I CAN HELP.
LET ME TALK TO HER ALONE, IF YOU DON'T MIND.
STAY WITH NURSE RHONDA.
THIS WILL ONLY TAKE A MINUTE.

JENNIE, I WANT YOU TO CLOSE YOUR EYES. THIS WILL ONLY TAKE A FEW SECONDS.

OKAY. WHAT SHOULD I DO?

TRY NOT TO SCREAM TOO LOUD.

AIEEEE!!

JENNIE!!

PLEASE, IT'S GOING TO BE OKAY.

WHAT IS HE DOING TO HER??

WHAT HAPPENED?

DOCTOR!

Ughhhh...

RHONDA, TAKE THEM BOTH TO THE LAB. RUN A COMPLETE SET OF TESTS.

YOU LOOK WORSE THAN USUAL.

I'LL BE FINE. DO AS I ASK.

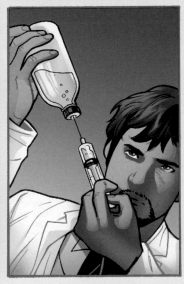

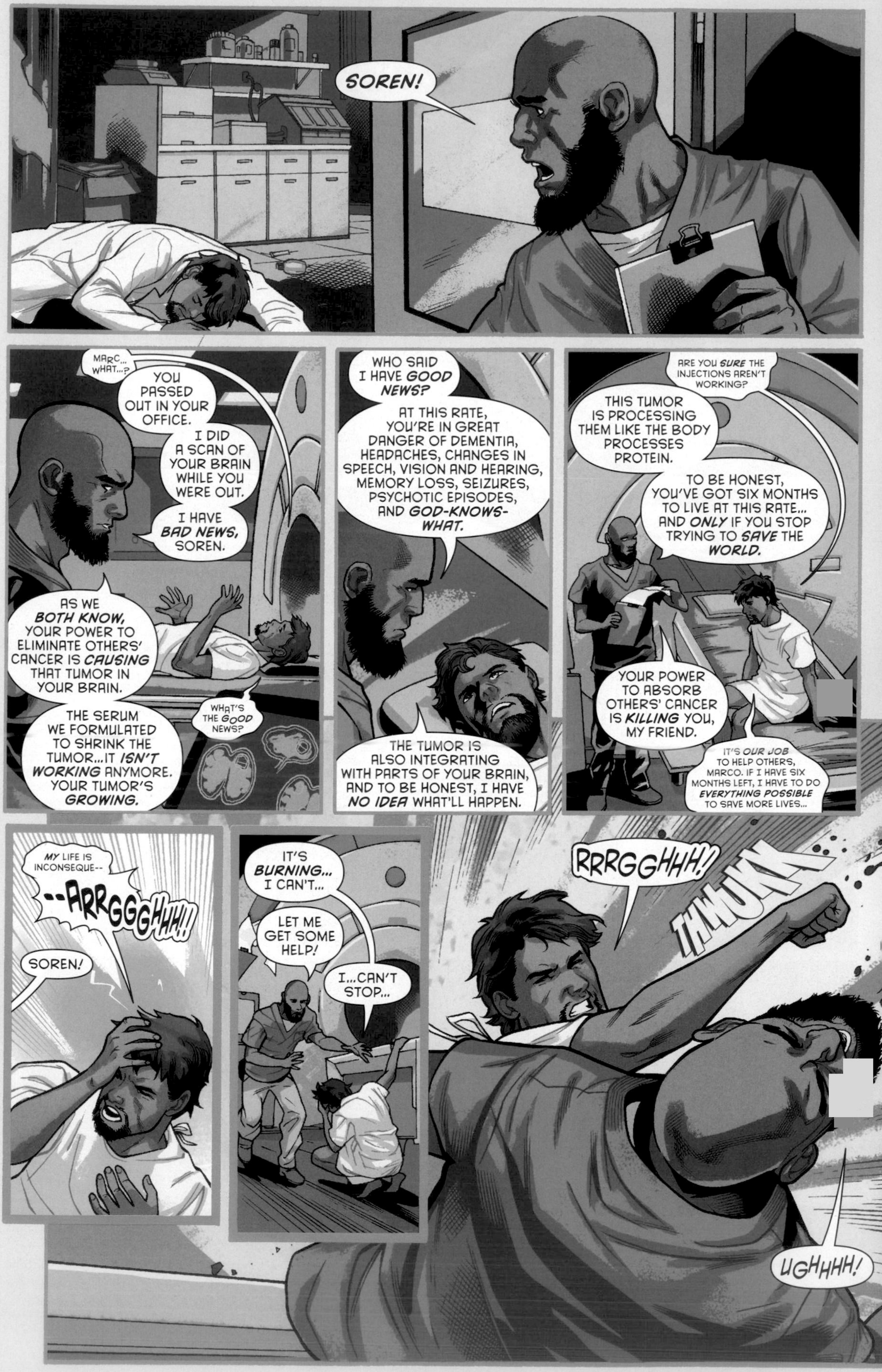
SOREN!
MARC... WHAT...?
YOU PASSED OUT IN YOUR OFFICE.
I DID A SCAN OF YOUR BRAIN WHILE YOU WERE OUT.
I HAVE BAD NEWS, SOREN.
AS WE BOTH KNOW, YOUR POWER TO ELIMINATE OTHERS' CANCER IS CAUSING THAT TUMOR IN YOUR BRAIN.
THE SERUM WE FORMULATED TO SHRINK THE TUMOR...IT ISN'T WORKING ANYMORE. YOUR TUMOR'S GROWING.
WHAT'S THE GOOD NEWS?
WHO SAID I HAVE GOOD NEWS?
AT THIS RATE, YOU'RE IN GREAT DANGER OF DEMENTIA, HEADACHES, CHANGES IN SPEECH, VISION AND HEARING, MEMORY LOSS, SEIZURES, PSYCHOTIC EPISODES, AND GOD-KNOWS-WHAT.
THE TUMOR IS ALSO INTEGRATING WITH PARTS OF YOUR BRAIN, AND TO BE HONEST, I HAVE NO IDEA WHAT'LL HAPPEN.
ARE YOU SURE THE INJECTIONS AREN'T WORKING?
THIS TUMOR IS PROCESSING THEM LIKE THE BODY PROCESSES PROTEIN.
TO BE HONEST, YOU'VE GOT SIX MONTHS TO LIVE AT THIS RATE... AND ONLY IF YOU STOP TRYING TO SAVE THE WORLD.
YOUR POWER TO ABSORB OTHERS' CANCER IS KILLING YOU, MY FRIEND.
IT'S OUR JOB TO HELP OTHERS, MARCO. IF I HAVE SIX MONTHS LEFT, I HAVE TO DO EVERYTHING POSSIBLE TO SAVE MORE LIVES...
MY LIFE IS INCONSEQUE--
--ARRGGGHHH!!
SOREN!
IT'S BURNING... I CAN'T...
LET ME GET SOME HELP!
I...CAN'T STOP...
RRRGGHHH!
THWUNK
UGHHHH!

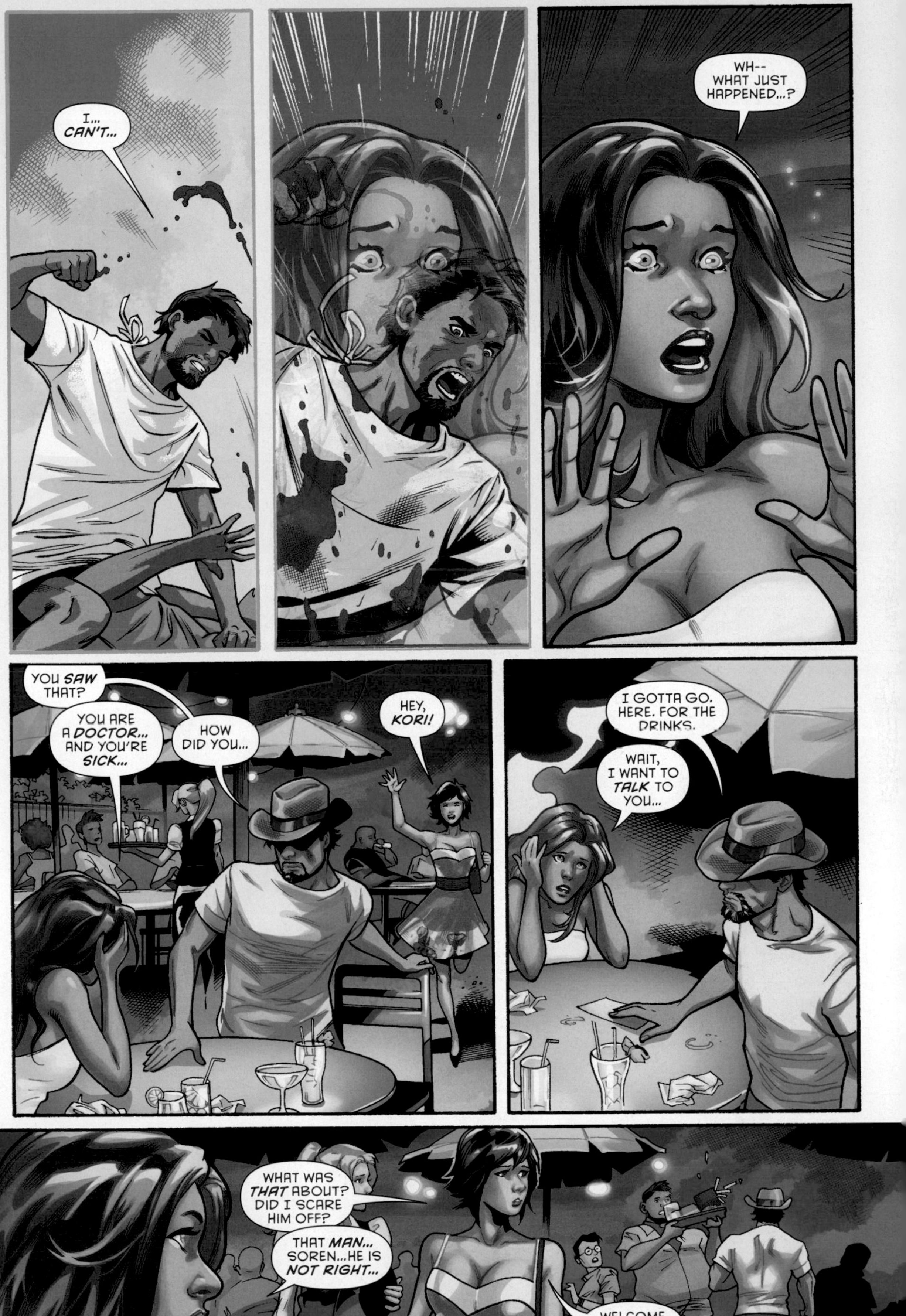

I... CAN'T...
WH-- WHAT JUST HAPPENED...?
YOU SAW THAT?
YOU ARE A DOCTOR... AND YOU'RE SICK...
HOW DID YOU...
HEY, KORI!
I GOTTA GO. HERE. FOR THE DRINKS.
WAIT, I WANT TO TALK TO YOU...
WHAT WAS THAT ABOUT? DID I SCARE HIM OFF?
THAT MAN... SOREN...HE IS NOT RIGHT...
WELCOME TO KEY WEST.

Missed Communication.

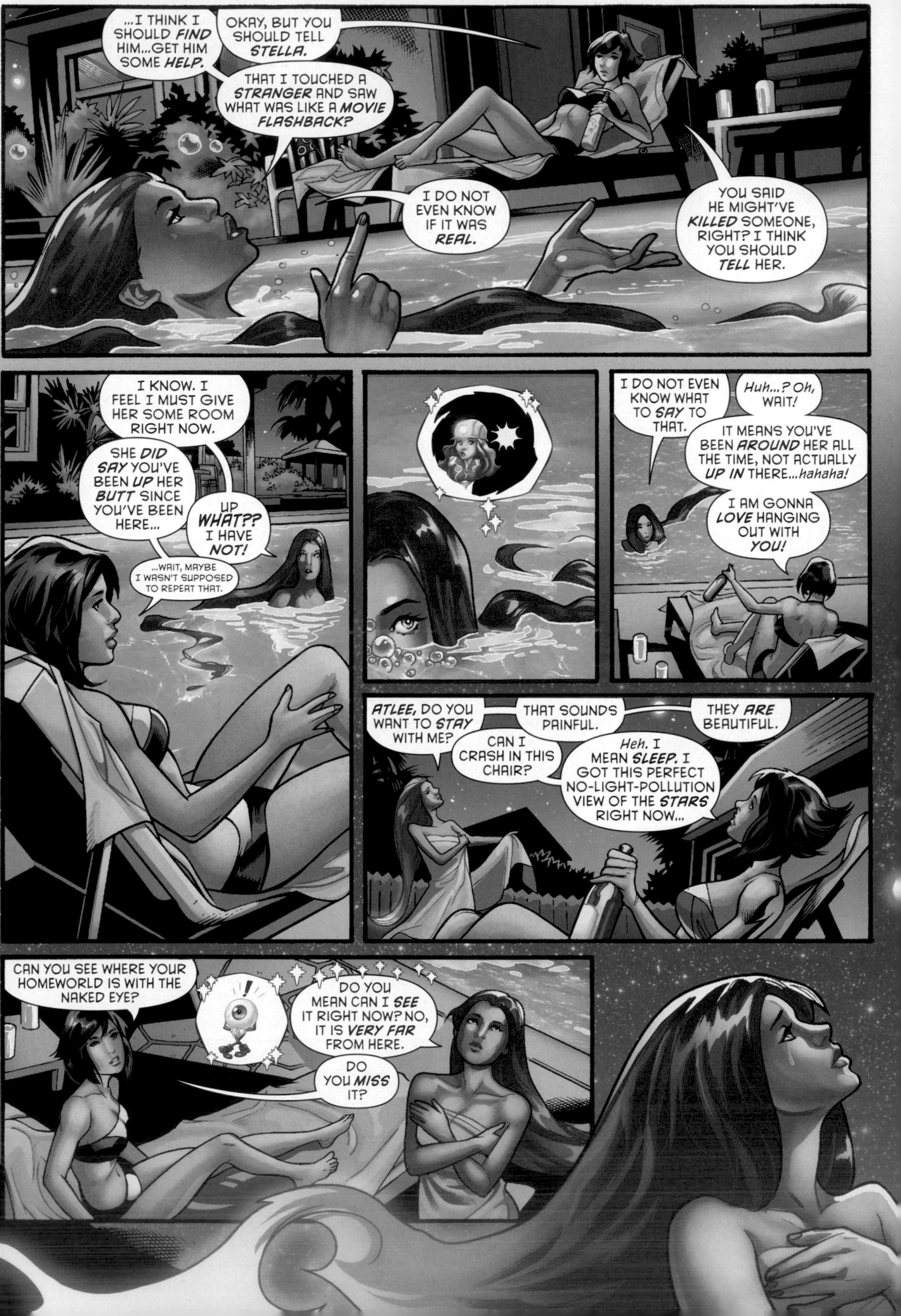

...I THINK I SHOULD FIND HIM...GET HIM SOME HELP.
OKAY, BUT YOU SHOULD TELL STELLA.
THAT I TOUCHED A STRANGER AND SAW WHAT WAS LIKE A MOVIE FLASHBACK?
I DO NOT EVEN KNOW IF IT WAS REAL.
YOU SAID HE MIGHT'VE KILLED SOMEONE, RIGHT? I THINK YOU SHOULD TELL HER.
I KNOW. I FEEL I MUST GIVE HER SOME ROOM RIGHT NOW.
SHE DID SAY YOU'VE BEEN UP HER BUTT SINCE YOU'VE BEEN HERE...
UP WHAT?? I HAVE NOT!
...WAIT, MAYBE I WASN'T SUPPOSED TO REPEAT THAT.
I DO NOT EVEN KNOW WHAT TO SAY TO THAT.
Huh...? Oh, WAIT!
IT MEANS YOU'VE BEEN AROUND HER ALL THE TIME, NOT ACTUALLY UP IN THERE...hahaha!
I AM GONNA LOVE HANGING OUT WITH YOU!
ATLEE, DO YOU WANT TO STAY WITH ME?
THAT SOUNDS PAINFUL.
THEY ARE BEAUTIFUL.
CAN I CRASH IN THIS CHAIR?
Heh. I MEAN SLEEP. I GOT THIS PERFECT NO-LIGHT-POLLUTION VIEW OF THE STARS RIGHT NOW...
CAN YOU SEE WHERE YOUR HOMEWORLD IS WITH THE NAKED EYE?
!
DO YOU MEAN CAN I SEE IT RIGHT NOW? NO, IT IS VERY FAR FROM HERE.
DO YOU MISS IT?

A New Plan.

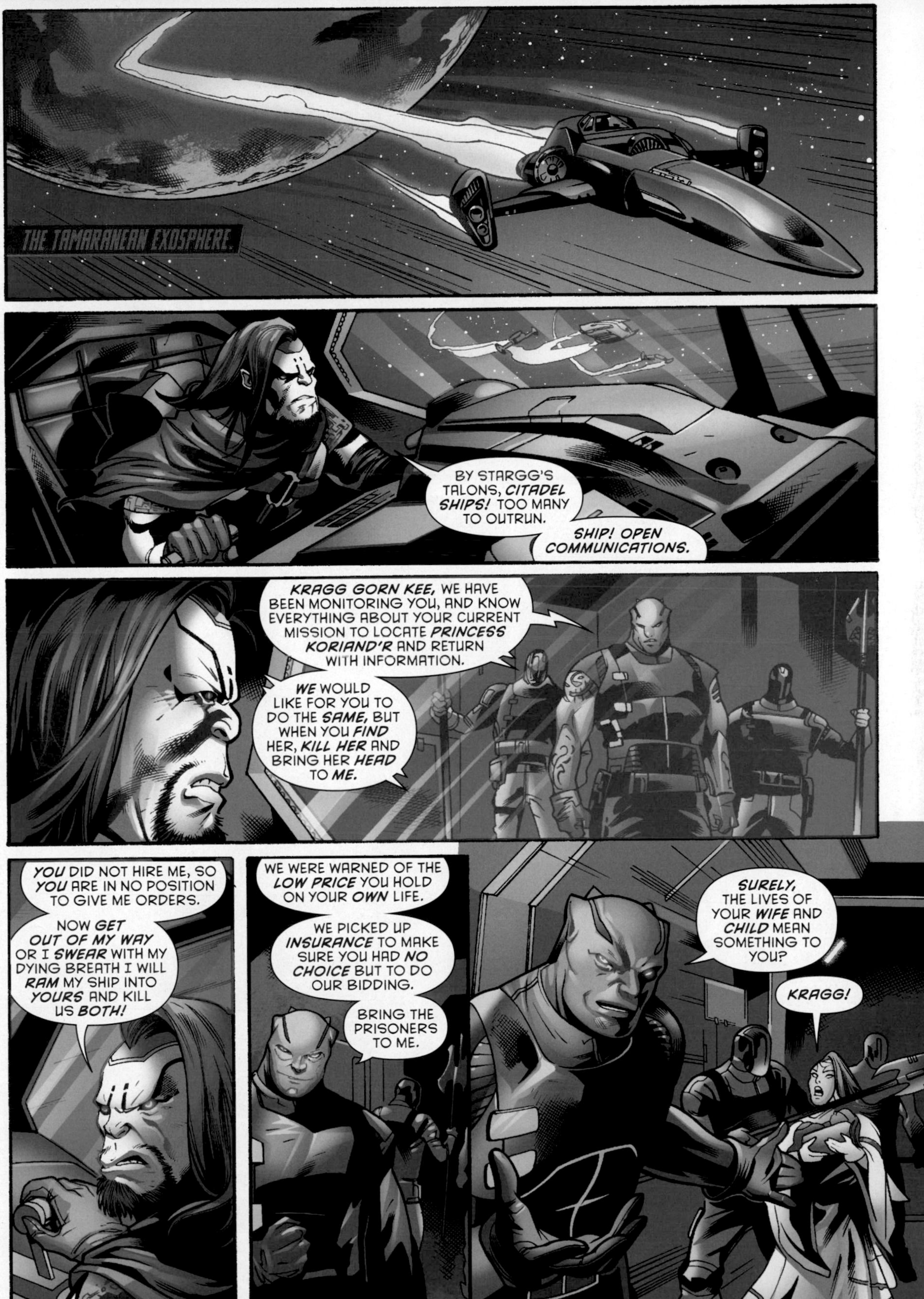
THE TAMARANEAN EXOSPHERE.
BY STARGG'S TALONS, CITADEL SHIPS! TOO MANY TO OUTRUN.
SHIP! OPEN COMMUNICATIONS.
KRAGG GORN KEE, WE HAVE BEEN MONITORING YOU, AND KNOW EVERYTHING ABOUT YOUR CURRENT MISSION TO LOCATE PRINCESS KORIAND'R AND RETURN WITH INFORMATION.
WE WOULD LIKE FOR YOU TO DO THE SAME, BUT WHEN YOU FIND HER, KILL HER AND BRING HER HEAD TO ME.
YOU DID NOT HIRE ME, SO YOU ARE IN NO POSITION TO GIVE ME ORDERS.
NOW GET OUT OF MY WAY OR I SWEAR WITH MY DYING BREATH I WILL RAM MY SHIP INTO YOURS AND KILL US BOTH!
WE WERE WARNED OF THE LOW PRICE YOU HOLD ON YOUR OWN LIFE.
WE PICKED UP INSURANCE TO MAKE SURE YOU HAD NO CHOICE BUT TO DO OUR BIDDING.
BRING THE PRISONERS TO ME.
SURELY, THE LIVES OF YOUR WIFE AND CHILD MEAN SOMETHING TO YOU?
KRAGG!

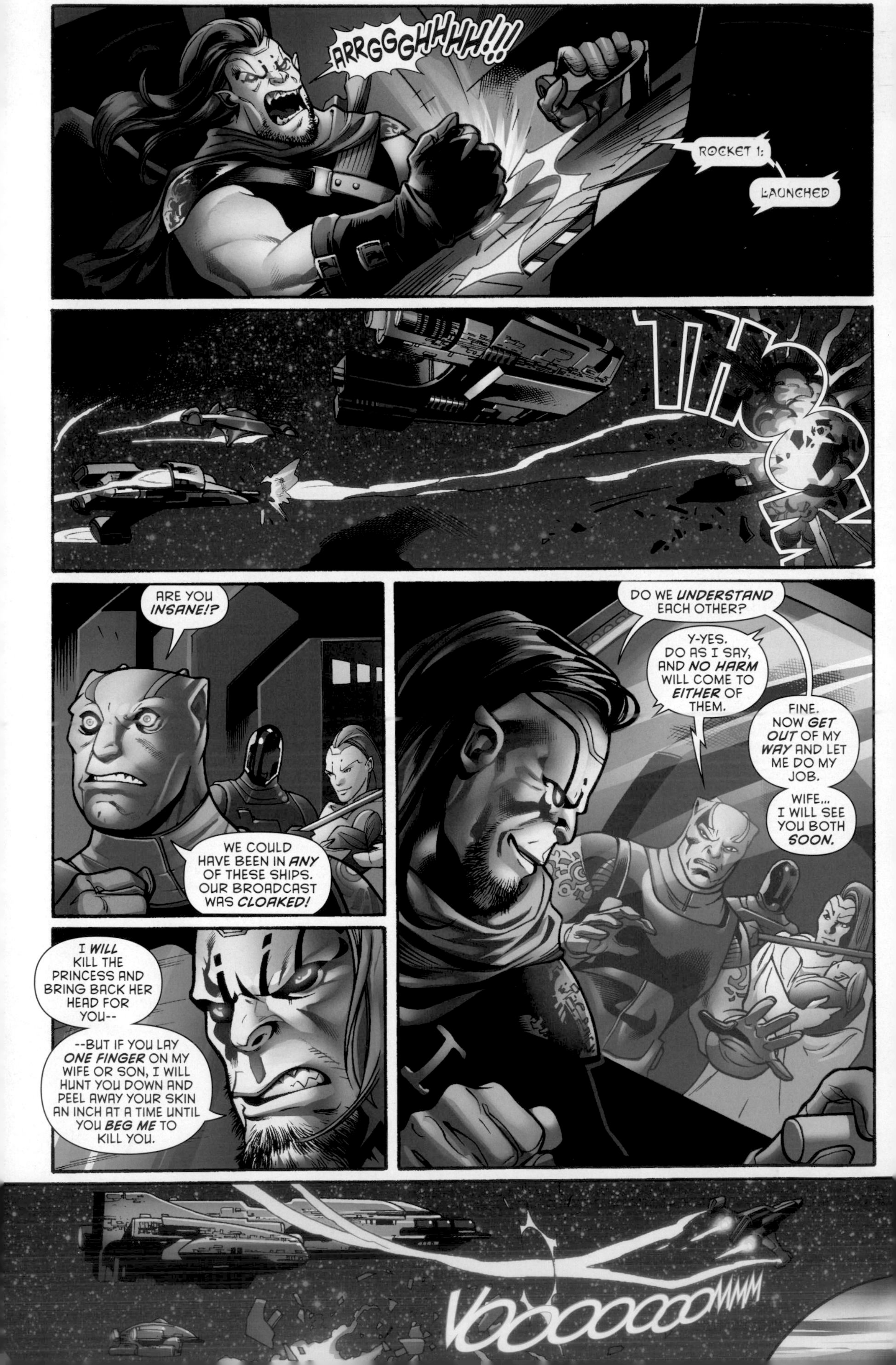
ARRGGGHHHH!!!
ROCKET 1:
LAUNCHED
ARE YOU INSANE!?
WE COULD HAVE BEEN IN ANY OF THESE SHIPS. OUR BROADCAST WAS CLOAKED!
I WILL KILL THE PRINCESS AND BRING BACK HER HEAD FOR YOU--
--BUT IF YOU LAY ONE FINGER ON MY WIFE OR SON, I WILL HUNT YOU DOWN AND PEEL AWAY YOUR SKIN AN INCH AT A TIME UNTIL YOU BEG ME TO KILL YOU.
DO WE UNDERSTAND EACH OTHER?
Y-YES. DO AS I SAY, AND NO HARM WILL COME TO EITHER OF THEM.
FINE. NOW GET OUT OF MY WAY AND LET ME DO MY JOB.
WIFE... I WILL SEE YOU BOTH SOON.
VOOOOOOOOMMM

Internal Maternal Nocturnal Kernel.

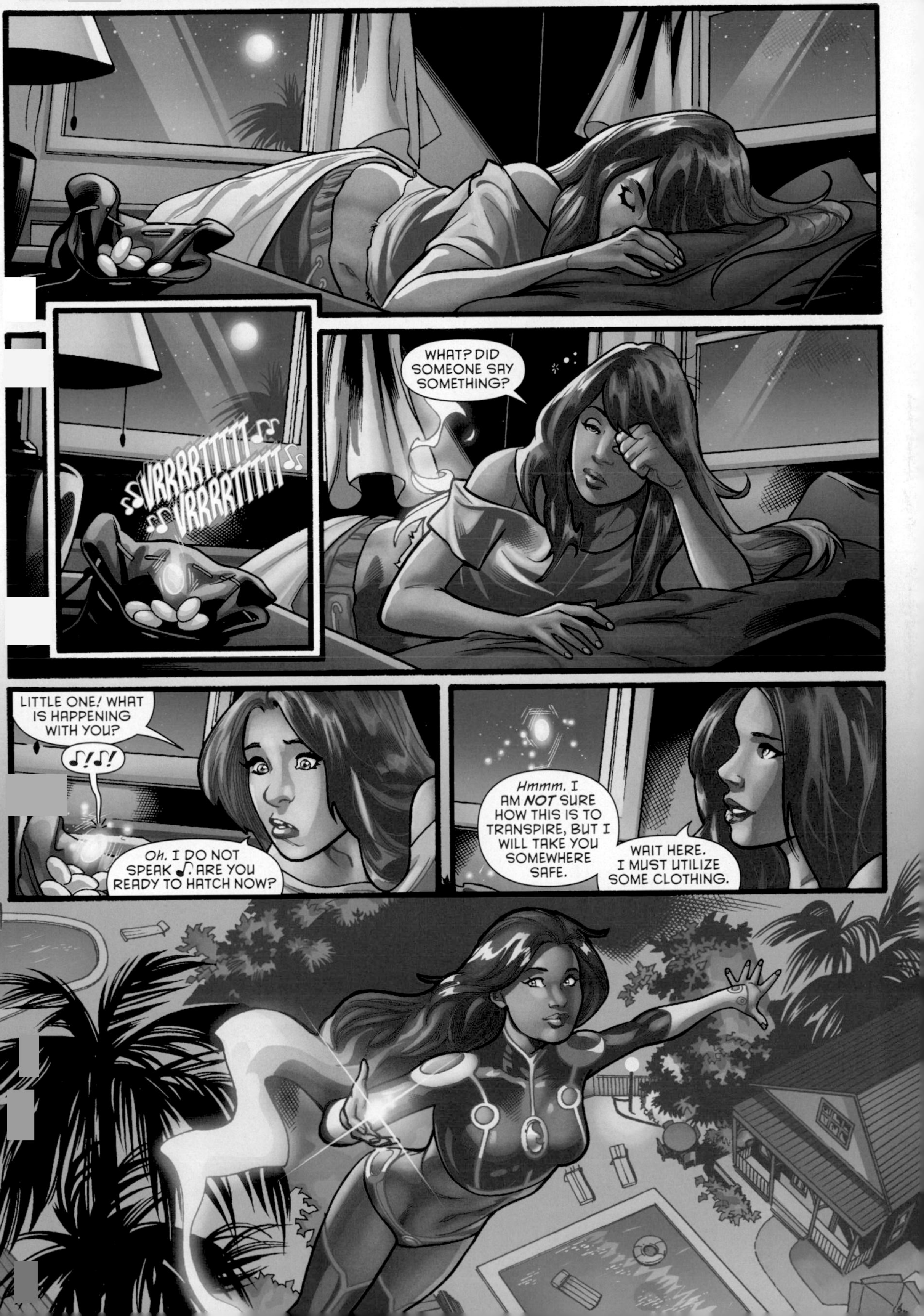

♫VRRRTTTTTT♫
♫VRRRRTTTTTT♫
WHAT? DID SOMEONE SAY SOMETHING?
LITTLE ONE! WHAT IS HAPPENING WITH YOU?
♪!♪!
Oh. I DO NOT SPEAK ♪. ARE YOU READY TO HATCH NOW?
Hmmm. I AM NOT SURE HOW THIS IS TO TRANSPIRE, BUT I WILL TAKE YOU SOMEWHERE SAFE.
WAIT HERE. I MUST UTILIZE SOME CLOTHING.

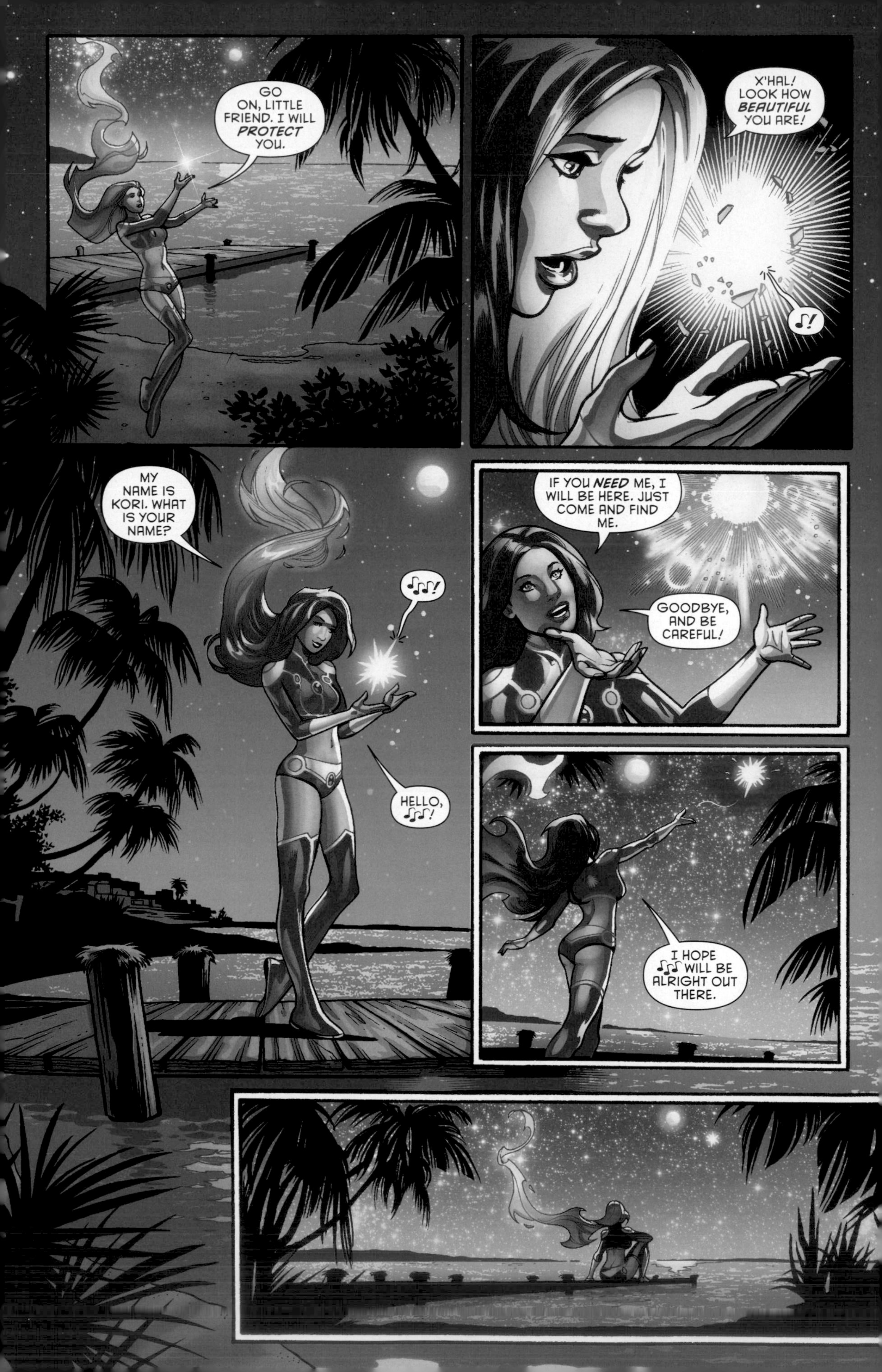
GO ON, LITTLE FRIEND. I WILL PROTECT YOU.
X'HAL! LOOK HOW BEAUTIFUL YOU ARE!
♪!
MY NAME IS KORI. WHAT IS YOUR NAME?
♫♪!
HELLO, ♫♪!
IF YOU NEED ME, I WILL BE HERE. JUST COME AND FIND ME.
GOODBYE, AND BE CAREFUL!
I HOPE ♫♪ WILL BE ALRIGHT OUT THERE.

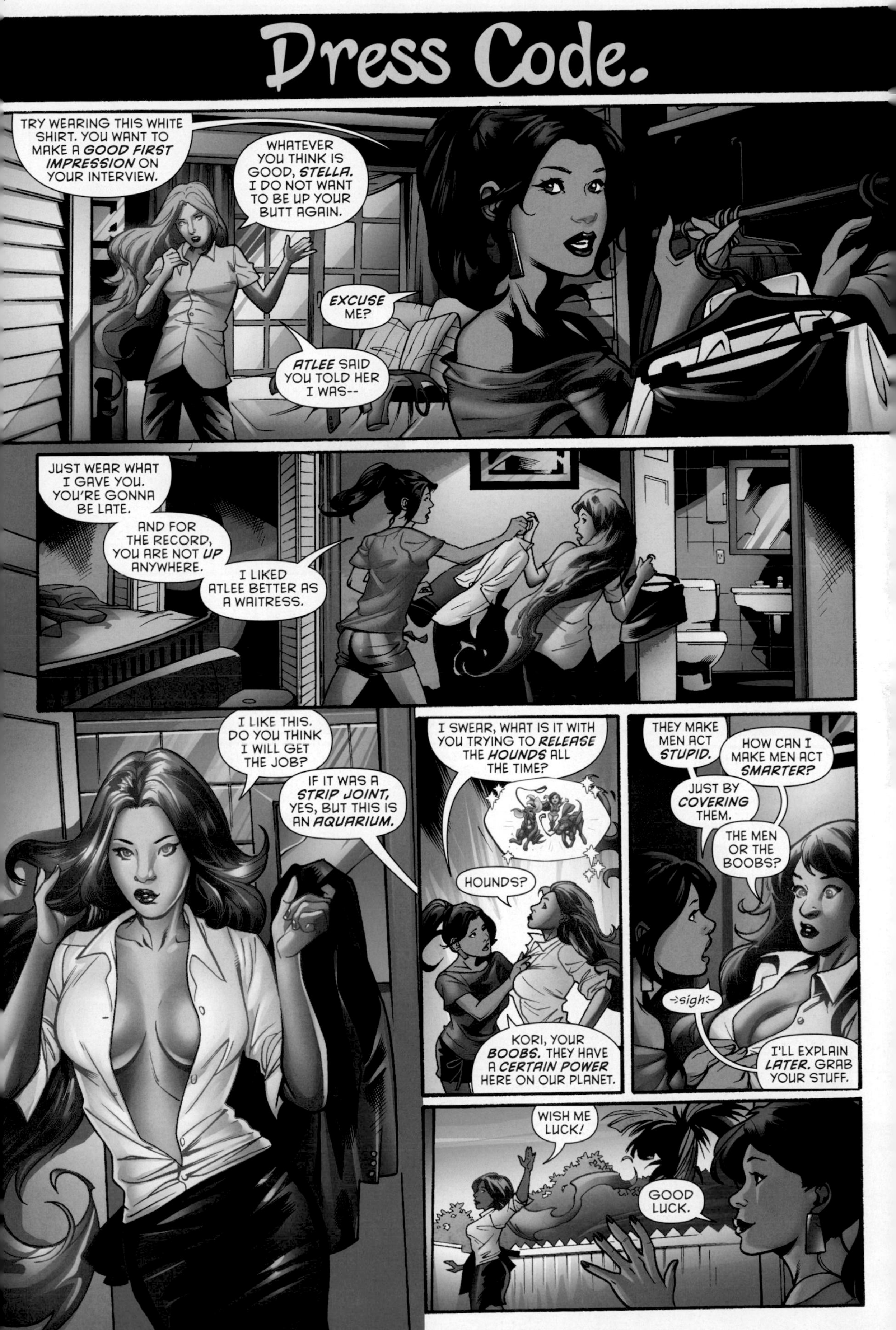
Dress Code.
TRY WEARING THIS WHITE SHIRT. YOU WANT TO MAKE A GOOD FIRST IMPRESSION ON YOUR INTERVIEW.
WHATEVER YOU THINK IS GOOD, STELLA. I DO NOT WANT TO BE UP YOUR BUTT AGAIN.
EXCUSE ME?
ATLEE SAID YOU TOLD HER I WAS--
JUST WEAR WHAT I GAVE YOU. YOU'RE GONNA BE LATE.
AND FOR THE RECORD, YOU ARE NOT UP ANYWHERE.
I LIKED ATLEE BETTER AS A WAITRESS.
I LIKE THIS. DO YOU THINK I WILL GET THE JOB?
IF IT WAS A STRIP JOINT, YES, BUT THIS IS AN AQUARIUM.
I SWEAR, WHAT IS IT WITH YOU TRYING TO RELEASE THE HOUNDS ALL THE TIME?
HOUNDS?
KORI, YOUR BOOBS. THEY HAVE A CERTAIN POWER HERE ON OUR PLANET.
THEY MAKE MEN ACT STUPID.
HOW CAN I MAKE MEN ACT SMARTER?
JUST BY COVERING THEM.
THE MEN OR THE BOOBS?
-sigh-
I'LL EXPLAIN LATER. GRAB YOUR STUFF.
WISH ME LUCK!
GOOD LUCK.

No One You See... Is Brighter Than She!

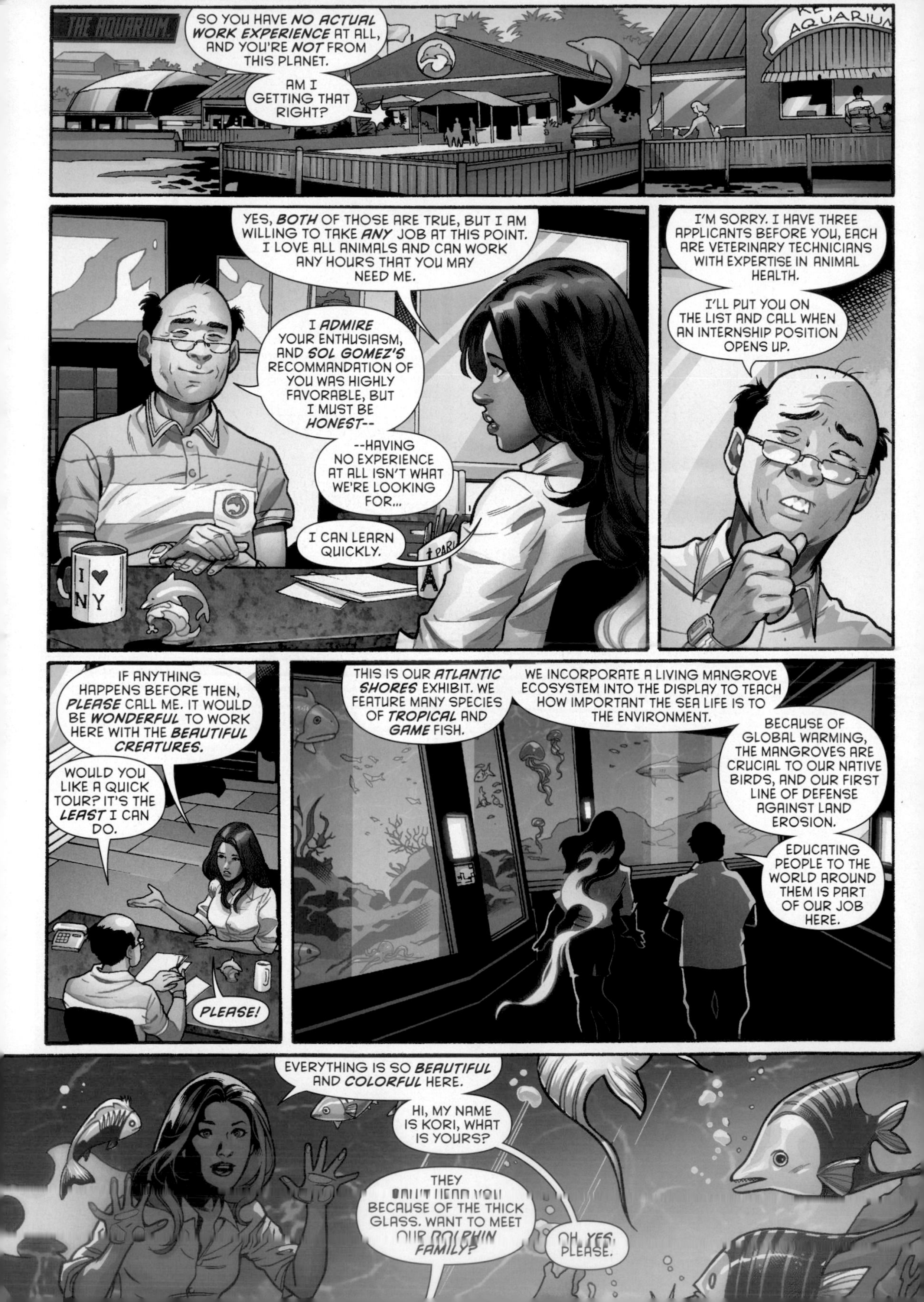
THE AQUARIUM.
KEY ... AQUARIUM
SO YOU HAVE NO ACTUAL WORK EXPERIENCE AT ALL, AND YOU'RE NOT FROM THIS PLANET.
AM I GETTING THAT RIGHT?
YES, BOTH OF THOSE ARE TRUE, BUT I AM WILLING TO TAKE ANY JOB AT THIS POINT. I LOVE ALL ANIMALS AND CAN WORK ANY HOURS THAT YOU MAY NEED ME.
I ADMIRE YOUR ENTHUSIASM, AND SOL GOMEZ'S RECOMMANDATION OF YOU WAS HIGHLY FAVORABLE, BUT I MUST BE HONEST--
--HAVING NO EXPERIENCE AT ALL ISN'T WHAT WE'RE LOOKING FOR...
I CAN LEARN QUICKLY.
I ♥ NY
PARI
I'M SORRY. I HAVE THREE APPLICANTS BEFORE YOU, EACH ARE VETERINARY TECHNICIANS WITH EXPERTISE IN ANIMAL HEALTH.
I'LL PUT YOU ON THE LIST AND CALL WHEN AN INTERNSHIP POSITION OPENS UP.
IF ANYTHING HAPPENS BEFORE THEN, PLEASE CALL ME. IT WOULD BE WONDERFUL TO WORK HERE WITH THE BEAUTIFUL CREATURES.
WOULD YOU LIKE A QUICK TOUR? IT'S THE LEAST I CAN DO.
PLEASE!
THIS IS OUR ATLANTIC SHORES EXHIBIT. WE FEATURE MANY SPECIES OF TROPICAL AND GAME FISH.
WE INCORPORATE A LIVING MANGROVE ECOSYSTEM INTO THE DISPLAY TO TEACH HOW IMPORTANT THE SEA LIFE IS TO THE ENVIRONMENT.
BECAUSE OF GLOBAL WARMING, THE MANGROVES ARE CRUCIAL TO OUR NATIVE BIRDS, AND OUR FIRST LINE OF DEFENSE AGAINST LAND EROSION.
EDUCATING PEOPLE TO THE WORLD AROUND THEM IS PART OF OUR JOB HERE.
EVERYTHING IS SO BEAUTIFUL AND COLORFUL HERE.
HI, MY NAME IS KORI, WHAT IS YOURS?
THEY CAN'T HEAR YOU BECAUSE OF THE THICK GLASS. WANT TO MEET OUR DOLPHIN FAMILY?
OH, YES, PLEASE.

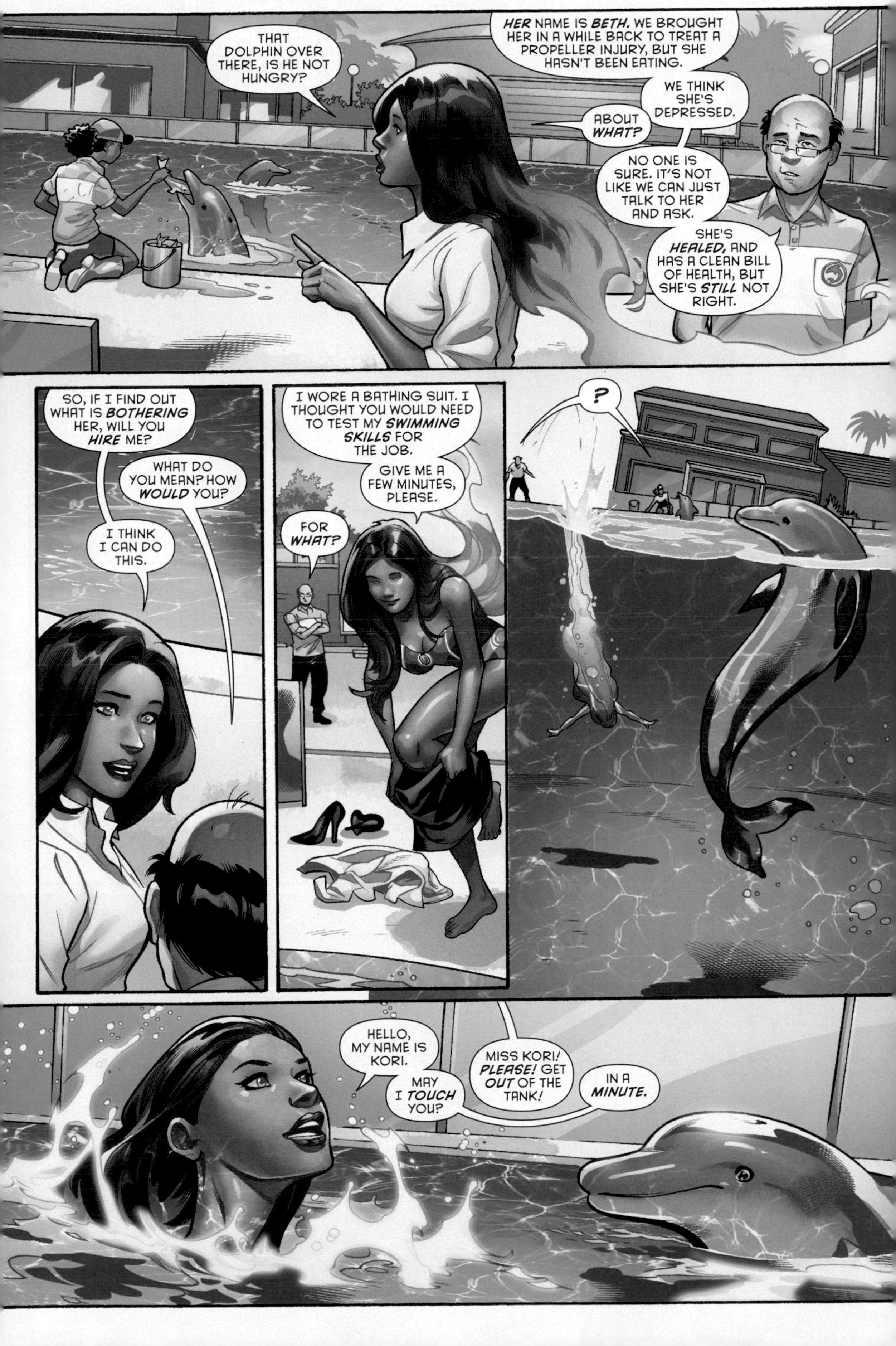

THAT DOLPHIN OVER THERE, IS HE NOT HUNGRY?
HER NAME IS BETH. WE BROUGHT HER IN A WHILE BACK TO TREAT A PROPELLER INJURY, BUT SHE HASN'T BEEN EATING.
WE THINK SHE'S DEPRESSED.
ABOUT WHAT?
NO ONE IS SURE. IT'S NOT LIKE WE CAN JUST TALK TO HER AND ASK.
SHE'S HEALED, AND HAS A CLEAN BILL OF HEALTH, BUT SHE'S STILL NOT RIGHT.
SO, IF I FIND OUT WHAT IS BOTHERING HER, WILL YOU HIRE ME?
WHAT DO YOU MEAN? HOW WOULD YOU?
I THINK I CAN DO THIS.
I WORE A BATHING SUIT. I THOUGHT YOU WOULD NEED TO TEST MY SWIMMING SKILLS FOR THE JOB.
GIVE ME A FEW MINUTES, PLEASE.
FOR WHAT?
?
HELLO, MY NAME IS KORI.
MAY I TOUCH YOU?
MISS KORI! PLEASE! GET OUT OF THE TANK!
IN A MINUTE.

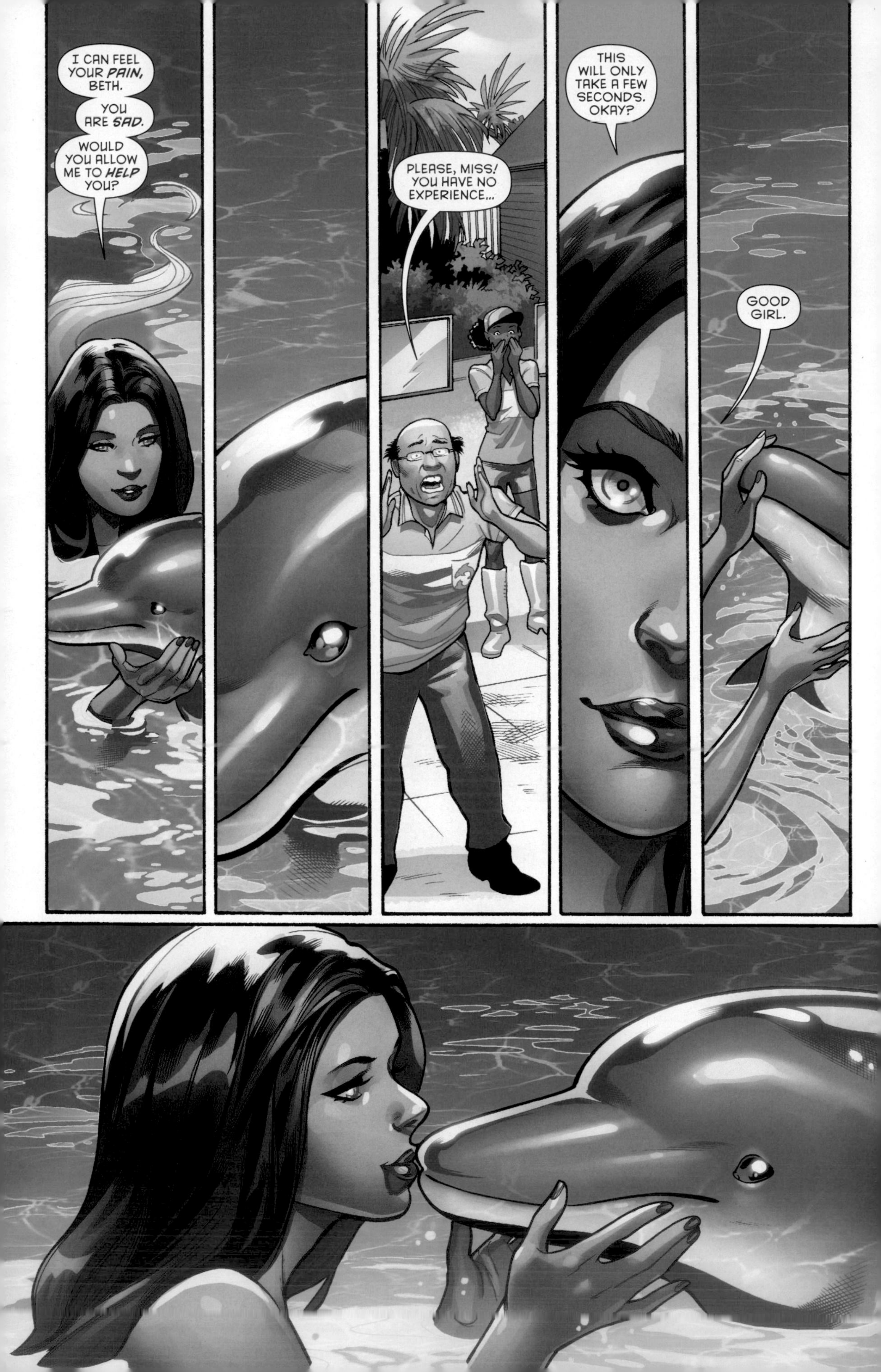
I CAN FEEL YOUR *PAIN*, BETH.
YOU ARE *SAD*.
WOULD YOU ALLOW ME TO *HELP* YOU?
PLEASE, MISS! YOU HAVE NO EXPERIENCE...
THIS WILL ONLY TAKE A FEW SECONDS. OKAY?
GOOD GIRL.

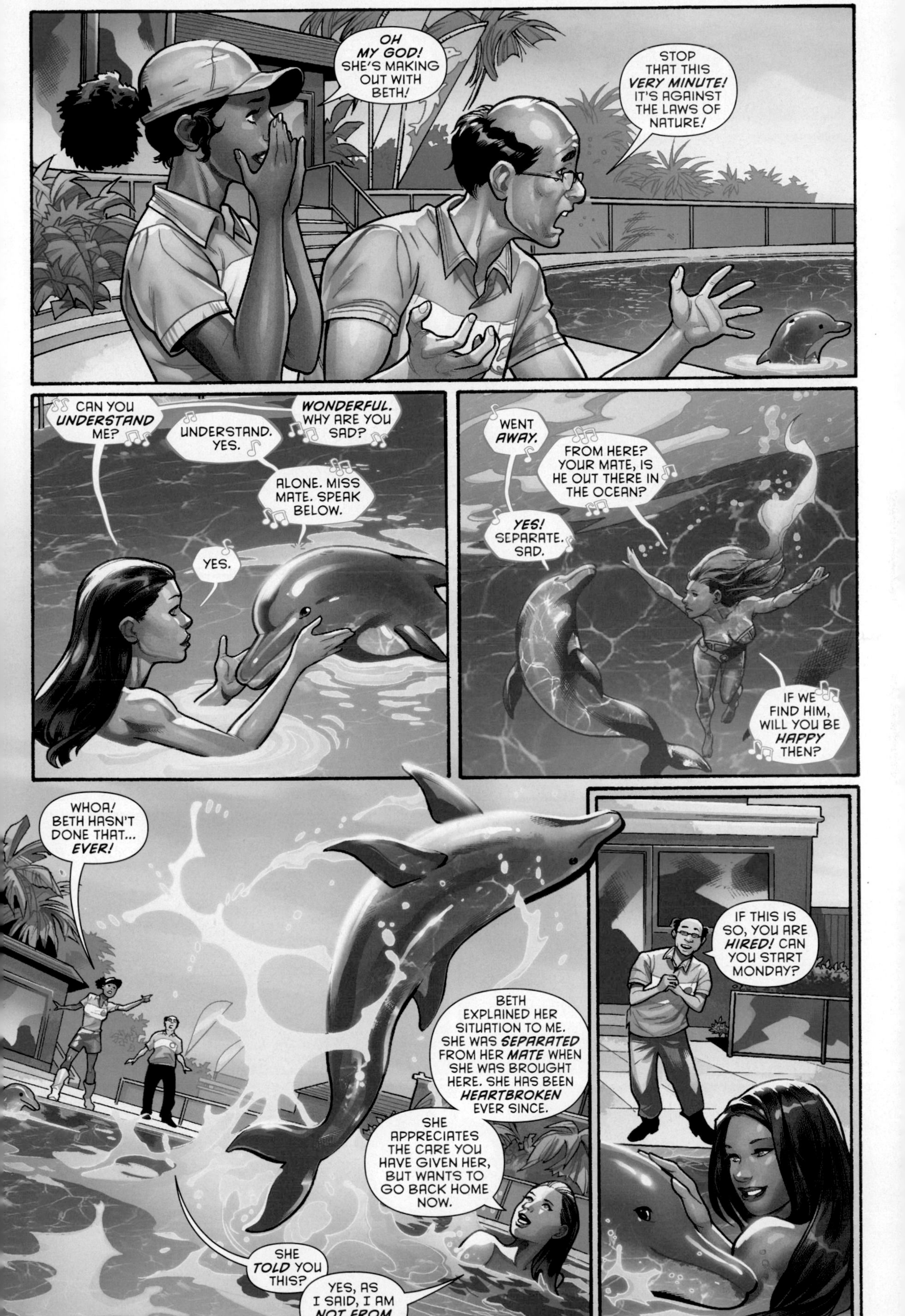
OH MY GOD! SHE'S MAKING OUT WITH BETH!
STOP THAT THIS VERY MINUTE! IT'S AGAINST THE LAWS OF NATURE!
CAN YOU UNDERSTAND ME?
UNDERSTAND. YES.
WONDERFUL. WHY ARE YOU SAD?
ALONE. MISS MATE. SPEAK BELOW.
YES.
WENT AWAY.
FROM HERE? YOUR MATE, IS HE OUT THERE IN THE OCEAN?
YES! SEPARATE. SAD.
IF WE FIND HIM, WILL YOU BE HAPPY THEN?
WHOA! BETH HASN'T DONE THAT... EVER!
BETH EXPLAINED HER SITUATION TO ME. SHE WAS SEPARATED FROM HER MATE WHEN SHE WAS BROUGHT HERE. SHE HAS BEEN HEARTBROKEN EVER SINCE.
SHE APPRECIATES THE CARE YOU HAVE GIVEN HER, BUT WANTS TO GO BACK HOME NOW.
SHE TOLD YOU THIS?
YES, AS I SAID, I AM NOT FROM THIS PLANET.
IF THIS IS SO, YOU ARE HIRED! CAN YOU START MONDAY?

Freaky Tiki Invitee.

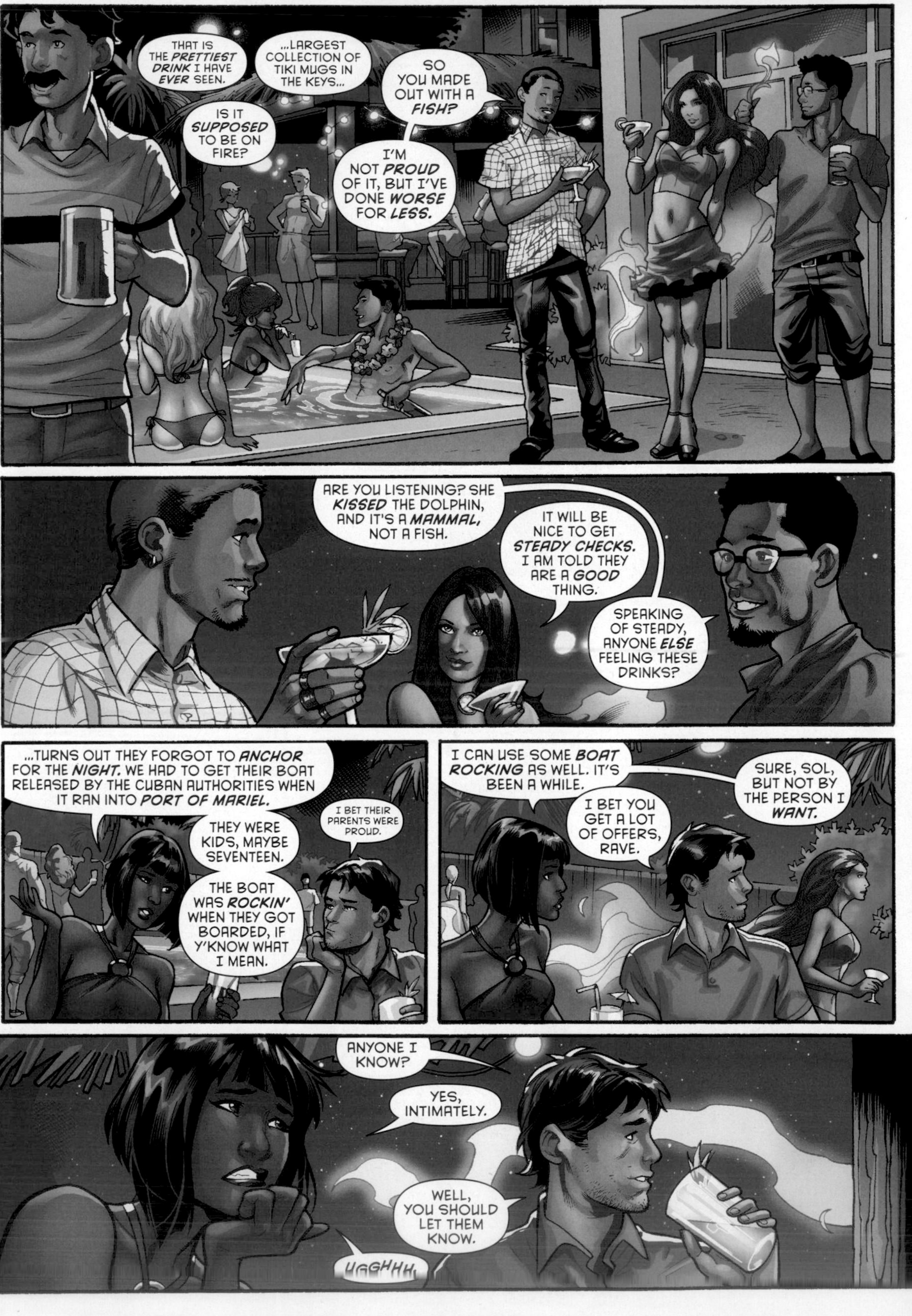

THAT IS THE PRETTIEST DRINK I HAVE EVER SEEN.
...LARGEST COLLECTION OF TIKI MUGS IN THE KEYS...
IS IT SUPPOSED TO BE ON FIRE?
SO YOU MADE OUT WITH A FISH?
I'M NOT PROUD OF IT, BUT I'VE DONE WORSE FOR LESS.
ARE YOU LISTENING? SHE KISSED THE DOLPHIN, AND IT'S A MAMMAL, NOT A FISH.
IT WILL BE NICE TO GET STEADY CHECKS. I AM TOLD THEY ARE A GOOD THING.
SPEAKING OF STEADY, ANYONE ELSE FEELING THESE DRINKS?
...TURNS OUT THEY FORGOT TO ANCHOR FOR THE NIGHT. WE HAD TO GET THEIR BOAT RELEASED BY THE CUBAN AUTHORITIES WHEN IT RAN INTO PORT OF MARIEL.
THEY WERE KIDS, MAYBE SEVENTEEN.
I BET THEIR PARENTS WERE PROUD.
THE BOAT WAS ROCKIN' WHEN THEY GOT BOARDED, IF Y'KNOW WHAT I MEAN.
I CAN USE SOME BOAT ROCKING AS WELL. IT'S BEEN A WHILE.
I BET YOU GET A LOT OF OFFERS, RAVE.
SURE, SOL, BUT NOT BY THE PERSON I WANT.
ANYONE I KNOW?
YES, INTIMATELY.
WELL, YOU SHOULD LET THEM KNOW.
UAGHHH

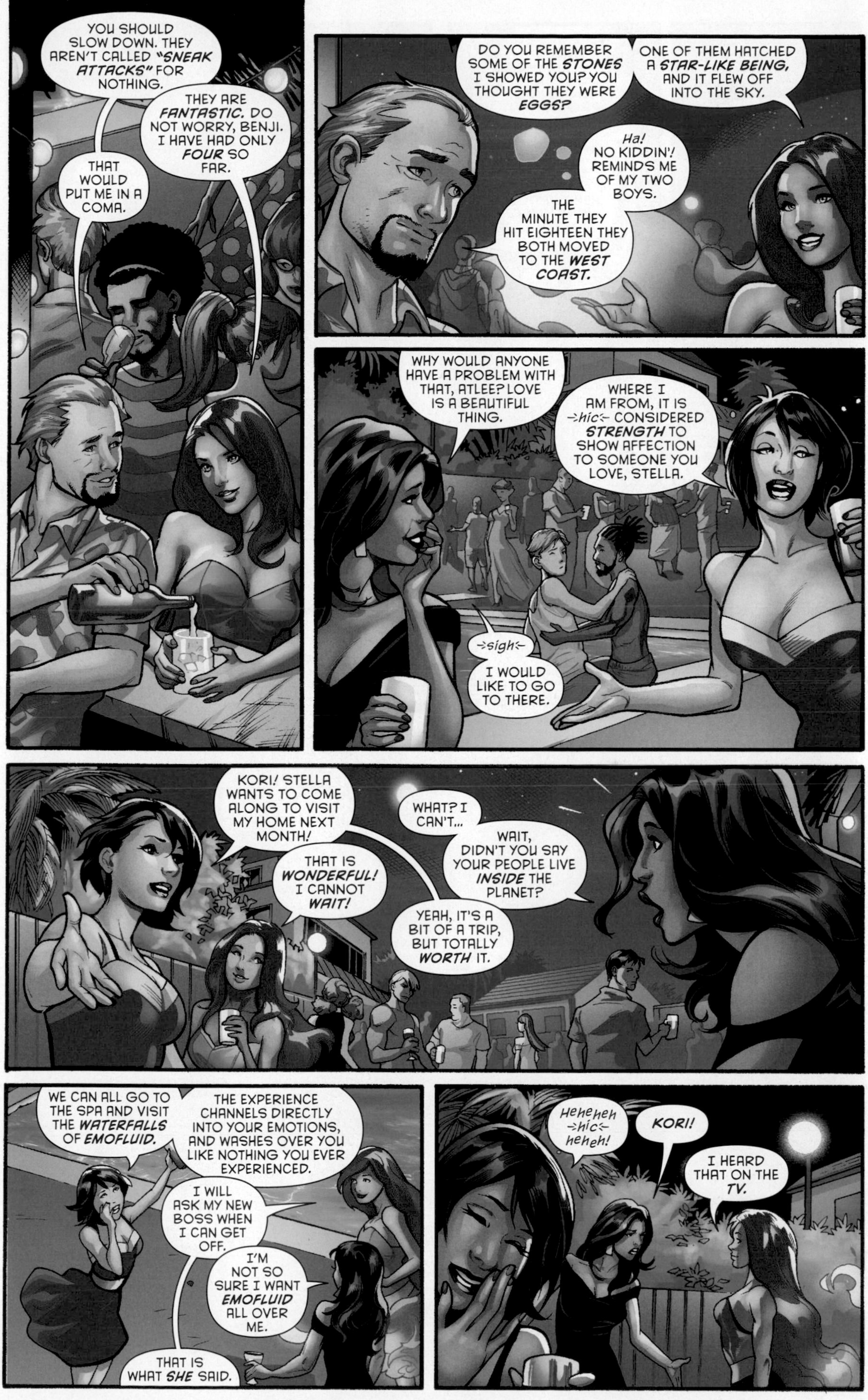
YOU SHOULD SLOW DOWN. THEY AREN'T CALLED "SNEAK ATTACKS" FOR NOTHING.
THEY ARE FANTASTIC. DO NOT WORRY, BENJI. I HAVE HAD ONLY FOUR SO FAR.
THAT WOULD PUT ME IN A COMA.
DO YOU REMEMBER SOME OF THE STONES I SHOWED YOU? YOU THOUGHT THEY WERE EGGS?
ONE OF THEM HATCHED A STAR-LIKE BEING, AND IT FLEW OFF INTO THE SKY.
Ha! NO KIDDIN'! REMINDS ME OF MY TWO BOYS.
THE MINUTE THEY HIT EIGHTEEN THEY BOTH MOVED TO THE WEST COAST.
WHY WOULD ANYONE HAVE A PROBLEM WITH THAT, ATLEE? LOVE IS A BEAUTIFUL THING.
WHERE I AM FROM, IT IS -hic- CONSIDERED STRENGTH TO SHOW AFFECTION TO SOMEONE YOU LOVE, STELLA.
-sigh-
I WOULD LIKE TO GO TO THERE.
KORI! STELLA WANTS TO COME ALONG TO VISIT MY HOME NEXT MONTH!
THAT IS WONDERFUL! I CANNOT WAIT!
WHAT? I CAN'T...
WAIT, DIDN'T YOU SAY YOUR PEOPLE LIVE INSIDE THE PLANET?
YEAH, IT'S A BIT OF A TRIP, BUT TOTALLY WORTH IT.
WE CAN ALL GO TO THE SPA AND VISIT THE WATERFALLS OF EMOFLUID.
THE EXPERIENCE CHANNELS DIRECTLY INTO YOUR EMOTIONS, AND WASHES OVER YOU LIKE NOTHING YOU EVER EXPERIENCED.
I WILL ASK MY NEW BOSS WHEN I CAN GET OFF.
I'M NOT SO SURE I WANT EMOFLUID ALL OVER ME.
THAT IS WHAT SHE SAID.
Heheheh -hic- heheh!
KORI!
I HEARD THAT ON THE TV.

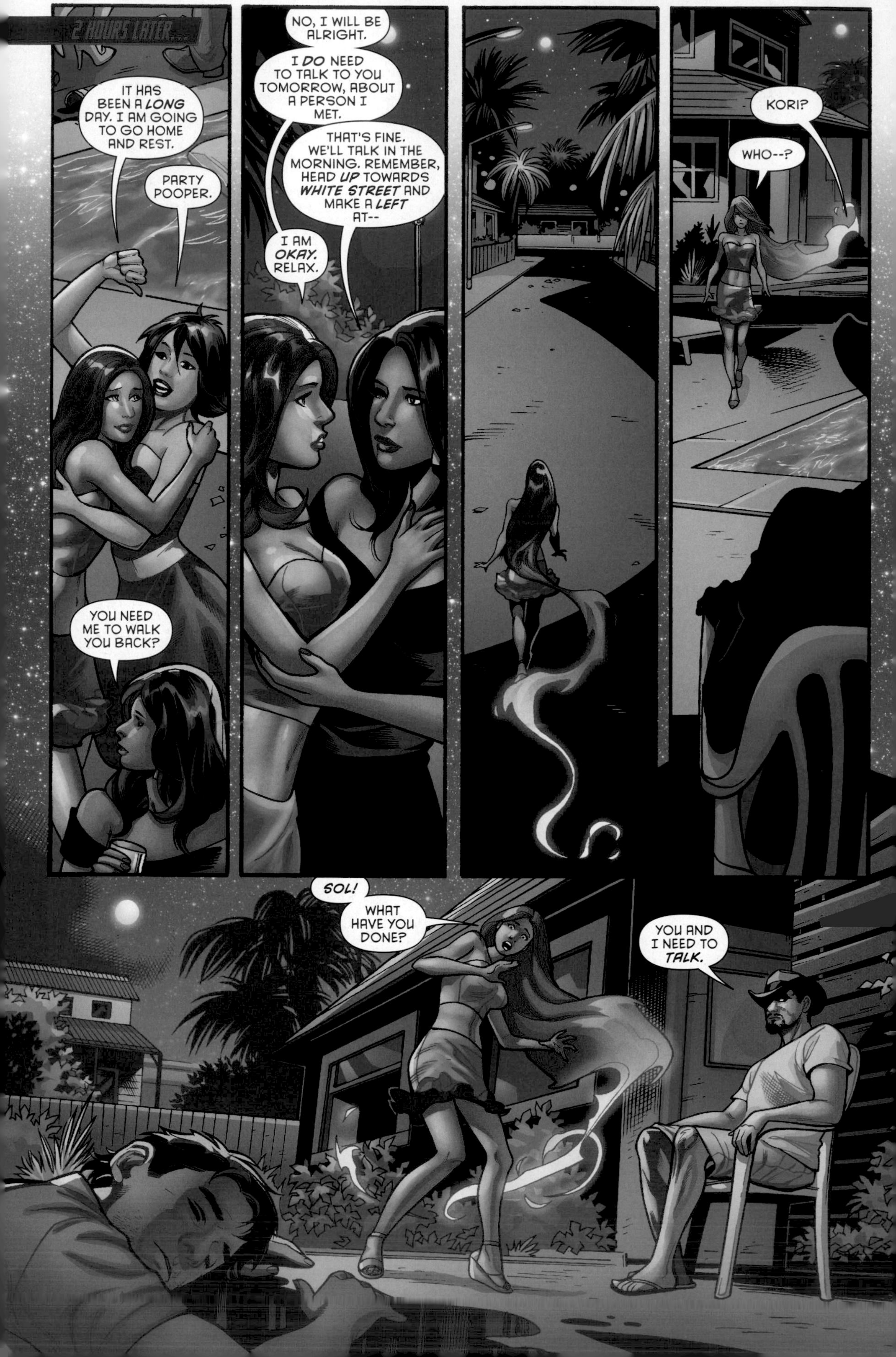
2 HOURS LATER...
IT HAS BEEN A LONG DAY. I AM GOING TO GO HOME AND REST.
PARTY POOPER.
YOU NEED ME TO WALK YOU BACK?
NO, I WILL BE ALRIGHT.
I DO NEED TO TALK TO YOU TOMORROW, ABOUT A PERSON I MET.
THAT'S FINE. WE'LL TALK IN THE MORNING. REMEMBER, HEAD UP TOWARDS WHITE STREET AND MAKE A LEFT AT--
I AM OKAY. RELAX.
KORI?
WHO--?
SOL!
WHAT HAVE YOU DONE?
YOU AND I NEED TO TALK.

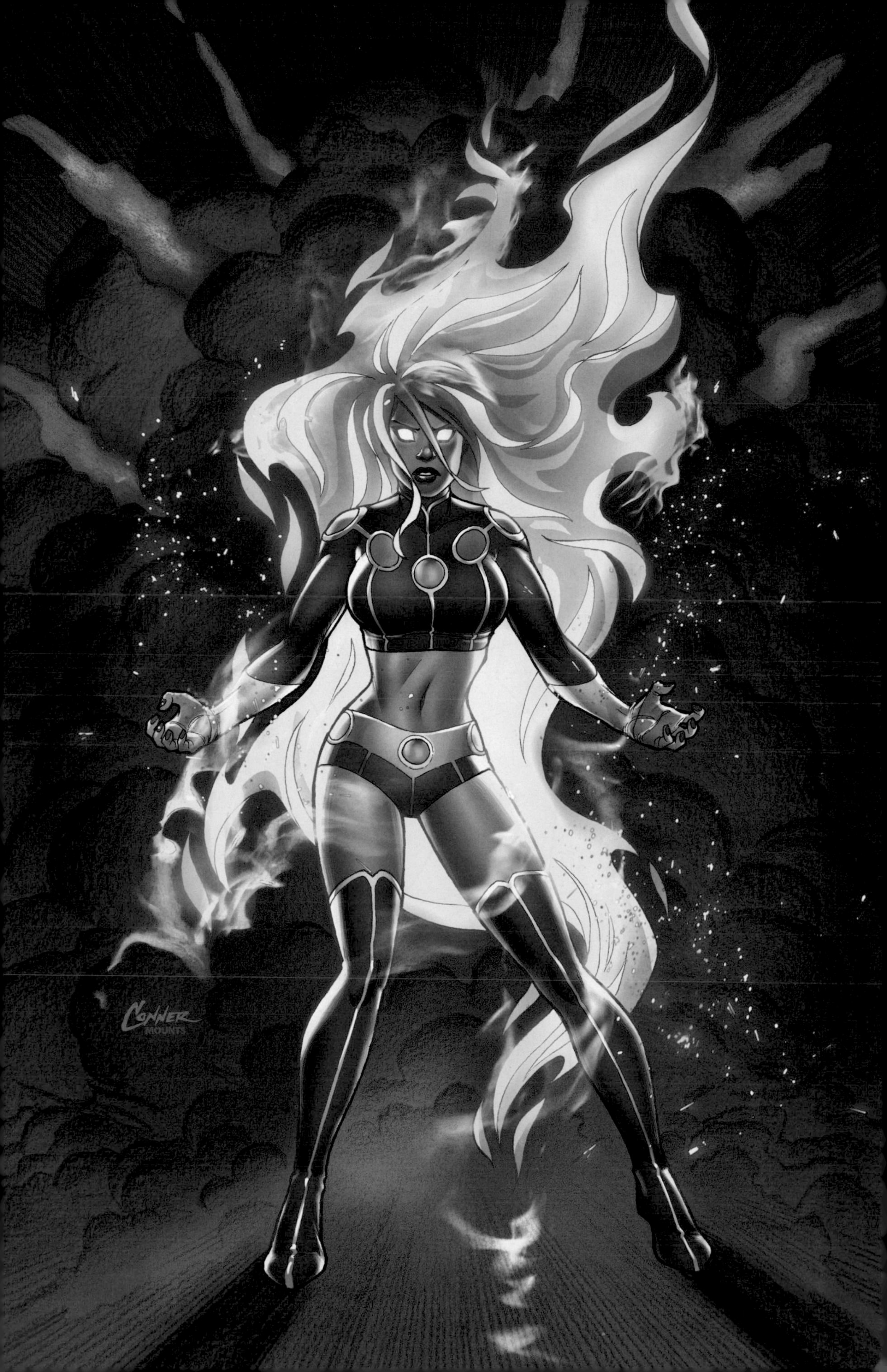
CONNER
MOUNTS

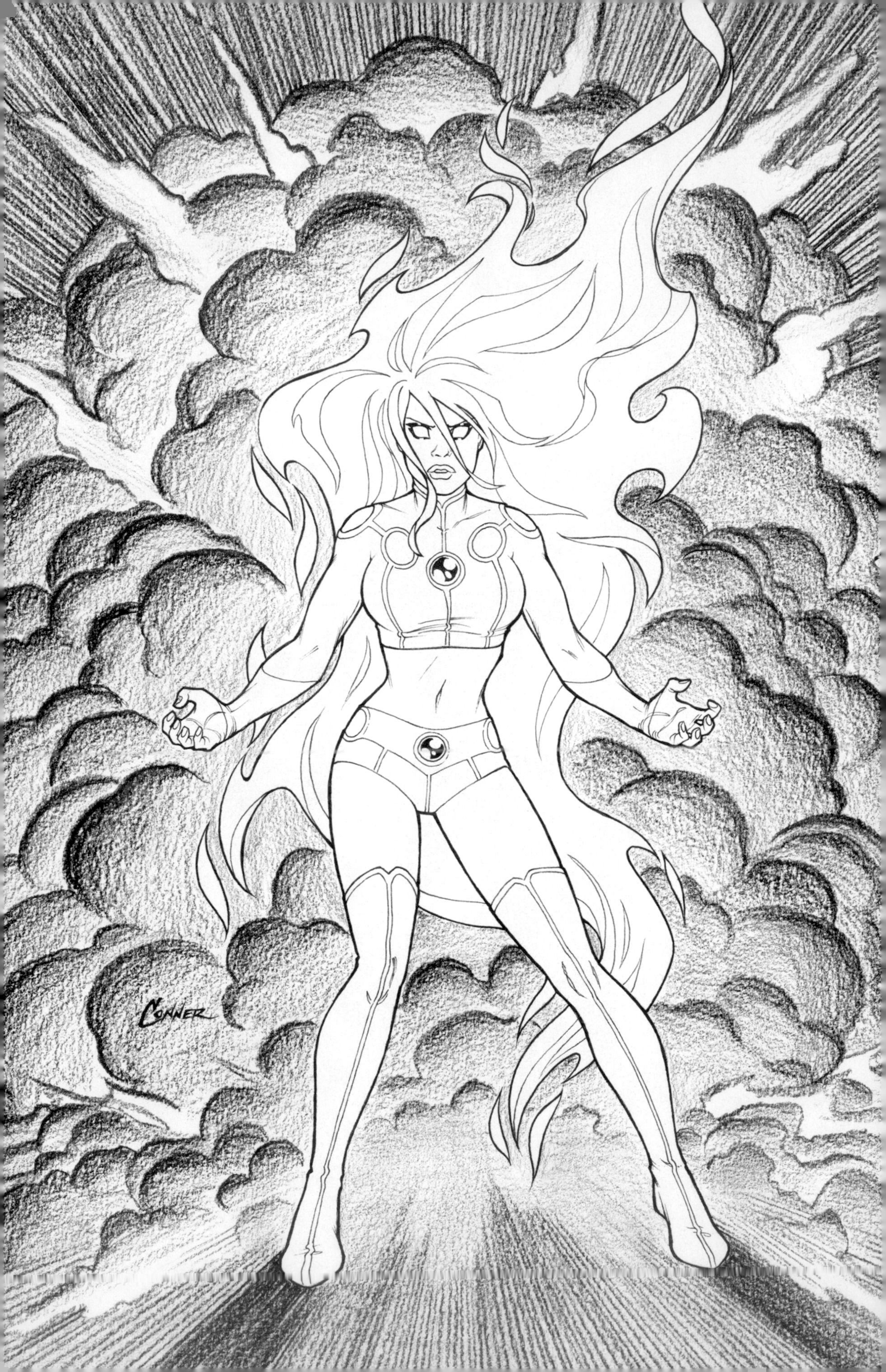
CONNER

Maria.

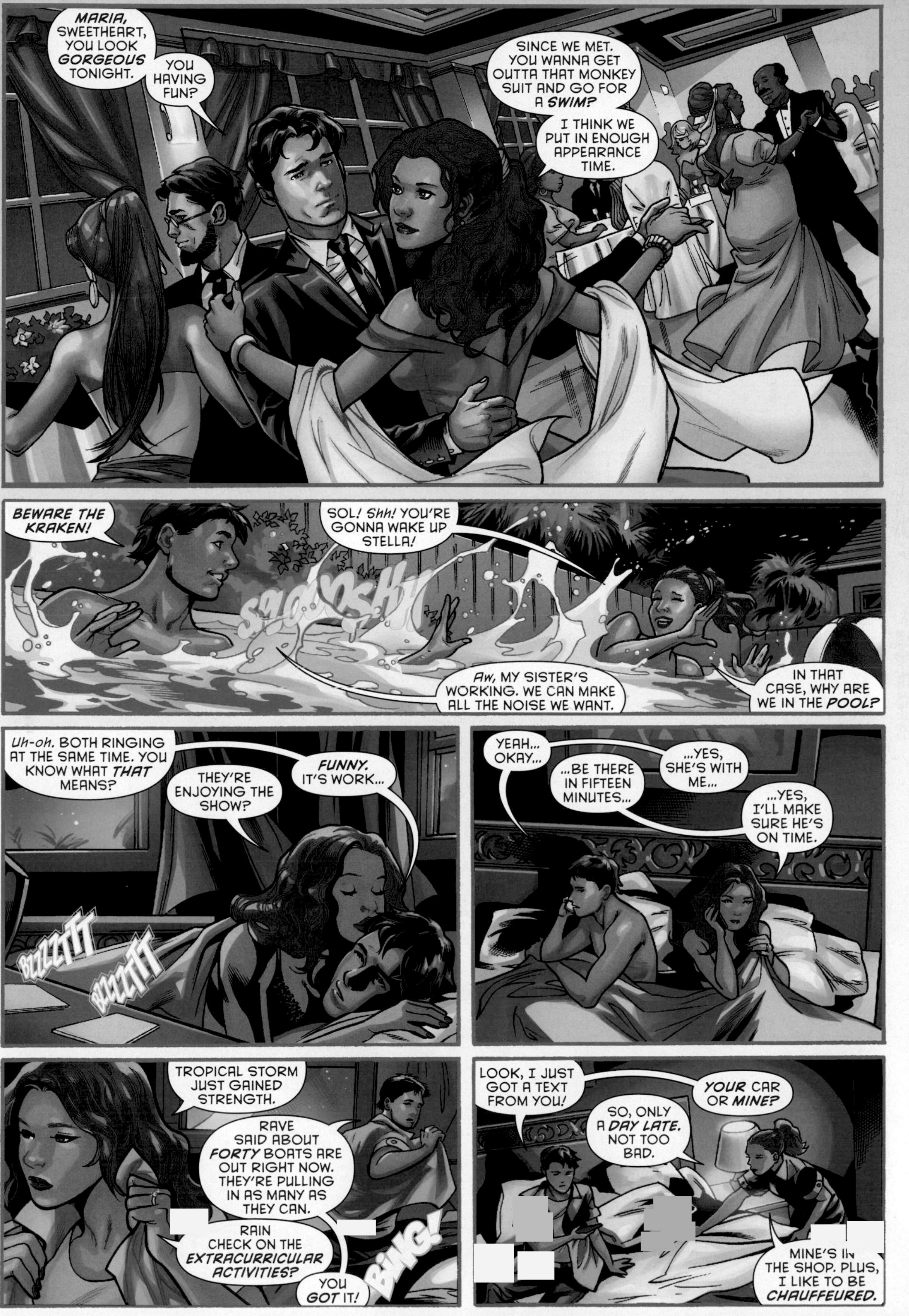

MARIA, SWEETHEART, YOU LOOK GORGEOUS TONIGHT.
YOU HAVING FUN?
SINCE WE MET. YOU WANNA GET OUTTA THAT MONKEY SUIT AND GO FOR A SWIM?
I THINK WE PUT IN ENOUGH APPEARANCE TIME.
BEWARE THE KRAKEN!
SOL! Shh! YOU'RE GONNA WAKE UP STELLA!
SPLOOSH!
Aw, MY SISTER'S WORKING. WE CAN MAKE ALL THE NOISE WE WANT.
IN THAT CASE, WHY ARE WE IN THE POOL?
Uh-oh. BOTH RINGING AT THE SAME TIME. YOU KNOW WHAT THAT MEANS?
THEY'RE ENJOYING THE SHOW?
FUNNY. IT'S WORK...
BZZZTTT
BZZZTTT
YEAH... OKAY...
...BE THERE IN FIFTEEN MINUTES...
...YES, SHE'S WITH ME...
...YES, I'LL MAKE SURE HE'S ON TIME.
TROPICAL STORM JUST GAINED STRENGTH.
RAVE SAID ABOUT FORTY BOATS ARE OUT RIGHT NOW. THEY'RE PULLING IN AS MANY AS THEY CAN.
RAIN CHECK ON THE EXTRACURRICULAR ACTIVITIES?
YOU GOT IT!
BING!
LOOK, I JUST GOT A TEXT FROM YOU!
YOUR CAR OR MINE?
SO, ONLY A DAY LATE. NOT TOO BAD.
MINE'S IN THE SHOP. PLUS, I LIKE TO BE CHAUFFEURED.

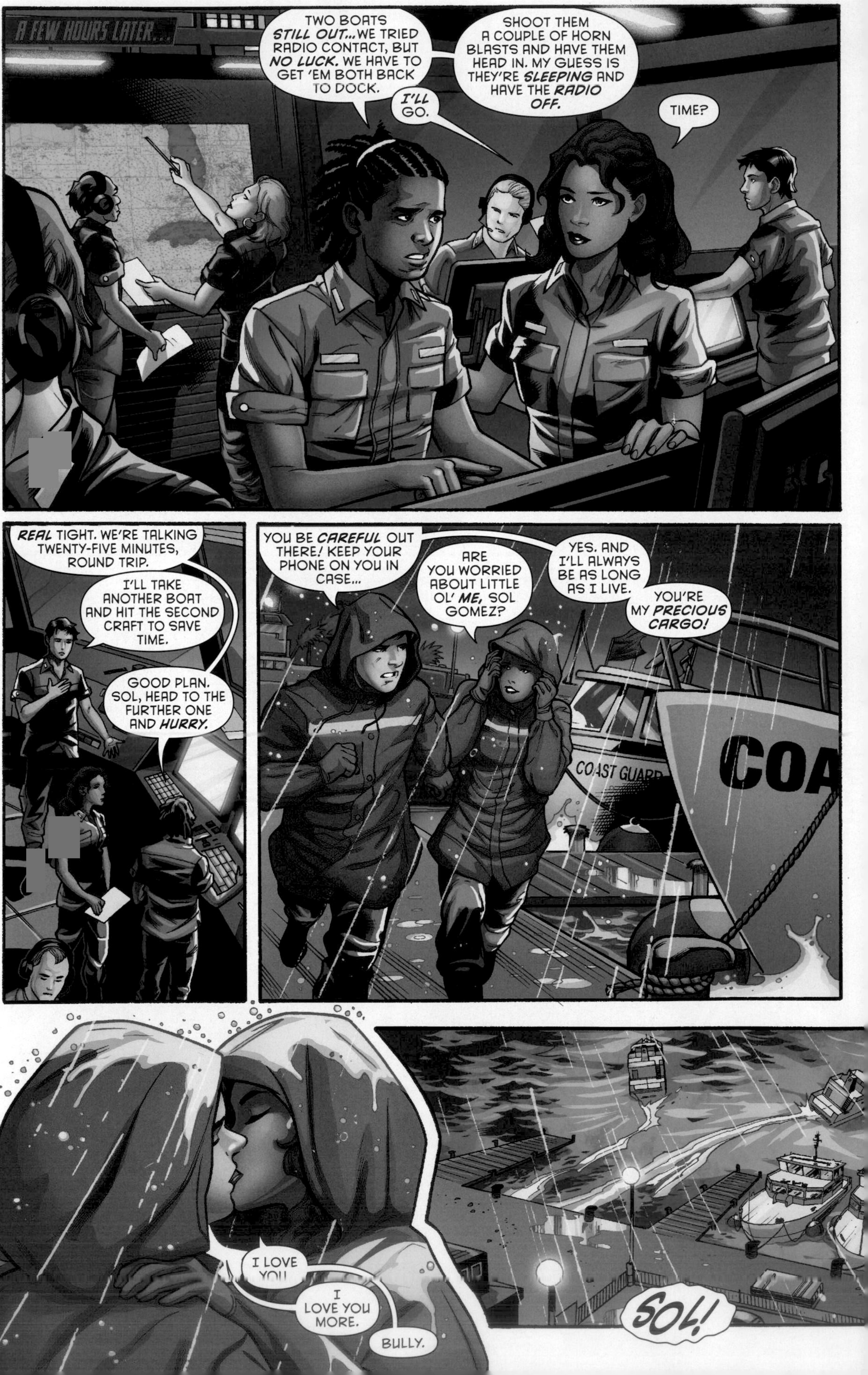
A FEW HOURS LATER...
TWO BOATS STILL OUT...WE TRIED RADIO CONTACT, BUT NO LUCK. WE HAVE TO GET 'EM BOTH BACK TO DOCK.
SHOOT THEM A COUPLE OF HORN BLASTS AND HAVE THEM HEAD IN. MY GUESS IS THEY'RE SLEEPING AND HAVE THE RADIO OFF.
I'LL GO.
TIME?
REAL TIGHT. WE'RE TALKING TWENTY-FIVE MINUTES, ROUND TRIP.
I'LL TAKE ANOTHER BOAT AND HIT THE SECOND CRAFT TO SAVE TIME.
GOOD PLAN. SOL, HEAD TO THE FURTHER ONE AND HURRY.
YOU BE CAREFUL OUT THERE! KEEP YOUR PHONE ON YOU IN CASE...
ARE YOU WORRIED ABOUT LITTLE OL' ME, SOL GOMEZ?
YES. AND I'LL ALWAYS BE AS LONG AS I LIVE.
YOU'RE MY PRECIOUS CARGO!
COAST GUARD
COA
I LOVE YOU.
I LOVE YOU MORE.
BULLY.
SOL!

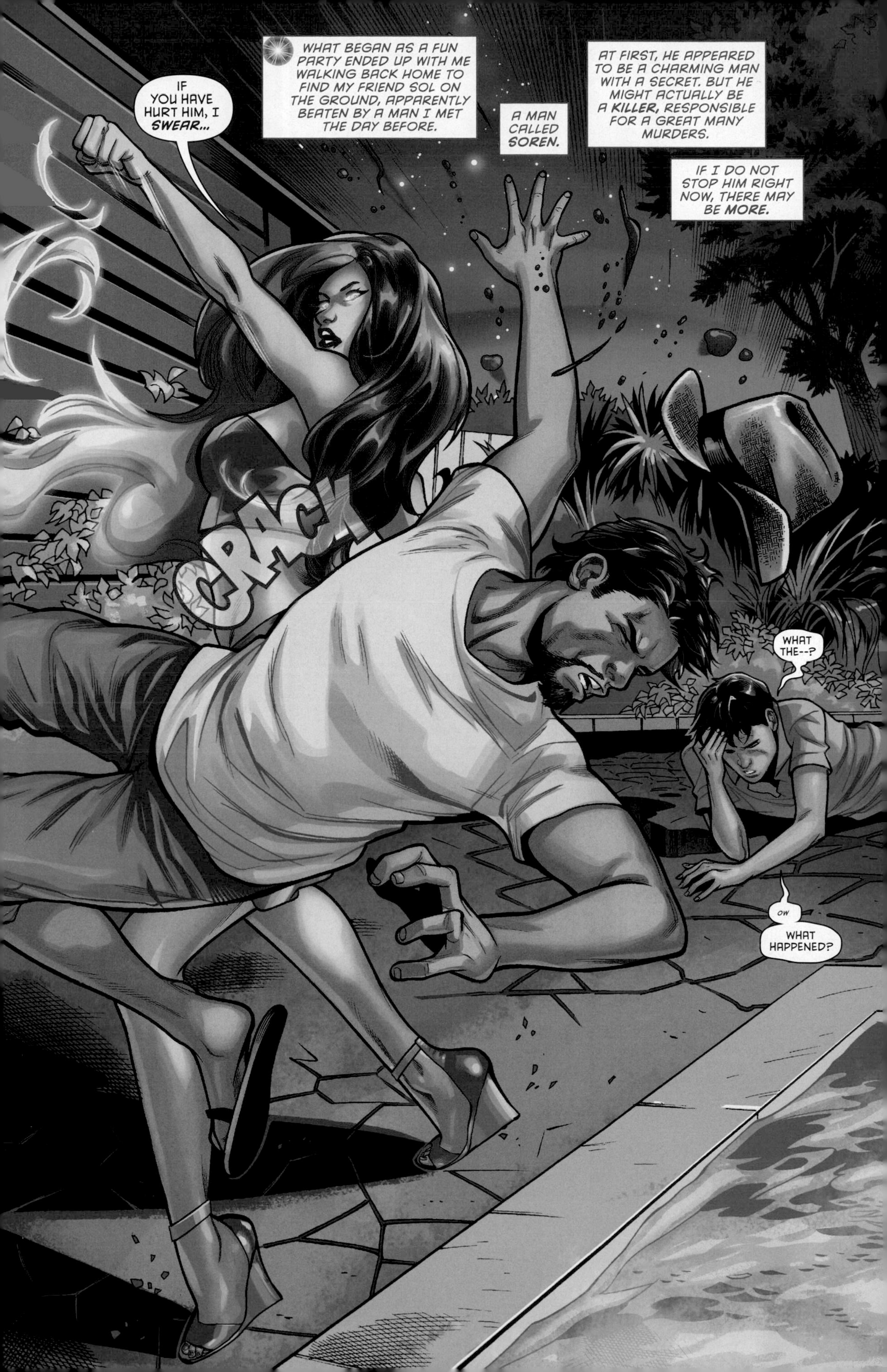
WHAT BEGAN AS A FUN PARTY ENDED UP WITH ME WALKING BACK HOME TO FIND MY FRIEND SOL ON THE GROUND, APPARENTLY BEATEN BY A MAN I MET THE DAY BEFORE.
A MAN CALLED SOREN.
AT FIRST, HE APPEARED TO BE A CHARMING MAN WITH A SECRET. BUT HE MIGHT ACTUALLY BE A KILLER, RESPONSIBLE FOR A GREAT MANY MURDERS.
IF I DO NOT STOP HIM RIGHT NOW, THERE MAY BE MORE.
IF YOU HAVE HURT HIM, I SWEAR...
CRACK
WHAT THE--?
OW
WHAT HAPPENED?

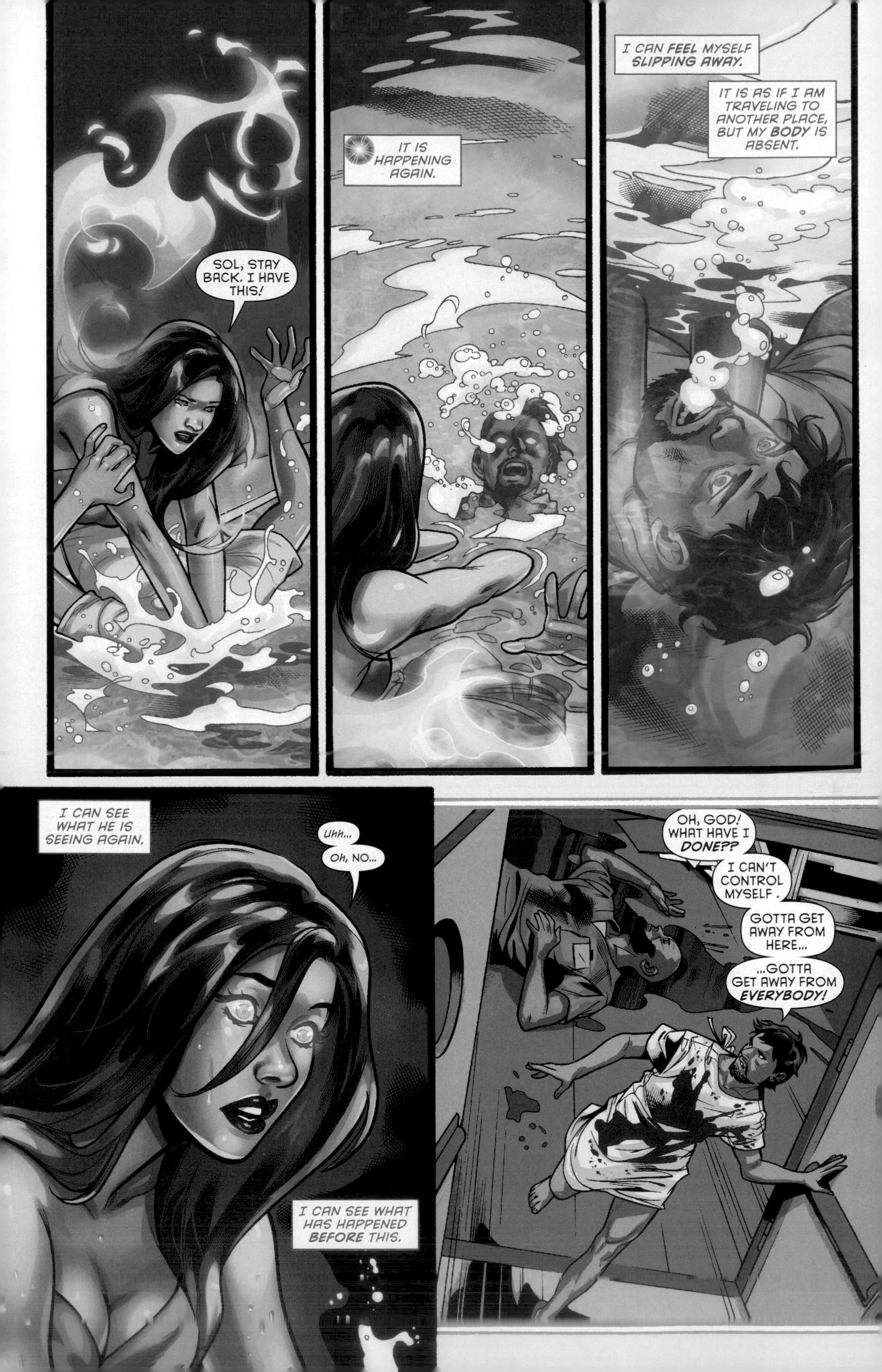
SOL, STAY BACK. I HAVE THIS!
IT IS HAPPENING AGAIN.
I CAN FEEL MYSELF SLIPPING AWAY.
IT IS AS IF I AM TRAVELING TO ANOTHER PLACE, BUT MY BODY IS ABSENT.
I CAN SEE WHAT HE IS SEEING AGAIN.
Uhh...
Oh, NO...
I CAN SEE WHAT HAS HAPPENED BEFORE THIS.
OH, GOD! WHAT HAVE I DONE??
I CAN'T CONTROL MYSELF .
GOTTA GET AWAY FROM HERE...
...GOTTA GET AWAY FROM EVERYBODY!

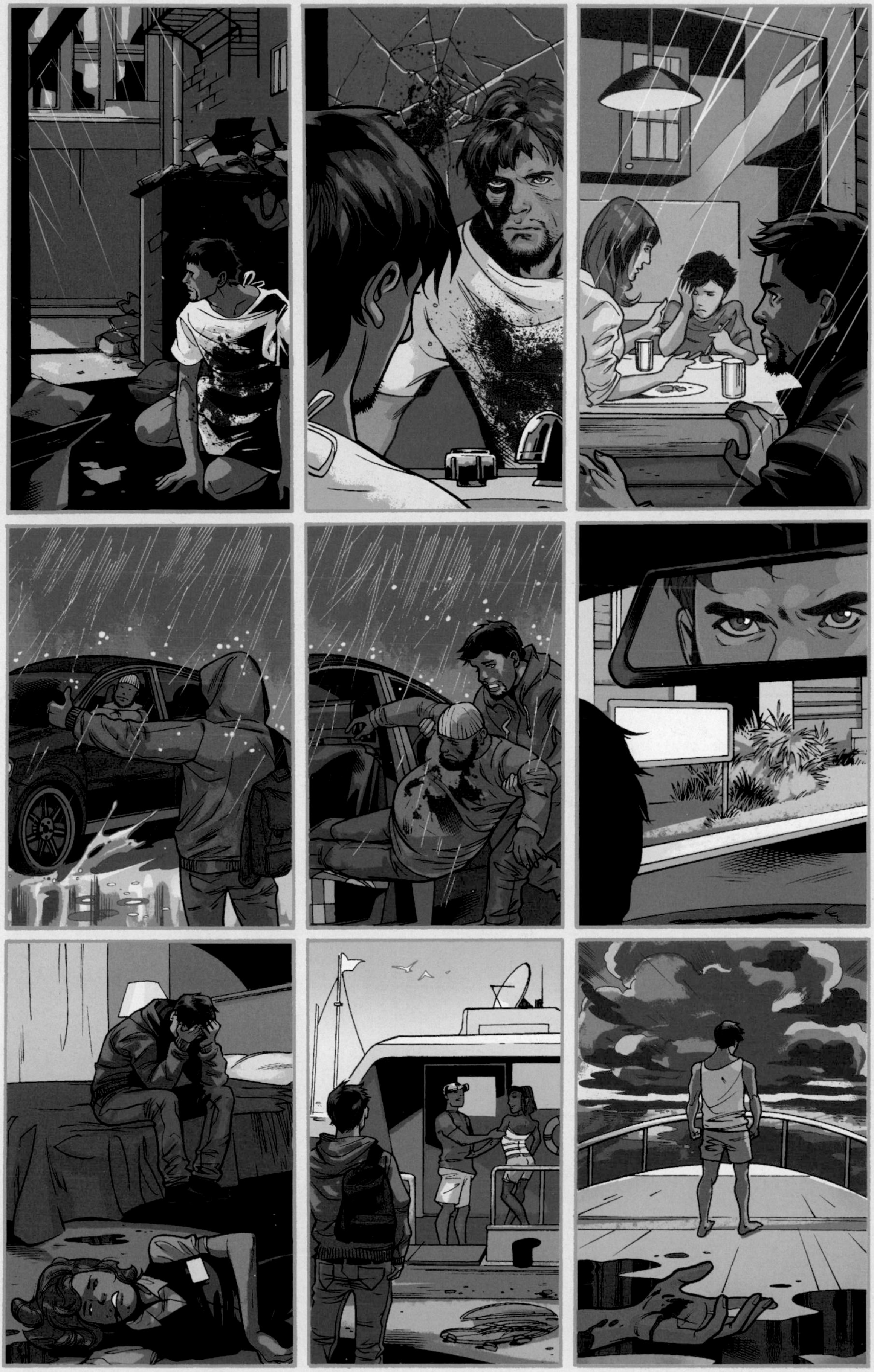

I RETURN, SLIPPING AWAY FROM WHAT HE SEES AND BACK TO MYSELF AGAIN.

THIS MAN...WHAT HE DID...

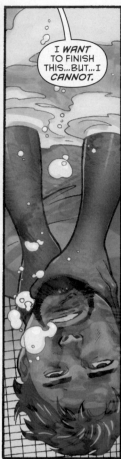

I *WANT* TO FINISH THIS...BUT...I *CANNOT.*

KORI, ARE YOU *OKAY?*

PHYSICALLY, YES.

SOL. WHAT THIS MAN *DID*...SO MANY *PEOPLE...*

LET'S GET HIM ON HIS BACK. I DON'T THINK HE'S BREATHING.

SOL IS TRYING TO *SAVE* THE VERY MAN THAT ATTACKED HIM.

SOL IS LIKE NO ONE I HAVE MET SO FAR. IT GIVES ME SUCH A GOOD FEELING TO HAVE HIM IN MY LIFE.

HE'S BREATHING...

WE CANNOT ALLOW HIM TO GET FREE.

I'LL CALL STELLA AND THE BOYS TO TAKE HIM IN. DON'T WORRY.

Wake Up And Smell The Prey.

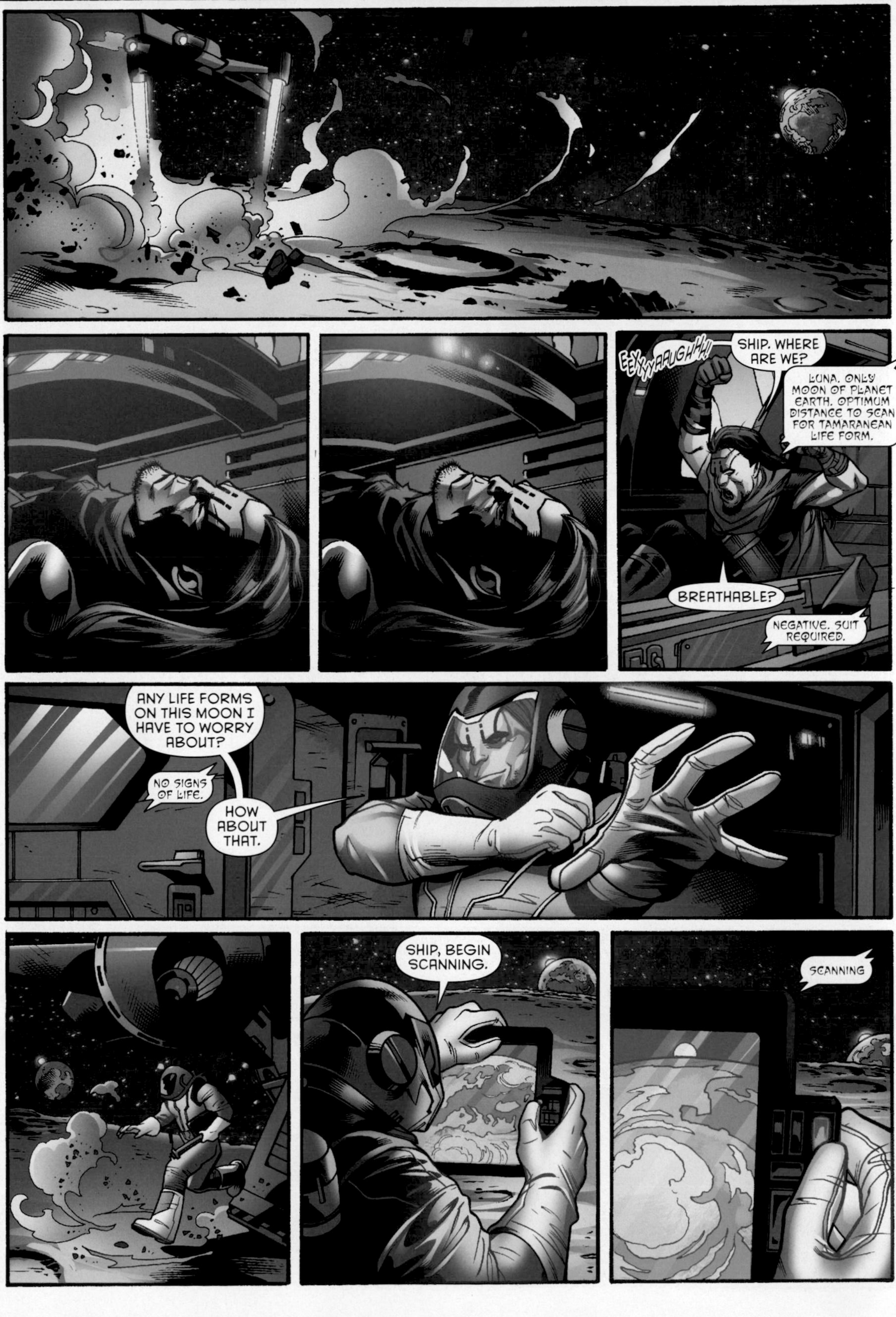
EEYYYYAARUGHHH!
SHIP. WHERE ARE WE?
LUNA. ONLY MOON OF PLANET EARTH. OPTIMUM DISTANCE TO SCAN FOR TAMARANEAN LIFE FORM.
BREATHABLE?
NEGATIVE. SUIT REQUIRED.
ANY LIFE FORMS ON THIS MOON I HAVE TO WORRY ABOUT?
NO SIGNS OF LIFE.
HOW ABOUT THAT.
SHIP, BEGIN SCANNING.
SCANNING

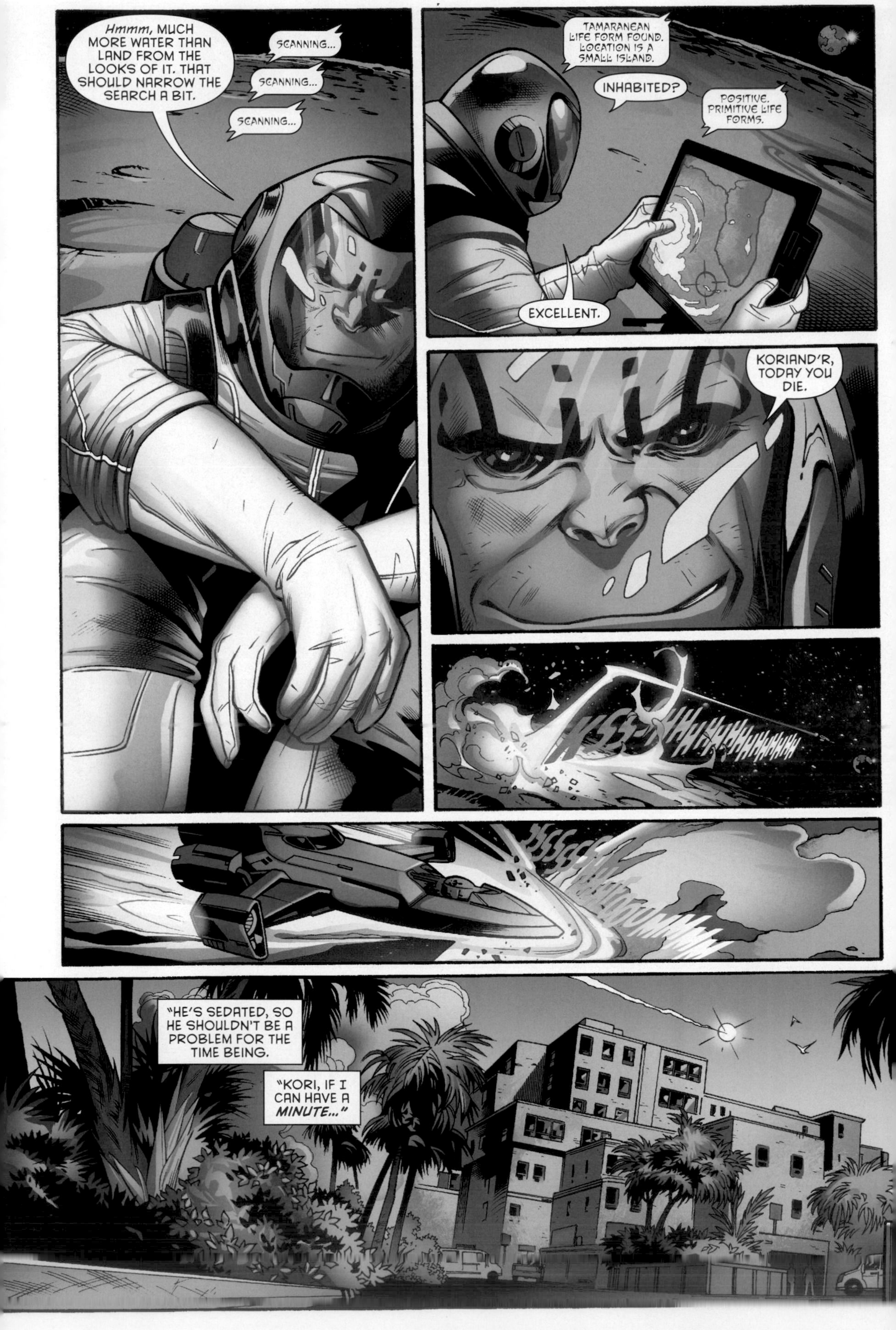

Hmmm, MUCH MORE WATER THAN LAND FROM THE LOOKS OF IT. THAT SHOULD NARROW THE SEARCH A BIT.
SCANNING...
SCANNING...
SCANNING...
TAMARANEAN LIFE FORM FOUND. LOCATION IS A SMALL ISLAND.
INHABITED?
POSITIVE. PRIMITIVE LIFE FORMS.
EXCELLENT.
KORIAND'R, TODAY YOU DIE.
"HE'S SEDATED, SO HE SHOULDN'T BE A PROBLEM FOR THE TIME BEING.
"KORI, IF I CAN HAVE A MINUTE..."

I'm Okay, You're Okay, Lets Eat.

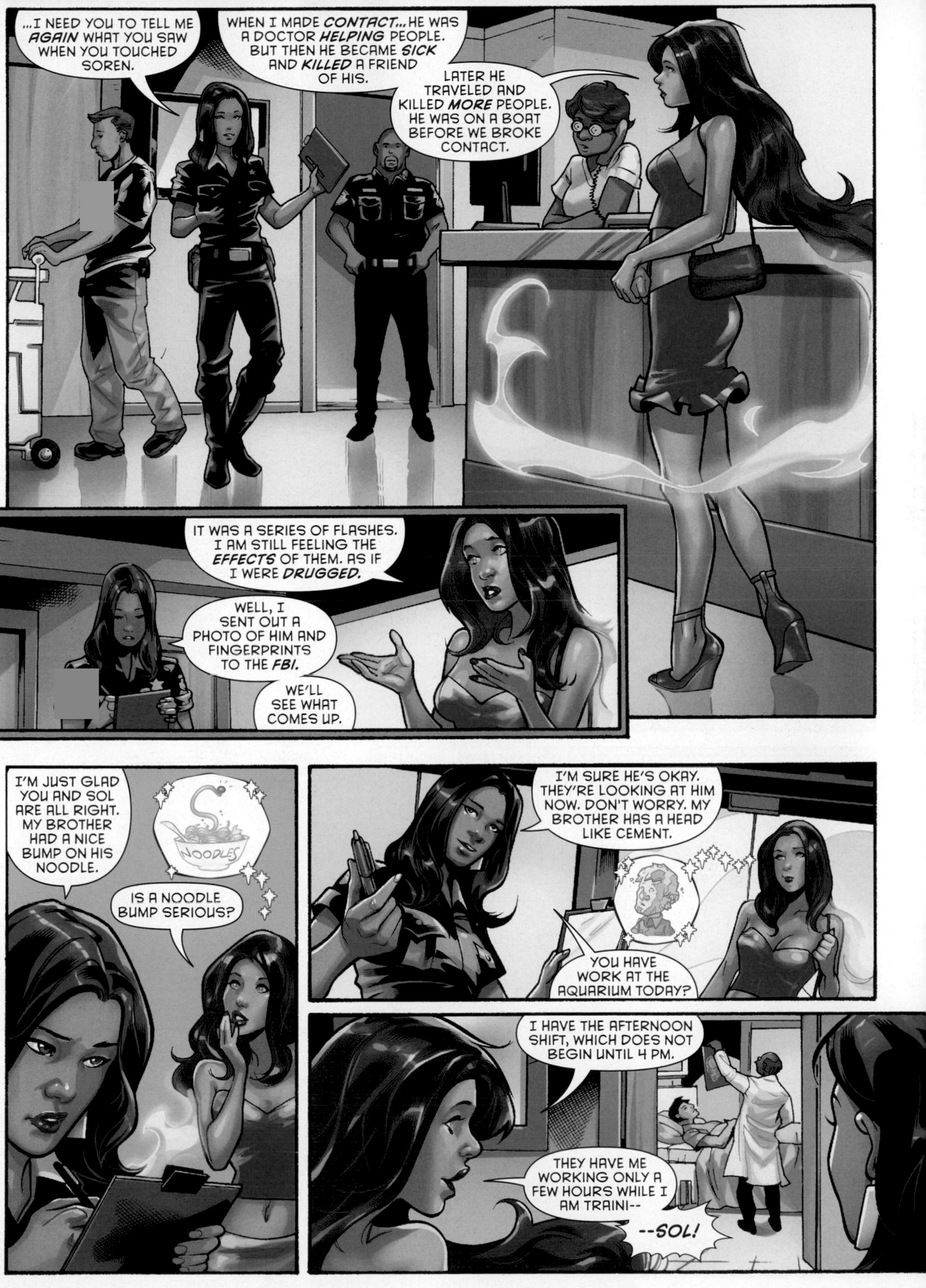

...I NEED YOU TO TELL ME AGAIN WHAT YOU SAW WHEN YOU TOUCHED SOREN.
WHEN I MADE CONTACT... HE WAS A DOCTOR HELPING PEOPLE. BUT THEN HE BECAME SICK AND KILLED A FRIEND OF HIS.
LATER HE TRAVELED AND KILLED MORE PEOPLE. HE WAS ON A BOAT BEFORE WE BROKE CONTACT.
IT WAS A SERIES OF FLASHES. I AM STILL FEELING THE EFFECTS OF THEM. AS IF I WERE DRUGGED.
WELL, I SENT OUT A PHOTO OF HIM AND FINGERPRINTS TO THE FBI.
WE'LL SEE WHAT COMES UP.
I'M JUST GLAD YOU AND SOL ARE ALL RIGHT. MY BROTHER HAD A NICE BUMP ON HIS NOODLE.
NOODLES
IS A NOODLE BUMP SERIOUS?
I'M SURE HE'S OKAY. THEY'RE LOOKING AT HIM NOW. DON'T WORRY. MY BROTHER HAS A HEAD LIKE CEMENT.
YOU HAVE WORK AT THE AQUARIUM TODAY?
I HAVE THE AFTERNOON SHIFT, WHICH DOES NOT BEGIN UNTIL 4 PM.
THEY HAVE ME WORKING ONLY A FEW HOURS WHILE I AM TRAINI--
--SOL!

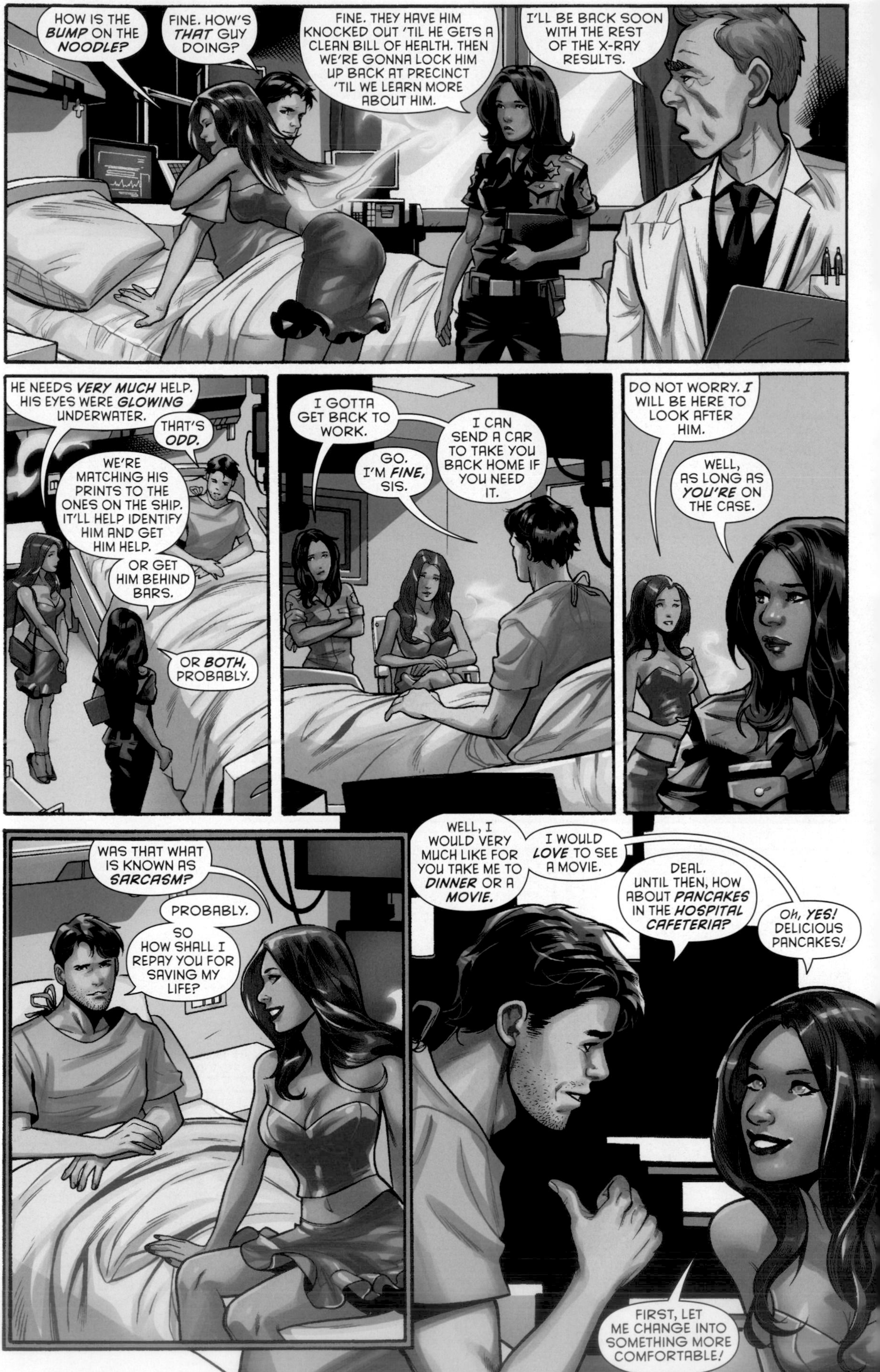
HOW IS THE BUMP ON THE NOODLE?
FINE. HOW'S THAT GUY DOING?
FINE. THEY HAVE HIM KNOCKED OUT 'TIL HE GETS A CLEAN BILL OF HEALTH. THEN WE'RE GONNA LOCK HIM UP BACK AT PRECINCT 'TIL WE LEARN MORE ABOUT HIM.
I'LL BE BACK SOON WITH THE REST OF THE X-RAY RESULTS.
HE NEEDS VERY MUCH HELP. HIS EYES WERE GLOWING UNDERWATER.
THAT'S ODD.
WE'RE MATCHING HIS PRINTS TO THE ONES ON THE SHIP. IT'LL HELP IDENTIFY HIM AND GET HIM HELP.
OR GET HIM BEHIND BARS.
OR BOTH, PROBABLY.
I GOTTA GET BACK TO WORK.
I CAN SEND A CAR TO TAKE YOU BACK HOME IF YOU NEED IT.
GO. I'M FINE, SIS.
DO NOT WORRY. I WILL BE HERE TO LOOK AFTER HIM.
WELL, AS LONG AS YOU'RE ON THE CASE.
WAS THAT WHAT IS KNOWN AS SARCASM?
PROBABLY.
SO HOW SHALL I REPAY YOU FOR SAVING MY LIFE?
WELL, I WOULD VERY MUCH LIKE FOR YOU TAKE ME TO DINNER OR A MOVIE.
I WOULD LOVE TO SEE A MOVIE.
DEAL. UNTIL THEN, HOW ABOUT PANCAKES IN THE HOSPITAL CAFETERIA?
Oh, YES! DELICIOUS PANCAKES!
FIRST, LET ME CHANGE INTO SOMETHING MORE COMFORTABLE!

Wrong Runway.

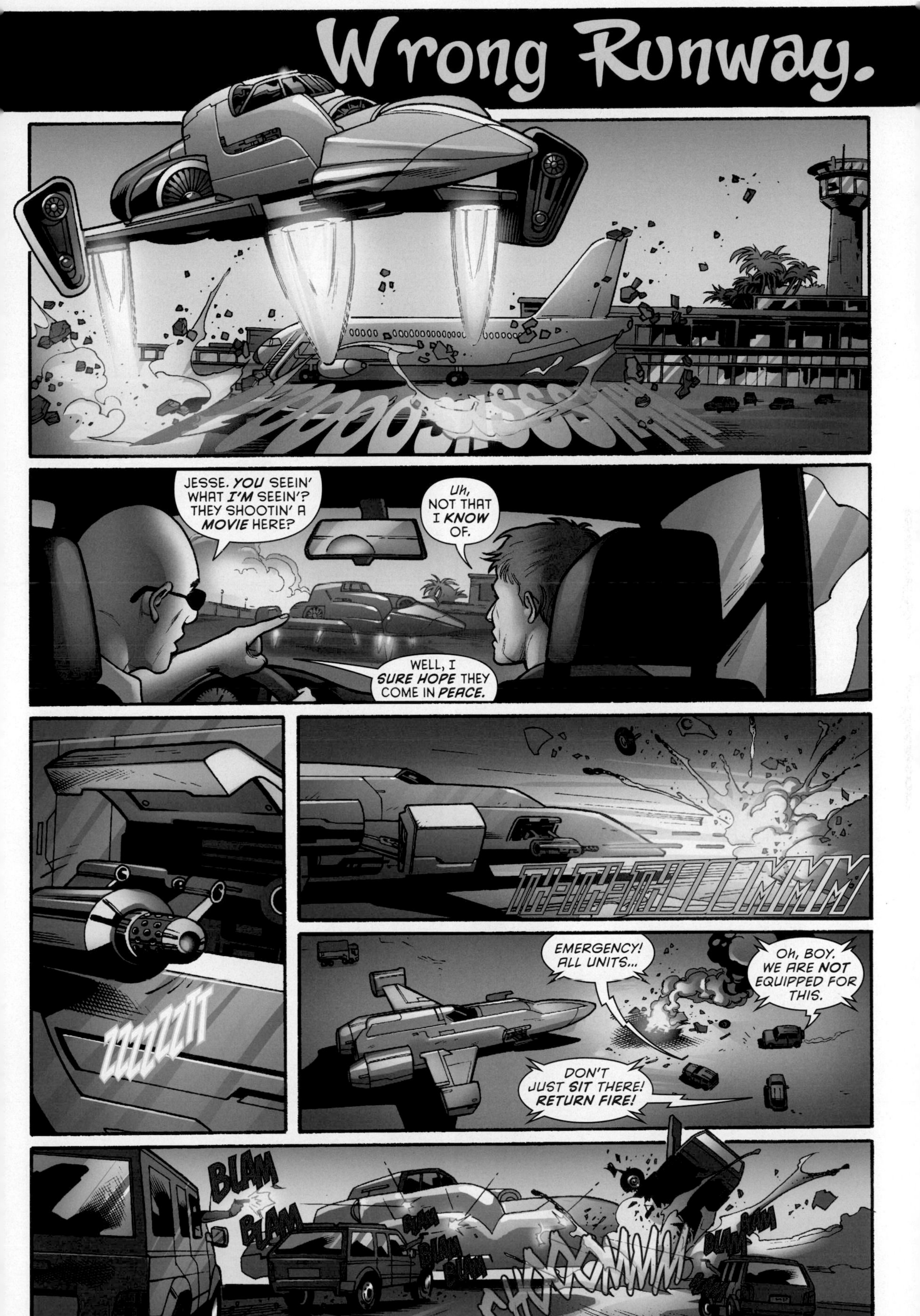

JESSE. *YOU* SEEIN' WHAT *I'M* SEEIN'? THEY SHOOTIN' A *MOVIE* HERE?
Uh, NOT THAT I *KNOW* OF.
WELL, I *SURE HOPE* THEY COME IN *PEACE*.
EMERGENCY! ALL UNITS...
Oh, BOY. WE ARE **NOT** EQUIPPED FOR THIS.
DON'T JUST **SIT** THERE! **RETURN FIRE!**
BLAM
BLAM

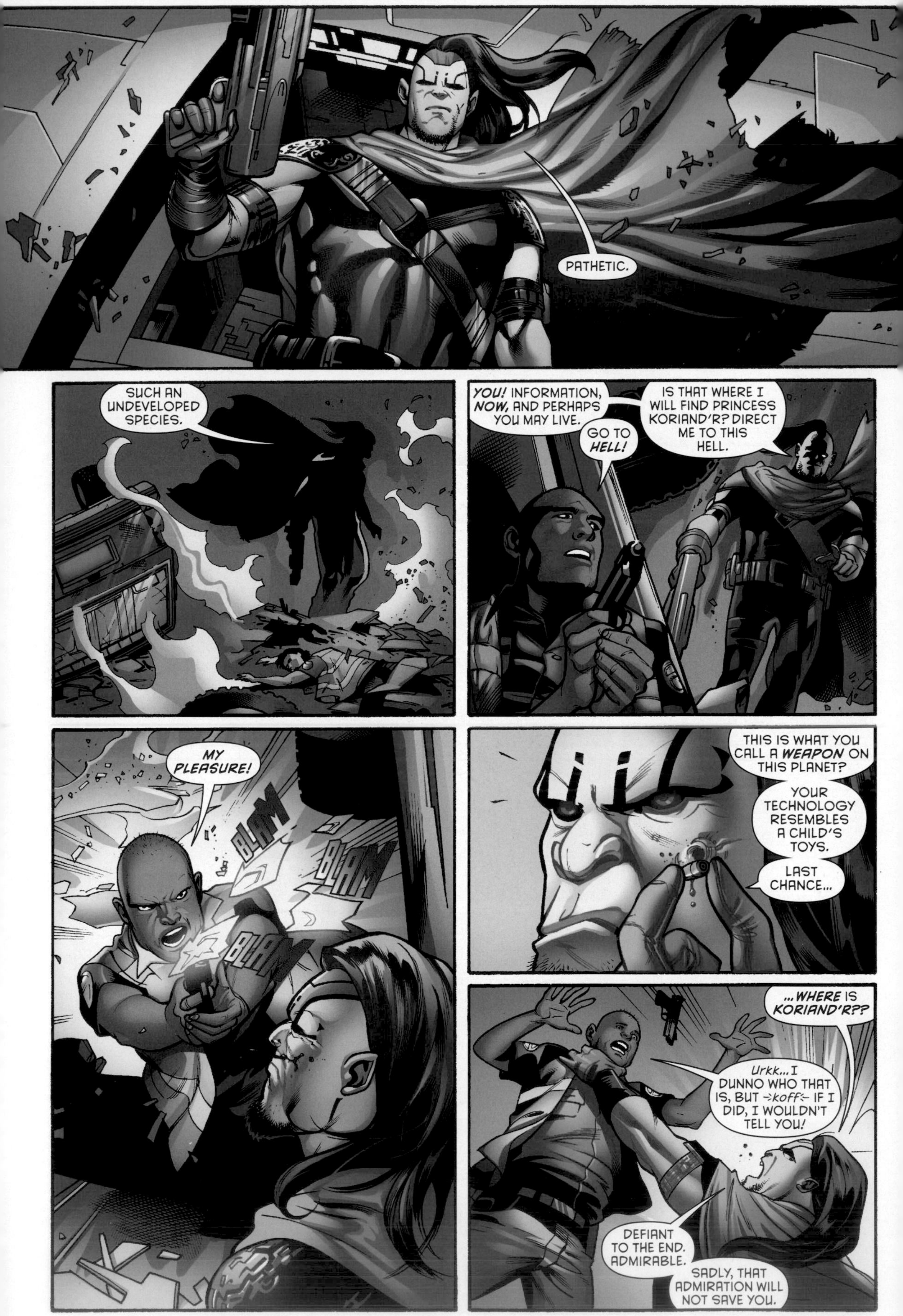
PATHETIC.
SUCH AN UNDEVELOPED SPECIES.
YOU! INFORMATION, NOW, AND PERHAPS YOU MAY LIVE.
IS THAT WHERE I WILL FIND PRINCESS KORIAND'R? DIRECT ME TO THIS HELL.
GO TO HELL!
MY PLEASURE!
BLAM
BLAM
BLAM
THIS IS WHAT YOU CALL A WEAPON ON THIS PLANET?
YOUR TECHNOLOGY RESEMBLES A CHILD'S TOYS.
LAST CHANCE...
...WHERE IS KORIAND'R??
Urkk... I DUNNO WHO THAT IS, BUT koff IF I DID, I WOULDN'T TELL YOU!
DEFIANT TO THE END. ADMIRABLE.
SADLY, THAT ADMIRATION WILL NOT SAVE YOU.

More Than A Mouthful.

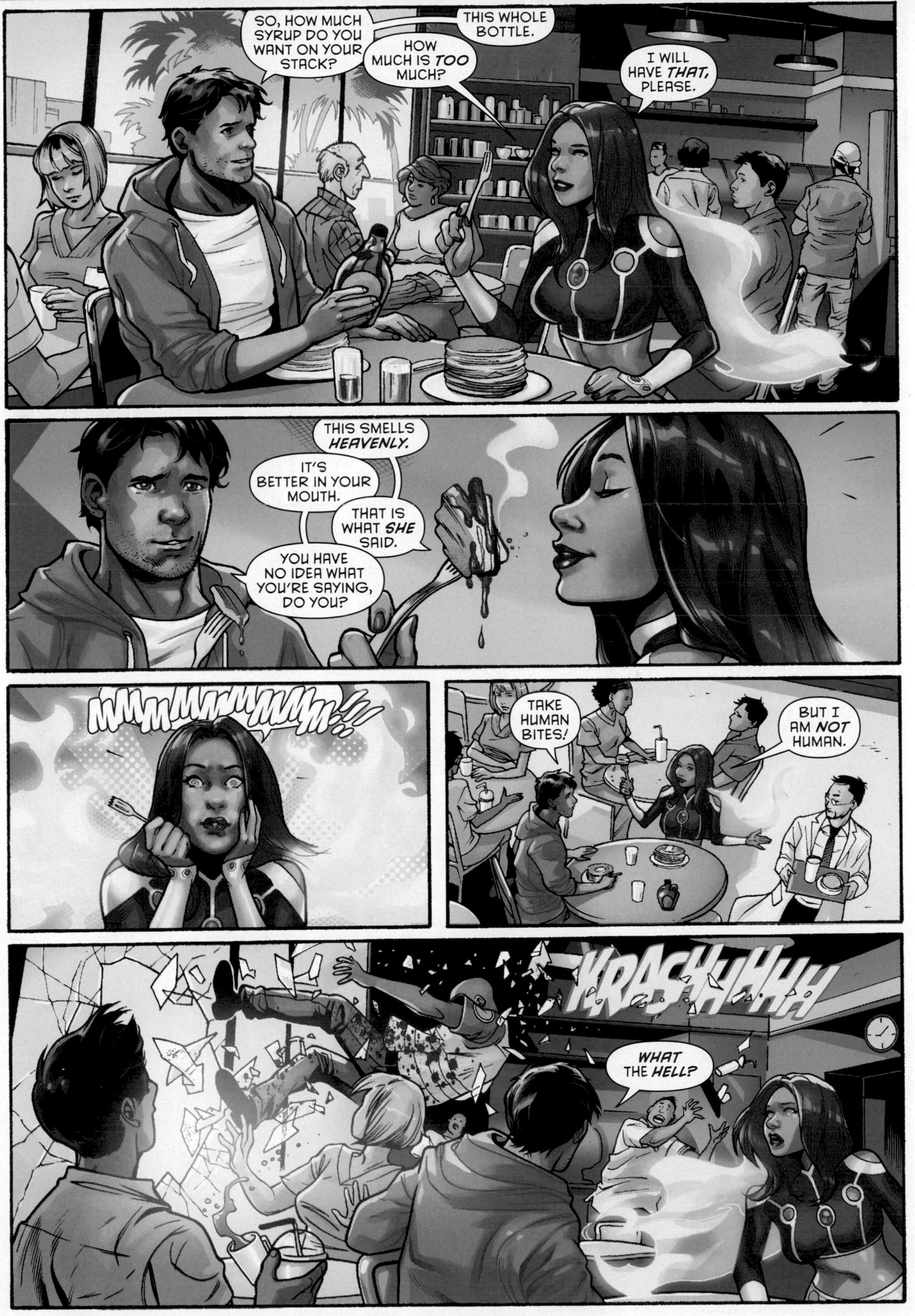
SO, HOW MUCH SYRUP DO YOU WANT ON YOUR STACK?
THIS WHOLE BOTTLE.
HOW MUCH IS *TOO* MUCH?
I WILL HAVE *THAT,* PLEASE.
THIS SMELLS *HEAVENLY.*
IT'S BETTER IN YOUR MOUTH.
THAT IS WHAT *SHE* SAID.
YOU HAVE NO IDEA WHAT YOU'RE SAYING, DO YOU?
TAKE HUMAN BITES!
BUT I AM *NOT* HUMAN.
WHAT THE *HELL?*

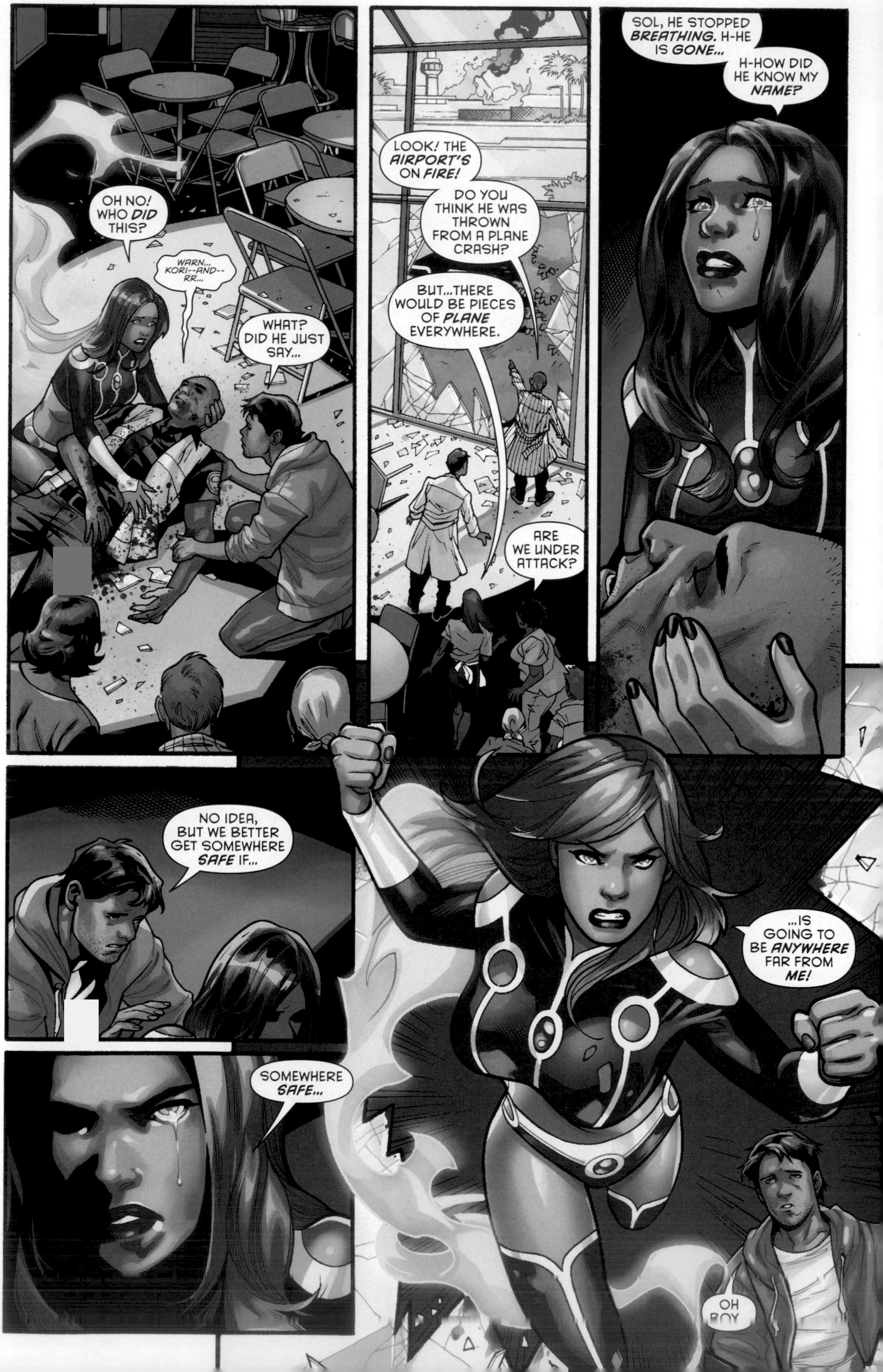
OH NO! WHO *DID* THIS?
WARN... KORI--AND-- RR...
WHAT? DID HE JUST SAY...
LOOK! THE *AIRPORT'S* ON *FIRE!*
DO YOU THINK HE WAS THROWN FROM A PLANE CRASH?
BUT...THERE WOULD BE PIECES OF *PLANE* EVERYWHERE.
ARE WE UNDER ATTACK?
SOL, HE STOPPED *BREATHING.* H-HE IS *GONE...*
H-HOW DID HE KNOW MY *NAME?*
NO IDEA, BUT WE BETTER GET SOMEWHERE *SAFE* IF...
SOMEWHERE *SAFE...*
...IS GOING TO BE *ANYWHERE* FAR FROM *ME!*
OH BOY

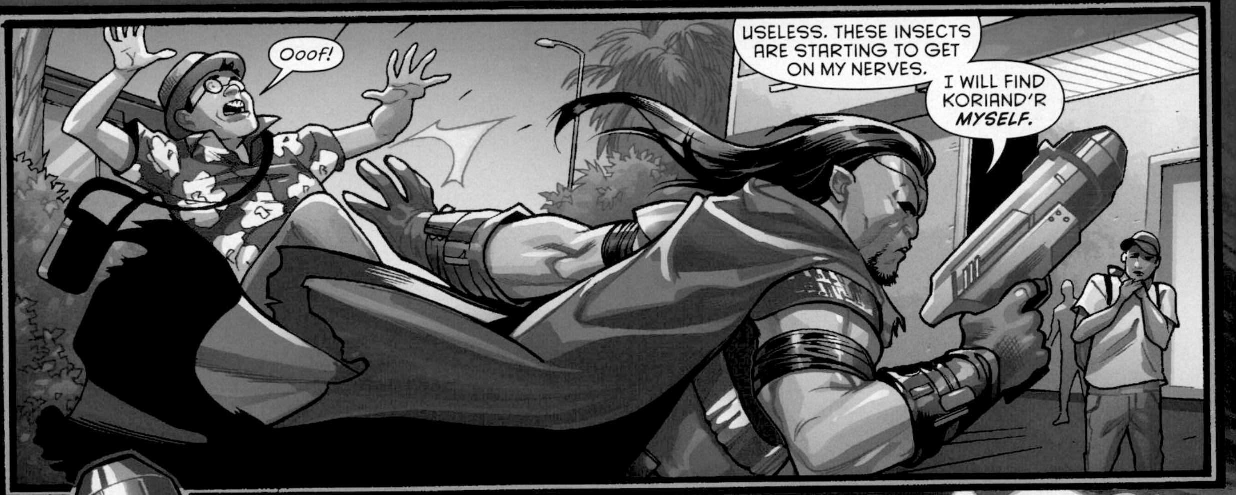
Ooof!
USELESS. THESE INSECTS ARE STARTING TO GET ON MY NERVES.
I WILL FIND KORIAND'R MYSELF.

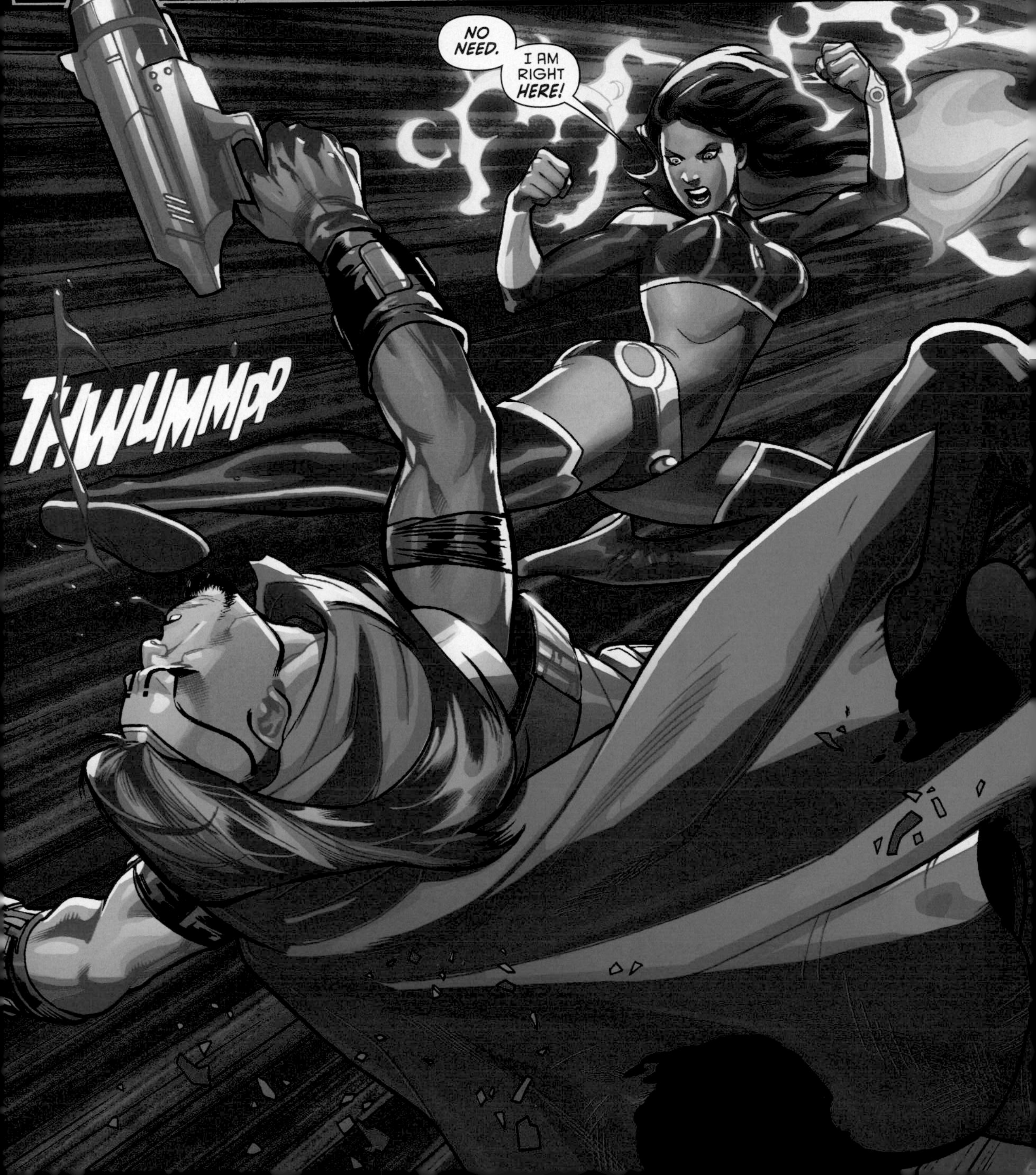
NO NEED.
I AM RIGHT HERE!
THWUMMPP

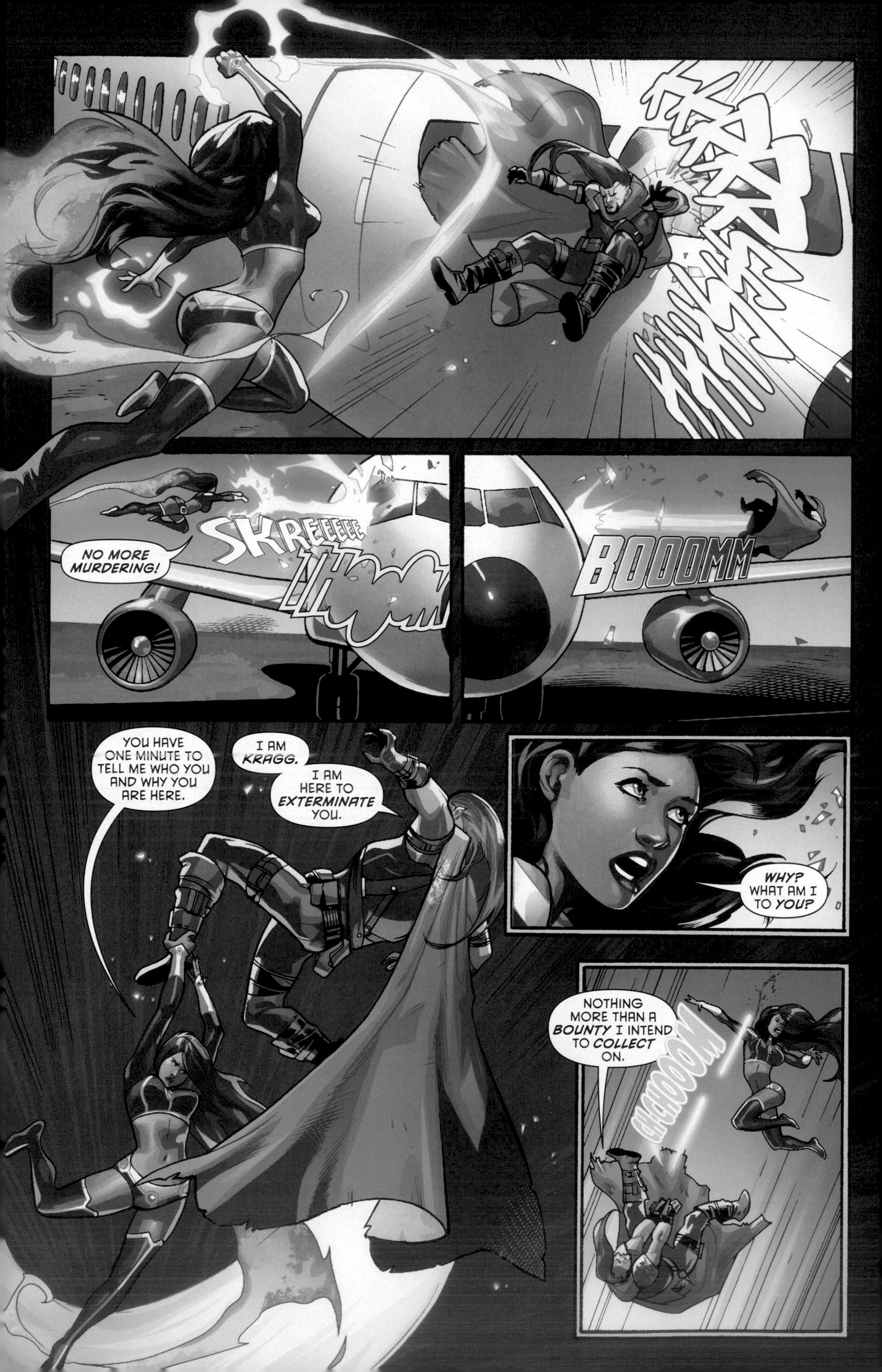

NO MORE MURDERING!
SKREEEEEE
BOOOMM
YOU HAVE ONE MINUTE TO TELL ME WHO YOU AND WHY YOU ARE HERE.
I AM KRAGG.
I AM HERE TO EXTERMINATE YOU.
WHY? WHAT AM I TO YOU?
NOTHING MORE THAN A BOUNTY I INTEND TO COLLECT ON.

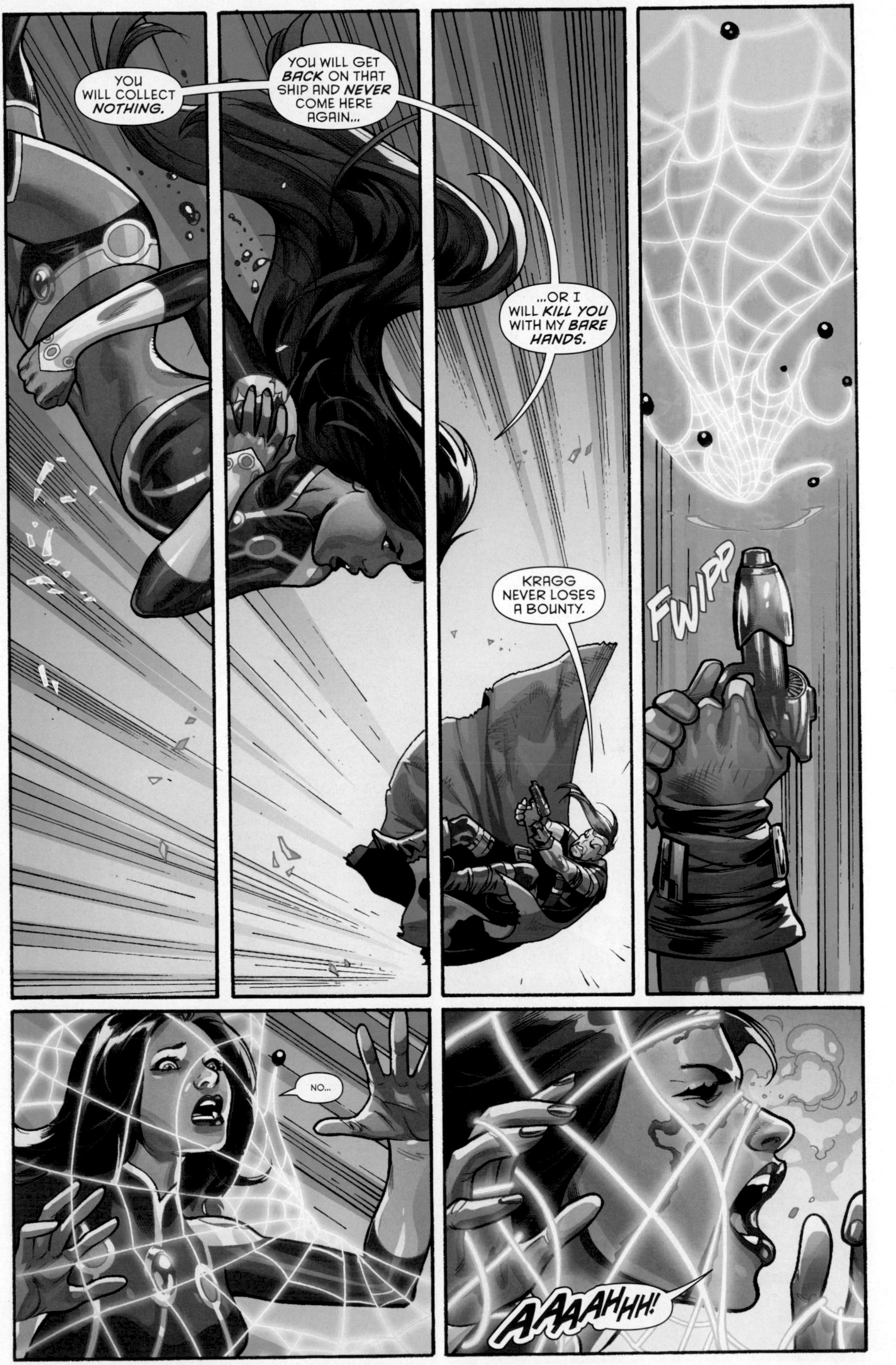
YOU WILL COLLECT NOTHING.
YOU WILL GET BACK ON THAT SHIP AND NEVER COME HERE AGAIN...
...OR I WILL KILL YOU WITH MY BARE HANDS.
KRAGG NEVER LOSES A BOUNTY.
FWIPP
NO...
AAAAHHH!

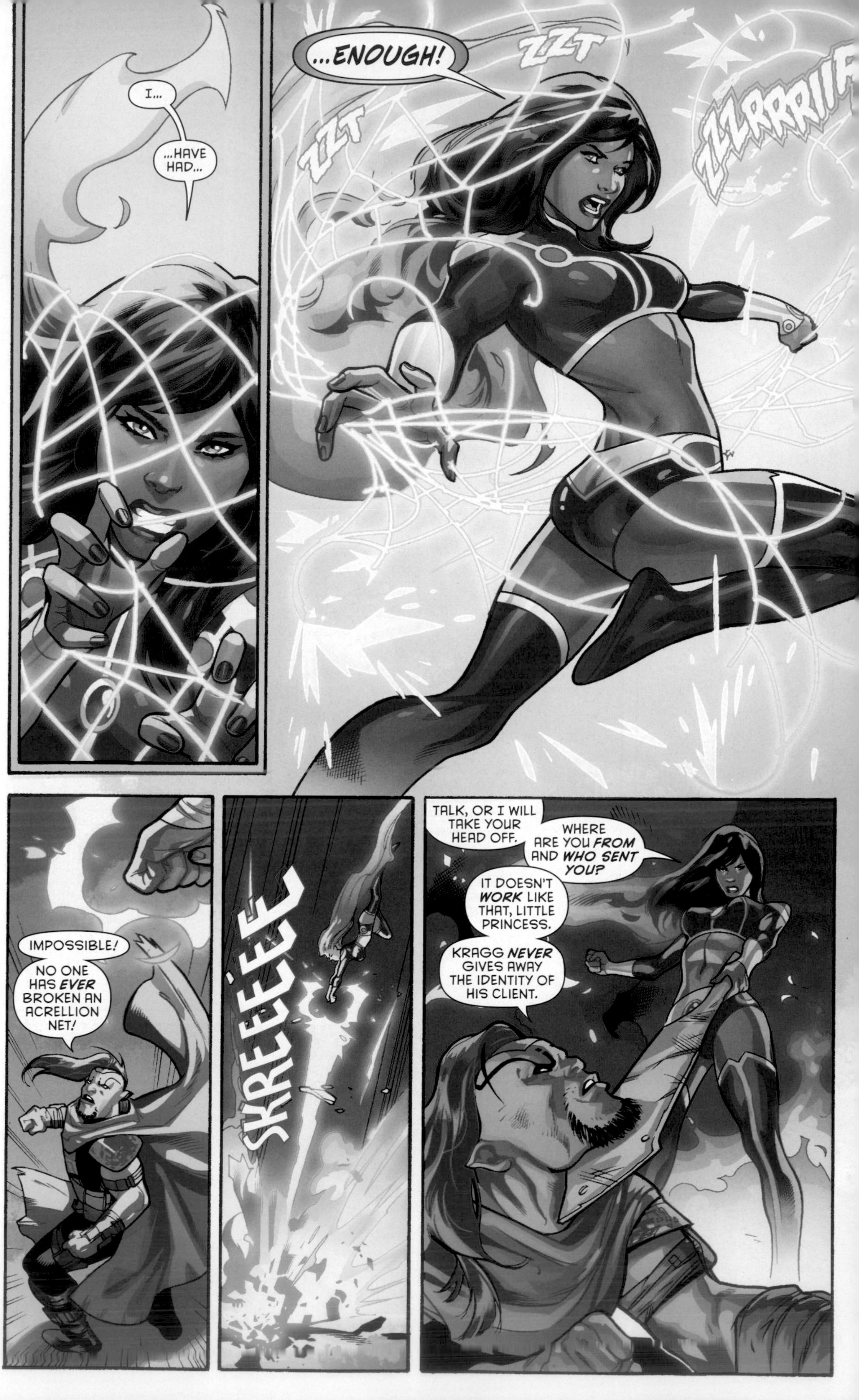

I...
...HAVE HAD...
...ENOUGH!
ZZZT
ZZZT
ZZZRRRIIIF
IMPOSSIBLE!
NO ONE HAS EVER BROKEN AN ACRELLION NET!
SKREEEEEEEE
TALK, OR I WILL TAKE YOUR HEAD OFF.
WHERE ARE YOU FROM AND WHO SENT YOU?
IT DOESN'T WORK LIKE THAT, LITTLE PRINCESS.
KRAGG NEVER GIVES AWAY THE IDENTITY OF HIS CLIENT.

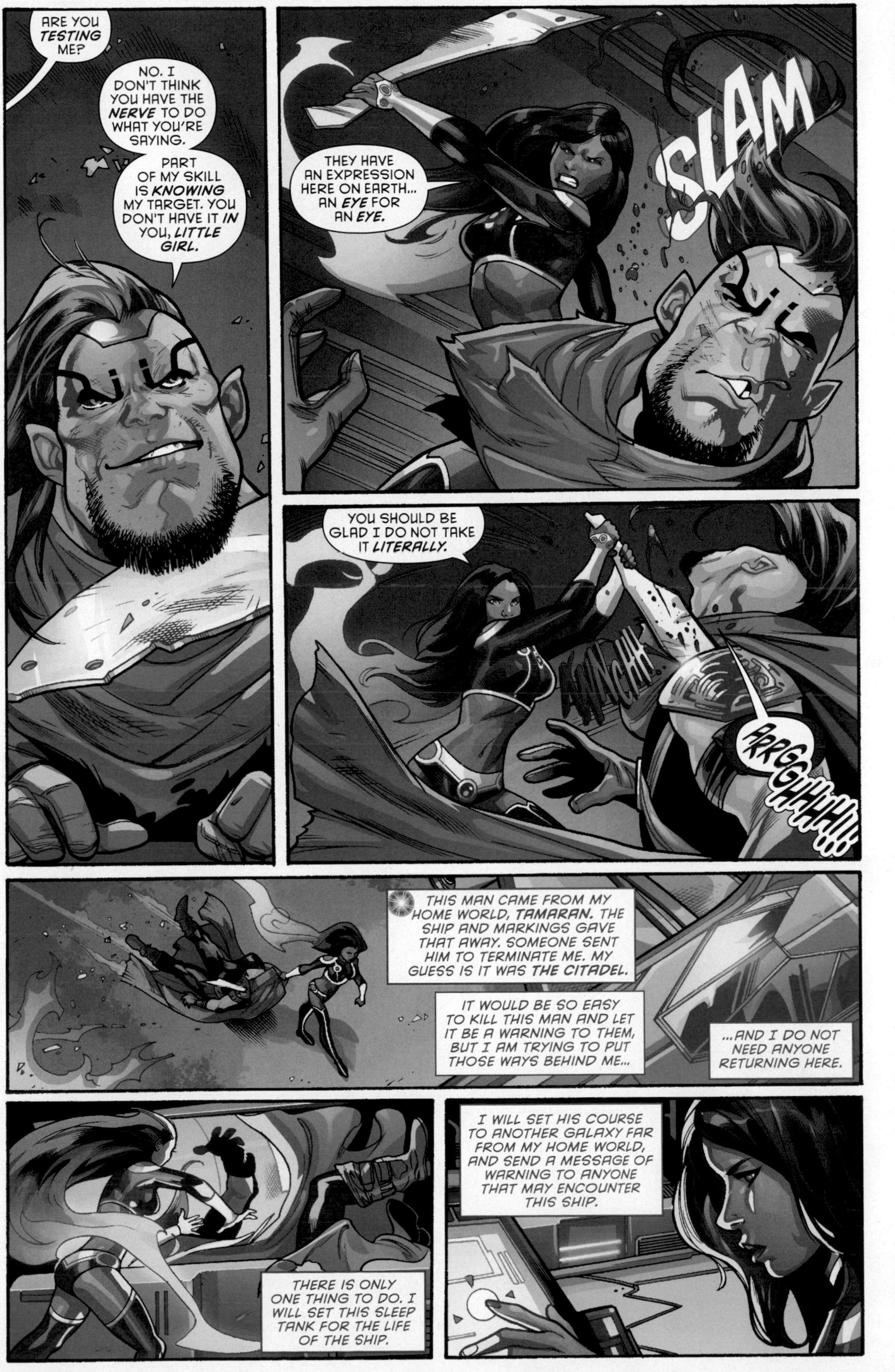
ARE YOU TESTING ME?
NO. I DON'T THINK YOU HAVE THE NERVE TO DO WHAT YOU'RE SAYING.
PART OF MY SKILL IS KNOWING MY TARGET. YOU DON'T HAVE IT IN YOU, LITTLE GIRL.
THEY HAVE AN EXPRESSION HERE ON EARTH... AN EYE FOR AN EYE.
SLAM
YOU SHOULD BE GLAD I DO NOT TAKE IT LITERALLY.
KLANCHH
ARRGGHHHH!!!
THIS MAN CAME FROM MY HOME WORLD, TAMARAN. THE SHIP AND MARKINGS GAVE THAT AWAY. SOMEONE SENT HIM TO TERMINATE ME. MY GUESS IS IT WAS THE CITADEL.
IT WOULD BE SO EASY TO KILL THIS MAN AND LET IT BE A WARNING TO THEM, BUT I AM TRYING TO PUT THOSE WAYS BEHIND ME...
...AND I DO NOT NEED ANYONE RETURNING HERE.
THERE IS ONLY ONE THING TO DO. I WILL SET THIS SLEEP TANK FOR THE LIFE OF THE SHIP.
I WILL SET HIS COURSE TO ANOTHER GALAXY FAR FROM MY HOME WORLD, AND SEND A MESSAGE OF WARNING TO ANYONE THAT MAY ENCOUNTER THIS SHIP.

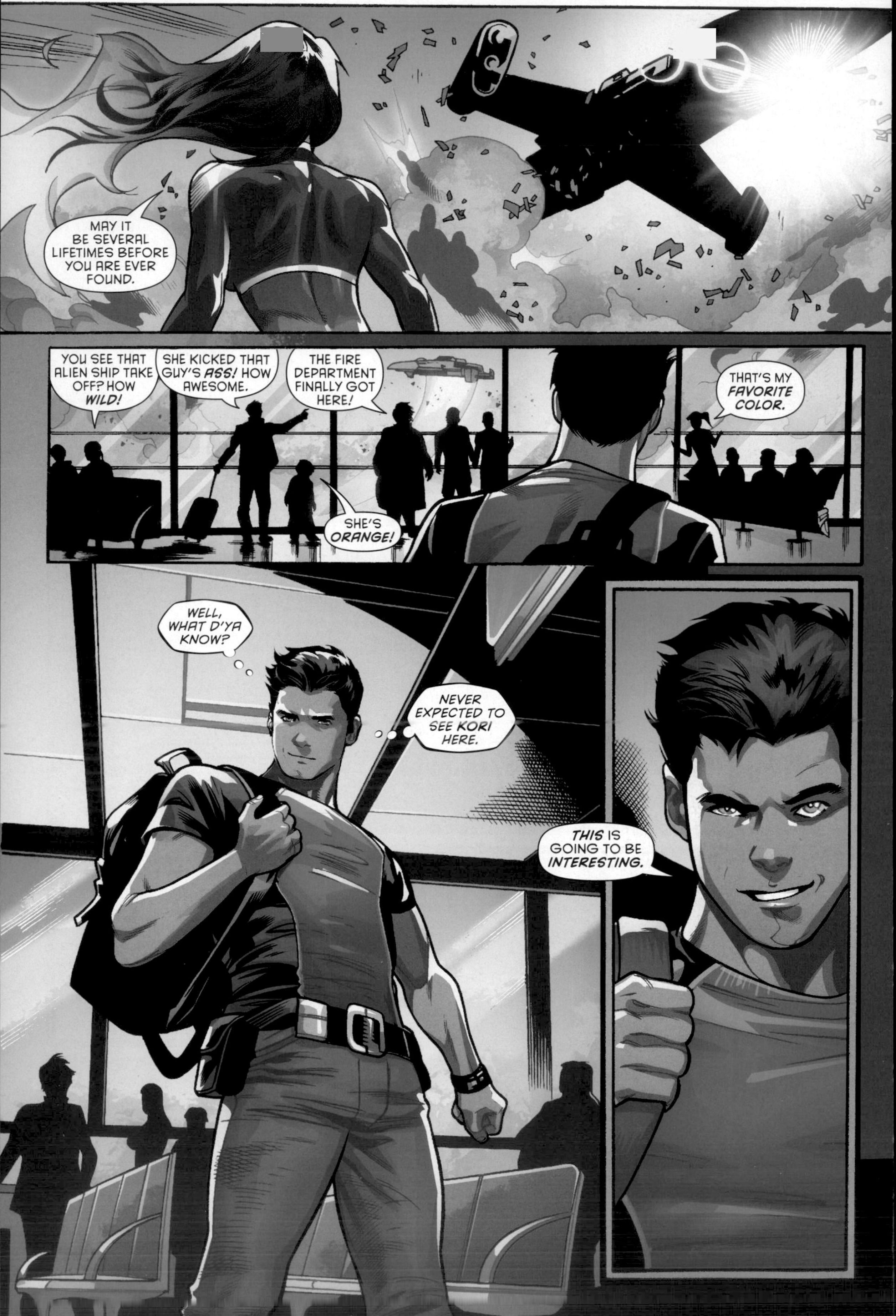
MAY IT BE SEVERAL LIFETIMES BEFORE YOU ARE EVER FOUND.
YOU SEE THAT ALIEN SHIP TAKE OFF? HOW WILD!
SHE KICKED THAT GUY'S ASS! HOW AWESOME.
THE FIRE DEPARTMENT FINALLY GOT HERE!
SHE'S ORANGE!
THAT'S MY FAVORITE COLOR.
WELL, WHAT D'YA KNOW?
NEVER EXPECTED TO SEE KORI HERE.
THIS IS GOING TO BE INTERESTING.

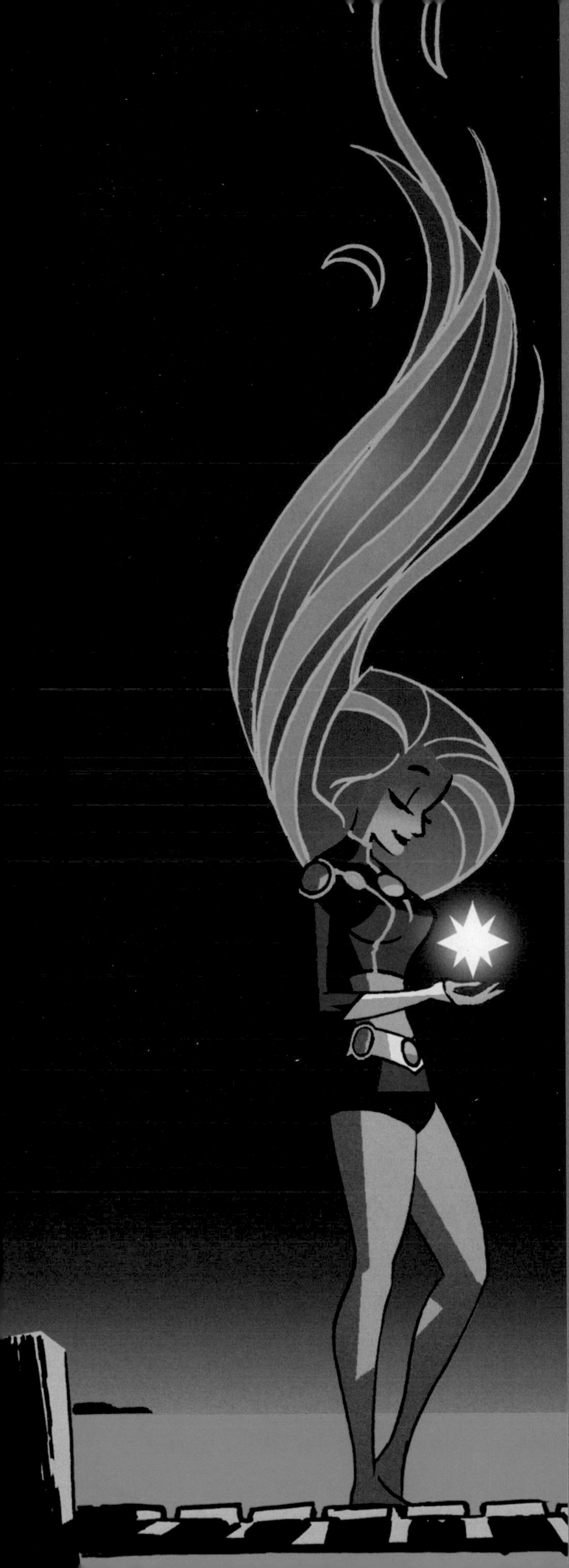

VARIANT COVER GALLERY

STARFIRE #1
VARIANT BY
EMANUELA LUPACCHINO & HI-FI

STARFIRE #2
VARIANT BY
EMANUELA LUPACCHINO & HI-FI

STARFIRE #3
VARIANT BY DARWYN COOKE

STARFIRE #4
GREEN LANTERN
75TH ANNIVERSARY
VARIANT BY LEE GARBETT

STARFIRE #5
MONSTER VARIANT BY
GUILLEM MARCH

STARFIRE #6
LOONEY TUNES VARIANT
BY EMANUELA LUPACCHINO,
TOMEU MOREY & SPIKE BRANDT

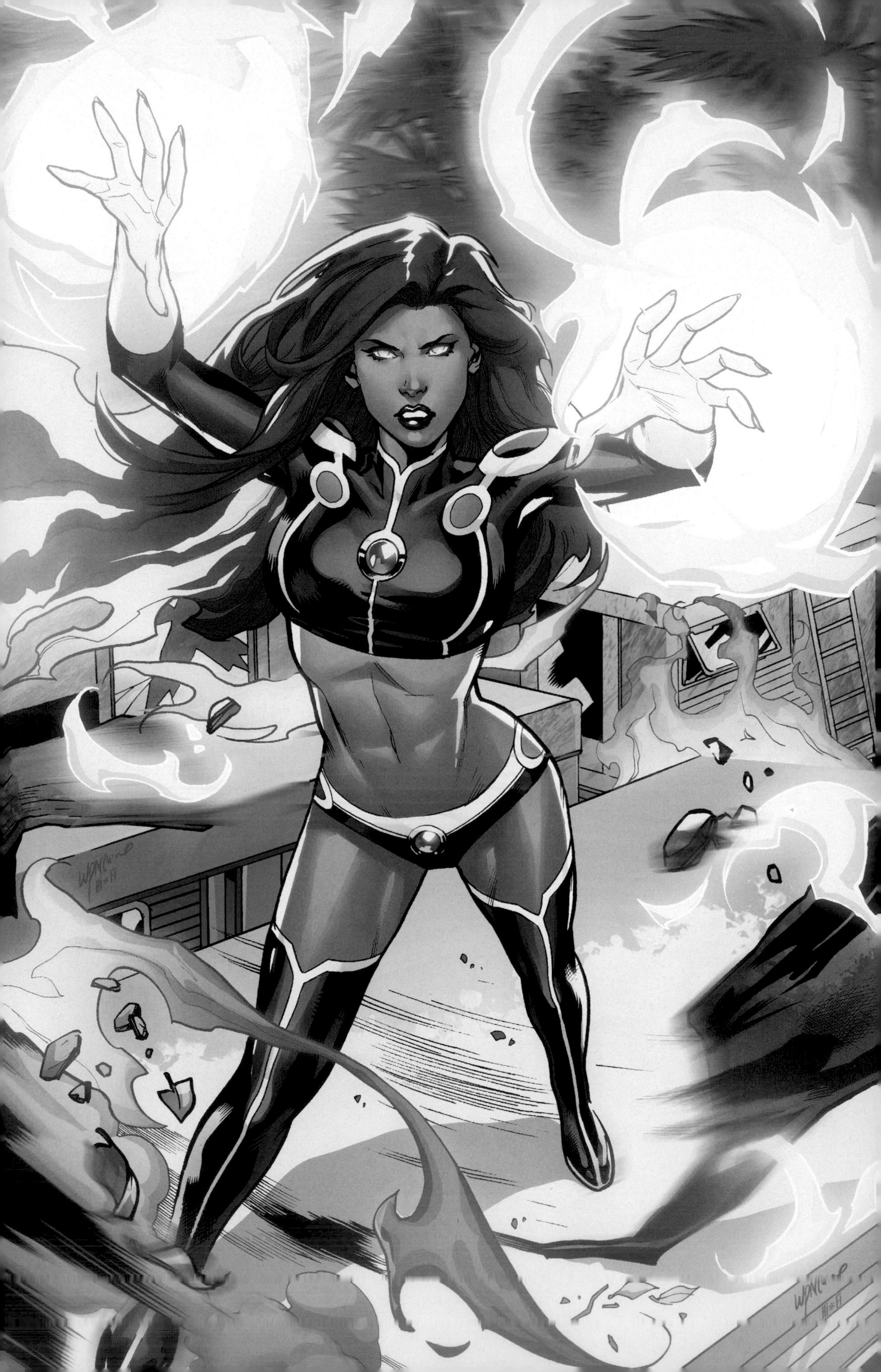

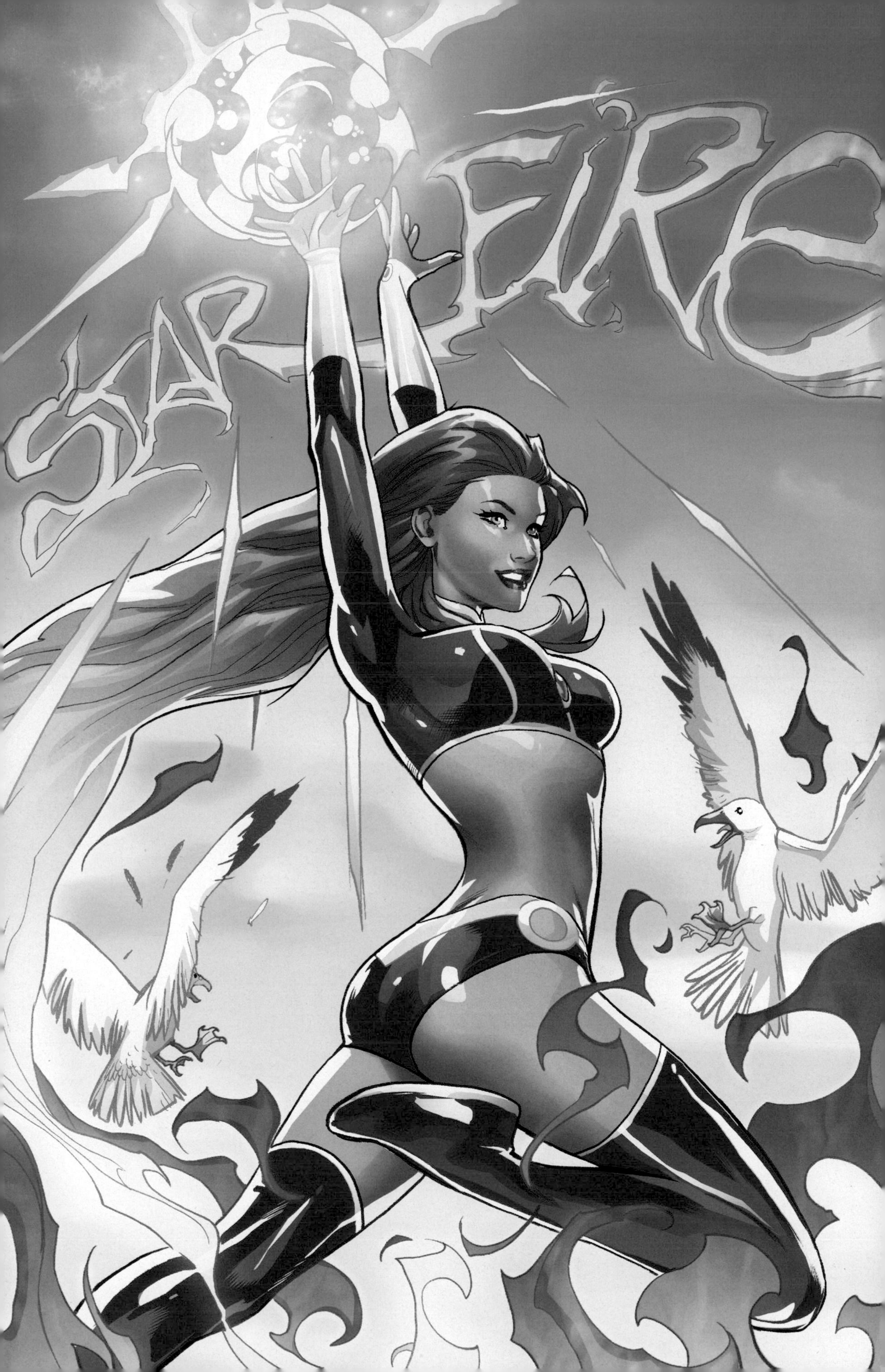
STARFIRE

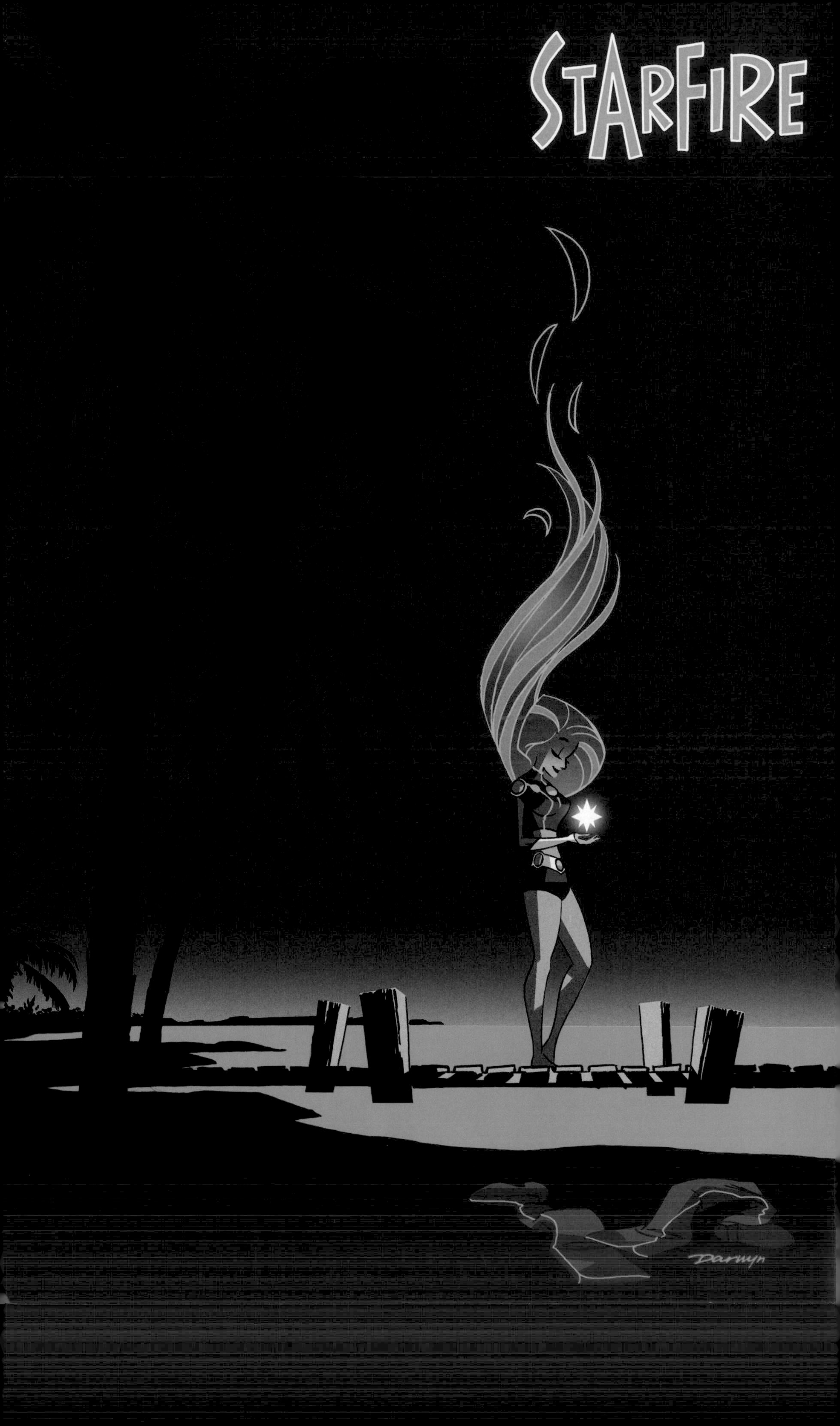
STARFIRE
Darwyn

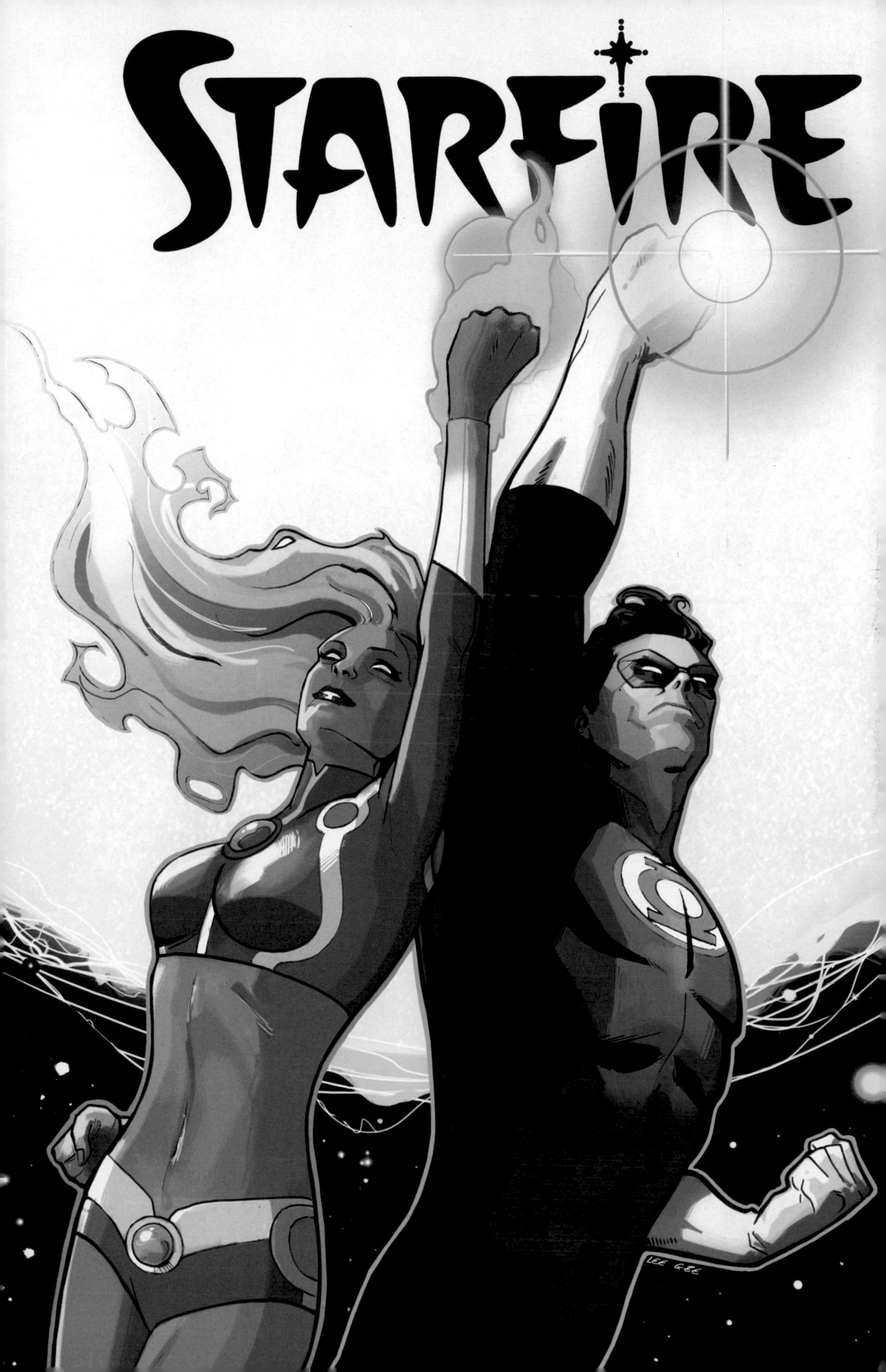
STARFIRE
LEE GEE

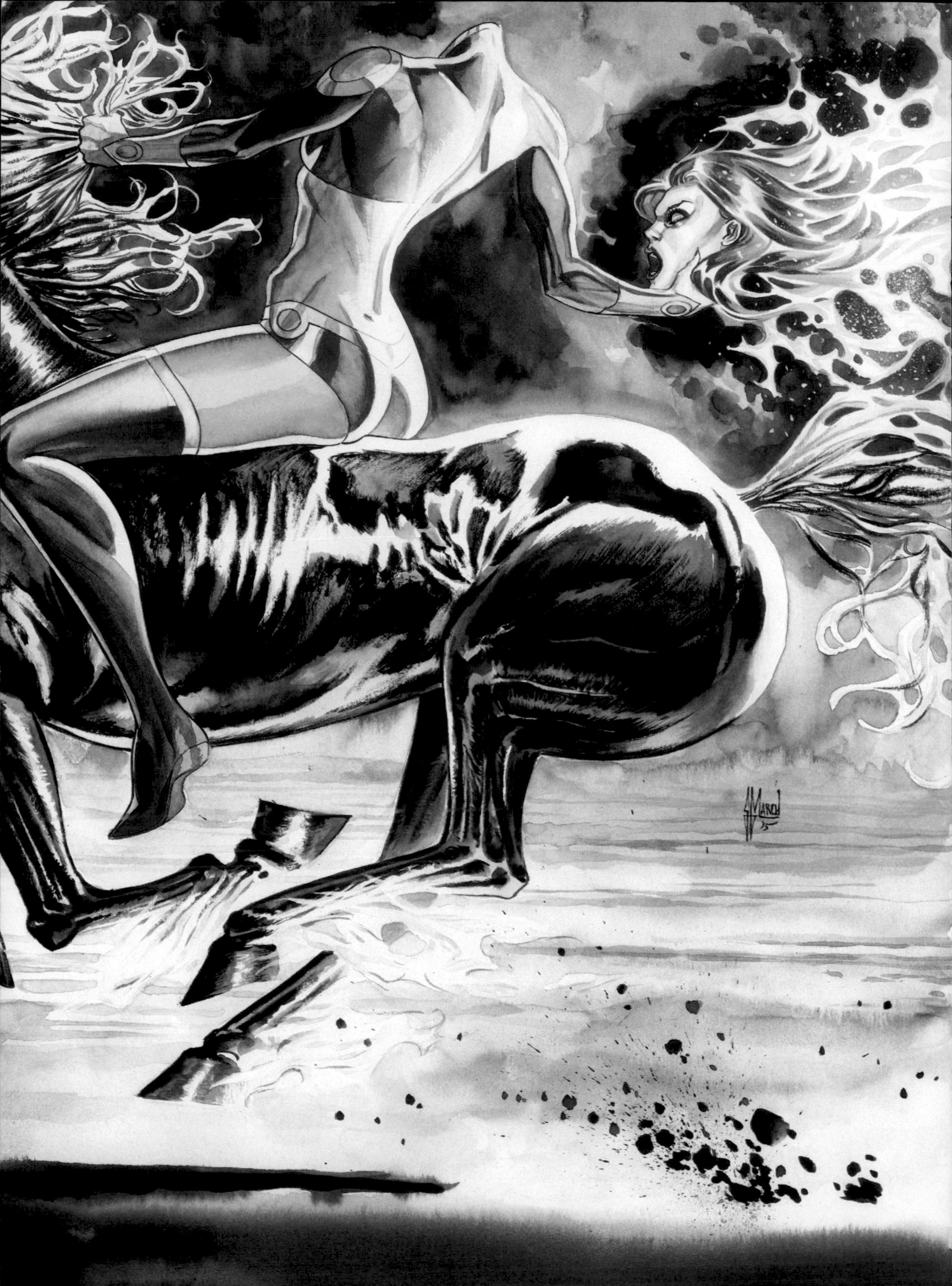

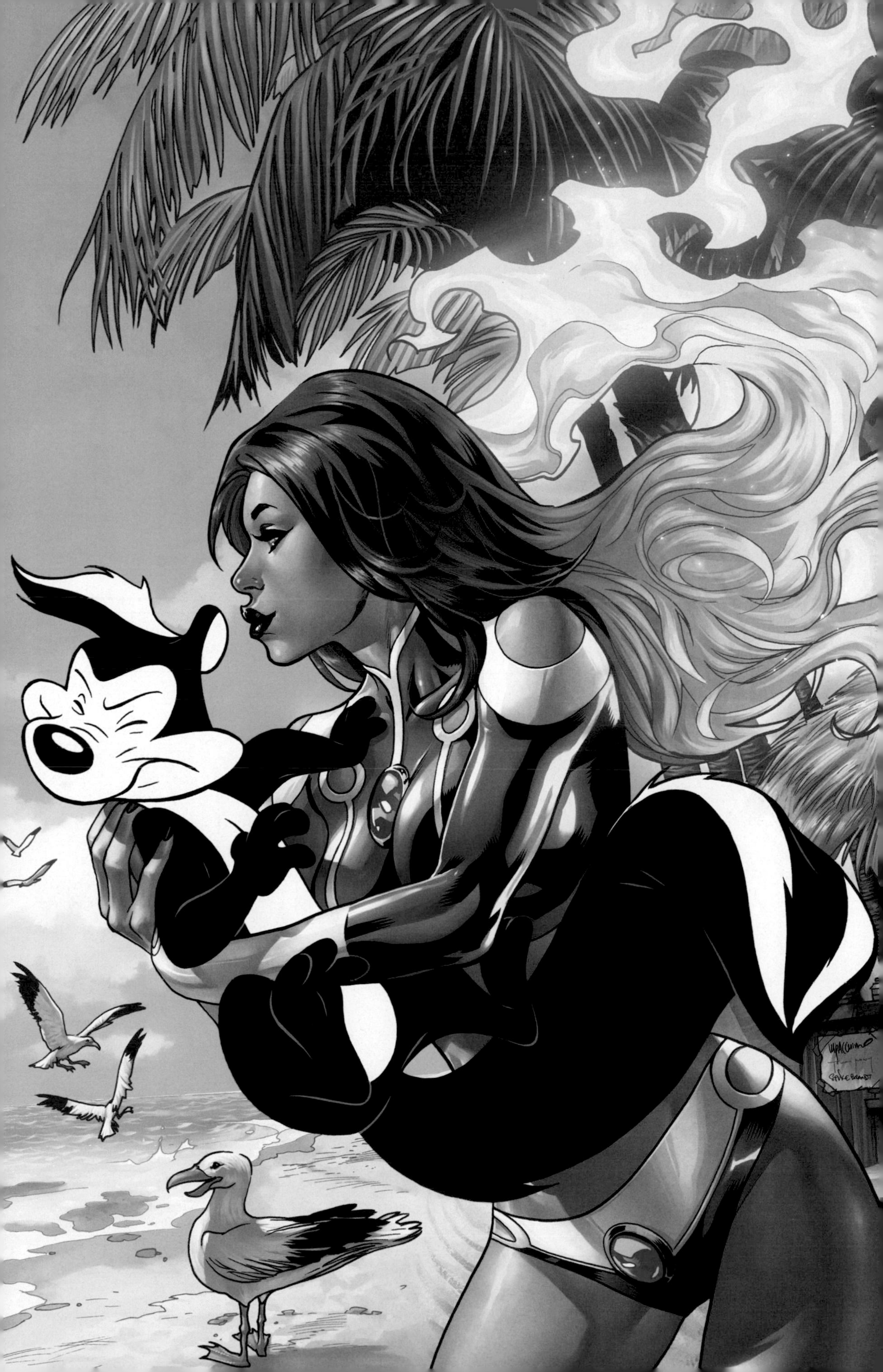

STARFIRE SKETCHBOOK

LAYOUTS AND PENCILS FOR STARFIRE #2 VARIANT COVER BY EMANUELA LUPACCHINO

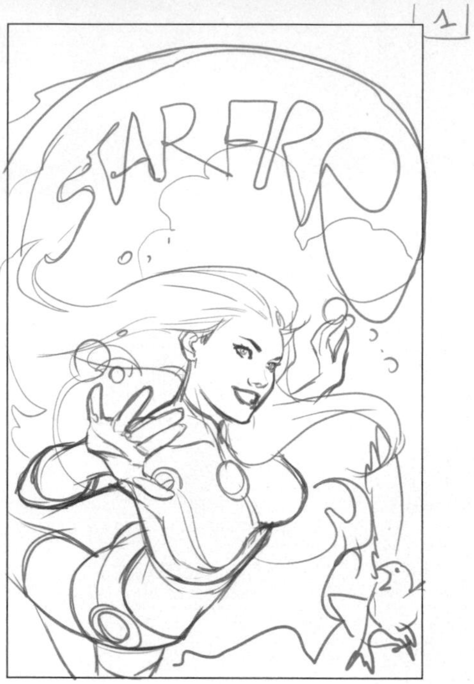
1
STARFIRO

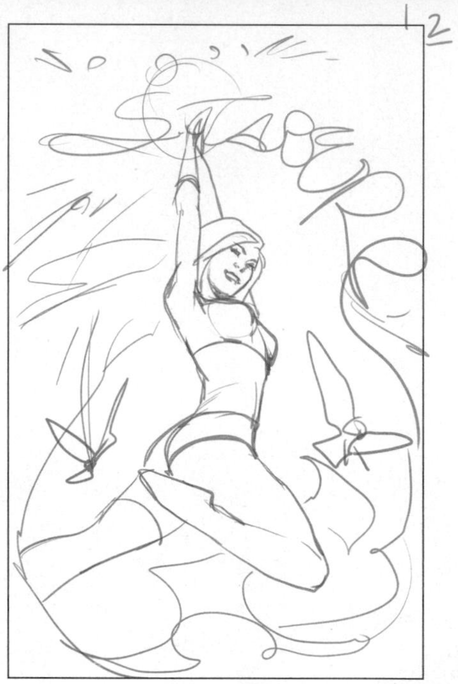
2

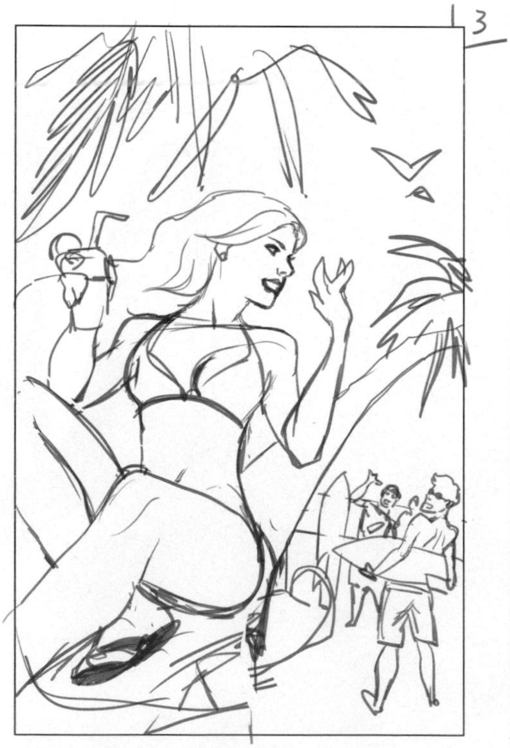
3

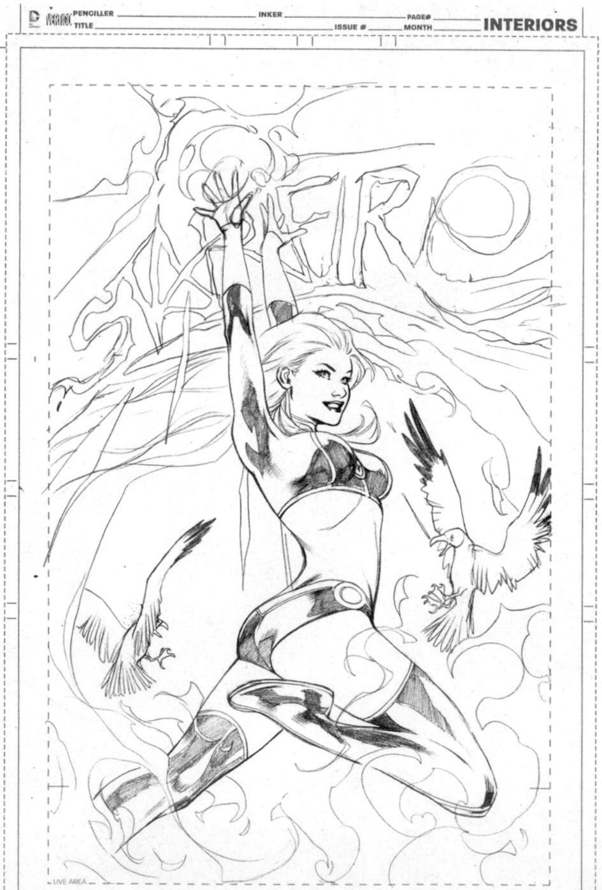
PENCILLER
INKER
PAGE#
TITLE
ISSUE #
MONTH
INTERIORS
LIVE AREA
CROP

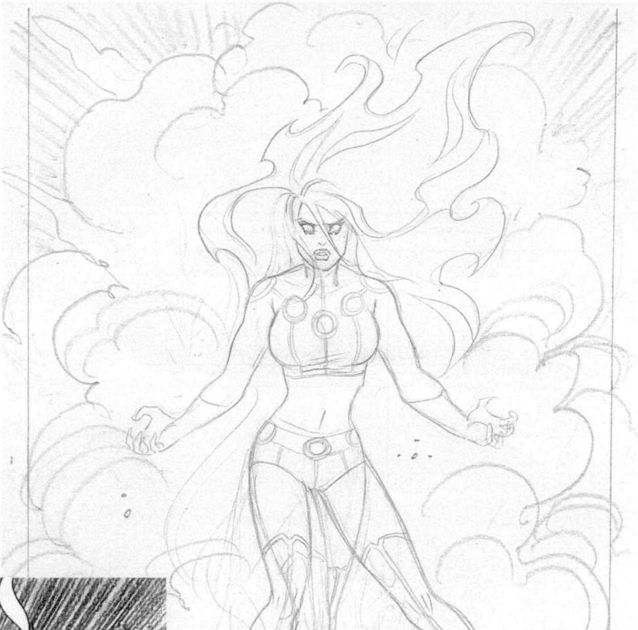

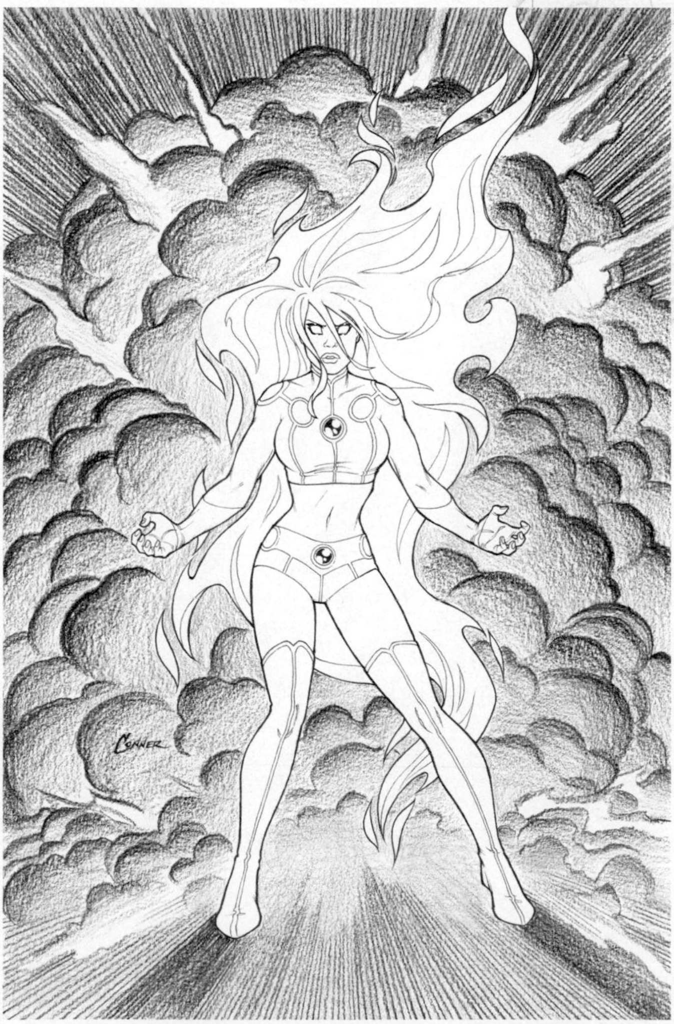
CONNER

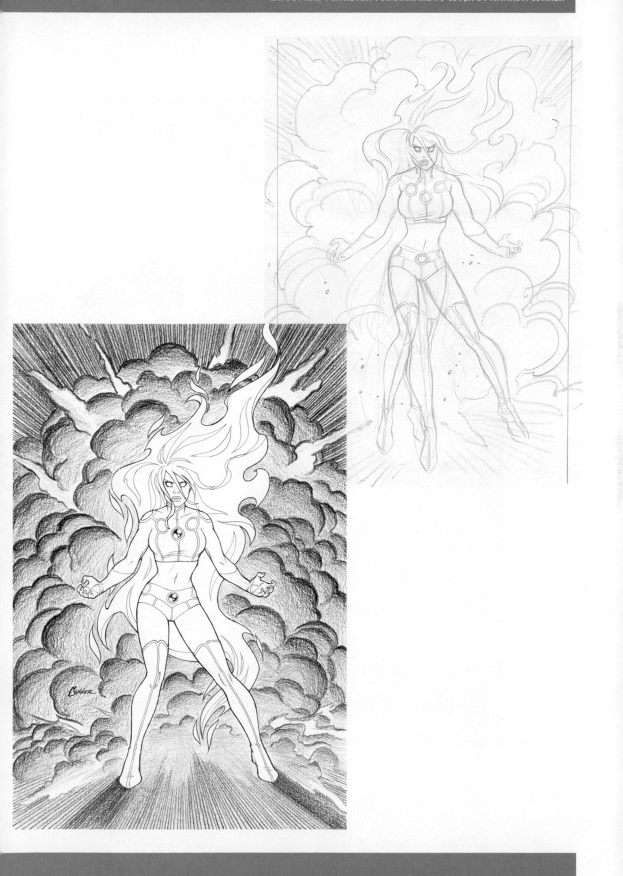

UNUSED COVER CONCEPT FOR STARFIRE #4 BY AMANDA CONNER

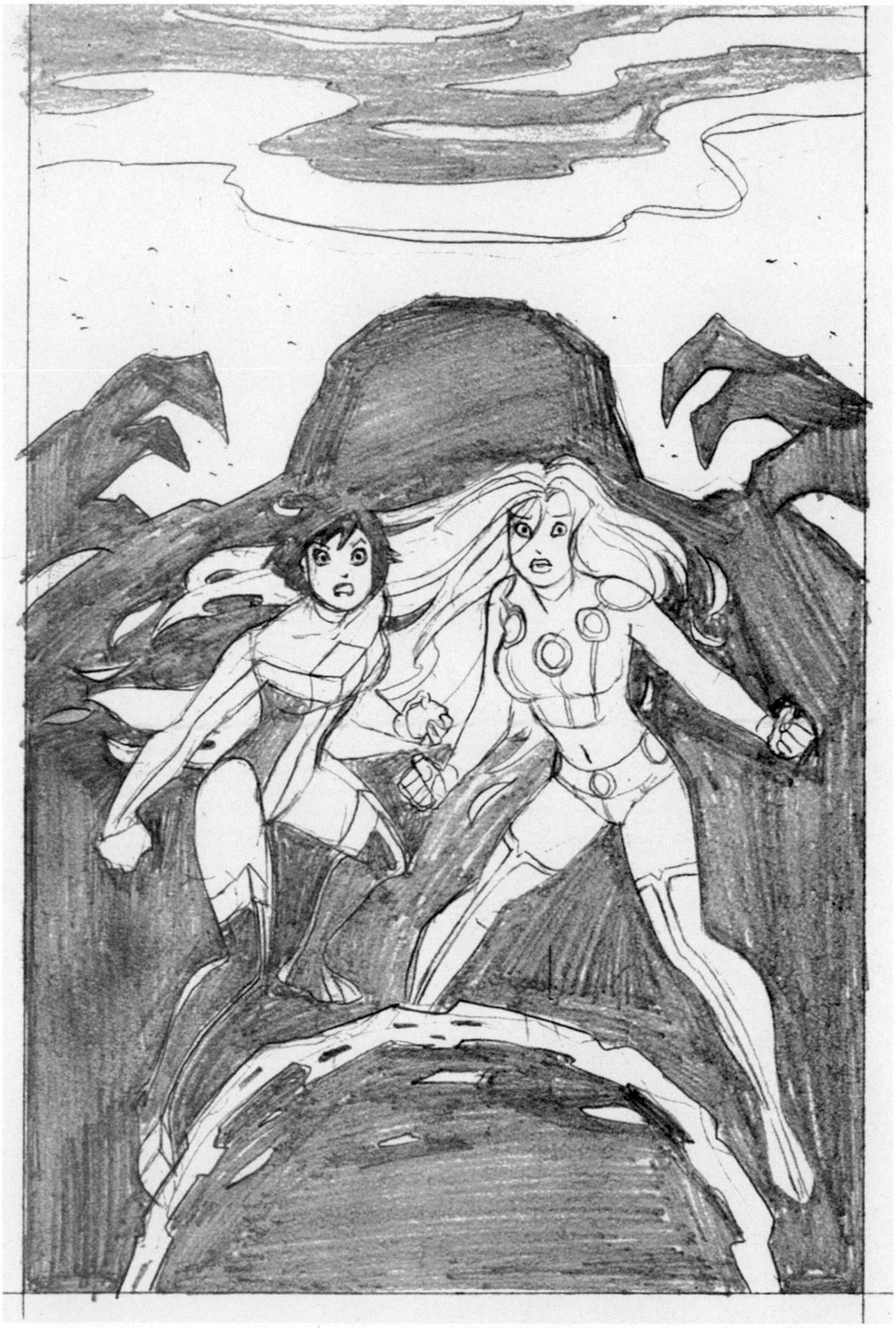

ATLEE COSTUME SKETCH AND COVER LAYOUTS FOR STARFIRE #3 AND #5 BY AMANDA CONNER

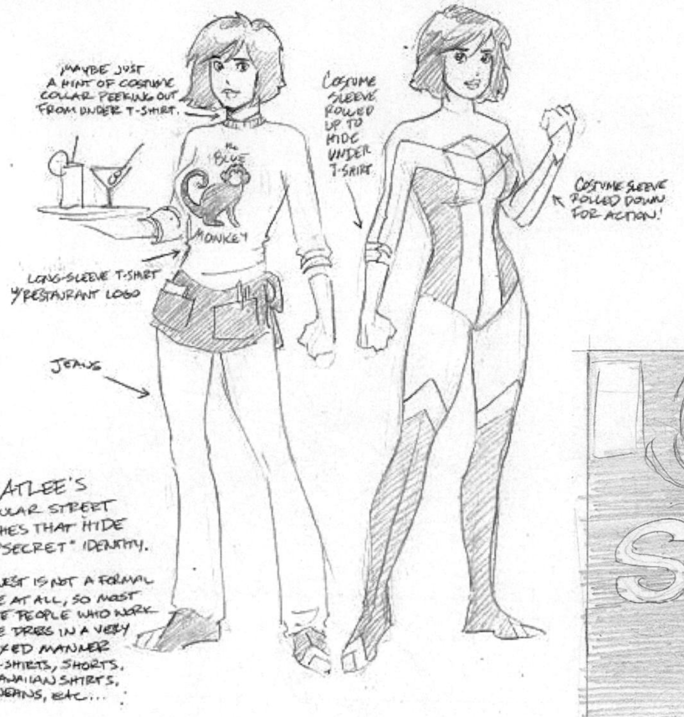
MAYBE JUST A HINT OF COSTUME COLLAR PEEKING OUT FROM UNDER T-SHIRT.
COSTUME SLEEVE ROLLED UP TO HIDE UNDER T-SHIRT
THE BLUE MONKEY
COSTUME SLEEVE ROLLED DOWN FOR ACTION!
LONG-SLEEVE T-SHIRT W/RESTAURANT LOGO
JEANS
ATLEE'S REGULAR STREET CLOTHES THAT HIDE HER "SECRET" IDENTITY.
KEY WEST IS NOT A FORMAL PLACE AT ALL, SO MOST OF THE PEOPLE WHO WORK THERE DRESS IN A VERY RELAXED MANNER ie: T-SHIRTS, SHORTS, HAWAIIAN SHIRTS, JEANS, ETC...

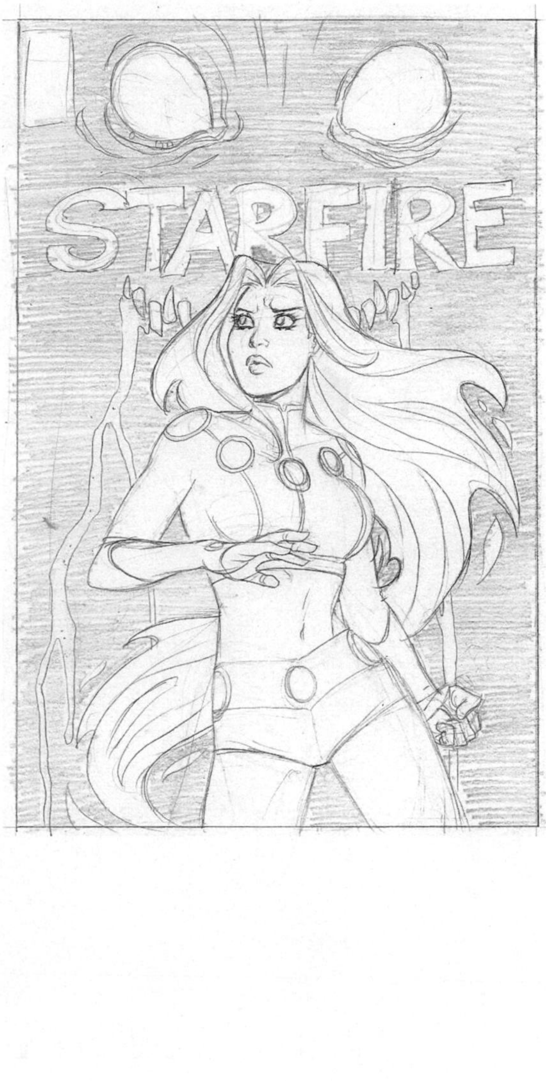
STARFIRE

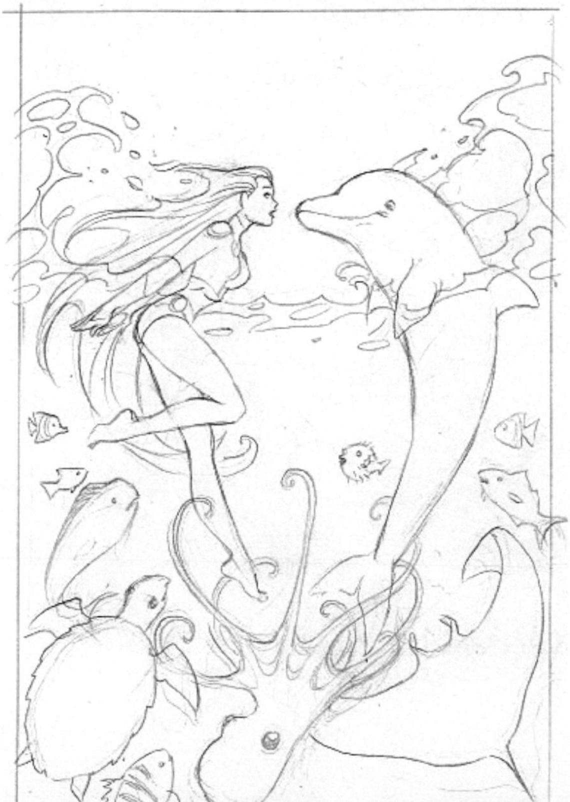

PAGE PROGRESSION FOR STARFIRE #2, PAGES 2-3
LAYOUTS AND PENCILS BY EMANUELA LUPACCHINO, INKS BY RAY McCARTHY AND COLOR BY HI-FI

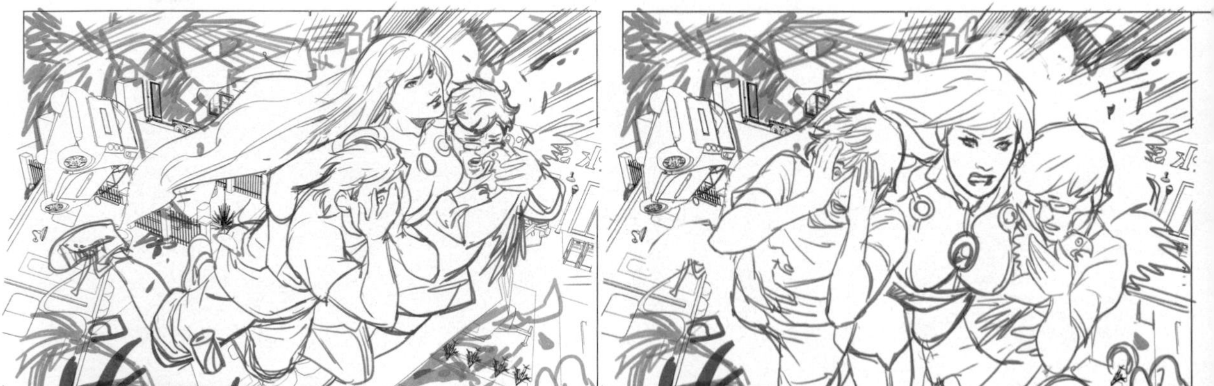

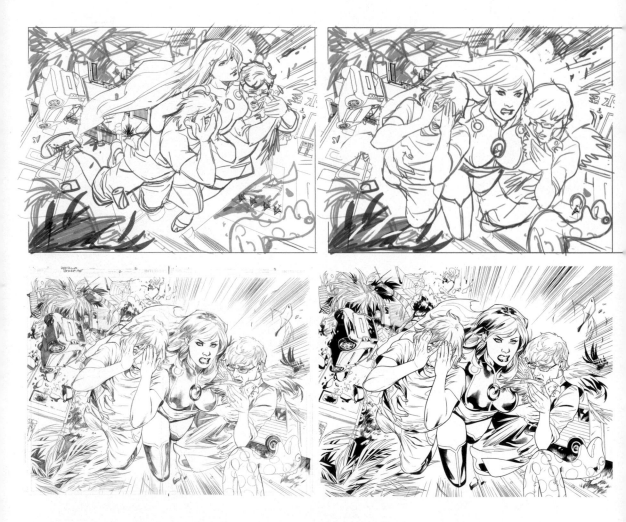

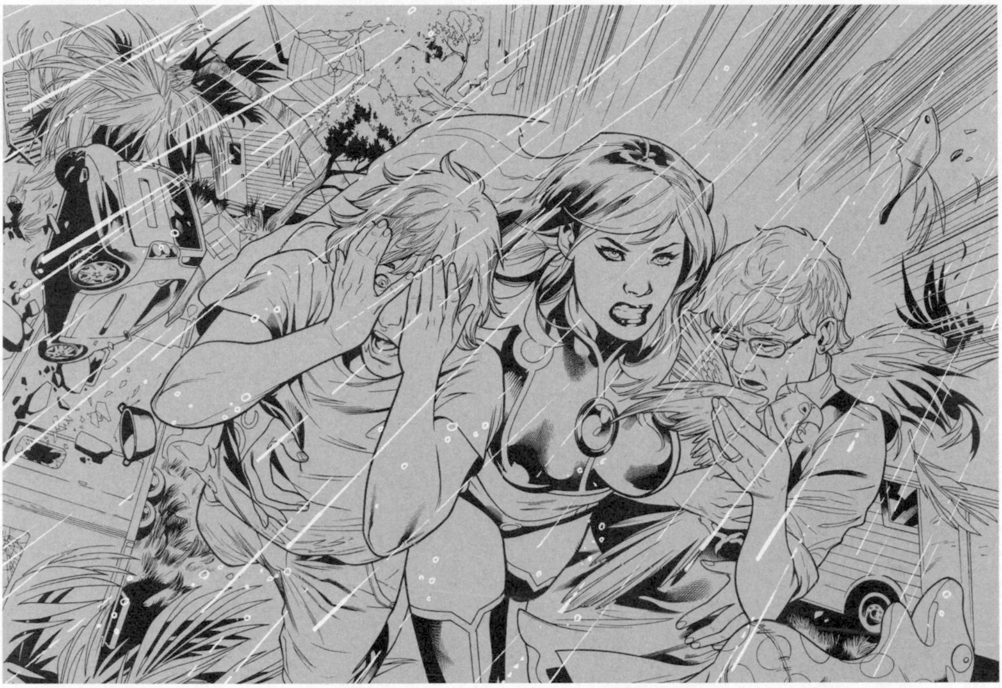

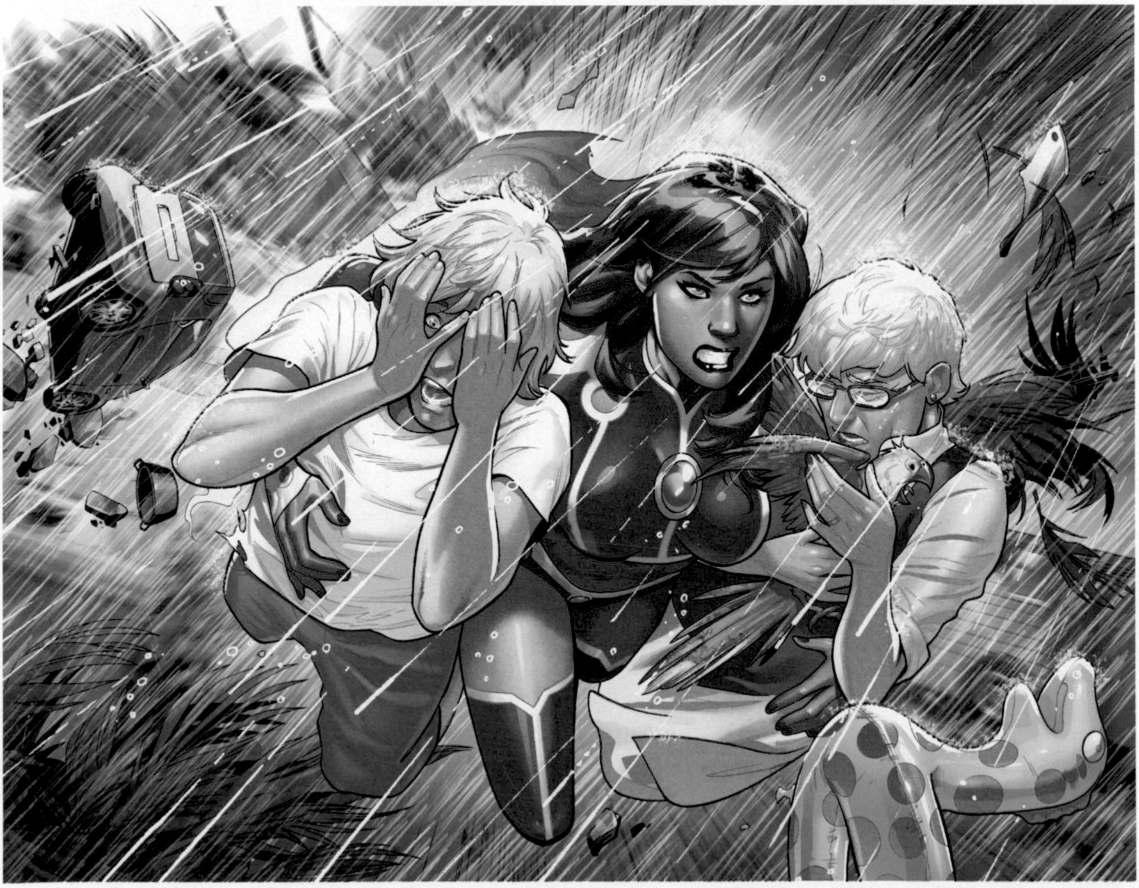

EMANUELA LUPACCHINO'S LAYOUTS FOR STARFIRE #1 PAGE 18, STARFIRE #3 PAGE 9, STARFIRE #4 PAGE 4, AND STARFIRE #5 PAGE 19

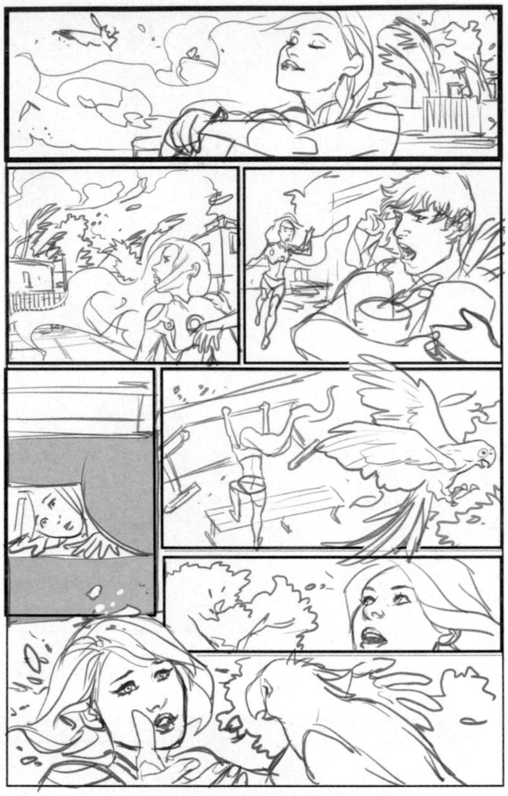

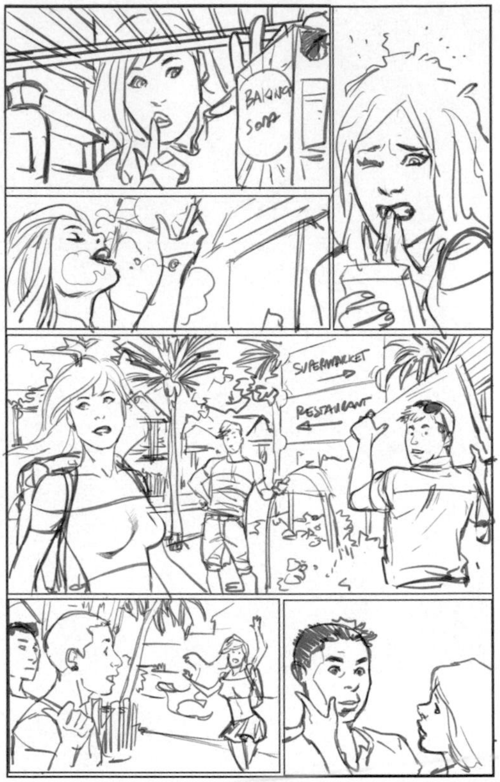
BAKING SODA
SUPERMARKET
RESTAURANT

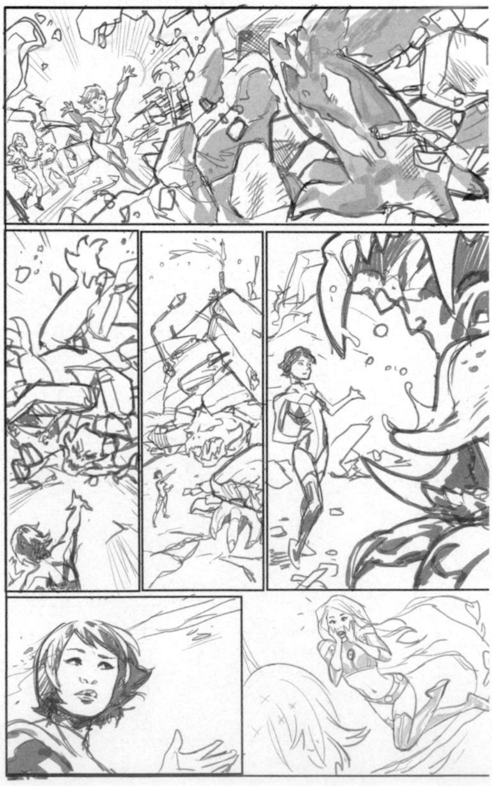

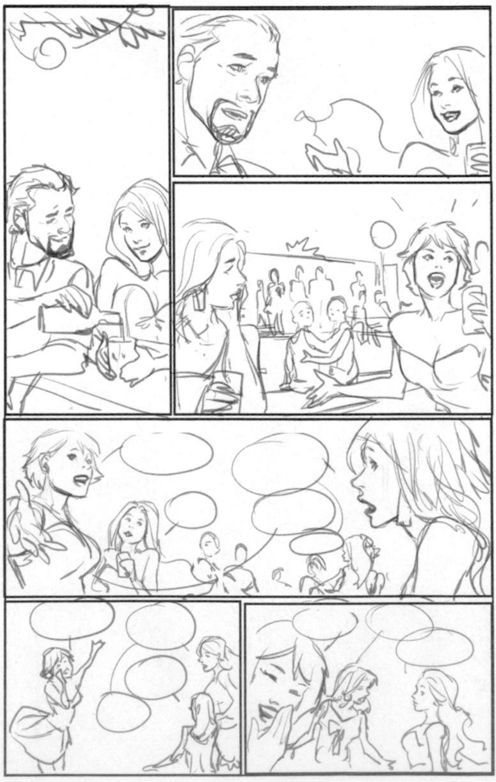

EMANUELA LUPACCHINO'S LAYOUTS FOR STARFIRE #5 PAGES 13-14 AND STARFIRE #6 PAGES 18-19

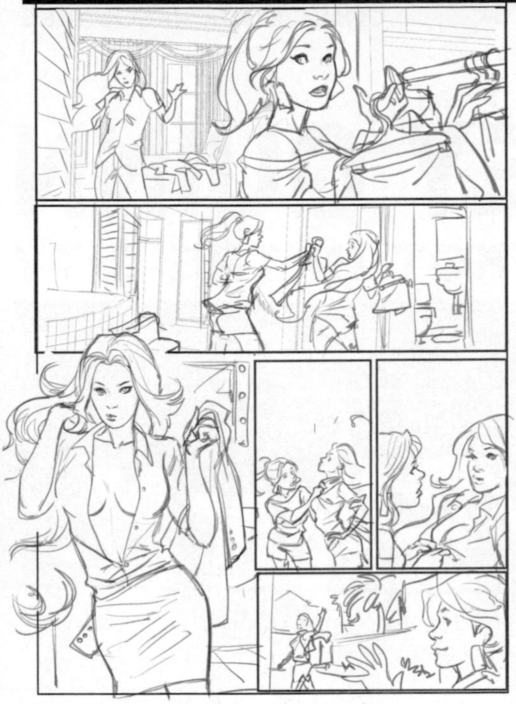

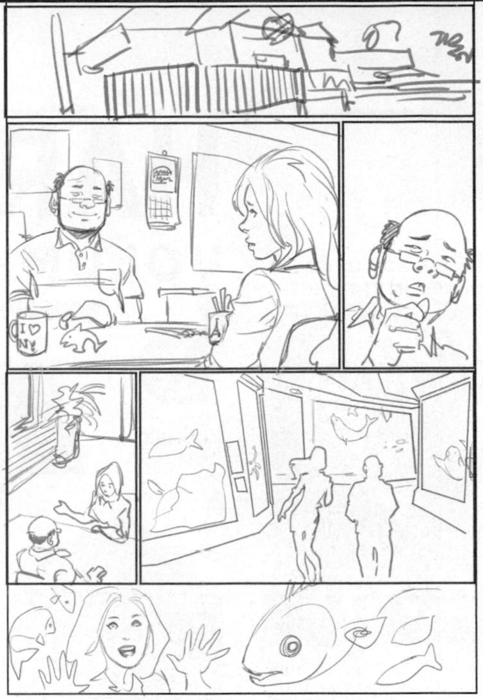

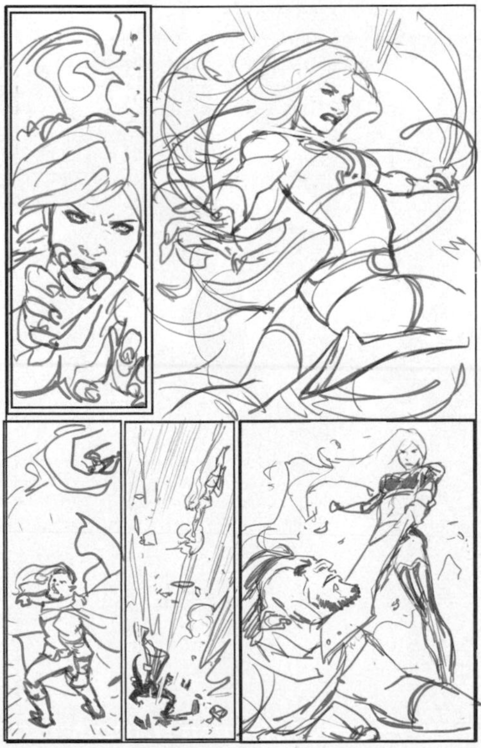

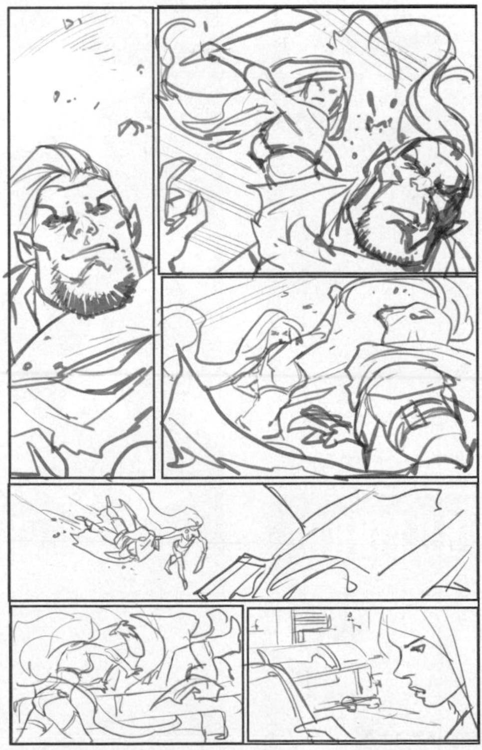

"Chaotic and unabashedly fun."—IGN

*"I'm enjoying HARLEY QUINN a great deal;
it's silly, it's funny, it's irreverent."*
—COMIC BOOK RESOURCES

HARLEY QUINN
VOLUME 1: HOT IN THE CITY

**SUICIDE SQUAD VOL. 1:
KICKED IN THE TEETH**

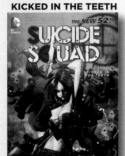

**with ADAM GLASS and
FEDERICO DALLOCCHIO**

**HARLEY QUINN:
PRELUDES AND
KNOCK-KNOCK JOKES**

**with KARL KESEL and
TERRY DODSON**

**BATMAN: MAD LOVE
AND OTHER STORIES**

**with PAUL DINI
and BRUCE TIMM**

DC COMICS™

THE NEW 52!

VOLUME 1
HOT IN THE CITY

"CHAOTIC AND UNABASHEDLY
FUN AS ONE WOULD EXPECT."
— IG

AMANDA **CONNER**   JIMMY **PALMIOTTI**   CHAD **HARDIN**
STEPHANE **ROUX**   ALEX **SINCLAIR**   PAUL **MOUNTS**